Nancy Chodorow and *The Reproduction of Mothering*

"Forty years ago, *The Reproduction of Mothering* introduced a groundbreaking approach to understanding capitalist patriarchy. By putting women at the center of analysis, Chodorow paved the way for feminist revolutions in sociology and psychoanalysis. Petra Bueskens' superb volume pays tribute to her intellectual legacy and the generations of scholars she inspired."

—Christine Williams, *Professor of Sociology, The Elsie and Stanley E. (Skinny) Adams, Sr. Centennial Professor of Liberal Arts, The University of Texas at Austin; President, American Sociological Association*

"Revisiting the impact of Nancy Chodorow's contribution to feminist scholarship is a critical task for our contentious times. Many recent debates seem to generate more passion and hostility than collective understanding, but Petra Bueskens' edited book deepens our grasp of culturally diverse patterns of gendered identity and social practice. In bringing together Chodorow's theoretical insights and the contributions of a wide range of contemporary feminist scholars, including Bueskens, she has produced a collection of important work that challenges and extends the earlier psychoanalytic feminist tradition."

—Kerreen Reiger, *Associate Professor, School of Social Sciences, La Trobe University, Melbourne; author of* The Disenchantment of the Home: Modernizing the Australian Family *(OUP)*; Our Bodies Our Babies: the Forgotten Women's Movement *(MUP)*

Petra Bueskens
Editor

Nancy Chodorow and *The Reproduction of Mothering*

Forty Years On

palgrave
macmillan

Editor
Petra Bueskens
University of Melbourne
Melbourne, VIC, Australia

ISBN 978-3-030-55589-4 ISBN 978-3-030-55590-0 (eBook)
https://doi.org/10.1007/978-3-030-55590-0

This Palgrave Macmillan imprint is published by the registered company Springer Nature Switzerland AG
The registered company address is: Gewerbestrasse 11, 6330 Cham, Switzerland

Acknowledgments

Bringing together an edited collection on Nancy Chodorow and her canonical work *The Reproduction of Mothering* has been a great honor. It began with meeting Nancy at the "Motherhood and Cultures" conference at Maynooth University, Ireland in 15–17 June 2015 where she was a keynote speaker. Although we had already corresponded around the reprinting of her essay "Too Late" in my edited volume *Mothering and Psychoanalysis*, we had not yet met. I was delighted to discover Nancy was so warm and friendly, and enjoyed several memorable conversations.

I would like to thank first and foremost Nancy Chodorow for her enthusiasm for this project, her willingness to write an original chapter, and to connect me to many of the authors in this book who were her contemporaries, colleagues, students, and friends. It has been a pleasure to work with these authors and to see the many and varied ways *The Reproduction of Mothering* has influenced their work theoretically, clinically, and personally.

I would like to thank Andrea O'Reilly at Demeter Press and Tanya Cassidy for originally working with me on this project and Valerie Heffernan for organizing the wonderful Maynooth University Motherhood and Cultures conference where I first met Nancy and discussed this project. Many thanks to Amelia Derkatsch, Commissioning Editor of Gender Studies at Palgrave Macmillan for her professionalism, warmth, and support. I would also like to thank the three anonymous reviewers for their helpful comments. Thanks also goes to Sharla Plant, Poppy Hull and

Nina Guttapalle, who came on as editors in the late stages of production and assisted me with matters large and small. I would also like to thank Karthika Purushothaman for expert copy-editing.

Gratitude is also extended to the Association for Research on Mothering, Australia for their support and cultivation of scholarly community. Parts of my chapter were presented and discussed at seminars and conferences over the past 2 years. I would also like to thank the wonderful maternal scholars Melbourne reading group including Carla Pascoe Leahy, Julie Stephens, Anne Manne, Barbara Matter, Emma Dalton, Kate Johnson-Ataata and Cindy Renate for intellectually stimulating conversations that nourish my thinking.

Finally, I would like to thank Sarah Hewat, Kim Toffoletti, Janet Fraser, Anne Manne, Julie Stephens, Fiona Giles, Andrea O'Reilly, Pia Cerveri, Miri Taube, Rebecca Lister, Jen Brownscombe and Susi Fox for friendship, support, and camaraderie. Each of you, behind the scenes, has nurtured this project.

I would also like to thank my parents Rolf and Jenny Bueskens, my adult daughter Mia, my partner Nick and my children Sophia and Tom. You are my inspiration and love.

This book is dedicated to Nancy Julia Chodorow for the great gift of her scholarship.

Contents

1 Introduction: *The Reproduction of Mothering* Turns Forty 1
Petra Bueskens

Part I Mothers

2 Women Mother Daughters: *The Reproduction of Mothering* After Forty Years 49
Nancy J. Chodorow

3 *The Reproduction of Mothering*: Forty Years on 81
Adrienne E. Harris

4 Reminiscing and Reflecting on Nancy Chodorow's *The Reproduction of Mothering* 87
Rosemary H. Balsam

5 Thinking Back Through Our Mothers: The Legacies of Nancy Chodorow 111
Elizabeth Abel

6 The Impact of Nancy Chodorow's *The Reproduction of Mothering* and Its Implications for the Future 125
Madelon Sprengnether

Part II Daughters

7 *The Reproduction of Mothering*: A Love Story 149
Ilene Philipson

8 Mothering in Life and Therapy: An Appreciation of Chodorow's Lifelong Contribution 159
Daphne de Marneffe

9 Mother Figures: On Becoming the Mother One Wishes One Had 169
Meg Jay

10 The Production of Male Mothering 191
Leslie C. Bell

11 Full Circle with Chodorow: Reflections on Women's Desire and Lesbian Sexuality 205
Jade McGleughlin

Part III Grand Daughters

12 Mother–Daughter Relations and the Maternal in Irigaray and Chodorow 239
Alison Stone

13 Mothers Reproducing the Social: Chodorow and Beyond 265
Petra Bueskens

14 Mirroring a Mother's Love: A Chodorowian Analysis of the Complicated Relationship Between Mothers and Nannies 301
Katie B. Garner

15 *The Reproduction of Mothering*: Unlocking Italian Women's Fiction from the *Fin-de-siècle* Onwards 329
Ursula Fanning

Index 353

Notes on Contributors

Elizabeth Abel is a Professor of English at the University of California, Berkeley. She is the author of *Virginia Woolf and the Fictions of Psychoanalysis* and *Signs of the Times: The Visual Politics of Jim Crow*; the editor of *Writing and Sexual Difference*; and the coeditor of *The Voyage In: Fictions of Female Development*, *The Signs Reader: Women, Gender and Scholarship*, and *Female Subjects in Black and White: Race, Psychoanalysis and Feminism*. She has published essays on gender, race, psychoanalysis, and visual culture. Her current project tracks the afterlives of Virginia Woolf in unexpected places.

Rosemary H. Balsam is an Associate Clinical Professor of Psychiatry Yale Medical School, Staff Psychiatrist, Yale University Student Mental Health and Counseling, and Training and Supervising Analyst, Western New England Institute for Psychoanalysis. Balsam has written extensively on issues of female development, the body, and gender, teaches and gives national and international presentations on these topics. Her latest book is *Women's Bodies in Psychoanalysis* (Routledge, 2012). She is a winner of the 2018 Sigourney Award for psychoanalytic achievements.

Leslie C. Bell, Ph.D., LCSW is a psychotherapist and sociologist in private practice in Berkeley, California, USA. Her empirical research on gender, sex, and sexuality integrates psychoanalytic and sociological theories and methods. Her work has appeared in various academic and popular publications and has been frequently featured in the news media. She is the author of *Hard to Get: Twentysomething Women and the Paradox of Sexual Freedom* (University of California Press, 2013) and the coeditor of *Gender, Sex, and Sexualities: Psychological Perspectives* (Oxford University Press, 2017). Nancy J. Chodorow chaired her dissertation in the sociology department at U.C. Berkeley.

Petra Bueskens, Ph.D. is an Honorary Fellow in the School of Social and Political Sciences at the University of Melbourne, a psychotherapist in private practice, and a freelance writer. She has written widely on motherhood, psychotherapy, social theory, and gender politics in both scholarly and popular fora. Her books include *Mothering and Psychoanalysis* (Demeter Press, 2014), *Modern Motherhood and Women's Dual Identities: Rewriting the Sexual Contract* (Routledge, 2018) and the coedited *Australian Mothering: Historical and Sociological Perspectives* (Palgrave, 2019).

Nancy J. Chodorow has a career that spans academia and psychoanalysis, and she has received many honors in both. She is Professor of Sociology Emerita at the University of California, Berkeley, where she also participated in creating the Gender and Women's Studies Department and taught in Clinical Psychology. She undertook psychoanalytic training in the 1980s and became a practicing analyst. She is currently Training and Supervising Analyst at the Boston Psychoanalytic Society and Institute and Lecturer Part-time in Psychiatry, Harvard Medical School/Cambridge Health Alliance. Her books include *The Reproduction of Mothering* (1978/1999); *Feminism and Psychoanalytic Theory* (1989); *Femininities, Masculinities, Sexualities: Freud and Beyond* (2004); *The Power of Feelings: Personal Meaning in Psychoanalysis, Gender, and Culture* (1999); *Individualizing Gender and Sexuality: Theory and Practice* (2012) and *The Psychoanalytic Ear and the Sociological Eye: Toward an American Independent Tradition* (2020). She is in private practice in Cambridge, MA.

Daphne de Marneffe, Ph.D. is a psychologist and author of *The Rough Patch: Marriage and the Art of Living Together* and *Maternal Desire: On Children, Love, and the Inner Life*. She has published scholarly papers on gender identity development, maternal subjectivity, and psychoanalytic history, and she teaches and lectures on couple therapy, adult development, and parenthood. She is a contributing editor to *Parents* Magazine, where she writes a monthly column on couple relationships. Her work has been featured in the *New York Times*, *NPR*, *Greater Good*, *Psychotherapy Networker*, and *Talks at Google*. She is in private practice in Corte Madera, CA.

Ursula Fanning is Associate Professor and Head of Italian Studies at the School of Languages, Cultures and Linguistics in University College Dublin. She is a member of the editorial board of the Women and Gender in Italy book series, published by Classiques Garnier. She has published extensively in the areas of nineteenth- and twentieth-century women's writing, as well as on the theater and narrative of Luigi Pirandello. Her recent monograph, *Italian Women's Autobiographical Writings in the Twentieth Century: Constructing Subjects* is published by Fairleigh Dickinson University Press.

Katie B. Garner, Ph.D. focuses on motherhood, childcare, and labor equality. She is thrilled to take the helm of the International Association of Maternal Action and Scholarship (IAMAS) (née MIRCI) based in Chicago, Illinois. In addition to teaching English and WGS courses, Katie runs consciousness-raising workshops for mothers. Her (in-progress) book covers interviews with nearly 100 US women. She has been featured in several podcasts and consulted with for a wide variety of mainstream articles. See more at: www.drkatiebgarner.com.

Adrienne E. Harris, Ph.D. is Faculty and Supervisor at New York University Postdoctoral Program in Psychotherapy and Psychoanalysis and at the Psychoanalytic Institute of Northern California. She is an Editor at *Psychoanalytic Dialogues*, and *Studies in Gender and Sexuality* and of the IPA ejournal, *Psychoanalysis.Today*. Lew Aron, Adrienne, and Jeremy Safran opened the Sandor Ferenczi Center at the New School in 2012. Her book *Gender as Soft Assembly* was published in 2005.

Meg Jay, Ph.D. is a clinical psychologist and associate professor of education at the University of Virginia. She received a doctorate in clinical psychology, and in gender studies, from the University of California, Berkeley. A narrative nonfiction writer, she is the author of two books, *The Defining Decade* and *Supernormal*, each of which interweave and translate clinical work, theory, and research for the general public.

Jade McGleughlin, L.I.C.S.W. is past president, personal and supervising analyst, board member, and faculty member of The Massachusetts

Institute for Psychoanalysis. She is on the editorial boards of *Psychoanalytic Dialogues* and *Studies in Gender and Sexuality*. She cofounded The Center for Alternative Families and is a former instructor in Psychiatry for Harvard Medical School, and former codirector of the Sexual Abuse Treatment Team, Psychiatry Dept., Children's Hospital Boston. She is in private practice in Cambridge, MA, providing consultation, supervision, psychotherapy, and psychoanalysis to children and adults. She specializes in consultations to difficult therapies. Her writing focuses on gender, the negative, the analysts' necessary nonsovereignty, and uses of visual art to articulate problems in representation. She is a portrait painter.

Ilene Philipson holds doctorates in sociology, clinical psychology, and psychoanalysis. She is a training and supervising analyst at the Institute of Contemporary Psychoanalysis in Los Angeles and is in the private practice of psychotherapy and psychoanalysis in Oakland, California. In addition to *On The Shoulders of Women: The Feminization of Psychotherapy*, her books include *Married to The Job; Ethel Rosenberg: Beyond the Myths*; and *Women, Class, and the Feminist Imagination* (ed). She has taught at UC Berkeley, UC Santa Cruz, and NYU.

Madelon Sprengnether is a poet, memoirist, and literary critic and Regents Professor Emerita of the Department of English at the University of Minnesota. Her publications include *The (M)other Tongue: Essays in Feminist Psychoanalytic Interpretation* (1985), *Shakespearean Tragedy and Gender* (1996), and *The Spectral Mother: Freud, Feminism and Psychoanalysis* (1990). In addition, she has published three memoirs and three collections of poetry. Her most recent books are *Great River Road: Memoir and Memory* (2015), *Near Solstice: Prose Poems* (2015), and *Mourning Freud* (2018). She is also a regular blogger for *Psychology Today*. For more information consult her website: www.madelonsprengnether.com.

Alison Stone is a Professor of European Philosophy in the Department of Politics, Philosophy and Religion at Lancaster University, UK. She writes about feminist philosophy and continental European philosophy. She is the author of several books and numerous articles on feminism, German Idealism, philosophy of nature, and maternal subjectivity. Stone coedits the journal the *Hegel Bulletin*. Her most recent books include *Being Born: Birth and Philosophy* (Oxford University Press, 2019); *Nature, Ethics and Gender in German Romanticism and Idealism* (Rowman & Littlefield, 2018); *Feminism, Psychoanalysis, and Maternal Subjectivity* (Routledge, 2012); *The Value of Popular Music: An Approach from Post-Kantian Aesthetics* (Palgrave, 2016); *The Routledge Companion to Feminist Philosophy*, coedited (Routledge, 2017).

CHAPTER 1

Introduction: *The Reproduction of Mothering* Turns Forty

Petra Bueskens

What is it that turns a book from a "product of its time" into a classic and, therefore, in some important respects, into something timeless? Is it the content or its reception? Is it the author or her readers? In truth, it is a mercurial combination of the two, producing "something more". Not unlike the "analytic third"[1] created between two people in psychotherapy, there is a magic in a classic that exceeds the sum of its parts. It is this relationship between the idea and the audience, between the book and its historical moment, that ignites and endures in a classic. As Victor Hugo memorably put it, "nothing is more powerful than an idea whose time has come".[2] Nancy Chodorow's *The Reproduction of Mothering: Psychoanalysis and the Sociology of Gender* is one such book. It speaks both to the universal: the mother at the centre of our collective psyche, and the

[1] Jessica Benjamin, *Beyond Doer and Done To: Recognition Theory, Intersubjectivity, and the Third* (New York: Routledge, 2018).

[2] Victor Hugo, *History of a Crime: The Testimony of an Eye-Witness*, trans. T.H. Joyce and Arthur Locker (New York: Mondial, 2005 [1852/1877]).

P. Bueskens (✉)
University of Melbourne, Melbourne, VIC, Australia
e-mail: petra.bueskens@unimelb.edu.au

P. Bueskens (ed.), *Nancy Chodorow and* The Reproduction of Mothering,
https://doi.org/10.1007/978-3-030-55590-0_1

particular: the historical moment of social change in which it was caught up and helped to create. More poignantly, it provides a framework for understanding our own unique relationships with our mothers. Like all good classics, we can read ourselves into its pages.

The Reproduction of Mothering is a tale told through the eyes of an acute observer who read and embodied the political moment—the zeitgeist—of her time, and transformed it into a language useable for scholars, clinical practitioners, activists, and laypeople. This too was integral to the appeal of Chodorow's book: it's broad, indeed profound, impact across the humanities and social sciences, including in sociology, anthropology, psychology, philosophy, psychoanalysis, literary theory, and in the emergent fields of women's and gender studies. In addition to its compelling subject matter—mothers and mothering—Chodorow's book endures because it integrates insights from several disciplines. As she says, *The Reproduction of Mothering* "… insists, as have all my writings since, upon the inextricable interconnectedness and mutual constitution of psyche, society, and culture".[3] This feat was recognized in several awards and symposia including the Jessie Barnard prize for Women in Society, a division of the American Sociological Association, in 1979, a special issue of *Signs* in 1981 and *Feminism and Psychology* in 2002 and, in 1996, it was voted one of the ten most influential books in the social sciences in the preceding twenty-five years by the flagship academic journal *Contemporary Sociology*.[4]

Forty years has passed since *The Reproduction of Mothering* was published (indeed forty-two years by the time this book is published). Nancy reminded me that in the Judaic tradition forty years is a biblically resonant passage of time: the time of wandering and reflection.[5] It is interesting to place a book so fundamentally about time—embodied,

[3] Chodorow, "Preface to the Second Edition," in *The Reproduction of Mothering*, x.

[4] Jessie Bernard Award of Sociologists for Women in Society, American Sociological Association (1979); Symposium, "On The Reproduction of Mothering: A Methodological Debate," *Signs* 6, no. 3 (1981): 482–514; named one of "Ten Most Influential Books of the Past Twenty-five Years," *Contemporary Sociology* 25, no. 3 (1996) 25th Anniversary Special Issue; "The Reproduction of Mothering: A Reappraisal." A symposium in *Feminism and Psychology* 12 (2002): 5–53. *The Reproduction of Mothering* has also been excerpted in numerous edited collections and translated into Japanese, Dutch, Spanish, German, Swedish, Portugese, Italian and Chinese.

[5] Personal correspondence, 2019.

generational, cyclical, maternal time no less!—outside time, in the preternaturally masculine realm of the transcendent. And yet any book that forms part of the canon is surely in the realm of the transcendent? It is that which stands apart crystallising insights that are both of their time and yet reach beyond and speak to those who come after. This book is arranged generationally for precisely this reason, to recognize the fertile ground of its birth, its reception by a generation of peers ("mothers") and grad students ("daughters"), many of whom were inspired and transformed professionally, and in some cases personally (see in particular Ilene Philipson, Adrienne E. Harris and Daphne de Marneffe), and a third generation of students and scholars ("granddaughters") who have taken up, used, critiqued and transformed *The Reproduction of Mothering* applying it to new ideas and social contexts.

The Reproduction of Mothering Revisited

The main thesis of the book—well known by now but worth rehearsing in broad outline—is twofold. First, there is the psychoanalytic component whereby Chodorow traces, through object relations theory, including what she now calls the "American independent school",[6] the internal psychic world of the infant daughter and son, and their intersubjective (conscious and unconscious) relationship with their mother, and she to them. Second, is the sociological component, woven throughout, whereby Chodorow traces the historically specific societal and familial constellation within which the development of gender takes shape. Chodorow begins with a seemingly obvious question: why do women mother? And her answer is a fascinating excursus into psychoanalytic theory, the sociological peculiarities of the late twentieth century nuclear family and the evolution of the male and female psyches produced therein. The short answer is *women mother because they were mothered*, which is, in important respects, a more psychologically potent experience (for both genders) in the context of the modern family with its highly specialized gender roles and relative isolation from kin and community. As Chodorow observes, the historical peculiarity of the modern western family with its asymmetrical gender roles, namely fathers at work and mothers at home

[6] Nancy Chodorow, *The Psychoanalytic Ear and the Sociological Eye* (London and New York: Routledge, 2019).

(in the middle-class and still at the time of Chodorow's writing), is that mothers largely mother in isolation.[7]

Sons and daughters are recreated, then, by mothers who have lost their traditional supports (a situation that remains the case today, even as women have entered the labour force *en masse*). For Chodorow, this social context shapes the internal worlds of familial protagonists in critical and enduring ways. Conventional sociological understandings of role learning and socialisation were insufficient to explain why women mother, suggested Chodorow, who turned rather to psychoanalysis to elucidate the complex internal worlds of (socially situated) mothers and the male and female children they birthed, nurtured and raised. For Chodorow, it is the intra-psychic dyad between mother and daughter, and its intergenerational transmission, that is central to the "reproduction of mothering". Here we see the confluence of gender and generation. As she says,

> I investigate the mother-daughter relationship and how women create and recreate this relationship internally. It is a cyclical process that I break into at the daughter's birth, but developmental outcomes in the mother already situate that birth and subsequent development and give it characteristic features.[8]

The mother is first a daughter. Through this experience of *being mothered*, she is able to regress to her own infancy[9] and more easily identify with the needs and subjective states of her infant. This unconscious and conscious process shapes her care of the infant, and his or her conscious and unconscious experience of that care, which, over time, and in the context of familial relationships and societal gender norms, is internalized. This process of regression and empathic identification is even stronger

[7] Contrary to later assertions of universalising, Chodorow was well aware of exceptions to this norm. In her assertion that the nuclear family is problematic for mothers, she contrasts it with other more economically and socially integrated models, "In a previous period, and still in some stable working-class and ethnic communities, women did support themselves emotionally by supporting and reconstituting *one another*. However, in the current period of high mobility and familial isolation, this support is largely removed, and there is little institutionalized daily emotional reconstitution of mothers. What there is depends on the accidents of a particular marriage, and not of the carrying out of an institutionalized support role." Chodorow, *The Reproduction of Mothering*, 36.

[8] Chodorow, "Preface to the Second Edition," *The Reproduction of Mothering*, vii.

[9] Chodorow is here outlining the normal regression experienced by psychologically healthy mothers.

with female infants, contends Chodorow, since this evokes the unconscious embodied experience for the mother of having been ***an infant daughter of a female mother*** herself. Similarly, the daughter identifies with her mother—both as her primary caregiver and as a person of the same sex—producing a mutual identification for mothers and daughters and, in turn, what Chodorow calls a "sense of self-in-relation".[10] Sons, in contrast, come to experience themselves as sexually and socially different from their mothers, in a process that is strengthened by the Oedipus complex and subsequent identification with the father. In this way, the boy's ego boundaries tend to be clearer and repression of his maternal identification and infantile dependence greater. Mothers, too, push their sons to differentiate, just as they typically hold their daughters closer.[11]

In broad terms, Chodorow argues—using psychoanalytic theory, case study and philosophical inference—that women and men are psychosocially shaped in and through the primary care of mothers: a same-sex parent for girls, and an opposite sex parent for boys. This produces different developmental trajectories and outcomes for each gender. Just as girls are drawn to connection and typically develop "selves-in-relation", boys are oriented to separation and individuation. Boys differentiate first as subjects in a process that is reinforced through sexual difference and grow up to identify with their symbolically stronger, but often absent, fathers. In the patriarchal family, the father's social and familial dominance is the boy's inheritance. This, in psychic terms, is the boy's "patriarchal dividend."[12] However, while boys come to identify with dominant fathers, daily father absence in industrial society means fathers are not typically introjected as primary attachment figures for boys or girls. For Chodorow this means boys, and the men they grow into, tend to have a more fragile and defensive masculinity, less founded in real attachment to fathers (and other adult men) and more on fantasy and projection. Being masculine, then, becomes in large part about being ***not feminine*** (or not mother).

[10] Chodorow, "Preface to the Second Edition," viii.

[11] Chodorow, *The Reproduction of Mothering*, 107.

[12] This is a term first coined by sociologist Raewyn Connell referring more specifically to the socio-economic (not psychic) currency of masculinity. See. R. W. Connell, *Masculinities* (Crows Nest: Allen & Unwin, 1993), 79.

Boys who resolve their Oedipus complex—the primary goal of which is masculine gender identification and heterosexual object choice—are able to substitute mothers with wives retaining a primary dyadic relational bond to a woman. Girls, on the other hand, are required to make the much more difficult shift from mother to father as primary love object—a process Freud already knew was fraught and incomplete.[13] As Chodorow shows, girls tend to triangulate—***adding*** their father to their pre-Oedipal internal object world rather than relinquishing their mother. This creates a more complex internal relational configuration; essentially girls layer a triangle (mother-father-child) on to a pre-existing female-female (mother-infant) dyad. The earlier relation sits, in Freud's terms, like a lost civilization at the core of the feminine self (indeed, Freud likened it to the discovery of Mycenaean civilisation prior to the Athenian one). It continues to inform her conscious and unconscious femininity, her internal and external object relations and her psychosocial development. Moreover, girls tended to retain deep attachments to both parents into adulthood. Critical here is the daughter's unwillingness to relinquish her mother or her emotional centrality even after the Oedipus complex is "resolved". Like Freud, Chodorow argued that this created a latent *emotional* homosexuality in girls and women. As she says,

> Girls emerge from this [oedipal] period with a basis for 'empathy' built into their primary definition of self in a way boys do not. Girls emerge with a stronger basis for experiencing another's needs or feelings as one's own (or of thinking that one is so experiencing another's needs and feelings). Furthermore, girls do not define themselves in terms of the denial of preoedipal relational modes to the extent as do boys. Therefore, regression to these modes tends not to feel as much a basic threat to their ego. From very early, then, because they are parented by a person of the same gender (a person who has already internalized a set of unconscious meanings, fantasies, and self-images about this gender and brings to her experience

[13] It took 35 years for Freud to grasp the significance of the mother-daughter relationship. Beneath the girl's Oedipus complex, he came to realise was a deep "homosexual" tie to her mother. The little girl never relinquished her (erotic) attachment to her mother, and as a consequence her Oedipus complex was never fully resolved. She was never fully reconciled with either femininity or heterosexuality, but would retain deep ties to her mother and, later, mother substitutes (daughters, sister, friends). Sigmund Freud, "Female Sexuality," 226.

> her own internalized early relationship to her mother), girls come to experience themselves as less differentiated than boys, as more continuous with and related to the external object-world and as differently oriented to their inner object-world as well.[14]

Chodorow illuminated the psychosexual as well as psychosocial dimensions of masculinity and femininity in conventional male-dominant, nuclear families in late-twentieth century western societies.[15] While women typically developed a sense of "self-in-relation", which often manifested as embeddedness in, and dependence on, relationship; men tended to shore up their ego boundaries, and remain differentiated, autonomous subjects.

Like Freud, Chodorow explored the shadow sides to these typical patterns too: for women it was boundary fusion, and a corresponding lack of a distinct and differentiated self (potentially giving rise to problems with excessive self-sacrifice, a lack of agency and autonomy, ambivalence in relation to their own mothers (or mother substitutes), resentment and narcissism); for men, this manifested in a defensive masculinity, including a defensive and potentially malignant homophobia or misogyny as well as a primordial fear of collapsing back into the mother/feminine, producing a defensive anxiety about dependence on, and relationship with, women. While women have more tenuous ego boundaries, they emerge from a mother-centred childhood more secure in their gender; men, on the other hand, have clearer ego boundaries, but a more fragile sense of gender-identity. This meant that while women in heterosexual relationships were more likely to desire emotional connection and intimacy than their male partner (and be frustrated by its lack), they were also more likely to have multiple close relationships, whereas men were typically more dependent on their primary intimate (dyadic) relationship, but also—and as a consequence—more defended against it.

In Chodorow's terms, men and women emerge through the Oedipus complex sexually attracted but emotionally incompatible. Most women

[14] Chodorow, *The Reproduction of Mothering*, 167.

[15] In my understanding Chodorow uses the term patriarchy in quite specific sociological and anthropological terms, to mean father dominance in social, political, legal and economic terms. This is distinct from more recent popular uses of the term, which refer to an ill-defined and all-inclusive male dominance.

end up "genitally heterosexual,"[16] but emotionally tied to their mothers (now introjected as dyadic, identificatory love). In this way, women's internal and external relational landscape continues to be animated by the pre-Oedipal dyadic relationship with their mother. In adult heterosexual relationships, men regain the pre-Oedipal dyad by having a substitute mother: a wife. Women do not have a wife, and so rarely receive the same kind of emotional or domestic support of a mother-substitute, while often having a longing and arguably even a need for this. In conventional heterosexual relationships, women thus often feel unsatisfied, and in need (or at least in want) of greater empathy, intimacy and connection. Thus, to answer Chodorow's abiding question: why do women mother? It is that they desire to recreate primary, dyadic intimacy (mother-child) within a triangulated (mother-father-child) relationship.[17] Women desire a primary identificatory love, then, like they had with their own mothers, that is created and re-created through becoming a mother. This, in essence, is "the reproduction of mothering". Again, social context is relevant for Chodorow, since women live in conditions of industrial-capitalist society, where female kin rarely live close by and so the longing for a mother—and for female companionship and nurture more broadly—is often acute. As Chodorow notes, while women reproduce men and children, with the attenuation of kin networks, women are essentially required to *reproduce themselves*.[18] The loss of adult female companionship produces a host of unmet needs and dependencies in women, that form part of the psychopathology of mothering under conditions of modernity. As she says,

> The very capacities and needs which create women as mothers create potential contradictions in mothering. A mother's sense of continuity with her infant may shade into too much connection and not enough separateness. Empathy and primary identification, enabling anticipation of an infant's or child's needs, may become an unconscious labelling of what her child ought to need ... The sense of autonomous self becomes difficult for children and leads to a mother's loss of sense of self as well. That women

[16] Chodorow, *The Reproduction of Mothering*, 128–129.

[17] Chodorow is here referring to an abstract, heuristic triangle that is both conventional—i.e., the norm in families, and a useful conceptual device for understanding and interpreting women's internal object world.

[18] Chodorow, *The Reproduction of Mothering*, 36.

> turn to children to complete a relational triangle, or recreate a mother-child unity, means that mothering is invested with a mother's often conflictual, ambivalent, yet powerful need for her own mother. That women turn to children to fulfil emotional and even erotic desires unmet by men or other women means that a mother expects from infants [or children] what only another adult should be expected to give.[19]

The second sociological part of *The Reproduction of Mothering* took up this point more substantially and was more socio-political in focus.[20] Chodorow expounded the psychic and social virtues of an egalitarian family structure in which men and women shared paid work and childcare with a view to expanding women's autonomy and reconnecting men to care. In her final chapter, "Women's mothering and women's liberation," Chodorow makes the point that the gendered division of labour, specifically women's responsibility for childcare, *produces* inequality.[21] It isn't a neutral division: different but equal; rather, the differential power assigned to each sphere—literally the power based on access to resources—created a hierarchy with men possessing power and control over women (and here Chodorow's foundational discipline of anthropology is brought to bear as she reflects on patriarchal hunter-gatherer and agricultural societies). Chodorow asserted that only men's active involvement in childcare from infancy would free women for more active participation in the public sphere, including independent access to the market economy. It was only then that women would have the material basis to cultivate autonomy. Men too could reconnect with children and play a more central role in their socialisation and care as they had done in pre-industrial society. For Chodorow this didn't mean reversal, rather it meant a rounding out. Men and women still had their positive qualities—autonomy and care respectively—but these would be tempered at the extremes, and each could more flexibly approach and undertake the tasks of the other. At a deeper level, this would also free children from singular emotional dependence

[19] Chodorow, *The Reproduction of Mothering*, 211–212.

[20] It is important to note that this is a heuristic distinction. The "two parts" I refer to—the psychoanalytic and sociological parts—are woven together through-out the book. They are integrated into the book, albeit as separate chapters, rather than constituting two separate sections.

[21] Chodorow, *The Reproduction of Mothering*, 214.

on women (as mothers) and assign the emotional work of socialising (and failing) children to both men and women. This would stop the asymmetries of gender resulting from the reproduction of (too much) mothering; that is, mothering from isolated mothers, without access to the social and emotional supports of kin and community.

Chodorow, the political idealist, wanted both a shared division of domestic and psychological labour with a view to reconstructing gender relations on a more egalitarian and humane footing. Autonomy and care were not *a priori* or essentially male and female, and gendered selves were malleable. While shared care invited men into more integrated and less defensive forms of masculinity, for women the stakes were higher: it had the potential to end sexism and misogyny, in its distinctly modern (or industrial-capitalist) form. Writing at roughly the same time, Dorothy Dinnerstein in *The Mermaid and the Minotaur* propounded a similar argument: misogyny was universal and endemic and grew out of asymmetrical parenting arrangements producing our primordial debt to and dependence on women.[22] This, she argued, was also the psychosexual basis of our rabid destruction of the earth. We resented women for the absolute power they wielded over life itself, and this was extended to "mother earth". Both were objectified and exploited. In Dinnerstein's view, this power needed to be democratized and its effects—both the love and the hate—more evenly distributed. Exclusive maternal care created self-sacrificing women and counter-dependent men who resented and refused women's authority. Both Chodorow and Dinnerstein conjectured that shared parenting would undermine industrial-capitalist patriarchy at its core, by knocking out its socio-economic, familial and unconscious foundations.

The Reproduction of Mothering Contextualised

This second part of *The Reproduction of Mothering* was much more programmatic and aligned itself with the goals of the second-wave women's movement. It bears the traces of Chodorow's youth, and of the counter-cultural movements of the era with their aspirations for a freer, more just society. As Jade McGleughlin argues (Chapter 11, this

[22] Dorothy Dinnerstein, *The Mermaid and the Minotaur: Sexual Arrangement and Human Malaise* (New York: Harper & Row, 1976).

volume), the women's movement was the political foundation for the feminist psychoanalytic work of Nancy Chodorow and Jessica Benjamin. It provided the fertile ground through which to base a theory of women's subjectivity, a critique of conventional masculinity, and for the real-world cultivation of intersubjectivity beyond the strictures of the nuclear family. As McGleughlin points out, within the women's movement *women could recognize each other's subjectivity* even if the men in their lives (and, in particular, their fathers, as Benjamin's work explored)[23] did not. Women could be emotional supports for each other, and they could recognize and reflect each other as writers, artists, intellectuals, political actors, sexual beings and autonomous agents. The women's movement declared that women were capable of generating meaning, including as authors of their own lives and as agents in the public sphere. As McGleughlin perspicaciously observes, this groundswell of feminist community made the theories of female subjectivity, like those promulgated by Chodorow and Benjamin, possible and constituted both the testing ground and support structure for their elucidation.

Psychoanalytic feminism was annexed to the women's movement and it is this fact that perhaps anchors *The Reproduction of Mothering* to place, periodising it in the progressive politics of the nineteen sixties and seventies. Importantly, the women's movement was generative of work like Chodorow's; it created the political and intellectual tools (not to mention the support and camaraderie) to question orthodox theories with their classically androcentric biases. Freud had been roundly rejected as a misogynist by second-wave feminists—Germaine Greer had referred contemptuously to the "psychological sell,"[24] while Kate Millet derided Freud's conflation of women's dissatisfaction and distress with causes rooted in the female condition.[25] In the polemical style characteristic of the time, Shulamith Firestone articulated the shared critique well,

[23] Jessica Benjamin, *The Bonds of Love: Psychoanalysis, Feminism and the Problem of Domination* (New York: Pantheon, 1988).

[24] Germaine Greer, *The Female Eunuch* (London: MacGibbon and Kee, 1970).

[25] Kate Millet, *Sexual Politics* (New York: Doubleday, 1970).

Interestingly, both Millet and Firestone granted Freud his peculiar genius while deriding his elevation of the masculine over the feminine. In many respects this anticipated Juliet Mitchell's work insofar as already, even in the midst of blistering critique, there was a distinction between Freud "the genius" and Freud "the patriarch".

> … Freudian theory, regroomed for its new function of 'social adjustment', was used to wipe up the feminist revolt. Patching up with band-aids the casualties of the aborted feminist revolution, it succeeded in quieting the immense social unrest and role confusion that followed in the wake of the first attack on the rigid patriarchal family. It is doubtful that the sexual revolution could have remained paralysed at half-way point for half a century without its help; for the problems stirred up by feminism are still not resolved today.[26]

While psychoanalysis had a comprehensive and layered account of subjectivity, then, it was largely an account of *men's subjectivity*: from fusion with the mother through differentiation and Oedipal rivalry with the father, through to the assumption of a masculine psychosexual subject position founded in dominance over women and a concomitant disparagement of femininity. In the prevailing trajectory, man transcends the particularity of his embodied and emotional foundations and becomes an autonomous subject. Conflated with the masculine norm and found deficient—infamously "lacking" (a penis)—women's internal worlds, sexuality and identity were subsumed and diminished within the Oedipal model, and while female analysts challenged the androcentrism and misogyny of Freudian psychoanalysis—notably, Karen Horney[27] and, to a lesser extent, Helene Deutsch[28] (lesser because her own views regarding female passivity were themselves quite sexist)—these pioneering analysts did not have the gust of wind called the women's movement behind them.

The reclamation and restitution of psychoanalysis began with a complex recognition of both its insights and its shortcomings. This work began in earnest with Juliet Mitchell's *Psychoanalysis and Feminism*[29] where she staked out a critical distinction between Freud's *description* of patriarchy (in psyche and society) and its endorsement. Her claim was that Freud was a master expositor of the patriarchal nuclear family, and its repressed sexual interior, rather than an apologist or propagator.

[26] Shulamith Firestone, *The Dialectic of Sex: The Case for Feminist Revolution* (New York: Morrow, 1970), 71.

[27] Karen Horney, *Feminine Psychology* (New York: W. W. Norton, 1967 [1926]).

[28] Helene Deutsche, *Psychology of Women*, vols. 1 and 2 (New York: Grune & Stratton, 1944/1945)

[29] Juliet Mitchell, *Psychoanalysis and Feminism* (Harmondsworth, Middlesex: Penguin, 1974).

He was the man in the wilderness marking the developmental and drive based territories of the psyche and, just like an intrepid explorer, what he brought back was a map, and one that feminists could avail themselves of. "However it may have been used", contended Mitchell, "psychoanalysis is not a recommendation *for* a patriarchal society, but an analysis of one. If we are interested in understanding and challenging the oppression of women, we cannot afford to neglect it."[30]

Second-Wave Feminism and Motherhood

Nancy Chodorow's work was groundbreaking insofar as she breathed new life into the bones of psychoanalytic theory imagining the female subject not as a defective male or embittered woman (defined by lack), but as a subject unto herself. As she has subsequently stated, her focus at this point in her career and development was that of the daughter rather than the mother, even as she saw these two subjectivities as mutually constitutive and interdependent.[31] Chodorow sought to explain and explore female subjectivity *on its own terms*, to reanimate psychoanalytic theory with the fullness of a theory not only of men's psychosexual identity formation, but also of women's. This work had begun in the 1920s with Karen Horney,[32] as had the synthesis of psychoanalysis and sociology, with both Horney's and Eric Fromm's work.[33] In this sense, Chodorow's "feminist foremothers" were not only those brilliant lights of the second-wave women's movement (Friedan, Firestone, Greer, Mitchell and Millet) they were also, and arguably more fundamentally, the first generation of women analysts.[34] While later theorists have identified an

[30] Mitchell, *Psychoanalysis and Feminism*, xv.

[31] Chodorow repeatedly refers to her work being produced in her 20s and being defined by developmental concerns that naturally focused more on the daughter (as future mother) than on the mother as past daughter. Chodorow, "Preface to the Second Edition," xvii.

[32] Freud's late reflections on women also identify the intensity of the girl's pre-Oedipal relationship to her mother. See Freud, "Female Sexuality," 225–243. See also, Chodorow, *The Reproduction of Mothering*, 95.

[33] See in particular, Horney, *Feminine Psychology*; Erich Fromm, "Psychoanalysis and Sociology," in *Critical Theory and Society: A Reader*, eds. Stephen Bronner and Douglas Kellner (New York: Routledge, 1989 [1929]), 37–39.

[34] Interestingly, as Chodorow shows, she went on to discover that most of these pioneering women analysts were *not* feminists. Chodorow makes a fascinating (to this editor) passing comment in a footnote, "Lurking in my unconscious was probably a

anti-maternal bias in the second-wave feminist writing on mothers,[35] and a bias toward the perspective of the "angry daughter," Chodorow was herself integral to this critique. In a paper written in 1980 with her colleague Susan Contratto, Chodorow argued that the feminist "consensus" on mothering in the 1970s presupposed that mothers and children were "adversaries" and that this relied on a reified conception of both mother and child.[36] The prevailing trope—evident in Dinnerstein, Rich, Rossi, Friday and Lazarre—was that mothers were the ambassadors of the patriarchy, albeit oppressed ones, crushing their daughters' sexuality and subjectivity. Chodorow and Contratto insightfully pointed out that these *feminist accounts* of the mother were characterized by a rigidity and splitting indicating an underlying idealization rooted "in unprocessed, infantile fantasies ...".[37] In this well-rehearsed, albeit unreconstructed, trope, "[m]othering either destroys the world or generates world perfection".[38] These analyses shared prevailing cultural tropes of mothering defined by two opposing and contradictory world views (frequently staged in the apocalyptic terms of life and death):[39] an omnipotent and devouring/castrating mother or the ever-giving "fantasy of the perfect mother" restoring plenitude.

What was required to offset this splitting, argued Chodorow and Contratto, was a greater sense of agency for the child rather than reducing him or her to a mere vessel of maternal socialisation (often cast as punitive) and for the mother to be seen as a person in her own right with

romanticized image of the reproduction of professional mothering." Nancy Chodorow, "Seventies Questions for Thirties Women: Gender and Generation in a Study of Early Women Psychoanalysts," in Nancy Chodorow, *Feminism and Psychoanalytic Theory* (New Haven and London: Yale University Press, 1989), 268.

[35] Daphne de Marneffe, *Maternal Desire: On Children, Love, and the Inner Life* (New York: Little, Brown & Co., 2004); Anne Manne, *Motherhood: How Should We Care for our Children?* (Crows Nest, Sydney: Allen & Unwin, 2005); Julie Stephens, *Confronting Postmaternal Thinking: Feminism, Memory, and Care* (New York: Columbia University Press, 2011).

[36] Nancy Chodorow and Susan Contratto, "The Fantasy of the Perfect Mother" in Nancy Chodorow, *Feminism and Psychoanalytic Theory* (New Haven and London, Yale University Press, 1989 [1980]), 82.

[37] Ibid.

[38] Chodorow and Contratto, "The Fantasy of the Perfect Mother," 88.

[39] See, in particular, Dinnerstein who believed women's "monopoly" on early childcare would lead to an environmental apocalypse because it generated a misogynist tendency to objectify women and nature, to treat them both as resources to exploit.

interests, relationships and desires beyond the mothering role and relationship. She would inevitably fail and yet she could, and most likely would, provide "good enough mothering". In Kleinian terms, feminism needed—and arguably still needs—to get beyond defensive splitting—the all-good or all-bad mother—and move towards a depressive position of integrated, imperfect, "good enough" mothers and mothering. Could a mature feminism, ask Chodorow and Contratto, accept maternal imperfection, and orient realistically to both mothers and motherhood?

Julie Stephens has written powerfully about the anti-maternal strands in second-wave feminism often manifesting in open hostility towards mothers and mothering. In Stephens' insightful view, the passionate desire of second-wave feminists to "give birth to themselves"[40] produced a negation, even a denial, of the maternal at the very core of feminist politics. Stephens' view is nuanced however insofar as she sees a kernel in feminism intersecting with a "collective memory" process that has reinforced "postmaternal thinking" as part of a more generalized denial of dependence and care under neo-liberalism. Stephens asks us to consider how memory is created both individually and collectively and wonders, "what does a feminist cultural memory that actively forgets the nurturing mother reveal …?"[41] For Stephens there is an active reinforcement of this collective forgetting in a new "postmaternal" zeitgeist in which mothers—including our feminist foremothers—are disparaged or simply eliminated from view (we see this also in the de-gendering of social policy that eliminates mothers and instead speaks of "parents", obscuring who does the work of care. Even worse, under neo-liberalism mothers at home are redefined as "unemployed").[42]

Now second-wave feminism is blamed for the mass movement of women into the labour market and for ostensibly valuing paid work over mothering. In reality, the women's movement articulated and fought for much broader, more meaningful and radical political goals including wages for housework, childcare, maternity leave, equal pay for equal work, economic independence and over-turning laws that allowed rape in marriage. Moreover, the paradigmatic protagonists, such as Firestone,

[40] Stephens, *Confronting Postmaternal Thinking*, 44.

[41] Ibid., 45.

[42] See Ann Orloff, *Farewell to Maternalism: Welfare Reform, Liberalism, and the End of Mothers' Right to Choose between Employment and Full-Time Care* (Illinois: Institute for Policy Research at Northwestern University, 2000).

Mitchell, Millet and Greer, argued for a wholesale transformation of society that did away with conventional constraints on women's sexuality and identity altogether. As much as we may critique these views as naïve, utopian or even destructive,[43] they were a very long way from a conventional endorsement of waged labour under capitalism! In the 2015 re-issue of *Women's Estate*,[44] Juliet Mitchell, for example, points out,

> When we said 'the personal was the political' it was certainly highlighting the formation of consciousness-raising groups but it was also the material presence of women's lives that was indicated. In a street group we took it in turns to share the child-care whether or not we had children: then childless, my turn was Tuesday afternoons when I would often pile a gaggle of toddlers into my old mini to allow them to slide along the polished floors of the Tate (now Britain), chase the pigeons on the lawns and love William Blake's Nebuchadnezzar. The press only mentioned American bra-burning and UK disruptions of Miss World … I say all this to counteract the impression so often given that women were not everywhere in the struggles … One tenet of the movement was that women who had had their educational potential realized should offer services to women who hadn't. It was from this seminar that the Peckham young mothers and housewives wrote a 'seminal' pamphlet and later Ann Oakley and I made it a founding strategy of the three collections of essays we edited on women.[45]

It is interesting that in our "collective memory" these diverse and arguably pro-mother strategies are edited out and reduced to "bra-burning" and "man hating" (another staple in the collective memory).

What second-wave feminism ***did do***, was uncouple the category of woman from the categories of wife and mother and while there have been both conservative and progressive backlashes against this historic uncoupling—and its paradigmatic expression in what Ann Snitow calls the "demon texts" that feminists have been "apologising for ever since"[46]—the separation was both fundamental and enduring. The idea that women could reject traditional roles, including those of wife and mother, and

[43] I am thinking here of familiar calls to "abolish the family". Or Firestone's insistence on the superfluity of the incest taboo in a free society.

[44] Juliet Mitchell, *Women's Estate* (London: Pelican, 1971).

[45] Juliet Mitchell, "Looking Back at Women's Estate," Verso Blog, February 3, 2015. https://www.versobooks.com/blogs/1836-juliet-mitchell-looking-back-at-woman-s-estate.

[46] Ann Snitow, "Feminism and Motherhood: An American Reading," *Feminist Review* 40, no. 1 (1992): 34.

invent themselves anew *was* truly revolutionary. It coalesced with, and gave social and political meaning to, the simultaneous development of the contraceptive pill. However, it wasn't the pill alone (which came into widespread use in 1965) which fundamentally broke the tie between women and motherhood, it was the pill *in combination with* the "consciousness raising" (not only of women, but of society at large) by first and second-wave feminism.[47] Second-wave feminism completed the cultural side of the political project which began in the Enlightenment with figures like Mary Wollstonecraft and Olympe de Gouges and came to fruition with the international suffrage movement of the late nineteenth and early twentieth centuries. In the western feminist conception, which grew out of and grappled with classical liberalism, women were conceptualised as ends-in-themselves who had a right, and indeed a duty, to determine their own lives. This meant women had a right to choose *if* they would be mothers, and if so, *when, how* and *with whom*. This separation of the category of woman from the category of mother—of which Chodorow's work, in a broader historical sense was part of—radically altered the sexual contract between men and women, and opened up new vistas for women as subjects and as mothers (see Bueskens, Chapter 13, in this volume).

However, in keeping with Stephens' critique, this uncoupling of woman and mother has also been problematized as "anti-maternal".[48] In Maura Sheehy's terms,

[47] This, of course, built on the first-wave feminist campaigns for reduced family size and contraception. In particular, the work of Margaret Sanger. All over the western world, this produced a demographic shift towards smaller families. As Alison Mackinnon's work shows, this was fundamentally connected to the new and radical view that women were ends-in-themselves and had a right to control their own reproductive destiny. See Alison Mackinnon, *Love and Freedom: Professional Women and the Reshaping of Personal Life* (Cambridge: Cambridge University Press, 1996).

[48] My own view differs from this, notwithstanding the "collective memory". In contrast, I argue that second-wave feminism broke the link between "woman" and "mother" that was integral to women's subordination. This freed women into a whole new way of being (or not being) mothers. Importantly, one needs to be able to say no to something in order to authentically choose it. It is because of second-wave feminism (building on the insights and activism of earlier waves) that women have this choice today. It is a fundamental right of world historic importance. This necessarily took precedence over, and underscored, the capacity to elaborate on maternal subjectivity in the terms discussed by contemporary feminist writers, which presuppose a level of choice and agency second wave (and earlier) writers could not.

> Second-wave feminism tried to take the door to female subjectivity off its patriarchal hinges altogether, but ultimately the goal wasn't to liberate *mothers* as much as to liberate women from motherhood. The thrust was a move to decouple the relation of women/mother as a given, rather than to enunciate maternal subjectivity.[49]

As Lisa Baraitser's more recent work shows, we need also to "repeat the second-wave move to uncouple maternity and femininity ... this time... for the sake of the maternal".[50] We need to look at maternal subjectivity on its own terms, as a valuable subjectivity rich with insights and meaning, not only as a ruse of oppression to be sloughed off (as if this were even possible) as we transcend to the lofty heights of unencumbered, individualist subjectivity.

Baraitser makes the insightful point that the otherness assigned to women in the familiar Cartesian binaries of order/chaos, reason/emotion, and nature/culture is now assigned to mothers. Mothers become the cypher for a subjectivity transcended by the childless woman in the disembodied spaces of neoliberal modernity. Interestingly, Baraitser identifies this in reverse too, observing how new mothers often construct the longed for, "lost" unitary self in retrospect against which a new messy, unruly, interrupted, maternal self emerges. In this way, *women* are autonomous and free while *mothers* are messy and chaotic.[51] The old rational man/chaotic woman split is now mapped onto the woman/mother dichotomy as women have increasingly ascended to individualist subjectivity and the realm of paid work.[52] Mother now

[49] Maura Sheehy, "Introduction: Writing of Mothers," in *Women, Mothers, Subjects: New Explorations of the Maternal*, ed. Maura Sheehy (London and New York: Routledge, 2014), 2.

[50] Lisa Baraitser, *Maternal Encounters: The Ethics of Interruption* (London: Routledge), 10.

[51] Lisa Baraitser, "Oi Mother, Keep Ye' Hair On! Impossible Transformations of Maternal Subjectivity," *Studies in Gender and Sexuality* 7, no. 3 (2006): 239–248.

[52] It might be, as I argue in my recent book *Modern Motherhood and Women's Dual Identities*, that women now have two modes of self, not easily reconciled given their foundations in the structural and symbolic separation of spheres produced by industrial modernity. It's not that the maternal self is simply a visage for projection, but that women have come to inhabit individualized selves in the past 40 years that are not easily reconciled with mothering selves, that are largely lived in domestic spaces sequestered from civil society. Petra Bueskens, *Modern Motherhood, and Women's Dual Selves: Rewriting the Sexual Contract* (London: Routledge, 2018), 172–176.

stands where woman used to: she is the unruly feminine Other, the dark and unknowable continent undoing women's hard won ego boundaries.

As Chodorow was at pains to point out, however, women always carried their mothers—or internal maternal object—with them, and perhaps the deeper (psychoanalytic) point is that we cannot jettison the messy, internal maternal object any more than we can jettison our "real" mothers. Psychically we are never done with our mothers. While Chodorow is sometimes held up as an example of the problem here—either as a theorist who was biased in favour of the daughter or as an advocate of egalitarian parenting—she was ever sensitive to the psychosocial (re)creation of maternal subjectivity. Even as she focused on the daughter, this daughter was conceived of as always already nested in the mother-daughter relationship. Even in her youth (and prior to having children), Chodorow was sensitive to the complex truth that we are all, in Shakespeare's—and later, Adrienne Rich's—terms, "of woman born".[53] Chodorow's work provided the foundation for this understanding with its sophisticated theorising of the nested intersubjectivity of both mother and daughter. In a twist on Freud's masterful point: that the ego is not master in its own house (there is always an unconscious provocateur prowling around in the basement), Chodorow noted that there is always a mother (who was once a daughter) reproducing herself inside the daughter's subjectivity, as captured so beautifully in the Matryoshka doll.

While this emphasis on female subjectivity and its locus in the mother-daughter relationship endures, the second more utopian part of Chodorow's thesis—that pertaining to egalitarian parenting—has come to be seen by some as anachronistic; a vain utopian wish to do away with the vulnerability and messiness of motherhood. In her twenty year reflections on *The Reproduction of Mothering*, Chodorow acknowledges that her call for equal parenting in many respects minimized the *emotional* centrality of mothering for both mother and child. Moreover, she contends that the two positions were "in contradiction" since to recognise this centrality, and its uniqueness, is to negate the idea that it can be shared.[54]

[53] Adrienne Rich, *Of Woman Born: Motherhood as Institution and Experience* (New York: W.W. Norton, 1976).

[54] Chodorow, "Preface to the Second Edition," xvi.

The Maternal Feminist Critique of *The Reproduction of Mothering*

In the early 2000s maternal feminist scholars—including, notably, Nancy Chodorow's former student Daphne de Marneffe and Australian social commentator Anne Manne—expressed concerns over the egalitarian vision of shared parenting and the *a priori* assumption that paid work was the royal road to autonomy. These maternal feminists were concerned about what they perceived as the denigration of motherhood in second-wave feminism, and the assumption that substitute care could replace mothers, or that most mothers even wanted to be replaced! As de Marneffe put it in *Maternal Desire*,

> Feminism has not always helped me. How many times I have encountered a feminist book filled with innovative ideas for changed gender relations, the acceptance of whose argument requires just one small price: that I relinquish my attachment to spending time caring for my children.[55]

de Marneffe identified a psychological shift for a new generation of daughters who wanted to reap the benefits of feminism alongside a commitment to mothering. This sentiment was echoed in a popular *New York Times* story in 2003 about the "opt-out generation": an elite strata of professional women choosing to "opt-out" of careers that demanded long-hours away from children.[56] For de Marneffe what was at stake in the battle between mothering and paid work was not only socio-economic equality but also moral and psychological commitments to children and the "inner life". She captured this through theorising the mother's desire *to be with* her children and how this desire was integral to the mother's own development and pleasure.[57] For de Marneffe mothering constituted a creative adult life path valid as an end-in-itself. In this way, she confounds the distinction between motherhood and autonomy by

[55] de Marneffe, *Maternal Desire*, 25.

[56] See Lisa Belkin, "The Opt-Out Revolution", *The New York Times*, October 26, 2003. https://www.nytimes.com/2003/10/26/magazine/the-opt-out-revolution.html. For a fuller analysis of this phenomenon see Pamela Stone, *Opting Out: Why Women Really Quit Careers and Head Home* (Berkeley: University of California Press, 2007).

[57] de Marneffe, *Maternal Desire*. See also her reply to critics, Daphne de Marneffe, "The (M)other We Fall in Love with Wants to Be There: Reply to Commentaries," *Studies in Gender and Sexuality* 10, no. 1 (2009): 27–32.

conceiving of an *autonomous mother* desiring “to be there”.[58] As part of this work, she observed a key generational shift from her feminist foremothers:

> Daughters of the 1940s and 1950s mothers, like Chodorow and Benjamin, were understandably motivated to analyse the problem of women trapped in a narrow domestic sphere ... But daughters of 1960s and 1970s mothers, like me, needed to solve something different: namely how to take advantage of the access women had gained in the workplace while not short-changing their desire to mother.[59]

Anne Manne also pointed to the flaws in a liberal feminist program that failed to properly account for the importance of mothers and mothering. In her influential book *Motherhood: How Should We Care for Our Children?* (2005) Manne made the insightful point that while infants were increasingly consigned to the undifferentiated group in feminist models of shared care, mothers were recast as unique “individuals”—differentiated, dynamic and free. While infants could suffice with a revolving cast of paid carers, mothers would charge into the sphere of worldly recognition and become subjects of history (like men). Manne likened the commodification of infant care to “the communist’s belief in the Collective Farm ... or an economic rationalist’s belief in the free market”.[60] In a Frankfurt school style critique, Manne called to account the colonization of the lifeworld and the unreconstructed, indeed naïve, assumption that institutionalization and commodification were preferable to home care.

Picking up on heated debates in Australia in the 1990s and 2000s, Manne observed, “the radical claim ... is that creche was better than home, that children were better off without full-time mothercare. All of them. *Always*.”[61] As Manne noted, this was wishful thinking at best, and unethical at worst, and here she called second-wave feminists to account,

> Thinkers such as Nancy Chodorow and Dorothy Dinnerstein came close to the utopian socialist hope that a new human being would be created by the

[58] Ibid.

[59] de Marneffe, *Maternal Desire*, 64.

[60] Manne, *Motherhood*, 41.

[61] Ibid., 41.

> abolition of 'exclusive' motherhood. Dinnerstein is particularly apocalyptic… [warning] her readers that if something is not done soon to 'break the female monopoly over early childcare', we can expect the imminent end of civilisation!"[62]

Manne acknowledged the important contribution the feminist argument for men's involvement in early child care had made, however she noted that both Chodorow and Dinnerstein "seesawed between the ideal of shared parental care and institutional daycare."[63] As she pointed out, it wasn't communal or shared care that replaced maternal care, but institutionalized childcare.[64] Importantly, as Manne argued, institutions tend to prioritize efficiency and routine over spontaneity, creativity or privacy, and they do not replace love. Manne observed an idealization of childcare that was the inverse of the earlier dictum of "biology is destiny" imposing compulsory motherhood on women. The new neoliberal discourse was tangled up with the anti-maternal strands in feminism, and each gave the other reinforcement. Home based mother care, we were told,[65] would produce selfish, neurotic children, objectifying nature and reproducing gender.

> The counterpoint, then, to the negative vision of mothercare was an idealized portrait of childcare. From daycare would emerge a new caring, sharing human being to begin the new world, free of sexism and all neuroses, eliminating both poverty and poor parenting in one fell swoop. Creches would replace the vagaries and imperfections of parental love with trained 'professional' care.[66]

[62] Ibid., 38. Dinnerstein believed that exclusive mother care was the cause of environmental destruction through a misogyny that extended to "mother earth".

[63] Ibid.

[64] In the last two decades, we have also seen a resurgence of nannies among the wealthy. See Cameron MacDonald, *Shadow Mothers: Nannies, Au Pairs, and the Micropolitics of Mothering* (Berkeley: California University Press, 2010); Megan K. Stack, *Women's Work: A Reckoning with Work and Home* (New York: Doubleday, 2019). See also, Katie Garner, Chapter 14, this volume.

[65] Manne's argument is based here on the heated feminist debate on childcare in Australia through the 1990s and 2000s. She draws on policy documents, research and statements made by prominent feminists in the media. Manne, *Motherhood*, 183–235.

[66] Manne, *Motherhood*, 40–41.

As Manne asks, was this really what feminists had fought for?

Arlie Hochschild similarly identified a "care deficit"[67] emerging from the exodus of white, middle-class women from the home into the world of work. A subtle shift had emerged, observed Hochschild, in which emotional needs and relationships were revised down, even away, to concord with market imperatives mandating the double-income family. As neo-liberalism usurped political and economic agendas, women's empowerment was falsely equated with career success—a point also made by Nancy Fraser in *Fortunes of Feminism*.[68] This denigrated the value of unpaid work—and mothering—in the domestic sphere. It also obliterated the second-wave feminist call for reduced paid work hours and greater time at home, in community, with loved ones and living creatively beyond the capitalist market.[69] It is interesting to read Chodorow's mature reflections (written in 1999) on this exact point. She highlights how her own egalitarian argument to bring fathers into childcare was premised on the post war, Keynsian social and economic structures, not the neoliberal ones that came to replace them. As she says,

> Nor could I foretell that a culture that advocated full-time mothering and an economy that permitted it [would] be replaced by workplace practices and economic transformations that erode the recognition of the mother-child relationship and often entail that neither mothers nor children have enough time together.[70]

The early utopian ideals of feminism—of which we can include Chodorow's—were co-opted by an inhumane and acquisitive economic rationalism that offered an elite strata of women a path into "equality" at the expense of the majority of women, and arguably also children. What the social theorist Jürgen Habermas calls the "lifeworld"[71]—namely, the private sphere including the familial and social relationships

[67] Arlie Hochshild, *The Commercialization of Intimate Life: Notes from Home and Work* (California: University of California Press, 2003), 214.

[68] Nancy Fraser, *Fortunes of Feminism: From State-Managed Capitalism to Neo-liberal Crisis* (London: Verso, 2013).

[69] See Kathi Weeks, *The Problem with Work: Feminism, Marxism, Antiwork Politics, and Postwork Imaginaries* (Durham: Duke University Press, 2011).

[70] Chodorow, "Preface to the Second Edition," xvi.

[71] Jürgen Habermans, *The Theory of Communicative Action*, vol. 1 (London: Heinemann, 1984 [1981]).

cultivated therein—was increasingly commoditized and "outsourced".[72] While the anti-maternal strands in second-wave feminism had important philosophical and ethical roots in the enlightenment assertion of female personhood, and in a contemporaneous push back against biological determinism, the assumption that children were better off *without mothers at home*, even in their early years, was political overreach. As I have written elsewhere, one of the reasons this is such an emotionally charged issue is because mothers are the last members of the western family institutionally mandated at home, and so their departure leaves "nobody home", at least not permanently. This leaves an existential crisis at the very heart of the west. Arguably, we have lost our secure base. It wasn't mothers' sole responsibility to keep the existential hearth fires burning, but their departure is certainly an opportunity to revisit the work/life question. [73]

This shift has resulted in a de-gendering of social policy across the western world[74] and the concomitant assumption of equality has resulted in a paradoxical situation: the more equal (some) women become (namely, the childless and the wealthy), the more unequal mothers become. This has caused feminists to pause. Neo-liberalism asserts that all individuals are free and equal, and must therefore earn their own living, turning motherhood from a recognised social good into an individualized risk. In this way, the economic costs of care have been returned to women. And yet, despite the considerable "price of motherhood" it remains a—if not the—fundamental life role and source of meaning for most women. Even in the advanced capitalist nations, being a wife and mother remains central for the great majority of women. As Catherine Hakim's large-scale research has shown, only a minority of women prioritize paid work over their maternal and domestic commitments. Most women are "adaptors" who seek to combine participation in paid work with mothering and domestic work.[75]

[72] See Arlie Hochschild, *The Outsourced Self* (New York: Henry Holt, 2011).

[73] See Bueskens, *Modern Motherhood*, 9.

[74] Ann Orloff, "From Maternalism to 'Employment for All': State Policies to Promote Women's Employment Across the Affluent Democracies," in *The State after Statism: New State Activities in the Age of Liberalization*, ed. J.D. Levy (Cambridge, MA: Harvard University Press, 2006), 230–270.

[75] Catherine Hakim, "Women's Lifestyle Preferences in the 21st Century," in *The Future of Motherhood in Europe*, eds. Gijs Beets, Joop Schippers, and Egbert te Velde (Dordrecht: Springer, 2009), 177–195.

Nonetheless, under the current social structure, there is an economic and a career cost for prioritising mothering. In an interesting article interviewing the "opt out" generation ten years on, Judith Warner found most of the mothers had either returned to paid work or were looking for work.[76] After somewhat grand assertions of "leaving the rat-race" and returning to the home to care for husbands and children, many found once their children were older, or if marriages fell apart, they wanted (or needed) to return to paid work. One divorced mother commented, "I was this woman who made this great 'choice,' [to stay at home] ... [and] It wasn't the perfect fairy-tale ending."[77] Pamela Stone's more detailed research into the opt-out mothers similarly found that elite women who had left the workforce to care for families in their 30s were often returning in their 40s, albeit often to jobs with less responsibility and lower rates of pay.[78] There is still a price for motherhood,[79] both in lost earnings for "time out" and in terms of the "motherhood wage penalty".[80]

The problem here—and one I take up in my own work on the "new sexual contract"—is that women shouldn't have to choose.[81] As Hakim's research shows, most women are "adaptors" combining mothering with paid work, even as the prevailing social structure makes this combination difficult.[82] In Australia, where this editor resides, mothers of dependent children are most likely to work part-time.[83] Similarly, where favourable

[76] Judith Warner, "The Opt-Out Generation Wants Back In," *The New York Times*, August 7, 2013. https://www.nytimes.com/2013/08/11/magazine/the-opt-out-generation-wants-back-in.html?pagewanted=3&smid=fb-share.

[77] Sheilah O'Donnel in Warner, "The Opt-Out Generation Wants Back In".

[78] Stone in Warner, "The Opt-Out Generation Wants Back In".

[79] Anne Crittendon, *The Price of Motherhood: Why the Most Important Job Is Still the Least Valued* (New York: Henry Holt, 2002).

[80] Michelle Budig and Paula England, "The Wage Penalty for Motherhood," *American Sociological Review* 66, no. 2 (2001): 204–225.

[81] Petra Bueskens, *Modern Motherhood and Women's Dual Identities: Rewriting the Sexual Contract* (London: Routledge, 2018), 142–145; Petra Bueskens, "Modern Mothers' Dual Identities and the New Sexual Contract," *Journal of the Motherhood Initiative* 10, no. 1 & 2 (2019): 59–82.

[82] Catherine Hakim, *Work-Lifestyle Choices in the 21st Century: Preference Theory* (Oxford: Oxford University Press, 2000).

[83] Sarah Charlesworth, Lyndall Strazdins, Léan O'Brien, and Sharryn Sims, "Parents' Jobs in Australia: Work Hours Polarisation and the Consequences for Job Quality and Gender Equality," *Australian Journal of Labor Economics* 14 (2011): 35–57; Marion

social conditions permit, such as in the Nordic countries, most women choose long periods of parental leave in combination with part-time work when they have infants and small children.[84,85] While women's part-time work has recently become politicized insofar as it is linked to ongoing inequality,[86] change is incremental. Indeed, tendencies toward convergence are also the result of men's higher rates of part-time work. What Hakim's "preference theory" shows is that when women have conducive policy and cultural contexts, most prioritize their home lives and choose work that fits in with mothering (between 60 and 80 percent), while only a minority are career-centred or home-centred (between 10 and 20 percent respectively).[87] What remains to be resolved at the policy level is how the majority of women who undertake mothering (and care work more broadly) can be compensated such that they are not left vulnerable to poverty in the event of divorce or separation.

Baird and Alexandra Heron, "The Life Cycle of Women's Employment in Australia and Inequality Markers," in *Contemporary Issues in Work and Organisations: Actors and Institutions*, eds. Russell Lansbury, Anya Johnson, and Diane van den Broek (London: Routledge, 2019), 42–56.

[84] This is sometimes referred to as the "Nordic paradox" insofar as greater choice has produced a greater divergence—or, in other words, greater inequality—between men and women. See Anne Lise Ellingsæter, "Scandinavian Welfare States and Gender (De) Segregation: Recent Trends and Processes," *Economic and Industrial Democracy* 34, no. 3 (2013): 501–518. Recent research indicates that it is primarily women who take "parental" leave and, moreover, that women take leave more frequently and for longer duration in turn disrupting their career trajectories and reducing their income, lifetime earnings and superannuation. OECD, "Is the Last Mile the Longest? Economic Gains from Gender Equality in Nordic Countries," Paris: OECD Publishing (2018). http://doi.org/10.1787/9789264300040-en; Kati Kuitto, Janne Salonen and Jan Helmdag, "Gender Inequalities in Early Career Trajectories and Parental Leaves: Evidence from a Nordic Welfare State," *Social Science* 8, no. 9 (2019). https://doi.org/10.3390/socsci8090253.

[85] While more women are entering the full-time workforce in recent decades after a substantial policy push, including "use it or lose it" leave entitlements designated for fathers only and universal high quality childcare, women still prevail in part-time work across the Nordic countries as recent research shows. See Aart-Jan Riekhoff, Oxana Krutova and Jouko Nätti, "Working-Hour Trends in the Nordic Countries: Convergence or Divergence?" *Nordic Journal of Working Life Studies* 9, no. 3 (2019). https://tidsskrift.dk/njwls/index; OECD, "Is the Last Mile the Longest?"; Anne Lise Ellingsæter, "Scandinavian Welfare States and Gender (De)segregation: Recent Trends and Processes," *Economic and Industrial Democracy* 34, no. 3 (2013): 501–518. https://doi.org/10.1177/0143831x13491616.

[86] Anne Lise Ellingsæter and Ragnhild Steen Jensen, "Politicising Women's Part-Time Work in Norway: A Longitudinal Study of Ideas," *Work, Employment and Society* 33, no. 3 (2019): 444–461.

[87] Hakim, "Women's Lifestyle Preferences in the 21st Century".

Across the lifecycle, we see that women's priorities also change, and we can assume that their maternal subjectivities do too. This was something touched on by Daphne de Marneffe in her reply to critics of *Maternal Desire*. She writes of wanting to write her book from *within* the visceral and emotional intensity of actively mothering young children because "childhood passes in a blink"[88] and so too does the maternal subjectivity that accompanies this phase.[89] Though it is rarely mentioned—and has certainly not been theorized in depth—*maternal subjectivity is dynamic across the lifecycle* and involves, as Chodorow now contends, generation as much as gender (see Chapter 2, this volume). Where a woman who is not yet a mother may be focused on her education and career, building partnership, friendships and life experiences, if she becomes a mother (still the majority preference) she may wish to reduce (paid) work time and concentrate her energies on her children and home life. She may, on the other hand, feel renewed creativity and energy for her work, and, if she has flexibility and support, combine both. This may shift again as children mature and a desire to return to the world of paid work, or simply to renew and/or shift her focus onto more worldly pursuits, arises. Middle and older age mothers experience developmental shifts such as the "empty nest", renewed autonomy and leisure time and the transition to grandparenthood—another "reproduction of mothering" (explored in more detail by Chodorow in Chapter 2 and Elizabeth Abel in Chapter 5, this volume). This thumbnail sketch contains many generalising biases regarding the standard female biography (my own departs from this substantially and so I understand its limitations). It also presupposes a level of choice not available to all. However, what we do know is that *when given the choice*, prioritising mothering in the early years of a child's life corresponds with most women's preferences, and arguably rather than pushing women into approximating male norms of full-time work across the lifecycle, recognising that mothers typically preference childrearing (if they have the economic and social options to do so) is critical. Again, de Marneffe is instructive here—in matters of equality, the "inner life" matters too.[90]

[88] de Marneffe "The (M)other We Fall in Love with Wants to Be There," 31.

[89] Ibid.

[90] Ibid.

It is my view that Chodorow offered a radical vision that combined an argument for women's autonomy—including our sexual, social, political and economic freedom—with an emphasis on maternal subjectivities transmitted from mother to daughter within the context of an (ideally) role-sharing family. Families where parents share the challenges and rewards of primary care (usually combined with some paid care), and the challenges and rewards of paid work[91] offer greater opportunities for whole personhood. Chodorow's vision, as I read it, was never for mothers to jettison their important mothering role, nor to assume that a neoliberal career could replace the precious intimacies of mothering, marriage or homemaking, it was rather to assert women's right to autonomous subjectivity and, importantly, the time and space to cultivate it. It was also about women's financial independence. In the last section of *The Reproduction of Mothering*, Chodorow proffers a sketch for how this might occur: bringing men into primary care, not simply as "babysitters" but as co-equal primary carers.[92] She now concedes that elements of this vision ran counter to her detailed account of maternal subjectivity insofar as it potentially undermined the primacy women place on mothering. Additionally, she observes that generalized political utopias are always contradicted by counter-veiling conceptions of "the good life".[93]

The Postmodern Critique of *The Reproduction of Mothering*

There are other well-rehearsed critiques of Chodorow—namely the postmodern critique of "grand theory" that emerged in the wake of Judith Butler's *Gender Trouble*[94] and the associated critique of "essentialism", which sent seismic waves through Women's and Gender Studies.[95] The

[91] Or unpaid work such as volunteering, creative pursuits, gardening, art etc.

[92] Chodorow now recognizes the call for shared parenting could be transformed into a claim for father's rights. Clearly this depends on fathers being loving, responsible parents. Chodorow, "Preface to the Second Edition," xvi.

[93] Ibid.

[94] Judith Butler, *Gender Trouble: Feminism and the Subversion of Identity* (New York: Routledge, 1990).

[95] Arguably the discipline has never been the same given the fundamental unit of analysis shifted from "women" to "gender" and the distinction between the two was hereafter collapsed.

political philosopher Carole Pateman refers to this period in the 80s and 90s as "essentialist hunting"[96] and certainly Chodorow's *Reproduction of Mothering* stood accused. She was accused of naturalising and universalising white, middle class women's experience.[97] In Evelyn Nakano Glenn's terms, while Chodorow (and here she also includes Sara Ruddick), decries the deleterious effects of the late twentieth century, male dominant, nuclear family, "the message that many readers ... take away [from *The Reproduction of Mothering*] is that this arrangement of 'biological mothers as sole and exclusive caretaker' is universal".[98] For Nakano Glenn,

> The problem for those attuned to the concerns of non-dominant groups is that the analyses do not sufficiently 'decentre' the dominant model. In trying to build a general or 'universal' theory, [Chodorow's] ... focus remains centred on a single, normative pattern, with variation relegated to the margins.[99]

Moving further into the territory of deconstruction, Parveen Adams' argued that Chodorow had falsely assumed a "core self" onto which a gendered (maternal) identity was mapped[100] and, from this putative ontological essentialism, extrapolated a Eurocentric model of mothering. Patrice DiQuinzio was similarly concerned about Chodorow's "false universalism". However, her critique was more specific: the problem resided not in Chodorow's analysis but in her conclusions. While Chodorow continually draws attention to the historical specificity of the family she's analysing, for DiQuinzio,

[96] Stephen On, "Interview with Carole Pateman by Steven On," *Contemporary Political Theory* 9, no. 22 (2010): 239.

[97] Evelyn Nakano Glenn, "Social Constructions of Mothering: A Thematic Overview," in *Mothering: Ideology, Experience, and Agency*, eds. Evelyn Nakano Glenn, Grace Chang, and Linda Rennie Forcey (London and New York: Routledge, 1994), 2–9.

[98] Nakano Glenn, "Social Constructions of Mothering," 5

[99] Ibid., 5.

[100] Parveen Adams, "Mothering," in *The Woman in Question,* eds. Parveen Adams and Elizabeth Cowie (Cambridge: MIT Press, 1990 [1983]), 324.

> ... whenever she draws conclusions she makes universalist claims about the sexual division of labor, the explanatory power of (at least certain) psychoanalytic approaches to personality development, and the cross-cultural relevance of the issue of the social reproduction of mothering.[101]

Like Nakano Glen, DiQuinzio argued that feminist analyses needed to focus on the plethora of sub-categories of mother. This would "enable a richer, more complex understanding of positions with respect to mothering such as 'single mother,' 'adoptive mother,' 'welfare mother,' 'lesbian mother,' 'foster mother,' 'surrogate mother,' and 'egg donor'."[102]

What I find disingenuous about much of the postmodern critique is the assumption that because a theorist is not specifically addressing a given phenomenon, such as a culturally marginalized form of mothering, that this means they are unaware of it or assume it is of lesser value. This is a significant slippage. The other problem, addressed more recently by Juliet Mitchell, is the erroneous assumption that generalisation is untenable.[103] This effectively puts an end to social theory, which is always in abstraction from the finely grained empirical reality on the ground. It is also important to note that *within* marginal groups there is variation too.[104] The assumption that "lesbian mothers" or "single mothers" are an undifferentiated monolith is equally fraught. Chodorow makes all kinds of qualifications and disclaimers in her text,[105] and indeed mounts her argument *against* the historically specific, atypical family arrangement of the

[101] Patrice DiQuinzio, "Exclusion and Essentialism in Feminist Theory: The Problem of Mothering," *Hypatia: A Journal of Feminist Philosophy* 8, no. 3 (1993): 9.

[102] DiQuinzio, "Exclusion and Essentialism in Feminist Theory," 15.

[103] Juliet Mitchell, "Reply to Lynne Segal's Commentary," *Studies in Gender and Sexuality* 3, no. 2 (2002): 219.

[104] Even Butler made this point in her succinct postmodern aphorism: "... there can be no subject without an Other." Judith Butler, "Gender Trouble, Feminist Theory, and Psychoanalytic Discourse," in *Feminism/Postmodernism*, ed. Linda J. Nicholson (New York: Routledge, 1990), 326. Behind the working-class mother is the lesbian, working-class mother. Behind the lesbian, working-class mother is the black, lesbian, working-class mother and so on ad infinitum. For the postmodernists this meant jettisoning "the subject", for those who didn't embrace the postmodern turn, it meant recognising that there are limits to generalisation, and an ever-present need for theorising that moves between generalisation and empirical specificity.

[105] As Chodorow says, "I am careful to point out that I am not describing a universal or essential story but a pattern ... We can generalize about patterns in these psychological processes, as I do in *The Reproduction of Mothering*, or we can look especially to clinical

late twentieth century that she is routinely accused of centring! Chodorow was describing, as she says, a, "... statistically prevalent rather than a morally normative model ...".[106] Importantly, there is value in generalising arguments about prevailing social patterns *and* value in identifying counter-trends and social practices that challenge and refine these generalisations. This is the process of inductive reasoning. Rather than define this in the either/or terms of margin *or* centre—an epistemological zero-sum game—why is it not possible to attend to both, to identify and theorize normative patterns and marginal ones? This does not obviate an analysis of power regarding the hegemony of the centre, nor oppose the development of critical theories regarding its deconstruction and reconstruction (or, for that matter, even conservative arguments that defend the *status quo*). The point is, if we are interested in truth claims rather than a moral superiority grounded in specious metaphysics we need to have theorising at large and small, examining prevailing and marginal patterns. This is the dialetic of "structure and agency" integral to sociology and social theory more broadly. Finally, the *a priori* assumption that Chodorow's theory of motherhood does not apply to the sub-groups in DiQuinzio's list—for example, "single mothers", "welfare mothers" or "lesbian mothers"—is a mistake. A lesbian, single mother may find her story reflected in Chodorow's analysis, and to assume otherwise is in fact exclusionary!

With the triumph of the post-modern and the post-gender within the academy many have forgotten or no longer engage with canonical second-wave work like Chodorow's content rather to dismiss it as an essentialist relic. This is a great shame, because *The Reproduction of Mothering* remains relevant and illuminating not only in the museum of classics, but also to reflect on contemporary issues related to sex, gender, identity, mothering, fathering and family. One of the challenging facts for feminism is precisely the tenacity of the gendered division of labour and women's attachment to mothering. Certainly, women in the middle-class

individuality and personal uniqueness: one approach informs and enriches the other." Chodorow, "Preface to the Second Edition," xv.

106 Chodorow, "Preface to the Second Edition," xi–xii. It is possible to argue this is akin to Mitchell's point that Freud was *describing* rather than *endorsing* patriarchy. This, of course, was not accepted by many feminists, and it seems Chodorow's claim that *The Reproduction of Mothering* was describing rather than endorsing the late-twentieth century nuclear family met the same fate at the hands of postmodern feminists.

have gone out to work over the last four decades (joining their working-class sisters), but most mothers do not have the same hours, incomes or career trajectories as men, indeed they continue to perform much more unpaid domestic and caring work, and here's the rub—at least for "post-gender" ideology—when it comes to motherhood, much of this is by choice.[107] Given this set of circumstance, Chodorow's analysis of the mother-daughter tie, and the "reproduction of mothering" continues to shed light on the emotional and psychological centrality of motherhood in women's lives.

Interestingly, where Chodorow has shifted in her thinking is toward the psychoanalytic and the individual, toward personal meaning and away from programmatic assertions based on "grand theory" or political utopias. She has returned to the *particular mother* at the heart of so many of her patient's lives, and psyches. What is it to have a mother, to be a mother and, more recently, to *not* be a mother? In her 2003 essay "Too Late" Chodorow turns to the *non-reproduction* of mothering, and the meaning of disruption and discontinuation (see also, Rosemary H. Balsam's Chapter 4, this volume).[108] Here her own subjectivity as a mother is brought to bear in an illuminating discussion on the clash between biological clocks, career imperatives (insensitive to women's reproductive window) *and* internalized self-sabotage. Again, we see Chodorow's exquisite capacity to balance social and cultural factors against the sharp silhouette of "clinical individuality". In one of

[107] I am not suggesting women *choose* the social and economic consequences of their preference for primary care (the double shift, reduced income, less superannuation); these are the consequences of outdated family and workplace structures and the exploitation of women's labour. However, the idea that women should adopt the masculine model of work—uninterrupted, full-time attachment to the labour force over a lifetime (now, no longer available to large swathes of working class men)—is false; nor is the conservative "solution" of marriage a viable answer to (single) mothers' poverty. Marriage is an institution that is clearly beneficial when it works, but needs to remain soluble; and while it does, women cannot rely on it. Women as mothers need remuneration that is not contingent upon marriage. As the political philosopher and women's rights advocate of the nineteenth century J.S. Mill said, this leaves women to the vagaries of luck. A woman is lucky, he noted, to have a good husband. We cannot assume this is a given, nor consign her entire life and future to the happenstance of luck. We would like to imagine we are a long way from this, but in fact, with few exceptions, a mother without a husband is still likely to be facing stark structural contradictions and economic deprivation.

[108] Nancy Chodorow, "'Too Late': Ambivalence About Motherhood, Choice, and Time," *Journal of the American Psychoanalytic Association* 51, no. 4 (2003): 1181–1198.

her layered insights Chodorow notes the veracity of external demands and constraints on professional women with *conscious* maternal aspirations, while also identifying how these constraints can be used to mask *unconscious* (or barely conscious) ambivalence. Here a neurotic or symptomatic relation to fertility is smuggled into a normalized trope of conflict between motherhood and career, thereby concealing the fact that it is, or will be, "too late". Chodorow writes, in an especially illuminating passage,

> This appropriation of cultural tropes as defenses obscures both conflicts about work and conflicts about motherhood. Work threatens too much involvement or fear of failure. On the other hand, it threatens success. Motherhood threatens, on the one side, a pull toward total envelopment in relation to a child, fantasies of triumph over one's mother, or fantasies of maternal-sexual voluptuousness and bountiful wombs and breasts. On the other hand, just as potent, lie fears of triumph over or regressive merger with one's internal mother, fears of losing oneself and one's identity, graphic fantasies about the ravages of pregnancy ... or imagining being too regressed to think. Divergent conscious and unconscious conflicts abut work on the one hand and motherhood on the other thus converge into a single conscious conflict, career versus motherhood, obscuring the anxieties and conflicts within each realm ... Our cultural climate ... and perhaps feminism itself, provide a cover for internal conflicts and fears.[109]

Acknowledging the centrality of the meaning of motherhood in women's psyches, including among those who are not (yet) mothers, or past the capacity to bear children, Chodorow identifies a different "reproduction of mothering".[110] The complex meaning of motherhood is still evident in chosen childlessness, in thwarted motherhood and in how a woman mothers step-children, her career, her home, her pets, her community and creative projects. Chodorow is not a maternal determinist. She reiterates her support for women's right to choose not to be mothers, for abortion, shared care and childcare, but she also sees the tenacity of motherhood—internal and external—in women's lives and the ways in which it continues to animate, or cast a shadow, over life choices, including those

[109] Chodorow, "'Too Late'," 1187.

[110] Ibid. See also, Chodorow, "Preface to the Second Edition," xiii.

below the level of awareness. Dominant cultural tropes about the "conflict" between motherhood and work, she insightfully observes, can mask more complicated layers of internal conflict.

As Chodorow now puts it, "the personal is personal" (Chapter 2, this volume, p. 49). The more programmatic dimensions of the second part of her thesis—changing the family through the greater participation of fathers in primary care—has yielded to an emphasis on individual meaning and solutions. In this revised conception, the psyche is an irreducibly personal configuration of real and abandoned object cathexes, a unique tapestry of drives, desires, internal object relations and external societal, cultural and familial pressures. Chodorow has not abandoned analysis of the social structure, power relations between the sexes, or the socio-economic and cultural pressures that are brought to bear on individuals, it is simply that she has recognized that there are a plethora of interpretations and answers to these "problems". As she says,

> If you take seriously that psychological subjectivity from within—feelings, fantasy, psychological meaning—is central to a meaningful life, then you cannot also legislate that subjectivity from without or advocate a solution based on a theory of political equality and a conception of women's and children's best interests that ignores that subjectivity.[111]

In this Chodorow contends that her two theses—the one promulgating egalitarian change to the sex-gender system through men's participation in early childcare, and the other pertaining to the creation and recreation of maternal subjectivity through the mother-daughter relationship—are in tension.[112] Chodorow notes that the insistence of the centrality of this relationship for both the mother's and the daughter's subjectivity means that engineering egalitarian social change may not be possible or desirable. Layered into this point is an epistemological one regarding the limits to truths claims and the need to square political utopias against experience and desire.

> As *The Reproduction of Mothering* made clear, mothering is not just another socially created unequal role that can be challenged, like the glass ceilings and discriminatory practices that keep women from achieving in

[111] Chodorow, "Preface to the Second Edition," xv.

[112] Ibid., xv–xvi.

> the educational, economic, and political worlds. Accordingly, a feminist recognition of the centrality of the realm of psychological reality would not have singled out a demand for equal parenting as a social goal—a goal that not only ignored many women's identities, wishes, and desires but that was also easily transformed into a claim for fathers' rights. Rather it would have focused on a variety of social goals and institutional and political supports that fostered and aided mothers to mother their children and to have a full life (this would include those women who found shared parenting appropriate to their family lives).[113]

While Chodorow has been periodized and her key arguments set into a particular narrative—whether that be one of feminist social engineering for the ideal-typical family, gender essentialism, falsely universalising, or providing a sensitive and nuanced account of maternal subjectivity—in reality, precisely because her work is complex and makes two distinct claims: that motherhood *is* interchangeable with parenthood and thus can be shared, and that motherhood is unique and central to female identity, and thus cannot be shared, it has produced a fruitful "intercourse of differences", to use Juliet Mitchell's felicitous expression.[114] It has created, in other words, a life of its own.

Overview of the Chapters

The chapters in this collection are organized into three sections: "mothers", "daughters" and "granddaughters," to reflect the generational distinctions between the authors as well as the chronology of their respective engagements with *The Reproduction of Mothering*. The first section includes an original essay from Nancy Chodorow and chapters by several of her contemporaries: Rosemary H. Balsam, Adrienne E. Harris, Elizabeth Abel and Madelon Sprengnether, each reflecting on the significance and influence of *The Reproduction of Mothering* both at the time of publication and forty years on. The next section includes chapters from several of Chodorow's graduate students: Ilene Philipson, Meg Jay, Daphne de

[113] Chodorow, "Preface to the Second Edition," xvi.

[114] Mitchell, "Reply to Lynne Segal's Commentary," 222.

Marneffe, Leslie C. Bell and Jade McGleughlin[115] all of whom have gone on to have important careers as clinical psychologists, authors and feminist theorists in their own right. These chapters reflect a shift in focus with a greater emphasis on critical engagement with *The Reproduction of Mothering* as well as exploring the enduring influence of Chodorow's mentoring. These "daughters of Chodorow" reflect on how her insights captured their imaginations and how they were able to utilize her dual emphasis on maternal subjectivity and the sociological reconstruction of gender norms in their own work. Finally, the next scholarly generation of "granddaughters"—where I situate myself—were not taught by Chodorow directly, but indirectly through the wide-ranging influence of her scholarship. These chapters by Alison Stone, Petra Bueskens, Katie B. Garner and Ursula Fanning apply Chodorow's ideas to novel contexts including comparing her analysis of maternal subjectivity with Luce Irigaray, an examination of how mothers are "reproducing the social", the mother/nanny relationship in contemporary literature and a Chodorowian analysis of Italian women's fiction. Taken together, the chapters are organized generationally to demonstrate a "reproduction of mothering scholarship". They comprise an eclectic mix of festschrift, memoir, reflection, reminiscence and original, contemporary engagement with Chodorow's ideas.

Nancy Chodorow leads this collection of essays with her chapter, "Mothering, Generation and the Life Cycle: *The Reproduction of Mothering* after Forty Years" situating her canonical work in a larger lifecycle frame connecting generation to gender. Chodorow comments on a poignant shift in her own thinking: from the second-wave feminist aphorism "the personal is political" to her more recent contention that the "personal is personal", even as the latter connects to the sociocultural and political-economic. Chodorow revisits *The Reproduction of Mothering* and charts how the focus on the psychodynamics of masculinity was widespread, from psychological anthropology and sociology to the Frankfurt School, but what was missing was attention to daughters and to the mother-daughter relationship, as well as an account of how girls grew up to *be* mothers. *The Reproduction of Mothering* therefore tied together the intrapsychic and interpsychic dynamics of individual gender-sexuality and the family to the sociology, political economy, and culture of

[115] Jade McGleughlin was not Chodorow's student but can be located here in terms of her generation and critical engagement with Chodorow.

gender. Chodorow describes how her own response to these insights was to undertake psychoanalytic training. Her contribution here brings this experience back to a reflection on *The Reproduction of Mothering*. She explores the tacit argument, expressed in its title, that in thinking about psychologies of gender, we are in the realm of generation. Chodorow explores how the inner mother-daughter world helps and hinders mothering and how it changes over the life cycle. She also honours some of the pioneering women psychoanalysts—her "mothers"—and acknowledges her colleague sisters, and her clinician and theorist daughters as well.

In her chapter, "*The Reproduction of Mothering*: Forty Years On", Adrienne E. Harris situates Chodorow's ground-breaking book in two traditions: 1970's second-wave feminism and in the transformations in psychoanalysis in which attachment, early object relations and intergenerational transmission became prominent areas of interest. Harris argues that Chodorow's book is a outstanding example of interdisciplinary thinking, bridging sociology, feminism and psychoanalysis in a unique mix that was transformative for each discipline.

In the fourth chapter, "Reminiscing and Reflecting on Nancy Chodorow's *The Reproduction of Mothering*," Rosemary H. Balsam reflects on the field of psychoanalysis in 1978 arguing that Chodorow's pioneering work regarding the mother's procreative life and its significant role in the daughter's mothering was a critical development in the field. Chodorow challenged the Freudian *status quo* of the Oedipal Complex. Balsam turns to Chodorow's insights from her 2003 "Too Late" paper to reflect back on *The Reproduction of Mothering*. She observes that Chodorow viewed the mother-daughter psychological process as an obstacle to women's liberation in her 1970s feminist phase. Now, in her seasoned psychoanalytic work, Chodorow patients illuminates the depth of the psychological process between mother and daughter. Balsam identifies Chodorow's ability to re-think complex theories and enrich them through her masterful synthesis of social theory and clinical practice.

In Chapter 5, "Thinking Back through our Mothers: Virginia Woolf, Nancy Chodorow, and Me," Elizabeth Abel offers a two-part reflection on Chodorow's profound influence on literary study and the new directions that influence might take. Coinciding with the feminist turn to women's literary genealogies, Abel shows how Chodorow's *Reproduction of Mothering* provided a theoretical framework for conceptualizing the dynamics of women's literary inheritance. These dynamics are echoed in

Virginia Woolf's *A Room of One's Own* (1929), whose narrator famously proclaimed that "we think back through our mothers if we are women." By making the psychoanalytic discourse of object relations available for literary study, Abel argues that Chodorow initiated a paradigm shift from the model of Oedipal rivalry presumed to characterize masculine literary inheritance to the dynamics of merger and separation that characterize the mother-daughter relations between and within books authored by women. Abel then shifts to the older adult daughter's perspective, observing that forty years later, feminist critics accustomed to thinking back through their literary mothers are learning to think forward through the object world bequeathed by the death of their literal mothers. In this second scenario, in which it is mothers who are separating from their daughters, lingering only in the things they leave behind, Abel asks how the "reproduction of mothering" might help to chart the material terrain of women's object relations.

In Chapter 6, "The Impact of Nancy Chodorow's *The Reproduction of Mothering* and Its Implications for the Future," Madelon Sprengnether argues that *The Reproduction of Mothering* altered the trajectory of second-wave feminism. Most feminists at this time identified psychoanalysis with its founder, Freud, rejecting him and his theories as a means of analyzing women's oppression. Chodorow argued, in contrast, that psychic structures were social, rather than fixed biological phenomena. Bypassing Freud, she made use of object relations theory to make the case that exclusive female mothering engenders psychic structures in boys and girls that reproduce themselves over time. Changing the social structure that ensured women's mothering would therefore lead to more flexible roles for women in society and a diminishment (if not end) of women's oppression. Sprengnether traces her indebtedness to Chodorow's core insight that psychic structures derive from social structures and how that conception has informed her own critique of the Oedipus complex, including how psychoanalytic theory has evolved after Freud, and how these altered conditions may better serve women.

In Chapter 7, "*The Reproduction of Mothering*: A Love Story," Ilene Philipson writes a poignant memoir as Chodorow's first Ph.D. student. She captures the intellectual, social and political context out of which *The Reproduction of Mothering* was written and received. As an undergraduate in the early 1970s, Philipson was searching for an intellectual foundation to explain women's second sex status that transcended the deliberate socialization model, which was hegemonic at the time. In finding the work of Chodorow, Philipson describes discovering a model for understanding the differences between men and women that finally spoke to the tenacity and emotional nature of our gendered sense of self. She argues that *The Reproduction of Mothering* continues to inspire through its message that while change is hard to effect, there is hope emanating from serious reflection, well-grounded and open intellectual inquiry and the capacity to see the world anew.

In Chapter 8, "Mothering in Life and Therapy: An Appreciation of Chodorow's Lifelong Contribution," Daphne de Marneffe makes the point that *The Reproduction of Mothering* is both a founding text for the psychoanalytic study of maternal subjectivity and the opening theoretical statement in Chodorow's lifelong investigation of subjective experience and its interaction with culture. De Marneffe argues that Chodorow's later psychoanalytic writings deepen her concern with individual psychic life and its necessary embeddeness in social context, while also observing that her exegesis of the work of the psychoanalyst Hans Loewald offers further reflection on the mother-child relationship. In this chapter, de Marneffe argues that Chodorow's humanistic psychotherapeutic perspective, combined with her spirit of searching and continual growth, is a precious resource for clinicians and a source of "intellectual mothering" to us all.

In Chapter 9, "Mother Figures: On Becoming the Mother One Wishes One Had," Meg Jay elicits Chodorow's opening line in *The Reproduction of Mothering*, "women mother", making the bold point that some women mother better than others. For daughters who were raised in "average, expectable" homes by "good-enough" mothers, the notion of the reproduction of mothering can seem full of promise. However, for daughters who were not so fortunate, the notion of reproduction can be terrifying. Such women may be afraid to become mothers or, more accurately, they may be afraid to become *their* mothers. In this chapter, Jay—a clinical psychologist and former graduate student of Nancy Chodorow—addresses the courage that is often required to become a mother when the mothering one received has been problematic. Often this courage comes from the mothering one glimpses, or receives in bits and pieces, from "mother figures" outside of the family, such as teachers, mentors, relatives, friends and therapists. Drawing on clinical work, empirical research and her own experiences with Chodorow as a mentor, Jay's message is hopeful about the possibility of "doing it differently" than one's own mother and claiming the reproduction of mothering for oneself.

In Chapter 10, "The Production of Male Mothering," Leslie C. Bell argues that men who serve as primary parents to their children are the product of changes wrought by the feminist movement, the LGBTQ movement, and changes in the economy that Chodorow advocated in *The Reproduction of Mothering*. According to Bell's research with stay-at-home fathers, in addition to needing a capacity for empathy, attachment, intimacy and dependency, men who serve as primary parents also require gender flexibility, a strong identity and a secure relationship with their female partner. Bell argues that we need Chodorow's formulation of gender now more than ever. Masculinity that denies and eschews dependency, vulnerability, relatedness and need is at the core of a masculinity that grounds itself in violence, aggression, domination, and radical independence. For Bell, stay-at-home fathers are at the vanguard of new articulations of masculinity.

In Chapter 11, "Full Circle with Chodorow: Reflections on Women's Sexual Desire and Lesbian Sexuality," Jade McGleughlin argues that Chodorow's seminal ideas in *The Reproduction of Mothering* offered a new way to understand gender differences in personality development that revalued women's relational capacities. However, she contends that women's sexual desire remained undertheorized. Based on her own unpublished work from the 1980s, McGleughlin pursues the possibility of women's sexual subjectivity by linking the work of Nancy Chodorow and Jessica Benjamin. She argues that conceptualisations of female subjectivity and desire are not just developmental projects, but emerged from the lived intersubjectivity of the women's movement. Looking back at the trajectory of tensions about women's desire in the movement, McGleughlin argues for the importance of sexual agency for women. Finally, she offers a personal story to imagine that the "queer art of failure" disrupts the reproduction of compulsory ways of loving and making family.

In Chapter 12, "Mother-Daughter Relations and the Maternal in Irigaray and Chodorow," Alison Stone's reprinted chapter argues that feminist theorists, writers, and artists have done much to bring mother-daughter relationships into representation and to reimagine the maternal beyond its traditional subservience to father-son dynasties. For Stone, Nancy Chodorow's important work in this area paints a portrait of contemporary mother-daughter relations which seems, at first sight, strikingly similar to Luce Irigaray's. Both thinkers suggest that mothers and their infant daughters experience a unique level of mutual identification.

However, under patriarchy—specifically, exclusive female childrearing for Chodorow and the absence of symbolization of female subjectivity for Irigaray—daughters are forced to turn to the father to achieve psychical independence from their mothers. Bringing Irigaray and Chodorow together across their different intellectual contexts, Stone compares and partially synthesizes their visions of the maternal and mother-daughter relations. By integrating their perspectives, Stone argues we can move beyond the impasse between Lacanian and object-relations feminisms that dominated psychoanalytic feminist debates in the 1980s and 1990s.

In Chapter 13, "Mothers Reproducing the Social: Chodorow and Beyond", Petra Bueskens summarizes Nancy Chodorow's important contribution to an understanding of female subjectivity grounded in mothering by women in gender asymmetrical families. This chapter takes Chodorow's psychoanalytic and sociological insights in *The Reproduction of Mothering* and asks: who is the maternal subject after 40 years of feminism? Drawing on the work of Alison Stone, Bueskens elucidates the process of not only reproducing but also reinventing mothering. From here, she explores how mothers are symbolically and actually "reproducing the social" through their transformative workforce patterns and preferences. Citizen mothers, Bueskens argues, have the potential to transform human relations, economies and polities, integrating an "ethic of care" with an ethic of justice". The last section of this article tentatively explores the emergence of "autonomous mothers" and their position as agents of history.

In Chapter 14, "Mirroring a Mother's Love: A Chodorowian Analysis of the Complicated Relationship Between Mothers and Nannies", Katie B. Garner extends Chodorow's ideas regarding the mother-daughter relationship to a new terrain: the mother/nanny relationship. Using three recent texts: Mona Simpson's *My Hollywood* (2010), Leila Slimani's *The Perfect Nanny* (2016), and Megan Stack's *Women's Work: A Reckoning with Work and Home* (2019), Garner applies Chodorow's theory to showcase how a mother's relationship with her nanny permits many unrecognized and ethically fraught psychological benefits including: recreating a triangulated relationship, receiving care from a woman while maintaining economic control and assuaging the ambivalence many mothers feel toward the demands of carework, while still vicariously adhering to culturally sanctioned tenets of intensive mothering. Garner analyses the complex emotional and ethical issues arising in these textual representations of the mother-nanny relationship.

In Chapter 15, "*The Reproduction of Mothering*: Unlocking Italian Women's Fiction from the Fin-de-Siècle Onwards", Ursula Fanning argues that Chodorow's *The Reproduction of Mothering*, is a groundbreaking work for feminist literary scholarship. Fanning finds echoes of Chodorow's ideas in the fiction of Italian women writers at the turn of the nineteenth and the beginning of the twentieth centuries. In the fiction of writers such as Matilde Serao (1856–1927) and Sibilla Aleramo (1876–1960), motherhood is a recurring focus and the mother-daughter relationship is frequently placed under the microscope in unexpected ways. These writers anatomize the mother-daughter relationship, and its significance, in strikingly modern ways. The process of modelling the (female) self on the mother is explored in these novels and, frequently, protagonists' heterosexual relationships are seen to be a poor second to the all-encompassing bond between mother and daughter. Fanning's chapter explores the mother-daughter bond in Serao and Aleramo's texts, showing how Chodorow's thesis allows us to read the texts against the grain. Through this process, Fanning highlights the influence of Chodorow in feminist literary criticism in the context of Italian Studies.

These diverse chapters are a testament to the influence, range and reach of Chodorow's *The Reproduction of Mothering* both at the time of publication and ongoing to today. This volume showcases and celebrates the enormous achievement of Chodorow's work while declaring its ongoing relevance for a new generation of scholars, analysts, students, women and men seeking to make sense of their primary relationships.

Bibliography

Adams, Parveen, "Mothering." In *The Woman in Question*, eds. Parveen Adams and Elizabeth Cowie. Cambridge, MA: MIT Press, 1990 [1983], 315–327.

Baird, Marion and Alexandra Heron, "The Life Cycle of Women's Employment in Australia and Inequality Markers." In *Contemporary Issues in Work and Organisations: Actors and Institutions*, eds. Russell Lansbury, Anya Johnson, and Diane van den Broek. London: Routledge, 2019, 42–56.

Baraitser, Lisa, *Maternal Encounters: The Ethics of Interruption*. London: Routledge, 2009.

———, "Oi Mother, Keep Ye' Hair On! Impossible Transformations of Maternal Subjectivity." *Studies in Gender and Sexuality* 7, no. 3 (2006): 239–248.

Belkin, Lisa, "The Opt-Out Revolution." *The New York Times,* October 26, 2003, https://www.nytimes.com/2003/10/26/magazine/the-opt-out-revolution.html.

Benjamin, Jessica, *Beyond Doer and Done To: Recognition Theory, Intersubjectivity, and the Third*. New York: Routledge, 2018 [2004].

———, *The Bonds of Love: Psychoanalysis, Feminism and the Problem of Domination*. New York: Pantheon, 1988.

Budig, Michelle and Paula England, "The Wage Penalty for Motherhood." *American Sociological Review* 66, no. 2 (2001): 204–225.

Bueskens, Petra, *Modern Motherhood and Women's Dual Identities: Rewriting the Sexual Contract*. London: Routledge, 2018.

———, "Modern Mothers' Dual Identities and the New Sexual Contract", *Journal of the Motherhood Initiative* 10, no. 1 & 2 (2019): 59–82.

Butler, Judith, *Gender Trouble: Feminism and the Subversion of Identity*. New York: Routledge, 1990.

———, "Gender Trouble, Feminist Theory, and Psychoanalytic Discourse." In *Feminism/Postmodernism*, ed. Linda J. Nicholson. New York: Routledge, 1990, 324–340.

Charlesworth, Sarah, Lyndall Strazdins, Léan O'Brien, and Sharryn Sims, "Parents' Jobs in Australia: Work Hours Polarisation and the Consequences for Job Quality and Gender Equality." *Australian Journal of Labor Economics* 14 (2011), 35–57.

Chodorow, Nancy J., "Preface to the Second Edition." In *The Reproduction of Mothering: Psychoanalysis and the Sociology of Gender*. University of California Press, 1999 [1978], vii–xvii.

———, *The Psychoanalytic Ear and the Sociological Eye: Toward an American Independent Tradition*. New York: Routledge, 2020.

———, *The Reproduction of Mothering*. Berkeley: University of California Press, 1978; second edition 1999.

———, "Seventies Questions for Thirties Women: Gender and Generation in a Study of Early Women Psychoanalysts." In *Feminism and Psychoanalytic Theory*, Nancy Chodorow. New Haven and London: Yale University Press, 1989, 199–218.

———, "'Too Late': Ambivalence About Motherhood, Choice, and Time." *Journal of the American Psychoanalytic Association* 51, no. 4 (2003): 1181–1198.

Chodorow, Nancy J., and Susan Contratto, "The Fantasy of the Perfect Mother." In *Feminism and Psychoanalytic Theory,* Nancy Chodorow. New Haven and London: Yale University Press, 1989 [1980], 79–96.

Connell, R. W., *Masculinities*. Crows Nest: Allen & Unwin, 1993.

Crittendon, Anne, *The Price of Motherhood: Why the Most Important Job Is Still the Least Valued*. New York: Henry Holt, 2002.

de Marneffe, Daphne, *Maternal Desire: On Children, Love, and the Inner Life*. New York: Little, Brown, 2004; second edition, 2016.

———, "The (M)other We Fall in Love with Wants to be There: Reply to Commentaries." *Studies in Gender and Sexuality* 10, no. 1 (2009): 27–32.
Deutsche, Helene, *Psychology of Women*, vols. 1 and 2. New York: Grune & Stratton, 1944/1945.
Dinnerstein, Dorothy, *The Mermaid and the Minotaur: Sexual Arrangement and Human Malaise*. New York: Harper & Row, 1976.
DiQuinzio, Patrice, "Exclusion and Essentialism in Feminist Theory: The Problem of Mothering." *Hypatia: A Journal of Feminist Philosophy* 8, no. 3 (1993): 1–20.
Ellingsæter, Anne Lise, "Scandinavian Welfare States and Gender (De) Segregation: Recent Trends and Processes." *Economic and Industrial Democracy* 34, no. 3 (2013): 501–518.
Firestone, Shulamith, *The Dialectic of Sex: The Case for Feminist Revolution*. New York: Morrow, 1970.
Fraser, Nancy, *Fortunes of Feminism: From State-Managed Capitalism to Neoliberal Crisis*. London: Verso, 2013.
Freud, Sigmund, "Female Sexuality." *Standard Edition*, vol. 21. London: Hogarth Press, 1961 [1931], 225–243.
Fromm, Erich, "Psychoanalysis and Sociology." In *Critical Theory and Society: A Reader*, eds. Stephen Bronner and Douglas Kellner. New York: Routledge, 1989 [1929], 37–39.
Greer, Germaine, *The Female Eunuch*. London: MacGibbon and Kee, 1970.
Habermans, Jürgen, *The Theory of Communicative Action*, vol. 1. London: Heinemann, 1984 [1981].
Hakim, Catherine, "Women's Lifestyle Preferences in the 21st Century." In *The Future of Motherhood in Europe*, eds. Gijs Beets, Joop Schippers, and Egbert te Velde. Dordrecht: Springer, 2009, 177–195.
———, *Work-Lifestyle Choices in the 21st Century: Preference Theory*. Oxford: Oxford University Press, 2000.
Hochshild, Arlie, *The Commercialization of Intimate Life: Notes from Home and Work*. California: University of California Press, 2003.
———, *The Outsourced Self*. New York: Henry Holt, 2011.
Horney, Karen, *Feminine Psychology*. New York: W. W. Norton, 1967 [1926].
Hugo, Victor, *History of a Crime: The Testimony of an Eye-witness*, Trans. T.H. Joyce and Arthur Locker. New York: Mondial, 2005 [1852/1877].
MacDonald, Cameron, *Shadow Mothers: Nannies, Au Pairs, and the Micropolitics of Mothering*. Berkeley: CA: California University Press, 2010.
Mackinnon, Alison, *Love and Freedom: Professional Women and the Reshaping of Personal Life*. Cambridge: Cambridge University Press, 1996.
Manne, Anne, *Motherhood: How Should We Care for Our Children?* Crows Nest, Sydney: Allen & Unwin, 2005.
Millet, Kate, *Sexual Politics*. New York: Doubleday, 1970.

Mitchell, Juliet, "Looking Back at Women's Estate." Verso Blog, February 3, 2015, https://www.versobooks.com/blogs/1836-juliet-mitchell-looking-back-at-woman-s-estate.

———, *Psychoanalysis and Feminism*. Harmondsworth, Middlesex: Penguin, 1974.

———, "Reply to Lynne Segal's Commentary." *Studies in Gender and Sexuality* 3, no. 2 (2002): 217–228.

———, *Women's Estate*. London: Pelican, 1971.

Nakano Glenn, Evelyn, "Social Constructions of Mothering: A Thematic Overview." In *Mothering: Ideology, Experience, and Agency*, eds. Evelyn Nakano Glenn, Grace Chang and Linda Rennie Forcey. London and New York: Routledge, 1994, 2–9.

On, Stephen, "Interview with Carole Pateman by Steven On." *Contemporary Political Theory* 9, no. 22 (2010): 239.

Orloff, Ann, *Farewell to Maternalism: Welfare Reform, Liberalism, and the End of Mothers' Right to Choose between Employment and Full-Time Care*. Illinois: Institute for Policy Research at Northwestern University, 2000.

———, "From Maternalism to 'Employment for All': State Policies to Promote Women's Employment Across the Affluent Democracies." In *The State after Statism: New State Activities in the Age of Liberalization* ed. J. D. Levy. Cambridge, MA: Harvard University Press, 2006, 230–270.

Rich, Adrienne, *Of Woman Born: Motherhood as Institution and Experience*. New York: W.W. Norton, 1976.

Sheehy, Maura, "Introduction: Writing of Mothers." In *Women, Mothers, Subjects: New Explorations of the Maternal*, ed. Maura Sheehy. London and New York: Routledge, 2014. Full page range.

Snitow, Ann, "Feminism and Motherhood: An American Reading." *Feminist Review* 40, no. 1 (1992): 32–51.

Stephens, Julie, *Confronting Postmaternal Thinking: Feminism, Memory, and Care*. New York: Columbia University Press, 2011.

Stone, Pamela, *Opting Out: Why Women Really Quit Careers and Head Home*. Berkeley: University of California Press, 2007.

Stack, Megan K., *Women's Work: A Reckoning with Work and Home*. New York: Doubleday, 2019.

Warner, Judith, "The Opt-Out Generation Wants Back In." *The New York Times*, August 7, 2013, https://www.nytimes.com/2013/08/11/magazine/the-opt-out-generation-wants-back-in.html?pagewanted=3&smid=fb-share.

Weeks, Kathi, *The Problem with Work: Feminism, Marxism, Antiwork Politics, and Postwork Imaginaries*. Durham: Duke University Press, 2011.

PART I

Mothers

CHAPTER 2

Women Mother Daughters: *The Reproduction of Mothering* After Forty Years

Nancy J. Chodorow

I, as a woman, ask in amazement, and what about motherhood?
Karen Horney, 1926[1]

[1]From Karen Horney, "The Flight from Womanhood: The Masculinity-Complex in Women, as Viewed by Men and by Women," *International Journal of Psychoanalysis* 7 (1926): 324–339. Reprinted with permission.

[2]From Virginia Woolf, *A Room of One's Own* (Hogarth Press, 1929). Reprinted with permission from Penguin Random House.

I presented an early version of this chapter in 2015 as a plenary address at the conference, "Motherhood and Culture," at Maynooth University, Ireland. There I discovered to my great pleasure that throughout the world, there is a thriving field of motherhood studies that draws scholars from disciplines across the social sciences and humanities. There I met Petra Bueskens, to whom I am so grateful for the honor of this book.

N. J. Chodorow (✉)
University of California, Berkeley, CA, USA
e-mail: Nancy_Chodorow@hms.harvard.edu

Harvard Medical School, Boston, MA, USA

P. Bueskens (ed.), *Nancy Chodorow and* The Reproduction of Mothering,
https://doi.org/10.1007/978-3-030-55590-0_2

For we think back through our mothers if we are women.
Virginia Woolf, 1929[2]

Women mother daughters who, when they become women, mother.
Nancy Chodorow, 1978

Women mother. So opens *The Reproduction of Mothering*.[3] Here is a book about mother and daughter, the intertwining of generation and gender, even as I myself have changed generations and developed. It is a great honor, and also daunting, to be invited to look back on this book after 40 years.

The Reproduction of Mothering comes from a time in second-wave feminism when the personal was political, but feminists were with rare exception hostile to psychoanalysis and suspicious of any account that began from the psyche rather than from political and economic forces. The book argues that the personal is *personal*, and that that's important in itself, even as it also shows how the personal connects to the socio-cultural and political-economic. I begin from the everyday, observing that the mother–daughter relationship—especially, being a daughter—seems important in women's experience and development. I explore, in an open-ended way, this relationship over the course of the daughter's development: how do we understand this important relationship, especially in the daughter's psyche and development? How is it being the mother of a daughter? How do women *become* mothers? I discover that these questions are connected, that it is through the mother-daughter relationship, through women's mothering, that daughters develop maternality. The female relatedness that develops in the mother–daughter relationship and goes into mothering is described by women writers in novels, autobiography, memoir, and poetry, even as this foundational emotional and relational experience and identity helps to put women into a psychosocial and psychocultural world of gender inequality and male dominance.

In articles that precede the book, I claim that women's mothering is fundamental to male dominance in culture and society. In my first publication, "Being and Doing: A cross-cultural examination of the

[3] Nancy Chodorow, *The Reproduction of Mothering: Psychoanalysis and the Sociology of Gender* (Berkeley and Los Angeles: University of California Press, 1978).

socialization of males and females,"[4] I suggest that male dominance is rooted in a defensive and aggressive psychology of male selfhood and masculinity that grows from the son's relationship to his mother. This territory—the mother-son dynamics of misogyny—had been explored (though not named as such) by theorists from psychological anthropology and sociology and the Frankfurt School (in Chodorow 2015, I call this mother-son theory the second-wave feminist theory of masculinity).[5] I wonder: if women's mothering universally grounds sociopolitical and cultural male dominance, how does this mothering come to be? It must be more than female biology and less than coercion: you can't coerce good-enough mothering. What seemed missing here, as in most of psychoanalysis (focused as it was on penis envy and the Oedipus complex), was attention to the experience of daughters and the mother–daughter relationship.[6] I wonder, what does it mean for *daughters* to be mothered, that mothers are *like them*?

More basically, I pose an open-ended question. What *about* mothers and daughters, "Family structure and feminine personality" (1974) asked.[7] In that early writing, I describe mother–daughter beginning in the preoedipal period, and I conceptualize women's flexible ego boundaries and relational self. The article was part of what became an influential tripartite theory of society, psyche, and culture, with Michelle Rosaldo's articulation of the domestic–public divide as sociopolitical anchor of male dominance and Sherry Ortner's "Is female to male as nature is

[4] Nancy J. Chodorow, "Being and Doing: A Cross-Cultural Examination of the Socialization of Males and Females," in *Feminism and Psychoanalytic Theory* (New Haven: Yale and London: Polity Press, 1989 [1971]), 23–44.

[5] Nancy J. Chodorow, "From the Glory of Hera to the Wrath of Achilles: Narratives of Second Wave Masculinity and Beyond," *Studies in Gender and Sexuality* 16 (2015): 261–270.

[6] At a recent panel, "Ghosts in the Nursery," the folklorist Maria Tatar drew on graphic illustrations from Grimm and Disney to remind us of the evil, terrifying mothers (often disguised as stepmothers) that terrorize beautiful, innocent daughters throughout folklore The devouring mother is of course exciting, and devoured by children, but then, the daughter becomes this very mother. See also Barbara Almond, *The Monster Within: The Hidden Side of Motherhood* (Berkeley and Los Angeles: University of California Press, 2010); Petra Bueskens, ed., *Mothering and Psychoanalysis: Clinical, Sociological and Feminist Perspectives* (Bradford, ON: Demeter Press, 2014).

[7] Nancy J. Chodorow, "Family Structure and Feminine Personality," in *Feminism and Psychoanalytic Theory*, Nancy J. Chodorow (New Haven: Yale and London: Polity Press, 1989 [1974]), 45–65.

to culture?" as cultural formulation.[8] That women mother, we suggest, underpins the domestic–public split that constitutes gender inequality in society and the polity and the division of nature and culture, in which men's appropriation of culture, against women's location in nature, gives men superiority. This was a time of integrative theory in the social sciences and a sense of right among feminists. We were all under 30 when we presented our papers at the 1972 Meetings of the American Anthropological Association.

The Reproduction of Mothering documents, in its theory and developmental story, how complicated and far-reaching something as everyday as the fact that women mother can be.[9] It takes this universal fact and shows how the psychology of women develops out of this fact of women's mothering, and the internal mother–daughter relationship, in all its ramifications. At the same time, in the book's instigating theoretical background, there is a noticing and a curiosity: in writings across a broad theoretical spectrum (psychological anthropology, psychoanalytic sociology, Frankfurt School theory) the psychodynamics of male dominance begin from the mother–son relationship.

The Reproduction of Mothering had impact and endured, I believe, because it had both experiential immediacy and theoretical-political complexity. First and foremost, it spoke to women personally. It made sense of, helped them to understand, a relationship, mother-daughter, that seems universally central in women's lives, and especially of the experience and intensity of that relationship for the daughter. It got to the heart of something central to women's sense of self and ways of being. By extension, it was usable by writers and thinkers from a wide variety of fields. Literary critics could draw upon it to reread women novelists and poets and understand women characters in novels. It provided

[8] Michelle Zimbalist Rosaldo and Louise Lamphere, eds., *Women, Culture, and Society* (Stanford, California: Stanford University Press, 1974); Sherry B. Ortner, "Is Female to Male as Nature is to Culture?" In Rosaldo and Lamphere, *Woman, Culture & Society*, 1974, 67–87.

[9] I come from fields that query the obvious. In anthropology, where I spent five years as undergraduate and graduate student, scholars (at least at that time) went to "other" cultures to learn about what, from the point of view of those cultures' members, was simply lived. My graduate training in sociology was rooted in ethnomethodology, a field that tried to unpack the taken-for-granted in everyday life (women mother). Psychoanalysis wants to get at the substance and roots of unconscious taken-for-granted pictures of self and world (transference) that inhibit and constrain living and being.

women in philosophy and political theory with a way of understanding certain characteristics of [male] thinking in their fields—an emphasis on autonomy and individuality, for example—while sociologists and anthropologists had a grand theoretical as well as on-the-ground guideline for studying women, men, and gender in society and culture.

Finally, the book contributed to transformations in psychoanalysis itself. First, it pointed to the need for, and helped to create, revision and reconsideration of the theory of femininity and clinical treatment of women, especially, excavating a past and anticipating later psychoanalytic attention to the mother–daughter relationship. Second, in its affirmation of a relational self, of relatedness and relationality in the internal world, it anticipated relational psychoanalysis. In "Gender, relation and difference in psychoanalytic perspective," an article that came out a year after the book, I claim that differentiation is a form of connection, a way of experiencing and relating to another.

Equally important, *The Reproduction of Mothering* took on, in a grand theoretical way, the question of inequality—women's oppression, the organization of gender and their dynamic bases. This was a time in second-wave feminism when the personal was political, but when feminists with rare exception were hostile to psychoanalysis. They were suspicious of Freud's sexist theories and their clinical application and suspicious in general, along with Marxist colleagues, of any account of the psyche and personal relations that didn't begin from determinative political and economic forces. The book, by contrast, not only made something substantial of the personal is political. It implied that the personal is *personal*—being a daughter, being a mother.[10] Within psychoanalysis, it brought back a relationship that had been unremarked since the 1930s (Deutsch extended these '30s accounts in her 1944–1945 volumes),[11]

[10] Now, in 2019, we are aware every moment of how the personal is personal, how feelings and culture as much as or more than economics, seem to drive people and politics nationally and throughout the world. We see rage, racial hatred and bigotry; an emotional virulence extending to violence in the anti-abortion movement; nationalisms and xenophobia that echo the 1930s and 1940s; more forms of misogyny and mistreatment of women and girls than can be counted; and the almost unthinkable separation of even the littlest children from migrant parents.

[11] Helene Deutsch, *The Psychology of Women*, Vols. 1 and 2 (New York: Grune & Stratton, 1944 and 1945).

just as, says Freud (incorrectly!) the daughter–mother relationship is buried in the female psyche.[12]

There are, then, two ways to read the book. *The Reproduction of Mothering* goes inward, to the deepest affects and conflicts of gender, especially of the mother–daughter connection, and herein, surely, lies its lasting appeal: it is a story about mothers and daughters, especially the mother in the daughter's psyche. Along with this, it is about ways of being, feeling and relating in women, women's sense of self and gender. The book also goes outward to the impact of women's mothering on everything. It is a "grand theory" of male dominance and the social organization of gender, of the organization and structure of the world, Western individualism, capitalism, politics and culture.[13] The book ties the intrapsychic dynamics of individuality, selfhood, and gender-sexuality to the sociology, political economy, and culture of gender. And it puts mothering at the center of psychoanalytic theories of women, femininity and feminism.

In what follows, I begin from my earliest observations. Mothering and maternal identity are internal mother–daughter experiences, and this internal mother–daughter maternality—identity, practices, and concerns, maternal sense of self, being a mother, having been mothered—goes through the life cycle. Mothering is generational and developmental, defined by internal and external place in the cycle of generations and by age as much as by gender. Because of these generational and developmental aspects, *time* is integral to mothering. Following my suggestion that sex-gender is composed of multiple components,[14] we notice varying components of maternality—what a woman makes of her maternal, gestational body; how she creates an inner mother–daughter world; her individual filtering of culture; her personal emotional mother–daughter tonality, and her fantasy animation of maternality.

When *The Reproduction of Mothering* was accepted for publication, my publisher suggested that mothering *wasn't a word*: couldn't I call the

[12] Sigmund Freud, "Female Sexuality," in *Standard Edition of the Complete Psychological Works*, Vol. 21 (London: Hogarth Press, 1931), 223–243.

[13] I myself first found psychoanalysis as grand theory when I was about 18, in Freud's *Civilization and Its Discontents* and Erikson's *Childhood and Society* (Chodorow, 2019, returns to these roots).

[14] Nancy J. Chodorow, *Individualizing Gender and Sexuality: Theory and Practice* (London and New York: Routledge, 2011).

book *The Reproduction of Motherhood*? My intuitive choice was mothering. Motherhood seemed static, to fix a woman in a *state*, to be a *status* that a woman takes on rather than a psychic constellation, identity, and activity. The psychological and cultural resonance of *motherhood*, even more than mothering, echoes mother and baby, a status or state, echoed in our extensive Madonna and child iconography, that changes when you have birthed a child.

In psychoanalysis also, most conceptualizations of mothering or maternality refer to mother-infant. Winnicott's "primary maternal preoccupation"[15] has in mind a mother's activity and attitude with her baby, and Loewald writes in several places of the "magical-evocational" mother–baby emotional communication that underpins language.[16] For Freud and Klein, mother *is* the maternal breast, seen from the viewpoint of the child and not from that of the maternal subject herself. As Freud puts it, "I can give you no idea of the important bearing of this first object upon the choice of every later object, of the profound effects it has in its transformations and substitutions in even the remotest regions of our sexual life".[17] For Klein, mother is both object and subject of all primal aggression and drive, all projection and splitting.

Horney is the exception (as she is in much of psychoanalysis). After asking "in amazement" about motherhood, she goes on:

> And the blissful consciousness of bearing new life within oneself? And the ineffable happiness of the increasing expectation of the appearance of this new being? And the joy when it finally makes its appearance and one holds it for the first time in one's arms? And the deep pleasurable feeling of satisfaction in suckling it and the happiness of the whole period when the infant needs her care?[18]

[15] Donald W. Winnicott, "Primary Maternal Preoccupation," in *Collected Papers: Through Paediatrics to Psycho-Analysis* (London: Tavistock, 1958 [1956]), 300–305.

[16] Hans W. Loewald, "Primary Process, Secondary Process, and Language," in *Papers on Psychoanalysis* (New Haven: Yale University Press, 1980 [1978]), 194.

[17] Sigmund Freud, *Introductory Lectures on Psychoanalysis: Standard Edition of the Complete Psychological Works*, Vol. 16 (London: Hogarth Press, 1916–1917), 314.

[18] Karen Horney, "The Flight from Womanhood: The Masculinity Complex in Women, as Viewed by Men and Women," in *Feminine Psychology* Karen Horney (New York: W. W. Norton, 1968 [1926]), 60.

Following Horney, *The Reproduction of Mothering* notices mothering as an ongoing identity, activity, and psychic constellation. Once you are a mother, it goes throughout your life and it never stops, even if your children are no longer alive. The gerund form, mothering, indicates the active nature (both intrapsychic and in the world) of being a mother, as well as a girl's orientation to *becoming a mother* and the maternal identity that she brings from her internal object-relational location as daughter.[19]

The Reproduction of Mothering thus invites considerations of generation and development, life history and history. It turns us toward Eriksonian considerations of generativity and the life cycle. I completed my dissertation, from which the book is virtually unchanged, when I was 30, and the book was published when I was 34.[20] In the preface to the book's second edition (1999), I notice that my 25–30-year-old self was very much a product of her personal, intellectual and political time. Further, the writer of this generation-centered book was a daughter, but not yet a mother. Now I am both mother and grandmother, and I am an academic mother and grandmother as well. My students have had students who have now had their own students, and my clinical trainees now have their own patients and practices.

The book, then, is written (as is most of psychoanalysis) developmentally, from the point of view of the daughter and the daughter's development. I begin from the daughter's infancy and describe the layerings of internal object-relations created by girls and women, in contrast to boys and men, over the course of development. When I asked about mothers and daughters and the mother–daughter relationship, I was more curious about daughters and their experience than about mothers, even as my account also paid close attention to maternal experience in relation to daughters versus sons. As a daughter, I had certainly noticed the absence of attention to daughters in the psychoanalytic literature, as in the literatures of psychological anthropology and sociology. I did not have available, it goes without saying, my colleagues' later investigations into

[19] Of course, not all women become mothers, and each mother's maternality is her own.

[20] This 1974 dissertation was called, after my first mother-daughter article, ***Family Structure and Feminine Personality***. Its subtitle was *The Reproduction of Mothering*, a formulation jointly discovered (or created) late in the process in a conversation with Egon Bittner, my dissertation advisor.

women's fantasies and psychic experiences of pregnancy and childbirth[21] or clinical investigations of daughter–mother attachment.[22] My developmental story, then, hinges on maternal experience of daughters versus sons, but I start from infancy.

At the same time, *The Reproduction of Mothering* also begins from maternal subjectivity. I notice those few psychoanalytic writers who consider pregnancy, childbirth, and inner genital experience,[23] as I develop an account (from a few scattered, not specific to the question, psychoanalytic articles) of how mothers experience their daughters in contrast to their sons. My intuitive choice to write of *mothering*, rather than *motherhood*, enabled an active, agentic focus often missing in the psychoanalytic literature. The book was published after what Fliegel called the "quiescent interval"[24] in psychoanalytic interest in women, and

[21] Barbara Almond, *The Monster Within* (Berkeley and Los Angeles: University of California Press, 2010); Rosemary Balsam, *Women's Bodies in Psychoanalysis* (London and New York: Routledge, 2012); Malkah Notman and Carol Nadelson, eds., *The Woman Patient, Volume 1: Sexual and Reproductive Aspects of Women's Health Care* (New York: Plenum, 1979); Dinora Pines, *A Woman's Unconscious Use of Her Body* (New Haven, CT: Yale University Press, 1993); Joan Raphael-Leff, *Pregnancy: The Inside Story* (London: Sheldon Press, 1993).

[22] See Nancy Kulish and Deanna Holtzman, *A Story of Her Own: The Female Oedipus Complex Reexamined and Renamed* (New York: Jason Aronson, 2008). Here and in the previous note I am making a point about what was available to me, in terms of psychoanalytic writing on pregnancy, childbirth, and maternality when I was writing *The Reproduction of Mothering*. Thus, I cite books rather than the articles (all written after my book) that are found within them, and I am not going up to the present, thereby giving short shrift to the continued generativity of these writers.

[23] For example, Benedek, 1956, 1959, 1960, Therese Benedek, "Psychobiological Aspects of Mothering," *American Journal of Orthopsychiatry* 26 (1956): 272–278; Therese Benedek, "Parenthood as a Developmental Phase," *Journal of the American Psychoanalytic Association* 7 (1959): 389–417; Therese Benedek, "The Organization of the Reproductive Drive," *International Journal of Psycho-Analysis* 41 (1960): 1–15; Grete Bibring, "Some Considerations of the Psychobiological Processes in Pregnancy," *Psychoanalytic Study of the Child* 14 (1959): 113–121; Grete Bibring, Thomas F. Dwyer, Dorothy S. Huntington, and Arthur F. Valenstein, "A Study of the Psychological Processes in Pregnancy and of the Earliest Mother-Child Relationship," *Psychoanalytic Study of the Child* 16 (1961a and 1961b): 9–72; Judith S. Kestenberg, "On the Development of Maternal Feelings in Early Childhood: Observations and Reflections," *Psychoanalytic Study of the Child* 11 (1956): 257–291; Judith S. Kestenberg, "Regression and Reintegration in Pregnancy," *Journal of the American Psychoanalytic Association* 24 (Suppl. 1976): 213–250.

[24] Zenia O. Fliegel, "Women's Development in Analytic Theory," in *Psychoanalysis and Women: Contemporary Reappraisals*, ed. J. L. Alpert (Hillsdale, NJ: The Analytic Press 1986), 17.

amidst a fair amount of hostility toward psychoanalysis among feminists. Mitchell's *Psychoanalysis and Feminism* appeared in 1974, the same year as "Family Structure and Feminine Personality."[25] It was followed by Gayle Rubin's brilliant "The 'Traffic in Women'"[26] in 1975 and in 1976 by a special issue on women of the *Journal of the American Psychoanalytic Association*.[27]

As I look back, my own life cycle and generational position enter in. I have returned to Erikson's understanding of the life cycle,[28] especially to his conceptualization of ego integrity as the stage when one looks back on oneself and one's life, holds oneself in mind as a parent once held us—as Erikson puts it, "the acceptance of one's one and only life cycle as something that had to be and that, by necessity, permitted of no substitutions."[29] I attend to the psychoanalyst Hans Loewald bringing in the parental, as he writes that internalization, making the external truly internal, requires us "to experience ourselves as agents notwithstanding the fact that we were born without our informed consent and did not pick our parents."[30] Indeed, psychoanalysis, beginning from Oedipus, has always centered on generation as much as on gender, as Janine Chasseguet-Smirgel and Joyce McDougall (1986) both notice,[31] along with the fact that generation is intrinsically linked to gender.[32]

[25] Juliet Mitchell, *Psychoanalysis and Feminism* (New York: Pantheon, 1974); Nancy J. Chodorow, "Family Structure and Feminine Personality".

[26] Gayle S. Rubin, "*The Traffic in Women*: Notes on the 'Political Economy' of Sex," in *Toward an Anthropology of Women*, ed. Rayna R. Reiter (New York: Monthly Review Press, 1975), 157–210.

[27] *Journal of the American Psychoanalytic Association*, 1976.

[28] Nancy J. Chodorow, *The Power of Feelings: Personal Meaning in Psychoanalysis, Gender and Culture* (New Haven, CT: Yale University Press, 1999); Nancy J. Chodorow, *Psychoanalytic Ear and the Sociological Eye: Toward an American Independent Tradition* (London and New York: Routledge, 2020).

[29] Erik H. Erikson, *Childhood and Society* (New York: Norton, 1950), 268.

[30] Hans W. Loewald, "The Waning of the Oedipus Complex," in *Papers on Psychoanalysis* (New Haven, CT: Yale University Press, 1980 [1979]), 392.

[31] Janine Chasseguet-Smirgel, *Creativity and Perversion* (London: Free Association Books, 1984); Joyce McDougall, *Theatres of the Mind: Illusion and Truth on the Psychoanalytic Stage* (London: Free Association Books, 1986).

[32] These psychoanalytic mothers proceeded me, but it took my own development and rereading, taking the point of view of the other and talking with them, to understand how insightful and pioneering they were. In her psychoanalytically-informed three generation

In *The Reproduction of* Mothering as in much of my subsequent work (for example, "Heterosexuality as a compromise formation"),[33] I notice the taken-for-granted (though it's probably the case that the fresh straightforwardness of my 20-something self has been layered over). "Women mother" is the book's opening sentence. Here is something very everyday: women mother, and women are mothers. Yet the mother–daughter dyad is absent in the family dynamics and psychoanalytic literature.

By contrast, as I note earlier, mothers and sons were well-observed and theorized. Popular psychology and culture had given us momism, maternal deprivation, maternal overprotection, and the "generation of vipers."[34] In psychoanalysis, Greenson described the masculine challenge of "dis-identifying" from mother and Stoller the developing boy's struggle with his mother-generated primary femininity.[35] In like vein, the Frankfurt Institute claimed that a decline in paternal authority and father absence—"society without the father"—underpinned authoritarianism and the rise of fascism.[36] Drawing on these writings, I argue in articles that preceded *The Reproduction of Mothering* and in the book itself that male dominance is rooted in a defensive and aggressive psychodynamics of masculinity that grows from the son's relationship to his mother. What about these mothers?

Cross-cultural commentators also made my case, as they described the defensive and aggressive psychodynamics of masculinity that grow from

interview study of Norwegian women and men, Harriet Bjerrum Nielsen documents the centrality of generation to gender. Nielsen, Harriet Bjerrum, *Feeling Gender: A Generational and Psychosocial Approach* (London: Palgrave Macmillan, 2017).

[33] Nancy J. Chodorow, "Heterosexuality as a Compromise Formation," in *Femininities, Masculinities, Sexualities: Freud and Beyond* (Lexington, KY: University of Kentucky Press and London, UK: Free Association Books, 1994 [1992]), 33–69.

[34] David Levy, *Maternal Overprotection* (New York: Columbia University Press, 1943); Philip Wylie, *Generation of Vipers: In Which the Author Rails against Congress, the President, Professors, Motherhood, Businessmen, and Other Matters American* (New York: Farrar and Rinehart, 1942).

[35] Ralph R. Greenson, "Dis-identifying from Mother: Its Special Importance for the Boy," *International Journal of Psycho-Analysis* 49 (1968): 370–374; Robert Stoller, *Sex and Gender*, Vol. 1 (New Haven, CT: Yale University Press, 1968).

[36] Max Horkheimer, "Authority and the Family," in *Critical Theory* (New York: Herder and Herder, 1972 [1936]), 47–128; Max Horkheimer and Theodor W. Adorno, *Dialectic of Enlightenment* (New York: Seabury Press, 1947); Alexander Mitscherlich, *Society without the Father* (New York: Schocken, 1970 [1963]).

the son's relationship to his mother. The anthropologist Margaret Mead observed how easily a girl, following her mother around from birth until marriage, could slip into becoming a woman and mother. Maleness, by contrast, "has to be kept and re-earned every day."[37] John Whiting, along with Beatrice Whiting, both undergraduate mentors of mine, suggested that the goal of tribal male initiation rites throughout the world is to wipe out femininity and enforce masculinity, and that these rites are more severe in cultures with exclusive mother-infant sleeping arrangements—again, too much of mother.[38] Philip Slater, also a teacher, claimed in *The Glory of Hera* that most of Greek mythology can be said to describe a vulnerable male omnipotence and narcissism that arises from the Greek mother–son relationship.[39] You could find in the literature occasional writing on fathers and daughters, though actually no one much noticed female development at all.

The Reproduction of Mothering begins, then, from these personal and intellectual roots. It tells a story of female development and female personality that is at the same time a story of how women develop intrapsychic maternality, of how women's internal world and intrapsychic life constitute an unconscious and conscious maternal identity, maternal capacities, and the desire to mother. I suggest that we cannot think of mothering nor conflicts about mothering and maternality without thinking of the mother–daughter relationship—a woman in relation to her own mother. Throughout, the book attends to this relationship itself, to its intensity, complexity, and pervasive internal presence in women's lives. Reading and interpreting psychoanalytic articles through a mother-daughter lens, I take the daughter (and mother) from the mother-infant and preoedipal dyad through the Oedipal triangle to what I called the adolescent daughter–mother replay.

[37] Margaret Mead, *Male and Female* (New York: William Morrow, 1949), 303. My first published paper, "Being and Doing," was partly inspired by this observation. See Nancy J. Chodorow, "Being and Doing," 1971.

[38] John W.M. Whiting, Richard Kluckhohn, and Albert Anthony, "The Function of Male Initiation Rites at Puberty," in *Readings in Social Psychology*, eds. Eleanor E. Maccoby, Theodore M. Newcomb, and Eugene L. Hartley (New York: Holt, 1958), 359–370.

[39] Philip E. Slater, *The Glory of Hera: Greek Mythology and the Greek Family* (Boston: Beacon, 1968).

Built into each girl's development is an internal early (preoedipal) mother–daughter dyad of both attachment/desire and oneness/identification. Layered onto that is an Oedipal triangle, a girl whose first sexual feelings develop in relation to mother rather than father, a girl who is then attached to both mother and father and wants to reproduce the mother–daughter relationship, whether she is straight or gay. The internal layerings of daughter-mother (and mother-daughter) go through the life cycle and into maternality.

I discovered (or excavated: we recall Freud's claim that the girl's preoedipal attachment to her mother is buried in the female psyche as the Mycenaean and Minoan civilizations were buried under the ruins of classical—Oedipal?—Greece) a buried classical psychoanalytic literature.[40] Several women analysts of the 1920s and early 1930s—Lampl-de Groot, Deutsch, and Brunswick, followed by Freud—had described features of the preoedipal and oedipal connections between mothers and daughters and the intrapsychic world in the developing girl that results.[41] These analysts described, and Deutsch named, the girl's bisexual triangle, noticing oscillation between Oedipal mother and Oedipal father and between preoedipal and Oedipal mother.

From these writings, I was able to elaborate an account of the layerings of connection between mothers and daughters in the developing girl, which I then extended to female sexuality, describing the "Oedipal asymmetries and heterosexual knots" of female sexual attachment. I described

[40] This is a personal as well as professional retrospective. I note that, inspired by a children's magazine that described Schliemann's discovery of Troy, I wanted as a child to be an archaeologist, and that I spent an undergraduate summer on an early Neolithic archaeological dig in Greek Macedonia.

[41] After I finished the book, I became curious. Who *were* these women, and how did it happen that there were so many early women analysts? I spent several years searching out this generation and interviewing those I could find. See for example, Nancy J. Chodorow, "Varieties of Leadership among Women Psychoanalysts," in *Women Physicians in Leadership Roles*, eds. L. Dickstein and C. Nadelson (Washington, DC: American Psychiatric Association Monograph, 1986), 45–54; Nancy J. Chodorow, "Seventies Questions for Thirties Women," in *Feminism and Psychoanalytic Theory* (New Haven, CT: Yale University Press and Cambridge, UK: Polity Press, 1989), 199–218; Nancy J. Chodorow, "Where Have All the Eminent Women Psychoanalysts Gone? Like the Bubbles in Champagne, They Rose to the Top and Disappeared," in *Social Roles and Social Institutions: Essays in Honor of Rose Laub Coser*, eds. J. Blau and N. Goodman (Boulder, CO: Westview Press, Second edition, 1995), 167–194; Nancy J. Chodorow, "Seventies Questions for Thirties Women: Some Nineties Reflections," in *Feminist Social Psychologies: International Perspectives*, ed. S. Wilkinson (Berkshire, UK: Open University Press, 1996), 21–50.

women's development of a self-in-relationship, in contrast to boys' need to differentiate themselves from their mother and their preoccupation with denying relationship and dependency. I remind the reader that the female "Oedipus" features the girl's continued attachment to her mother and an oscillation between mother and father: an internal and external bisexual triangle. I investigate the multiple *mother-centered* reasons for penis envy and the turn to the father.

For girls, both the preoedipal daughter–mother dyad and the Oedipal triangle, in which there is *always* mother-daughter in addition to daughter-father, begin to generate an intrapsychic reproduction of mothering. Revisited and consolidated in adolescence, this maternal orientation—choice to become a mother, sense of self as mother, and differential relation to daughters and sons—draws upon these preoedipal and Oedipal mother–daughter constellations. Later I call this Freud's Persephone story, a girl's continued attachment to her mother and reluctance to give up mother for father.[42] I suggest that it is both Freud's story of normal female development and one of his stories of "abnormal" development.[43] Here is the book's conclusion:

> Women's mothering capacities and commitments, and the general psychological capacities and wants which are the basis of women's emotion work, are built developmentally into feminine personality. Because women are themselves mothered by women, they grow up with the relational capacities and needs, and the psychological definition of self-in-relationship,

[42] Nancy J. Chodorow, "Freud on Women," in *Femininities, Masculinities, Sexualities: Freud and Beyond*, Nancy J. Chodorow (Lexington, KY: University of Kentucky Press and London, UK: Free Association Books, 1994 [1991]), 1–32. See also Nancy Kulish and Deanna Holtzman, "Persephone, the Loss of Virginity, and the Female Oedipal Complex," *International Journal of Psycho-Analysis* 79 (1998): 57–71.

[43] My first mother-daughter article, "Family Structure and Feminine Personality," was reprinted in a classics anthology, *The Homeric "Hymn to Demeter": Translation, Commentary, Interpretive Essays*, ed. Helena Foley (Princeton, NJ: Princeton University Press, 1994), 243–265. Later, in a chapter called "Rethinking Freud on Women" (Chodorow 1994, pp. 1–32), I notice that Freud's second "abnormal" developmental pathway—the girl who rejects her mother, but not for her father as object—also finds a mythic analogue. This girl remains virginal, identifies with her father, and "cling[s] with defiant self-assertiveness to her threatened masculinity" (Freud 1931, p. 229). As I suggest (Chodorow 1994, p. 31): Athena. "Rethinking Freud on Women" remarks in passing on several mythic analogues for Freud's theories and patients, including, in addition to Demeter and Persephone, Cassandra, Iphigenia, Aphrodite, Hera, Medusa, and, from the Old Testament, Judith [needs reformatting in Chicago style].

> which commit them to mothering .... Women mother daughters who, when they become women, mother.[44]

The Reproduction of Mothering, then, is both grand theory—a complex and detailed investigation of maternality, female development,and psychology, the mother–daughter relationship, and patriarchy—and a simple story.[45] I claim that the mother is central to the daughter's psyche and sense of self and that core bodily, psychological and interpersonal experiences for women, culminating in women's orientation to mothering, can be understood in terms of this internal mother–daughter lineage.

These were generalizations. The internal mother–daughter constellation is central to the feminine psyche, but each internal mother–daughter relationship is its own. Yet my clinical experience, garnered well after I wrote the book, also confirms the book's argument.[46] Each woman, whether she has children or not, brings something of daughter-mother/mother-daughter to her concerns, conflicts, and sense of self. Each in her own individual way brings her conscious and unconscious relation to her mother into a psychological and psychophysical maternal identity (another way of putting this, drawing on Harris, 2009, would be to say that mother-daughter is by each individual and each dyad softly assembled).[47] As each clinician brings some preconceptions, a pre-attuned ear, to her listening, I am perhaps more attuned than others to mother–daughter resonances. These are patterns, theories held in the back of the mind and clinical discovery at the same time.[48] If a clinician notices one element in a pattern, she is alerted to other elements that might (but also might not!) be around. *The Reproduction of Mothering* describes a pattern that revolves around the mother–daughter relationship, dyadically and as part of the Oedipal triad.

[44] Chodorow, *The Reproduction of Mothering*, 209.

[45] *How* simple? When my son's fourth grade class was "writing books," I gave a presentation on book writing. Some of the children were puzzled, but one little girl said, "It's easy! Mommies have daughters, and when they grow up, they become mommies!"

[46] My own (complex and overdetermined) response to my insights, that moved many people and seemed true to me, was to undertake psychoanalytic training: I could not go deeper without clinical experience.

[47] Adrienne Harris, *Gender as Soft Assembly* (New York and London: Routledge, 2009).

[48] Chodorow, *Individualizing Gender and Sexuality*.

Patterns illuminate the everyday. A young woman talks longingly of childhood memories when her father traveled or worked late and her mother made her comfort food for supper—noodles with butter and cheese, scrambled eggs and toast, tomato soup, and grilled cheese—which she ate at the kitchen counter. Her mother let her fall asleep in the parental bed. Another weeps, as she reports that her mother always puts her phone on speaker mode when she calls, so father can participate. I might say, very simply, "you want your mother all to yourself." I was reminded of these everyday wants when reading *Lost and Wanted*,[49] a novel that focuses partly on a little girl, Simmi, who has lost her mother and tries to keep her alive through texting in her mother's voice on the mother's secretly purloined cell phone. Simmi says, "They forget how much they used to love their own parents … when they were kids."[50]

I notice, as I sit in my consulting room, that I am attentive to daughter-mother/mother-daughter. This must be both because of what my patients bring—the centrality of daughter-mother for women—and because, in some way, I notice, or elicit, such fantasies and transferences. In *The Power of Feelings*, I describe a woman who devalues her mother (and her female analyst) in favor of her father (and her employer). As a child, she hated the weekly post-divorce return from a day with her father to her mother and her mother's run-down house. Now, she feels torn when she has to leave work to come to her analytic hour. I describe another woman who is preoccupied with invidious, shaming, and shameful bodily comparisons between her own felt little girl body and that of mature women like her mother. A third woman feels sadness and longing. She can never seem to engage women in close relationships, because they would always rather be with men. For me, she imagines, all my women patients are alike.[51]

I also notice mother-daughter in cultural-psychological patterns, for example, "weeping for the mother" in women from patriarchal cultures.[52] Women who weep for their mothers, often in spite of conscious feminism, cannot enjoy life and undermine their own freedoms and pleasures. They feel guilty and sad: their mothers could not go out alone, could not enjoy the lights of the city or a meal or drink with friends. They

[49] Nell Freudenberger, *Lost and Wanted* (New York: Knopf, 2019).

[50] Freudenberger, *Lost and Wanted*, 197.

[51] Chodorow, *The Power of Feelings*, 79–90.

[52] Ibid., 121–126.

had to endure the rage of their husbands, my patients' fathers. These are not universals, not the experience of all women from patriarchal cultures, but my attunement to mother-daughter interacted with my patients' self-descriptions (sometimes also their choice of analyst) and the transference-countertransference that emerged between us.

I attend to reported maternal communications: a mother who told her daughter that children destroy a woman's career, another who claimed that pregnancy and nursing ruin a woman's body and brains. We sometimes give shape to these internal mothers by calling up culturally resonant images—the 13th fairy in *Sleeping Beauty*, the witch in *Rapunzel*, or *The Snow Queen*. When I wished to describe women for whom becoming a mother was "too late," I was attuned to mother–daughter resonances, whereas previous analysts were more likely to focus on penis envy, Oedipal fixation on the father, or a rejection of femininity.[53] We pay attention to the internal mother, to how the woman's own and their mother's imagined uterus are deadened, collapsed, the opposite of generative.

Clinical experience has also expanded into a rethinking that grows from what I call clinical individuality. *The Reproduction of Mothering*, like most developmental theorizing, offers a generalized account, yet within this widespread phenomenon, we find a range of experience. Even as many women experience what feels like a drive or biological urge to become a mother, yet this biology is itself shaped through a daughter's internal, individual relation to her own mother, her unconscious fantasies and affects that cast what becoming pregnant and being a mother mean.[54] For each woman, her internal mother–daughter world, her sense of self as maternal and her actions that express these are individual. It is each girl's particular mother (and father or other-mother, whether the one in

[53] Nancy J. Chodorow, "'Too Late': Ambivalence about Motherhood, Choice and Time," *Journal of the American Psychoanalytic Association* 51 (2003): 1181–1198.

[54] I note in the preface to the book's second edition that *The Reproduction of Mothering* does not address the psychobiology of mothering or the rootedness of maternality in the female body, even as an internal mother-daughter bodily story can be taken from it. The physicality of childbirth, the stirrings of body in the young girl observing her mother's pregnancy, menstruation, with its promise and danger of pregnancy—these all help constitute maternal experience. There were political, professional and personal reasons for this choice. When I was writing *The Reproduction of Mothering*, and long afterwards, women were not getting into graduate school or getting fellowships and jobs because, as they were told, "you will just get pregnant and leave."

the home or a fantasied father[55]) whom she takes in and internally transforms, whom she brings to mothering? Does she want boys or girls? Does she see mothering as an overwhelming burden or in psychic terms that echo an idealized nineteenth-century maternal perfection? Does she see mothering as no different than fathering? Does she become a mother at all? How does she experience pregnancy, childbirth, lactation, and nursing? A mother-daughter lens affirms that gender is intrapsychically always same-gender/cross-generation—mother and daughter/daughter and mother—as much as it is gender difference. An internal, conscious and unconscious mother-daughter/daughter-mother helps to shape the individuality of maternal identity and mothering. And each daughter, as infancy research has shown, brings her own psychophysical propensities and emotional vulnerabilities.

Reciprocally, mothers are as varied psychologically as people in general, ranging across character and personality. They are permanent worriers or confident that a child will be fine, attuned to nonverbal communication or not. A daughter takes a *particular* mother into her own maternality, her own internal reproduction of mothering.

Of course, all parental figures have some impact. I focus in *The Reproduction of Mothering* on mother-daughter, and even after these many years, I still find that it is key. Women of whatever age, mothers and non-mothers, live internally, in conscious as well as unconscious reality, with their mothers in mind. Becoming a mother and mothering occur as a woman psychically takes, or begins to take, or shifts—but never completely, and that is my point—her internal mother–daughter constellation toward the maternal side.

An important outcome of the book was my undertaking psychoanalytic training. I have always been a theorist, but I felt that to understand the psyche more deeply, I needed clinical experience. Accordingly, as I have developed and changed, and as I have engaged in clinical work, I have come to extend my original account, to see mother-daughter and maternal identity as psychological constellations that go across the life cycle. We can see developmental and generational components as we look at mothering and maternality in women of different ages, and in women who have different relations to being mother and daughter.

[55] Diane Ehrensaft finds that children and parents both imagine a father in the parental constellation, even if there is not one in the actual family. See Diane Ehrensaft, *Mommies, Daddies, Donors, Surrogates* (New York: Guilford Press, 2005).

In what follows, I explore some generational, developmental, and life cycle components of mothering and maternality in three periods in women's lives. I look at early maternal identity, the worries of a young mother about her own external and internal mother's effect on her maternality. I consider mothering in later life—an older woman's maternal feelings that are also shaped by being a daughter. Finally, I consider how the internal mother-daughter bodily and relational constellation affect non-maternality, in some women who do not become mothers. Becoming a mother and maternal identity involve an internal mother–daughter world, even as, for each woman, the mother–daughter world is clinically individual. Maternality may include psychic representations and experiences of the mother's and daughter's reproductive body, a psychological filtering of culture, and emotional tonalities, affect and fantasy that do not initially seem to be about mothering. I affirm the tacit argument, expressed in my title, that in the realm of psychologies of gender, we are also in the realm of generation. The inner mother–daughter world helps and hinders mothering and maternal identity, and it changes over the life cycle.[56]

Danielle, an academic and mother of a daughter and son, began treatment when her daughter was a toddler and her son was a baby. Danielle hadn't been able to nurse her daughter and was feeling self-critical and a failure. She also worried that she might become angry like her mother, someone who could harm her children psychologically. She felt like a lucky survivor, but not sturdy or secure. No matter whether she felt good about an achievement or bad about something that had gone wrong, she heard a sarcastic internal maternal voice: "Everyone finishes their dissertation! You still have to get a job and tenure!" "Getting pregnant is easy! It's raising children that's hard!" Danielle felt that she carried this scornful maternal voice within 24/7.

Danielle told me that before she had her daughter, she had had a pregnancy that terminated spontaneously in the 11th week. This completely common occurrence had happened to several of her friends, but for Danielle it was grounds for self-blame. "I wasn't a safe place for a baby to grow," she said. "I was too preoccupied with finishing my thesis, TA-ing and not taking care of myself *or* the baby! What baby would want to grow inside such an overwhelmed mother?"

[56] My clinical examples are disguised and composite.

Danielle's daughter had been born early, just as she was finishing her dissertation. Her milk didn't come in, and her daughter was bottle fed throughout her infancy. Danielle felt that this was her own fault. She was working too hard to complete her degree, keep up with her field, and applying for her first academic position. She worried that she could not be a good mother to a daughter, feeling that her mother had done okay with her brothers but not with her and her sister: "You mess daughters up! I'll mess her up!" Moreover, she felt, as she put it, that between her early miscarriage and her premature baby "I never got to be big and pregnant! I never got to be Mother Earth."

Danielle wanted to have a second child as soon as possible and got pregnant easily. As she had hoped, her second child was a boy, but again she was unable to nurse. Her son was colicky and not gaining weight, and she felt bereft and a failure. Even holding and cuddling him was difficult. Danielle blamed herself, felt depressed, and sought treatment. Her last child, another daughter, was born a few years later after a relatively uneventful pregnancy. Her milk came in, and her daughter latched on and nursed actively.

We see a correlation here and internal sense making, though certainly not causation. As Danielle began to come to terms with her internal disparaging mother and to recognize some of the psychic costs of her attachment, she could relax into her own motherhood psychologically, relationally, and even, it seemed, physically. Her progression from miscarriage, premature birth, and difficulty nursing—all within normal range, all seen as her fault—to a full-term birth and lactation mirrored Danielle's progression, one that remained a challenge, in recognizing the destructive particulars of her experiences with her mother. Along the way, she formed attachments to maternal figures—a couple of senior women in her department, me, her mother-analyst who wrote *The Reproduction of Mothering*. She became increasingly able to modulate these attachments, to see how she had overidealized women mentors (and her analyst!), women who had, it turned out, both good and bad aspects. Her internal maternal world and division of older women was no longer all good or all bad. She noticed how her own mothering became more spontaneous, and she helped form a junior faculty mothers' group.

Though we get some sense here of how mother-daughter plays out, I do not mean to be causal. I do not suggest that Danielle's disentangling from her mother, or her treatment with me as a different mother, enabled her physiologically to carry a baby to term and to nurse. What we learn clinically is about personal experience: for both Danielle and me, there was a shift.

As Danielle was expecting her third child, there was leftover fear and hope. She worried that she should not plan ahead, pack a bag for the hospital, or pick names. All this would be tempting fate, and I myself might weigh in, a maternal 13th fairy who would ruin everything. "If I plan too much, it's dangerous. It's me acknowledging I'm going to have a baby and bring it home." Then there's the thought, "you're not clairvoyant! You're not going to have a baby today!" Danielle decided that if you don't plan, just *maybe* things will be okay. One day, when she came in en route to a department meeting wearing sexy designer pregnancy jeans, I found myself feeling jealous. Designer pregnancy *jeans*? Not, as I remembered my own pregnant academic self, pregnancy *schmatas*?

It is impossible to describe fully how the mind works, including the relation of the physical and the psychological in reproduction. Yet somehow, Danielle and I could both see—or it was important for us to think—that via her attachment to (and struggle with) me, and our beginning to uncover unconscious fears and forbidden thoughts, Danielle was able to rework her internal mother-daughter/reproduction of mothering world. After she had her third child (another daughter), Danielle said, "I wanted to be the Great Mother, a woman who's soft, warm, and comfortable in her own skin, a safe, warm place for the baby to be, not in a rush, not having a preemie. I've had no trouble getting pregnant, but then there's this fear: I'm cold, I'm a bad environment, what baby would want to grow in there? And I had – I now realize that I *created* – this dissertation deadline, so I was working too hard, drinking too much coffee. Now, I see I'm not such an unsafe host, not so toxic. My uterus can be warm and safe. The baby can think 'OK, I'll stay here.' As if embryos have free will! But then, there's always my mother's voice, my own [she now recognized] internal voice: "Women have had children since time immemorial! What's the big deal?"

We notice how pregnancy, birth, and mothering changed over Danielle's treatment, as we were able, to some extent, to disentangle her conflictual, complicated loyalty to her mother. Childbirth and nursing are largely bio-physical: therapy and analysis don't causally transform the fertile body, as analysts may once have thought.[57] But we would be wrong if we did not also recognize that in mothering, as in so much else, body and mind go together. Analysis and psychotherapy do not create the fertile body, but we are nonetheless lucky that new relationships, reworking the mother-relation in treatment or elsewhere, may help shift things internally, so that the experiences of pregnancy, childbirth, or nursing may themselves, in their felt biology, shift.[58]

We notice also a not-negligible cultural component. The United States (including its academic institutions) has the shortest maternity leave policies (and highest infant and maternal mortality rate) in the developed world. Danielle's miscarriage took place and her babies were born during grueling academic years, and any time off was at the expense of her dissertation. After her second child, she had to return to teaching when her baby was just three months old. One day, when her third child was a baby, Danielle noticed with wonder that when she woke up, breasts engorged, at 6:45, and knew that she would have to leave for her 8 o'clock class by 7:30, she chose to awaken her baby to nurse, rather than pumping and leaving her milk behind.

We see the reproduction of mothering not only in young mothers but also in mothers at the other end of the life cycle. Older women often enter treatment because of concerns about themselves as mothers or about their children. One of the greatest tragedies as you age is when an adult child is suffering or not doing well, or when there is estrangement, and you feel helpless or at fault. If things are mended, these mothers often feel that they no longer need treatment.

Frances, in her late 70s, had four children. She had lost her mother in her mid-40s. Yet she remained both mother and daughter. One day I say to Frances, "We're noticing that in order to keep your mother idealized, you are in danger of losing your daughter." When Frances was young, and also now, it turns out, there was no one more perfect than her mother. Her mother never made a mistake. At the same time, she remembers a

[57] We recall Apfel and Keylor's cautionary warning about thinking that sterility, infertility and other reproductive challenges are mainly psychogenic and best addressed through analysis or therapy rather than through infertility treatment. Roberta J. Apfel and Rheta G. Keylor, "Psychoanalysis and Infertility: Myths and Realities," *International Journal of Psycho-Analysis* 83 (2002): 85–104.

[58] Almond, Pines, and Raphael-Leff provide clinically rich, biologically attuned accounts of these processes. See Almond, *The Monster Within*; Pines, *A Woman's Unconscious Use of her Body*; Raphael-Leff, *Pregnancy*.

mother who was rarely home, who was out most of the day playing golf, tennis, or bridge, or was at luncheons with her friends. Her mother had told Frances that she didn't particularly like children and had agreed to two. An unplanned-for third child, Frances had been taken care of by nannies, who could be fired if she became too attached to them. Even as Frances had had a successful career, marriage and children, her mother once said to her, "I thought you'd take after me, but you haven't."

Frances's mother had expected deference, and Frances now feels that her own daughters have not been properly deferential. She describes how, 20 years earlier, her older daughter, proudly married, a mother, and in a new home, had expressed a wish to host the family Christmas. Frances was humiliated, and furious. The offer, as we came to recognize, was a devastating challenge to her own status and sense of self. She and her husband had recently sold the family home and downsized. Now, she was no longer the center of the family, no longer even a mother!

In the experience prompting my remark, a dinner at a local restaurant had been planned for some relatives and family friends. When Frances and her husband arrived, she found that one of her daughters had invited a few friends of her own, had arrived early, had already ordered hors d'oeuvres for the table, and had asked her brother to select the wine. She suggested where her parents might sit. An otherwise lovely dinner, with people whom parents and children had known forever, became an experience of insult and indignation. *Frances* was the hostess: *she* should oversee the menu and the seating, and her husband should choose the wine. She was not being respected—was not being allowed to inhabit her maternal heritage.

Here we see mother-daughter across the generations, with no easy solution. Frances has long been without her mother, yet internally her attachment remains fiercely strong, almost a matter of survival. She cannot bear, consciously and, we infer, unconsciously, to lose her idealized inner mother–daughter world, even as she watches herself over and over driving a wedge between herself and her daughters, the people whom she now loves and counts upon most. Mothers deserve respect, Frances repeats, which includes being recognized as the arranger of family events.

But there is another side to her feelings. Whenever we get close to exploring Frances's relationship with her daughters, who do not call her every day as she called her own mother, and who have professional ups and downs, tears well up. She worries about her daughters (and her daughters' children), and the worry feels unbearable. Such worries and tensions contrast with her less intense, more modulated concerns about her sons. Repeatedly, as we move toward the end of a session, Frances's face collapses and her tears begin: her concern over one or the other daughter is unbearable. The same concerns that evoked criticism now take on a different tonality: *How* is this daughter's marriage going? *Will* she be okay? *Will* her other daughter's children be all right? *Can* the one hold onto her professional life? Frances says, "This is the saddest thing in my life now! This is all that matters, all that I care about."

One day, Frances came in frantic. One of her daughters was en route to a meeting in the south, and Frances had heard reports of a possible hurricane. Would her daughter's plane be okay? She remembers trying to forbid this daughter from travelling to Europe on her own when she was in her early 20s. And will her granddaughter, about to start at a faraway university known for its student politics and alternate lifestyle, be safe? Where are the dorms? She is always anxious about her daughters, and by extension, her granddaughters. It is all danger and fear of loss. By contrast, she notices, she does not worry about men. She didn't worry about her husband's professional travel or now about her sons: of course they fly to meetings! And what if one of her professionally successful daughters takes a job elsewhere? She will have to move as well.

"We're noticing that in order to keep your mother idealized, you are in danger of losing your daughter." Which is worse, losing mother or daughter? On the one side is an identification with, connection to, and deep love for a mother that goes back 70-plus years. Part of this identification is maternal entitlement—being in charge of dinners and holidays. Yet there is agonizing worry and sadness on the other side. Anything might happen to daughters—a professional problem or move, planes blown away during a hurricane. To get away from these thoughts and feelings, it seems easier to hold onto entitlement and to a mother with whom Frances's relationship is now internal and eternal—part of who she is. Yet, my words, maybe my tone, evoke not only Frances now but also layers of bodily and emotional memory, known in the ways that we retain images of particular childhood times, the longings and disappointments of our earliest years, and our earliest connections to our mothers. The reproduction of mothering.[59]

In "Too late: The Reproduction and non-reproduction of mothering,"[60] I turn to another facet of the reproduction of mothering, a disruption in gender, generation and the life cycle. At some point, I noticed patients who had put off motherhood or possibly sabotaged their fertility, and who had done so partly through the denial of time and age (my original subtitle was "ambivalence about motherhood, choice, and time"). I noticed the cultural and personal settings and sets of meanings in which this may happen, the regret that (some) women may feel, and the reparation in which they may engage. Of course, in drawing upon this article, and in the article itself, I do not prescribe. I hope to illuminate further the internal mother–daughter world, not to suggest that not being a mother is bad or that infertility is a woman's fault.

Jenny, in her early 40s, was childless and desperately wanted a child.[61] During her 20s and 30s, Jenny had had six pregnancies, all of which she had chosen to abort. She described a drivenness to these pregnancies and the slightest and briefest of reasons and reasoning for their not being kept. Looking back, it sometimes seemed to us both that Jenny had gotten pregnant almost in order to have an abortion. In like vein, about the time in her mid-30s that she decided that she wanted children, now, Jenny chose as her boyfriend an unreliable, divorced man who was uninterested in his children. Jenny's abortions were a source of self-punishment, a constant reminder that she had only herself to blame for ruining her chances to become a mother. She thought that her abortions had destroyed her capacity to get pregnant, and her belief seemed not unrealistic.

Jenny told a mother-daughter story. She was the oldest of five children, and she reported feeling from early childhood protective toward her younger siblings, and guilty when their lives were harder than hers. Her

[59] The child analyst Calvin Settlage describes his centenarian patient's reaction when both her daughter and her analyst were to be out of town at the same time and how this reaction echoed pre-oedipal separation fears from a century earlier. See Calvin F. Settlage, "Transcending Old Age: Creativity, Development and Psychoanalysis in the Life of a Centenarian," *International Journal of Psycho-Analysis* 77 (1996): 549–564.

[60] Chodorow, "'Too Late'".

[61] In "Too Late," I call Jenny and Susan (not their real names) "J" and "S."

parents had been off-and-on separated for several years when an unanticipated pregnancy brought her father back to the home. Shortly after this sibling was born, her mother had a miscarriage, along with severe hemorrhaging. As she was rushed off to the hospital for a hysterectomy, Jenny was left to take care of her younger siblings. She was terrified that her mother would die but at the same time relieved to learn that there could no more babies.

As she reached her mid-40s, Jenny realized that she would never be a biological mother. We also came to understand that for Jenny, getting pregnant would have meant not so much becoming a mother as making reparation, undoing the damage she felt she had done to herself, her body, her siblings, and her mother. She felt that she could never undo this damage nor get over the sadness, guilt, and anger about her own self-destructiveness. She had harmed, not protected, her younger siblings and had to destroy her own potential children.

Like Jenny, Susan came from a large family, in which she was the youngest of six. She always felt that there was not enough to go around, that by the time she was born, her mother was tired, depleted, and unable to give. Susan was angry at her mother for being unavailable, but at the same time, she believed that her mother's exhaustion was entirely her own (Susan's own) fault: last born, she was the last straw. Her own birth, feeding and care were responsible for her mother's depletion. When she was younger, Susan had had risky, unprotected sex. As she had never gotten pregnant, she speculated that she herself had ruined her fertility.

Jenny and Susan filtered maternality through an internal mother–daughter psyche—constellations of unconscious mother–daughter–sibling fantasies, and rage and destructive wishes toward their own and their mothers' wombs. We learned how these feelings and fantasies led to behaviors that may have sabotaged fertility and pregnancy. Not having children was felt as their own internal doing.

The Reproduction of Mothering makes generation intrinsic to gender, and generation points us toward time, which, Kristeva suggests, is intertwined with maternality.[62] Over the course of our work together, Susan and I discovered her unconscious belief in, and commitment to, time standing still, how she kept her analysis and her life timeless. From her late 20s well into her 40s, Susan thought of herself as a girl, at most a young

[62] Julia Kristeva, "Women's Time," in *The Kristeva Reader*, ed. Toril Moi (New York: Columbia University Press, 1986 [1979]), 187–213.

woman. She did not notice her friends marrying and getting pregnant, or, if she noticed, she thought she herself was not old enough. She talked of "keeping things timeless," "rolling back the clock," and "running in place," and she had fantasies of playing family movies backward.

Along similar lines, Jenny often came late for her appointments or had to leave early, frequently because she was meant to be in three places at once, in her therapy hour and at two different meetings. For Jenny, time needed not to exist, because to acknowledge that time moves forward would be to acknowledge that she was too old to have children. Jenny and Susan both had to deny or stop time.

Mothering is generational, and generations involve time. Denying or playing with time has now become a marker that I am attuned to (so that it is sometimes *not* too late) in women who have put off pregnancy and motherhood, and as a wider index of conflicts about generativity. As Susan and I discussed time standing still, she was able to move forward not only in her career but also in finding a relationship in which she could be a stepmother. For Jenny, by contrast, the denial of time was a weaker psychic element, and her sabotage of her fertility more virulent.

Women for whom mothering is too late may begin from conscious or unconscious feelings that there was not enough of mother. Mother seemed depressed, downtrodden, and tired. Jenny, Susan, and others may feel that they themselves destroyed their mother with greed or envy. They also sometimes discover an envy of siblings and memories of destructive wishes toward them, furthering guilt. Contrary to what the analyst Melanie Klein might predict, however, daughters like Susan and Jenny do not fear maternal retaliation for these destructive wishes. Their mothers are already tired and weakened by motherhood, perhaps especially by this particular daughter's demands and attacks on her very being and her uterus. It is the mother herself who needs protection, and her daughter who has to take destruction, and non-maternality, upon herself.

My clinical observations reflect back upon and extend my original theorizing. Each woman's internal world includes pre-Oedipal and Oedipal (Persephonal and post-Persephonal? Persephonal and Demeterian?) layerings of the mother–daughter relationship. Mother-daughter figures throughout the life cycle, for foundational experiences like being or not being a mother and for the everyday worlds of grilled cheese or organizing a family dinner.

I first described the daughter–mother/mother–daughter relationship in a book that was basically written before I was thirty. I was young, then, and not yet a mother. Here, well along in the cycle of personal and professional generations and (hopefully) of generativity, shading over (also hopefully) toward ego integrity, I consider and expand upon the psychological dilemmas and developmental formulations I describe in the book. Perhaps because they were rooted intrapsychically as much as intellectually, my insights have for me, and it seems for others, withstood the test of time, even as I, along with others, have challenged and revised them.

"Women mother daughters who, when they become women, mother." Here, I describe a young mother whose biological and psychic maternality changes over time and a grandmother who feels as psychically tied to her own mother as she is to her adult daughters. I describe women whose internal relation to their mother has led them, through conscious and unconscious processes, not to become a mother. Throughout, we find identifications with and fears of a fantasied internal mother and of the mother whom one remembers, a mother felt as generative or a toxic mother who can never be given up. For each woman who mothers (or who does not), we find that specific, individual internal experiences go into how she feels about her children and herself as mother.

In *The Reproduction of Mothering*, we see mothering through the lenses of development and time. Throughout the life cycle, mothering and maternal identities and practices are for women generational and gendered, for those who become mothers and those who do not. Mothering, just as being mothered, reflects a mother–daughter constellation that inheres in the psychic and physical body and in the effects of the psychic body on the "real" body, as well as the reverse, in the sense of self as daughter and the sense of self as mother. Gender and generation, development and time, are fundamental components of maternality throughout the life cycle.

I wanted to understand female development and the mother–daughter relationship, and I began from an open-ended, inductive query: What about mothers and daughters? What do we know about them? What is the effect of mothers on daughters? How do mothers come into being? What resulted was at the same time a simple answer to a simple question that spoke to women personally and a complex theory that described female development, male development, and the strains in romantic and sexual relationships, that proposed a grand theory about the sociology of sex-gender. Maternality and its daughterly reciprocal are central, in manifold clinical and cultural variations, in women's lives and psyche and in the social and cultural organization of gender.

When I am fortunate enough to visit the Louvre, I glance at the *Mona Lisa*, but it is essential that I spend time with Leonardo's *The Virgin and Child and St. Anne*. Here, Mary sits on her mother's lap and holds her son, who himself holds a sort of lovey, a little lamb (the lamb of God, of course, but also ....) as he looks back at his mother.[63] Whereas we find countless portrayals throughout Western history of Mary and the baby Jesus, iconic, often astonishingly gorgeous and moving images of *motherhood*, it was Leonardo's genius to depict the reproduction of *mothering*—motherhood, certainly, but also a maternal mother–daughter lineage. In this extraordinary painting, St. Anne holds the *adult* Mary on her lap and looks benevolently upon her, as Mary leans forward to hold the baby Jesus (not negligibly, a son who seems to have caregiving capacities). In a lovely related sketch, Mary sits facing forward on her mother's lap, and their legs are so intertwined that you cannot tell whose legs are whose. St. Anne, holding Mary, the post-partum adult mother, but also, in fantasy for both of them, Mary her mother's little girl, who can be held on her lap. Women mother daughters who, when they become women, mother.

References

Almond, Barbara, *The Monster Within: The Hidden Side of Motherhood*. Berkeley and Los Angeles: University of California Press, 2010.

Apfel, Roberta J. and Rheta G. Keylor, "Psychoanalysis and Infertility: Myths and Realities." *International Journal of Psycho-Analysis* 83 (2002): 85–104.

Balsam, Rosemary, "Freud, the Birthing Body and Modern Life." *Journal of the American Psychoanalytic Association* 65 (2016): 61–90.

———, "The Pregnant Mother and Her Daughter's Body Image." In *Women's Bodies in Psychoanalysis*. London and New York: Routledge, 2012 [1996], 55–75.

———, *Women's Bodies in Psychoanalysis*. London and New York: Routledge, 2012.

Benedek, Therese, "Parenthood as a Developmental Phase." *Journal of the American Psychoanalytic Association* 7 (1959): 389–417.

[63]In "Leonardo da Vinci and a Memory of his Childhood," Freud (1910) writes about the *Mona Lisa* and what he calls "St. Anne with two others," about how they stand near one another in time of painting and also in the Louvre. My observations here are, unlike Freud's, not psychobiographical (or if they are, they draw from my own associations and psychobiography, not from Leonardo's or Freud's).

———, "Psychobiological Aspects of Mothering." *American Journal of Orthopsychiatry* 26 (1956): 272–278.

———, "The Organization of the Reproductive Drive." *International Journal of Psycho-Analysis* 41 (1960): 1–15.

Bibring, Grete, "Some Considerations of the Psychobiological Processes in Pregnancy." *Psychoanalytic Study of the Child* 14 (1959): 113–121.

Bibring, Grete, Thomas F. Dwyer, Dorothy S. Huntington, and Arthur F. Valenstein, "A Study of the Psychological Processes in Pregnancy and of the Earliest Mother-Child Relationship." *Psychoanalytic Study of the Child* 16 (1961a and 1961b): 9–72.

Bjerrum-Neilsen, Harriet, *Feeling Gender: A Generational and Psychosocial Approach*. London: Palgrave Macmillan, 2017.

Bueskens, Petra, ed., *Mothering and Psychoanalysis: Clinical, Sociological and Feminist Perspectives*. Bradford, ON: Demeter Press, 2014.

Chasseguet-Smirgel, Janine, *Creativity and Perversion*. London: Free Association Books, 1984.

Chodorow, Nancy J., "Being and Doing: A Cross-Cultural Examination of the Socialization of Males and Females." In *Feminism and Psychoanalytic Theory*, Nancy J. Chodorow. New Haven: Yale and London: Polity Press, 1989 [1971], 23–44.

———, "Family Structure and Feminine Personality." In *Feminism and Psychoanalytic Theory*, Nancy J. Chodorow. New Haven: Yale and London: Polity Press, 1989 [1974], 45–65.

———, "Freud on Women." In *Femininities, Masculinities, Sexualities: Freud and Beyond*. Lexington, KY: University of Kentucky Press and London, UK: Free Association Books, 1994 [1991], 1–32.

———, "From the Glory of Hera to the Wrath of Achilles: Narratives of Second Wave Masculinity and Beyond." *Studies in Gender and Sexuality* 16 (2015): 261–270.

———, "Heterosexuality as a Compromise Formation." In *Femininities, Masculinities, Sexualities: Freud and Beyond*. Lexington, KY: University of Kentucky Press and London, UK: Free Association Books, 1994 [1992], 33–69.

———, *Individualizing Gender and Sexuality: Theory and Practice*. New York and London: Routledge, 2011.

———, "The American Independent Tradition: Loewald, Erikson, and the (Possible) Rise of Intersubjective Ego Psychology." *Psychoanalytic Dialogues* 14 (2004): 207–232.

———, *The Power of Feelings: Personal Meaning in Psychoanalysis, Gender and Culture*. New Haven, CT: Yale University Press, 1999.

———, *The Psychoanalytic Ear and the Sociological Eye: Toward an American Independent Tradition*. London and New York: Routledge, 2020.

———, *The Reproduction of Mothering*, second edition 1999. Berkeley and Los Angeles: University of California Press, 1978.

———, "'Too Late': Ambivalence about Motherhood, Choice and Time." *Journal of the American Psychoanalytic Association* 51 (2003): 1181–1198 (reprinted in Chodorow, *Individualizing Gender and Sexuality*, as "Too Late": The Reproduction and Non-reproduction of Mothering").

Deutsch, Helene, *The Psychology of Women*, Vols. 1 and 2. New York: Grune and Stratton, (1944–1945).

Ehrensaft, Diane, *Mommies, Daddies, Donors, Surrogates*. New York: Guilford Press, 2005.

Erikson, Erik H., *Childhood and Society*. New York: Norton, 1950.

Female Psychology. *Journal of the American Psychoanalytic Association*, Vol. 24S, *Supplement* (1976).

Fliegel, Zenia O., "Women's Development in Analytic Theory." In *Psychoanalysis and Women: Contemporary Reappraisals*, ed. J. L. Alpert. Hillsdale, NJ: The Analytic Press, 1986, 3–31.

Foley, Helena, ed., *The Homeric "Hymn to Demeter": Translation, Commentary, Interpretive Essays*. Princeton, NJ: Princeton University Press, 1994.

Freud, Sigmund, *Introductory Lectures on Psychoanalysis: Standard Edition of the Complete Psychological Works*, Vol. 16. New York: W. W. Norton, 1916–1917.

Freudenberger, Nell, *Lost and Wanted*. New York: Knopf.

Greenson, Ralph R., Dis-identifying from Mother: Its Special Importance for the Boy. *International Journal of Psycho-Analysis* 49 (1968): 370–374.

Harris, Adrienne, *Gender as Soft Assembly*. New York and London: Routledge, 2009.

Horkheimer, Max, "Authority and the Family." In *Critical Theory*. New York: Herder and Herder, 1972 [1936], 47–128.

Horkheimer, Max and Theodor W. Adorno, *Dialectic of Enlightenment*. New York: Seabury Press, 1947.

Horney, Karen, "The Flight from Womanhood: The Masculinity Complex in Women, as Viewed by Men and Women." In *Feminine Psychology*, Karen Horney. New York: W. W. Norton, 1968 [1926], 54–70.

Kestenberg, Judith S., "On the Development of Maternal Feelings in Early Childhood: Observations and Reflections." *Psychoanalytic Study of the Child* 11 (1956): 257–291.

———, "Regression and Reintegration in Pregnancy." *Journal of the American Psychoanalytic Association* 24 (1976, Suppl.): 213–250.

Kristeva, Julia, "Women's Time." In *The Kristeva Reader*, ed. Toril Moi. New York: Columbia University Press, 1986 [1979], 187–213.

Kulish, Nancy and Deanna Holtzman, *A Story of Her Own: The Female Oedipus Complex Reexamined and Renamed*. Lanham: Jason Aronson, 2008.

———, “Persephone, the Loss of Virginity, and the Female Oedipal Complex.” *International Journal of Psycho-Analysis* 79 (1998): 57–71.
Lampl-de Groot, Jeanne, “The Evolution of the Oedipus Complex in Women.” *International Journal of Psycho-Analysis* 9 (1928): 333–345.
Levy, David, *Maternal Overprotection*. New York: Columbia University Press, 1943.
Loewald, Hans W., “Primary Process, Secondary Process, and Language.” In *Papers on Psychoanalysis*. New Haven: Yale University Press, 1980 [1978], 178–206.
———, “The Waning of the Oedipus Complex.” In *Papers on Psychoanalysis*. New Haven: Yale University Press, 1980 [1979], 384–404.
McDougall, Joyce, *Theatres of the Mind: Illusion and Truth on the Psychoanalytic Stage*. London: Free Association Books, 1986.
Mead, Margaret, *Male and Female*. New York: William Morrow, 1949.
Mitchell, Juliet, *Psychoanalysis and Feminism*. New York: Pantheon, 1974.
Mitscherlich, Alexander, *Society without the Father*. New York: Schocken, 1970 [1963].
Notman, Malkah and Carol Nadelson, eds., *The Woman Patient, Volume 1: Sexual and Reproductive Aspects of Women's Health Care*. New York: Plenum, 1979.
Pines, Dinora, *A Woman's Unconscious Use of Her Body*. New Haven, CT: Yale University Press, 1993.
Raphael-Leff, Joan, *Pregnancy: The Inside Story*. London: Sheldon Press, 1993.
Settlage, Calvin F., “Transcending Old Age: Creativity, Development and Psychoanalysis in the Life of a Centenarian.” *International Journal of Psycho-Analysis* 77 (1996): 549–564.
Slater, Philip E., *The Glory of Hera: Greek Mythology and the Greek Family*. Boston: Beacon, 1968.
Stoller, Robert, *Sex and Gender*, Vol. 1. New Haven, CT: Yale University Press, 1968.
Stone, Alison, ed., *Feminism, Psychoanalysis and Maternal Subjectivity*. New York and London: Routledge, 2013.
Whiting, John W.M., Richard Kluckhohn, and Albert Anthony, “The Function of Male Initiation Rites at Puberty.” In *Readings in Social Psychology*, eds. Eleanor E. Maccoby, Theodore M. Newcomb, and Eugene L. Hartley. New York: Holt, 1958, 359–370.
Winnicott, D.W., “Primary Maternal Preoccupation.” In *Collected Papers: Through Paediatrics to Psycho-Analysis*. London: Tavistock, 1958 [1956], 300–305.
Wylie, Philip. *Generation of Vipers: In Which the Author Rails against Congress, the President, Professors, Motherhood, Businessmen, and Other Matters American*. New York: Farrar and Rinehart, 1942.

CHAPTER 3

The Reproduction of Mothering: Forty Years on

Adrienne E. Harris

It is such a pleasure to be able to write about a book that has companioned my generation across decades, into and out of, different fields and enterprises, different meanings of motherhood, of reproduction, and perhaps, above all, of gender. My contact with the book goes back to its point of publication. My deep friendship with Nancy Chodorow begins at the point of powerful change for both of us as we moved from academic pursuits into a clinical engagement with psychoanalysis.

I want to start at the point of publication. *The Reproduction of Mothering*, in concert with only a few other books at that time (Dinnerstein's *The Mermaid and the Minotaur*[1]; Juliet Mitchell's *Psychoanalysis and Feminism*)[2] had an important and powerful effect upon feminism. Perhaps intended simultaneously for sociologists and for psychoanalysts, I want to notice the particular importance of this book for second-wave feminism in the 1970s, the women's movement in North America.

[1] Dorothy Dinnerstein, *The Mermaid and the Minotaur: Sexual Arrangements and Human Malaise* (New York: Harper & Row, 1976).

[2] Juliet Mitchell, *Psychoanalysis and Feminism: Freud, Reich, Laing and Women* (New York: Pantheon Books, 1974).

A. E. Harris (✉)
New York University, New York City, NY, USA

P. Bueskens (ed.), *Nancy Chodorow and* The Reproduction of Mothering,
https://doi.org/10.1007/978-3-030-55590-0_3

Activism, consciousness-raising, and the creation of a broad and important movement were the hallmarks of that time. The women's movement was built along the arc of movements for liberation and social change, from civil rights, from anti-imperialism, and the opposition to the war in Vietnam and leading into gay liberation (I deliberately use the language of the period). It was a time of extraordinary growth and expansiveness for many in my generation. I was supposed to have had a very serious and superior education but I actually only began to grow up intellectually in the period of the late '60s in the context of these social movements and the unexpected but hugely welcome demand to be reading and thinking of questions of political theory and social formation.

But, however engaged and crucial the projects of social activism, abortion rights, reproductive freedom, and many other liberatory projects, the psychological theory that underwrote feminism in that era was behavioralist. We could talk about roles and behavior. We could talk about cognitive structure. Carol Gilligan's use of theories of moral thought transformed into women's grappling with empowerment or eclipse.[3] But the early period of 70s second-wave feminism did not have a very profound theory of subjectivity or a considered role for unconscious experience. Franz Fanon, working in an even earlier period, on racism could deploy psychoanalytic ideas in an extremely potent form.[4] I would not say that the comparable movement in early feminism got so far into psyche and unconscious forces.

The Reproduction of Mothering, in my view, did something both necessary and useful for feminism and women's liberation by deepening our capacities to understand the strengths, the flaws, and the complexities of social change. I think that part of the power of Chodorow's work came from its radical and new argument and part from its interdisciplinarity. Now thinking through a concept in Rosi Braidotti[5] and Gilles Deleuze[6] I see this kind of theoretical practice as a *nomadic* or *migrant* theory,

[3] Carol Gilligan, *In a Different Voice: Psychological Theory and Women's Development* (Cambridge, MA: Harvard University Press, 1982).

[4] Frantz Fanon, *Black Skin, White Masks* (New York: Grove Press, 1967 [1952]).

[5] Rosi Braidotti, *Nomadic Subjects: Embodiment and Sexual Difference in Contemporary Feminist Theory* (New York: Columbia University Press, 2011 [1994]).

[6] Gilles Deleuze, *Difference and Repetition* (New York: Columbia University Press, 1994).

a theory whose concepts moved through, into and out of various disciplinary pockets, finding traction and energy in new constellations, and operating as a radical force against single-mindedness.

The Reproduction of Mothering was drawn from sociology and from psychoanalytic ideas and these concepts in coordination create a new field. One of the groups that most benefited from this form of analysis was feminism—its practices and its theories. Field theory, starts not with Bion, but in the 1920s by Kurt Lewin where it influenced social psychology, experimental psychology, perception, language studies, and other domains where experience "in context" is always in view.[7] Now we take field theoretical concepts for granted in many psychoanalytical areas and traditions, but in the 1970s Chodorow was doing something new, I think in melding a one-person and two-person perspective.

The Reproduction of Mothering offered an in-depth understanding of the complexity of mother–child, particularly mother–daughter, interaction and unpacked these relational configurations with a clear commitment to the intrapsychic (internal unconscious, drive inflected experience) as well as the relational and intersubjective experiences. Mothers' and women's relationality, the propensity for thinking dyadically, and intersubjectively, the maternal focus (Winnicott would say preoccupation)[8] on linking and interaction, are all produced and reproduced intergenerationally.

Feminist women and feminist practices and theories could mine a more complex structure of political groups and personal life. The personal is political was the resounding call of second-wave feminism.[9] We could look at envy, at competition and betrayal among women, at the powerful pull of maternal practices and the difficulty in managing power and equality with men. None of this can reduce the political to the intrapsychic. Nomadic like movements across her two target disciplines—sociology and psychoanalysis—kept Chodorow and her feminist audiences

[7] Kurt Lewin, *Principles of Topological Psychology* (New York: McGraw-Hill, 1936).

[8] Donald W. Winnicott, "Primary Maternal Preoccupation," in *The Maternal Lineage: Identification, Desire and Transgenerational Issues*, ed. Paola Mariotti (New York: Routledge, 2012 [1955]), 59–66.

[9] Muriel Dimen, "Between Lust and Libido Sex, Psychoanalysis, and the Moment Before," *Psychoanalytic Dialogues* 9, no. 4 (1999): 415–440; Muriel Dimen, "The Body as Rorschach," *Studies in Gender and Sexuality* 1, no. 1 (2000): 9–39.

always deepening the understanding of the psychological matters which impeded political action and underwrote it.

I also want to advance what I am sure is a personal opinion and one borne out of living through the complex and often terrible experiences in which various political movements turned to violence. Zwerman (1997) wrote a thesis on the kind of gender politics that appeared prominent in various far left groups whose activism turned increasingly to violence.[10] What she discovered is that the gender politics within such groups was astonishingly reactionary, whatever the intensity or activism or violence of the work against imperialism and the dominant neoliberal political culture. For me, that has led me to consider the way feminism—and feminism of the sort Chodorow's work privileged and aided, was an important prosthetic against the self-destruction and destruction of groups like Weatherman.[11] The politics of self-interest was a useful corrective to the politics of sacrifice and violence.

The bath that feminism and feminists took in the rich waters of *The Reproduction of Mothering* created more robust ideas and practices, more subtle politics, and a more informed psychodynamic theory of the subject: political, domestic, personal, gendered. Later movements wanted more about class and race and cultural difference but for a first mix-up of these theoretical worlds, the brew was intoxicating. Sorry to be mixing metaphors.

I am pursuing a helix-structured, dialectical model of development here when I say that this psychoanalytically invigorated feminism then began to repenetrate and demandingly interact with psychoanalysis. Certainly, the figures and characters of the relational movement imagined we were doing just that.[12] If the activism of the 70s was replaced by the immersion in clinical work in the 80s onward, the politics and the interest in the way history and the state became so deeply imbricated in psychic

[10] Reference required.

[11] Weatherman was an underground militant radical left student organisation founded at the University of Michigan in the late 1960s.

[12] In addition to Nancy Chodorow's seminal work in *The Reproduction of Mothering* there was also Jessica Benjamin, *The Bonds of Love: Psychoanalysis, Feminism and the Problem of Domination* (New York: Pantheon, 1988); *Jessica Benjamin, Beyond Doer and Done to: An Intersubjective View of Thirdness* (London and New York: Routledge, 2004); Muriel Dimen (2003), *Sexuality, Intimacy, Power* (Hillsdale, NJ: The Analytic Press, 2003); Adrienne Harris, *Gender as Soft Assembly* (NY: The Analytic Press, 2005); Ken Corbett, *Boyhoods: Rethinking Masculinities* (New Haven: Yale University Press, 2009).

experience. One way to say this is that we brought a feminist inflected theory of maternality and gender and sexuality back into psychoanalysis. Alpha work across groups and disciplines.

One process that Chodorow evolves and develops in her book is the notion of reproduction. This seems now very contemporary as we see, given a highly elaborated understanding of attachment experiences in all their variations. Chodorow was beginning to examine and make space for what has come to be called intergenerational transmission of traumatic experience. This work has been evolving through a very powerful international group of theorists including Haydée Faimberg, Maurice Apprey, Madeleine and Willy Baranger, Jill Salberg, and Sue Grand, among others.[13]

We can now look at the subtle microprocesses and transactions through which many powerful forms of experience involving many aspects of sexuality and subjectivity flow through the generations and think how well Chodorow's account of the emergence of psychic life from relational matrices frames this kind of understanding. Tracking complex sites of influences and evolutions across decades and across disciplines is a sensitive and difficult process. We need to think of a concept like *nachtraglichkeit* to be applied to process and change within our discipline. Looking 40 years back to the first appearance of *The Reproduction of Mothering* we see ideas cross over, move back, remark the source material, and plunge ahead into new realism of understanding. *Nachtraglichkeit* is our most nonlinear experience of time, change the past. 40 years after this book, we re-examine the book, its effects, and its shaping of a number of futures. We see things in the book we might not have seen at the beginning Migrant and nomads theorists and concepts.

[13] Haydée Faimberg, *The Telescoping of Generations: Listening to the Narcissistic Links between Generations* (London and New York: Routledge, 2005); Maurice Apprey, "The Pluperfect Errand: A Turbulent Return to Beginnings in the Transgenerational Transmission of Destructive Aggression," *Free Associations: Psychoanalysis* and *Culture*, *Media*, *Groups*, *Politics* 77 (2015): 15–28; Madeleine Baranger and Willy Baranger, "The Analytic Situation as a Dynamic Field," *International Journal* of *Psychoanalysis* 89 (2008): 795–826; Madeleine Baranger and Willy Baranger, "Spiral Process and the Dynamic Field," in *The Work of Confluence: Listening and Interpreting in the Psychoanalytic Field* (London: Routledge, 2009), 45–62; Jill Salberg and Sue Grand, eds., *Wounds of History: Repair and Resilience in the Trans-Generational Transmission of Trauma* (London: Routledge, 2017).

I will end with another metaphor. Chodorow's *Reproduction of Mothering* is one of our mother lodes. A spring turns into a strong coursing river. There are waterfalls, dams, and droughts. Returns to the source and a powerful new reservoir made when disciplines come together and mutate. We might even think, as many are trying to do about the ways the maternal links, their power and regressive pull both require us and disable us from thinking about various political formations maybe in particular climate change.

CHAPTER 4

Reminiscing and Reflecting on Nancy Chodorow's *The Reproduction of Mothering*

Rosemary H. Balsam

Nancy Chodorow has been one of the most outstanding feminist thinkers in psycho-sociology and psychoanalysis since the 1960s. At the time of publication in 1978 of the first edition of the extraordinary award-winning and now classic work *The Reproduction of Mothering: Psychoanalysis and the Sociology of Gender*—the fortieth anniversary of which we are celebrating in this volume—she was a young lecturer and Associate Professor in the University of California at Santa Cruz (1974–1986).[1] Later she moved to Berkeley (1986–2005), where she created the second edition of the book that updated her views in 1999. There she was a Professor in the University of California, Berkeley Department of Sociology. She also trained in clinical psychoanalysis at the San Francisco Center for Psychoanalysis through the early 1990s, combining all her fields, and now, through clinical practice with her own patients, she was able to approach even more closely the individual mind in all its variety:

[1] Nancy Chodorow, *The Reproduction of Mothering: Psychoanalysis and the Sociology of Gender* (Berkeley, CA: University of California Press, 1978).

R. H. Balsam (✉)
Yale Medical School, New Haven, CT, USA
e-mail: rosemary.balsam@yale.edu

P. Bueskens (ed.), *Nancy Chodorow and* The Reproduction of Mothering,
https://doi.org/10.1007/978-3-030-55590-0_4

plus in 1999, she added the Department of Psychology to her teaching and mentoring purview. Then in 2006 she retired as Professor of Sociology in Berkeley, changed coast in the United States, and moved, or (as she says sometimes), "returned East" to where her parents had originally belonged, this time to Cambridge, Massachusetts, to become a full time psychoanalyst. Shortly thereafter she became a Training and Supervising analyst at the Boston Institute, and had and still has educative roles in the Cambridge Health Alliance. Obviously, she kept writing throughout these developmental career and coast shifts, ever elaborating her fascinating topic of sexualities and genders, especially those of women. We psychoanalysts have been honored with her scholarly academic genius and delighted with her active clinical and theoretical presence and friendship in the national and international psychoanalytic world.

Dr. Chodorow, as one of the few and distinguished CORST (Committee on Research and Special Training) members of the American Psychoanalytic Association, has thus successfully mutually energized her several fields. She has kept her focus on feminism and issues of female concern and development in the forefront of her oeuvre, using especially the writings of the creative ego psychological theoretician Hans Loewald. What makes her productivity so important and enduringly special to her chosen fields? And what makes her work so special to me as a psychiatrist, fellow psychoanalyst, and feminist—besides the pleasure of her friendship? I will attempt in this chapter to answer both of these questions, at times weaving them together.

Nancy Chodorow's Creative Thinking

It is hard to separate the music from the lyrics of Nancy Chodorow's song, and her body of work from the quality of her thinking (She actually does have a beautiful singing voice, and can play a guitar with the best of them!). In a lively published interview with a young psychologist colleague, Mengchun Chiang in 2017, she explained her thought process:

> From the margin I'm always trying to see what the presuppositions are, to see what other people are taking for granted, that they don't even notice ... It's also [about] *going up against core thinking*. Originally, I wrote

about how sociologists should think about the psychological, and reciprocally these days, I write about how psychoanalysts should think about the social.[2]

The latter emphasis will be the topic of her next book in 2019. This style is one key to her ability to have been able to notice what was basic, common, and present in family and social life, but what was a missing link in Freudian psychoanalysis and in feminist scholarship, i.e., the average expectable living, thinking, interactive impact of a mother upon her daughter. "Women mother"[3] is the first brilliant sentence of Chodorow's book. It arrests the obvious, and that will then be examined in every dimension. Her searching attitude to this theme is the part of the book that endures. The other part, electrifying at the time with its recommendations for social feminist action, insisted that men take over more of the childcare with the implication that *that* would mitigate consuming or destructive gendered reactions to the unconscious all-powerful mother of the nursery. Psychologically that is moot. But men helping at home did become more common in the subsequent generations as a result of the feminist movement raising such awareness among men about the sheer unfairness of the conventional domestic labor division. Their own mothers' expectations of men's greater domestication changed during their upbringing after this era, but the psychological argument in this book for the hope that its remedial impact would significantly shift the influential archaic power of the mother in the internal life of her daughters is probably more of historical interest at this point.

Later Chodorow would say that her cornerstone book was written "from the point of view of a daughter".[4] That profound personal emotional experience is what she likely drew upon unconsciously as well as consciously in her early thirties, in addition to her scholarship. She

[2] Mengchun Chiang, "'You Just Know It's the Only Thing You Can Think': A Conversation with Chodorow," *Women & Therapy* 40, nos. 3–4 (2017): 318.

[3] Chodorow, *The Reproduction of Mothering*, 3.

[4] Marilyn Metzl, "From Sociology to Psychoanalysis: The Works of Nancy J. Chodorow," review of *The Reproduction of Mothering; Feminism and Psychoanalytic Theory; Femininities, Masculinities and Sexualities;* and *The Power of Feelings*, by Nancy Chodorow, *Psychoanalytic Psychology: The Journal of the American Psychological Association Division* 39 (2003): 55, https://www.apadivisions.org/division-39/publications/reviews/chodorow?_ga=2.221348312.1187038323.1565886747-1511100991.1563445240.

had courage and confidence in her observations, like Freud, to assume that she was Everywoman (He was more omnipotent though, in thinking of himself as Every*man* in an old-fashioned universalist sense, and not confined to his own sexed gender). Chodorow's upbringing with a loved and well-educated social worker mother, and a father who was a Professor of Physics and Applied Physics, plus her own education in Radcliffe College and Brandies University supported her intellectual interests and originality. Feminism in the early 1970s was so necessarily embattled against the domestic role of a woman with the intention of liberating her from the oppressions of confinement of "Kinder, Küche, Kirche," that no-one had really stopped to wonder *why* did women seem so driven to have children. And to look after them? *How* does that exactly work? The fact that the phenomenon of mothers and babies existed, yes. The observation that the three Ks were linked to a lack of involvement in "outside work" as the domain of men, yes. The fact that this position led to being taken less seriously by society than men who did not interrupt their careers to have a family, yes. The fact that this domestic role aided and abetted male dominion in society, yes. The fact that it was time to break up this sequence vigorously if women in society were going to be able to progress in power financially and in equality to men and support their own independence, yes. But it was Nancy Chodorow as a sociologist and anthropologist, who stopped to ask *why and how* does this happen to women not only externally, but within their internal lives. She turned to psychology and psychoanalysis to help illuminate the quest. In order to do that, she needed to separate herself from an all-encompassing notion that the source of the paucity of women's power was all due to man's ability to overpower her. I quote from a section where she tells of various opinions and experiments in social biology about men and women, and disagrees, say, with Polatnick who, in asking why men do not "mother," develops a thesis about their enforcing their power over women's powerlessness in this regard. In a passage where Chodorow is building her argument for mothering being shaped as an interior condition she says strongly, "Nor can men's power over women explain women's mothering".[5] I infer that Chodorow's own mind was independent enough of male/female gender enmeshments to be able to take an outsider stance and ask this key question about women. She looked to women's *inner* lives to search

[5] Chodorow, *The Reproduction of Mothering*, 33.

for additional answers. This search of internal life was an approach shared by the English, (formerly) Lacanian psychoanalyst and academic Juliet Mitchell in 1974[6]—the other noted feminist of that era whose knowledge and ideas helped Freud become less damned in academic feminist circles for his undiluted phallocentrism. Chodorow saw that Freud's tale of sex and gender dimorphism also importantly attempted to account for the undoubted inequalities in society, thus sharing common ground with her that these asymmetries not be taken for granted. She needed to be able to assume that, given a chance, women could function independently from men—a radical idea at the time, given society's myths since ancient times, such as the male God and Adam's (ever so generous) gift of his own rib to create the prototype female Eve all for himself. Regrettably psychoanalytic theory shared a version of that male possession of women, but at least Freud had asked "how and why?"

Chodorow communicates an appetitive passion for theory that is infectious, exciting and organizes her own mind. She readily appreciates its aims, virtues, and limitations for any given question. Chiang, reporting from her 2017 interview, says, "[Nancy] drew parallels between her way of thinking ("I have a structural mind") and her father's ability to "see how physics principles from widely disparate theories could be brought together in an instrument."[7] Quoting still from the Chiang interview, Chodorow reflects:

> I have a very structural mind. Doing anthropology, you could think about the structure and organization of societies. In contrast, I don't have a very narrative mind, and that's actually a challenge as a clinician. I don't think intuitively metaphorically; I think intuitively structurally. I was really well-placed for the period of structural anthropology and structural sociology—Levi-Strauss and his model, more than the post-modern, non-literal, associative ways of thinking....[8]

In *Reproduction* also one observes Chodorow as a great teacher. As I re-read the book, now senior in my own psychoanalytic career, I thought that her explanation of psychoanalysis in Chapter 3 was one of the best

[6] Juliet Mitchell, *Psychoanalysisand Feminism: Freud, Reich, Laing and Women* (London: Vintage Books, 1974).

[7] Chiang, "A Conversation with Chodorow," 311.

[8] Ibid., 312.

I've ever read for those outside the discipline. It is deceptively simple, but it captures everything of basic significance that one would ever need to know—even as a practicing analyst. One can also see the seeds of many ideas that became much more sophisticated later in her career and remain important today—such as her contributions to the debate about the nature of psychoanalysis which she sees as an intersubjective science or a subjective science operating with a model of the mind that could be called, "intersubjective ego psychology".[9]

Even back in 1978, Chodorow was thinking about the sexed and gendered world of women in a way approved by her later beloved psychoanalytic guru, the psychoanalytic scholar, Hans Loewald, in approaching a potential analysand. Loewald offered that: "The patient, by revealing himself to the analyst, provides rudiments of... an image which the analyst has to... hold... in safe keeping for the patient to whom it is mainly lost".[10] Chodorow knew intuitively how to "hold in safe-keeping" a vision of female lives, while she carefully explored their troubled phenomena.

Chodorow had and still has a remarkable ability to analyze critically with alacrity, read with astuteness and clarity, yet ultimately approach these fundamental psychological issues also intuitively, as she penned this doctoral thesis that ultimately became her famous book. It is a gift of genius to be able to tap into an idea that is so utterly unacknowledged but is so common that when people hear it they say—"Of course, that was always true."

The Reproduction of Mothering

When *Reproduction* was first published four decades ago, it was quickly appreciated that it put the mother–daughter relationship and female psychology "on the map".[11] In the 1990s, for example, it was chosen by *Contemporary Sociology* as one of the ten most influential books of the previous 25 years. Marilyn Metzl, reviewing the second edition in 2003 in

[9] Nancy Chodorow, "The American Independent Tradition: Loewald, Erikson, and the (Possible) Rise of Intersubjective Ego Psychology," *Psychoanalytic Dialogues* 14, no. 2 (2004): 209.

[10] Hans Loewald, "On the Therapeutic Action of Psycho-Analysis," *The International Journal of Psychoanalysis* 41 (1960): 18.

[11] Metzl, "From Sociology to Psychoanalysis," 55.

the journal of the American Psychological Division 39, noted that "Her points in this book can be separated into four main ideas: 1) How most women come to think of themselves as heterosexual, 2) Why women have the urge to mother, 3) What personality traits are specific to women, and 4) How the pattern of male dominance might be understood and might be changed."[12]

The first two of these wonderful topics are, I think, the enduring gems of the book. How women come to activate their heterosexuality is still just as good a question now as in 1978, (challenging the older psychoanalytic question—how do women come to activate their *homo*sexuality?—in turn displacing heterosexuality as the unquestioned norm). The same goes for why women want to "mother"—defined here as taking on primary nurturing responsibility for children in the family. How is that situation generationally reproduced, Chodorow asked. First, she challenged in a scholarly way the biologically determinist notion that women are simply born with maternal instinct. For example, she examined existent hormonal research, and also animal research and declared that this is a "problematic claim about natural or instinctual motherliness in women".[13] Persuasively she picks apart research papers and sees that other scientists too have admitted that the evidence for some kind of hormonal readiness for motherliness in females is flimsy, or perhaps applies to women only immediately after childbirth, quickly to disappear. Males and non parturient women seem similar in terms of readiness also. Oxytocin, associated with infant bonding, can be detected in both women and men who are close to infants. Yet, how irrationally tenacious *still* is that notion that women are assumed biologically to possess a "natural" motherliness! Society hates news that this certitude is in error and is actually a *problem*. This was so at the birth of psychoanalysis too. Margarete Hilferding, in 1910—among the first women to be accepted to the Vienna Medical School and also the first into the membership of Freud's new Vienna Psychoanalytic Society—gave as her initiation paper one entitled "On The Basis of Mother Love," the contents of which were based too on her medical obstetrical experiences and observations

[12] Ibid.

[13] Nancy Chodorow, "Preface to the Second Edition," in *The Reproduction of Mothering*, 15 [Petra: vii–xix].

of maternal hate.[14] Like Chodorow in the 1970s, Hilferding was beginning to be fascinated by looking to the inner life of women to study how mothers, pregnancy, and their babies interacted with each other.[15] Hilferding also declared "there is no innate mother love".[16] One could practically hear the gasp of disbelief in the male, mainly medical audience! The doctors enveloped in cigar smoke that evening took up fairy tales in their discussion, and evaded her message. She reported great disappointment. Not long afterwards she departed along with Adler, with whom Freud also parted company.[17] What a pity Hilferding did not remain in Freud's circle. Our current societal progress can be measured positively as Chodorow's and others' statements on behalf of women have been more clearly heard from 1978 onward. We who are particularly interested in this topic do recognize, however, that it is still an inconvenient truth that we are investigating with Chodorow's balance as exemplary, and with the help of the scholarly tools she provided by examining, "*Why* females mother."

Regarding the other two points of Chodorow's book as specified above by Metzl[18]—I have some problems these days going along with her idea of categorizing specific personality traits as belonging to "men" as opposed to "women." I believe that she herself in her later transformations might agree, having come to appreciate the opportunity to listen to more women talk individually and in depth from the couch. For example, her sensitive understanding for individual differences was an inherent part of her later highly influential thesis that renders gender in the plural rather than the old-fashioned singular.[19] That plurality itself sets free categorical

[14] Margarete Hilferding in Rosemary Balsam, "Women of the Wednesday Society: The Presentations of Drs. Hilferding, Spielrein and Hug-Hellmuth," *American Imago* 60, no. 3 (2003): 308.

[15] I discuss the figure of Hilferding and the dissonance between her insights and those of the essentially male Viennese medical establishment more fully in Rosemary Balsam, "Freud, Females, Childbirth, and Dissidence: Margarete Hilferding, Karen Horney and Otto Rank," *The Psychoanalytic Review* 100, no. 5 (2013): 695–716 and "The War on Women in Psychoanalytic Theory Building: Past to Present," *The Psychoanalytic Study of the Child* 69 (2015): 83–107.

[16] Hilferding in Balsam, "Wednesday Society," 309.

[17] Balsam, "Wednesday Society," 314.

[18] Metzl, "From Sociology to Psychoanalysis," 55.

[19] Nancy Chodorow, *Femininities, Masculinities and Sexualities: Freud and Beyond* (Lexington: University Press of Kentucky, 1994).

notions that this or that style of thinking belongs monolithically either to "women" or to "men." Chodorow has written vehemently against psychoanalytic theory as a monolithic mindset. However, as far as opening up descriptively some of the assumed and expectable traits that women or men are supposed to display societally, the text of *Reproduction* is rich.

Chodorow's Theory

In *Reproduction* Chodorow began to question thoughtfully Freud's version of the Oedipal conflict. Sooner or later if one is pursuing the theory of sex and gender one simply has to see the limitations of this discovery of Freud. Questioning such shibboleths in psychoanalysis is far from easy politically though, because I think that the field came (or indeed has come) to depend upon upholding this central formula of Freud's version to sustain its identity and cohesion, and to differentiate psychoanalysis from other forms of mental health study. Clinging doggedly to the Oedipal myth as central and exclusive is a continuation of Freud's own international movement-building activities, and of his behavior toward those who disagreed with him (like Jung, Horney or Rank) who were thus cast out.[20] A case can be made that many of these fights were over female development and the role of the female in interior psychic life.[21] Thus when Chodorow mentions in her 2017 interview[22] how her own manuscripts were initially rejected by editors, *Reproduction* among them, she highlights a profound uphill battle in the psychoanalytic field even to this day—an automatic support for male Oedipus almost as a flag of identity. In spite of improvement over the years since Freud versus Horney, challenging psychologically a vision of analytic theorists as less than fair-minded regarding sex and gender and issues concerning women's equality, still is an unwelcome criticism.

Chodorow gives a lovely and interactive portrait of the way the baby depends on the mother, persuasively showing that in an infant's life that mothering or sensitive caretaking is not psychologically optional. She leans on Winnicott, the Balints (who advocated in contrast to Freud

[20] George Makari, *Revolution in Mind: The Creation of Psychoanalysis* (New York: Harper/HarperCollins, 2008), 214.

[21] Rosemary Balsam, "Oedipus Rex: Where Are We Going, Especially with Females?" *The Psychoanalytic Quarterly* 84 (2015): 556.

[22] Chiang, "A Conversation with Chodorow," 319.

and the ego psychologists, a theory of primary love that included even antenatally a powerful registration of its emotional handling and environs), Fairbairn, and Bowlby, for example, all of them, the British Middle (or Independent) Group of analysts. None of them fully agreed with Freud's physiological base for psychoanalytic theory. This also sat right with Chodorow, basically trained as a social psychologist, unlike Freud's grounding in medicine. I read and I wonder now, how did she know so much of the comparative theoreticians of psychoanalysis without having been in analytic training than herself, or having done any clinical work? She read imaginatively—avidly, and with acute cognitive and emotional intelligence. Here is an example of her brilliant vigilance about differing theoretical ideas that bear on a similar psychological outcome. In a footnote she makes a sweeping, accurate and integrative comment that is for her, I think, a throwaway comment:

> As many critics of ego psychology have pointed out, Hartmann, in extolling the adaptive ego, and Anna Freud, Edith Jacobson and others, in claiming that defenses are the basis of ego formation, verge on making a necessary virtue out of what object relations theorists (Laing, Guntrip, Fairbairn, Winnicott) and non-psychoanalytic critics of the contemporary family consider a product of specific modes of child care and family organization.[23]

Many may not have quite noticed that or been able to express it so succinctly after far more years of study. She gives strong support for the notion that a continuity of attentive caretakers (not necessarily in the singular) is the important issue in early child care, and she criticizes psychoanalytic ideas that imply an unquestioned necessity for an infant's need for exclusivity with the biological mother. Women at the time no doubt liked very much to hear that well-argued basis for this claim. "Psychoanalysis does not describe those parenting arrangements that have to be for infants to become people"[24] she points out. She explores both the child's relation to the mother and also the mother's to the child. The latter is an area that had been, and continued to be slow to come into focus for psychoanalysis. All the focus then was on the interior life of the offspring reared by an assumed exclusive mother figure.

[23] Chodorow, *The Reproduction of Mothering*, 60.

[24] Ibid., 76.

Chodorow's view of the father reflects strongly the psychoanalytic view of that time. It was an era in psychoanalysis when, with an increased emphasis on studying "mother and child" and the flourishing of so-called preoedipal dynamics and a girl's independent establishment of core gender identity before age three[25] the role of the previously assumed dominant father (after Freud) was being redefined. The father was now described as quite separated from the dyad of mother and baby, and used by the child as a figure primarily to promote further separation from the early mother (The followers of Klein had then and now a different take on the father who, like the mother, was more of a paternal/generic male phantasy present all along in the infant's mind. Their assumption however was of an inbuilt knowledge of the primal scene. Contemporary eclectic analysis sees the father's role, while different from the mother's and not dominant as in Freud, as more intimate in the child's mind than was described in the 1970s). A reader can see the value of Chodorow's anthropological and sociological training that allowed her, in 1978, to question analytic elements such as the universality of the Oedipus complex on behalf of women and girls living in post-war Western culture and being reared hopefully in a less markedly and overtly patriarchal society than that of turn-of-the-century Vienna.

Having examined with an analytic lens up to that point in the book, attachment and caretaking of the child, Chodorow acknowledged, that the methodology (if not the theory of psychoanalysis about women) was leading us "in the right direction." She then sharpens the question—"Because neither the theory nor the clinical accounts directly ask why women, and not men, parent, they cannot provide a complete answer".[26] She wants to be very clear for her readers that her building thesis about the reproduction of mothering will depend on the fact that boys and girls have a very separate line of attachment to the mother, precisely because of their sex and gender. Chodorow's female "Oedipus" in this book recognizes the normative closeness of a mother and daughter than goes far beyond what Freud and many others believed (and *still* can believe) is

[25] See, for example, Phyllis Greenacre, "Early Physical Determinants in the Development of a Sense of Identity," *Journal of the American Psychoanalytic Association* 6 (1958): 612–617; James Kleeman, "The Establishment of Core Gender Identity in Normal Girls. II. How Meanings Are Conveyed between Parent and Child in the First 3 Years," *Archives of Sexual Behavior* 1, no. 2 (1971): 117–129.

[26] Chodorow, *The Reproduction of Mothering*, 91.

"pathological." She says that psychoanalytic accounts show that girls do *not* in fact turn away from their mothers toward the fathers, leaving the mother as past tense. This observation was dynamite in 1978. She was absolutely right of course, and in tune with the other analysts she cites. In her introduction to *Freud on Women*[27] in 1992, Young-Bruehl later asks the same question, but from a different angle, implying that the question itself remained (and possibly still remains) far from consensually settled in our field. In considering a vagueness about penis envy and its origins, elaborating on feminist criticisms of Freud's ideas on women, Young-Bruehl wondered, among other issues, what benefit it could be for a girl to "turn away" to the father against the mother.[28] There has been a great lag in the psychoanalytic field between teaching the received Freudian theory of girls' Oedipal story involving this fantasy—a "turn" to the father against the mother—and overt acceptance of Freud's errors which should by now be history.[29] While the clinical literature shows girls can be very angry and repudiating of their mothers, and daughters can and do compete for who is the better wife and the better mother, that is not the same issue as an unconscious *dissociation* from or desire for extreme distance from the mother such as Freud and many of his followers claimed was normative. Chodorow was one of the first to draw attention to this, and she went on in 1994 to be an early psychoanalytic author to articulate the myth of Demeter and Persephone as a possibly more fitting female developmental myth.[30]

Subsequently, Kulish and Holtzman[31] put this in the forefront of female development, emphasizing also that Persephone *kept* relationships with *both* her mother, Demeter and her husband Hades. Continued closeness between mother and daughter still lacks general acknowledgment, and thus in a low-grade way remains controversial. Our contemporary

[27] Elisabeth Young-Bruehl, *Freud on Women: A Reader* (New York: W. W. Norton, 1992).

[28] Ibid., 43.

[29] Balsam, "Oedipus Rex."

[30] Nancy Chodorow, "Family Structure and Feminine Personality," in *The Homeric Hymn to Demeter: Translation, Commentary, and Interpretive Essays*, ed. Helene P. Foley (Princeton: Princeton University Press, 1994), 243–264.

[31] Nancy Kulish and Deanna Hotzman Deanna, *A Story of Her Own: The Female Oedipus Complex Re-examined and Renamed* (Hillsdale: Jason Aronson Inc., 2008).

field is more likely to evade such unworked-through discomforts in developmental theory, and just change paths to emphasize some different theoretical position given less to developmental sequencing than Freud—such as the Kleinian "positions," where there are only two choices, the paranoid-schizoid or the depressive. The latter is a more mature psychological state, but nothing is said about body evolution in the life cycle, which is also occurring in development. Chaos theory applied to modern psychoanalysis, in spite of its liberating freshness of ideas on gender complexity, also soft-pedals emphasis on mentalized body development. Sustained structural patterning of internal life, through that theoretical lens is deemed at best evanescent (Harris "Soft Assembly").[32] According to Freud's psychoanalytic theory, then, a girl's intense involvement with the mother beyond about 5 or 6 years—the "classical" height of the Oedipal period—becomes suspect for a kind of infantilism of her character formation. The girl's ability to relate to boys and men and enjoy her heterosexuality *necessarily* then would be restricted, if she continued in a close tie to her mother. This was part of the early explanation of how female heterosexuality and homosexuality emerged, the latter as a form of "deviant" sexuality. The best that can be said is it was at least *an attempt* at some psychodynamic explanation. Early on Chodorow appreciated Freud for an open quality of thinking about gender that was not common in his time. Also, of course, she drew attention to his errors. (Many other analysts interested in sexuality and gender since Horney, mostly women—if spottily and in waves that somehow fade—have continued to question, add to and subtract from Freud).

Chodorow goes to some lengths to show how a mother will treat her son differently to her daughter. This basic point surely abides, even if some of her certainties about females' greater proclivities for boundary diffusion may prove clinically to be more dubious. It was certainly the coinage of the analytic theory of the sixties and seventies, and it was cited in feminist circles about how the mother distanced herself from her son earlier than from her daughter, and thus socialized him for independence. But, as Chodorow elaborates, in theory it cost him dearly in terms of gifts for social intimacy and pushed him to more "external" interests than girls (Greenson, for example, had articulated that understanding in

[32] Adrienne Harris, *Gender as Soft Assembly* (Hillsdale: Analytic Press, 2005).

1968,[33] naming it a necessary "disidentification" from mother that little boys manifested in order to assure their masculinity). "Sameness" between mother and daughter lent itself to less need for the push to differentiate from the mother.

These steps then began to show the way logically for Chodorow's theory about how mothers "reproduced" themselves inevitably across generations. The mother was (and is) the person whom the child loves with all the force of its egoistic primary love and attachment. Chodorow believed, following Alice Balint, that this early love for the mother was not under the sway of the "reality principle," whereas love for the more distant father was. As a clinician, I have some problem in seeing the image of the father operating *so* clear of irrationality in the child's mind, and *so* clearly representing "culture". By now in the twenty-first century many more women in Western societies are educated and in the work force as well as heading more single-mother families. This theory of a boy's *need* to "disidentify" from the mother perhaps has most significance for highly patriarchal systems of heterosexual family life. Work such as Michael Diamond's[34] on how boys and men develop their masculinities, though, challenges this conceptualization. Modern psychoanalytic theory softens this supposed male early "turning away" from the mother. Many men in fact are ongoingly deeply affected internally by continuing to identify with their early caretaking mothers, or the unconscious masculinity of the mother. The line of modern clinical argument then casts into question Chodorow's 1978[35] (and others') certainties about male development dealt with as a whole. Some theoreticians, like Kristeva[36] too highlight and explicate the poor treatment of women by men, (and of women by women) instead return to Freud's stress on the male horror of the female sexed body, recognizing deeply in general the sense of the importance of the morphology and function of the body to the psyche. Others have been primarily interested in investigating subjective

[33] Ralph Greenson, "Disidentifying from Mother: Its Special Importance for the Boy," *The International Journal of Psychoanalysis* 49 (1968): 370–374.

[34] Michael Diamond, "The Shaping of Masculinity: Revisioning Boys Turning away from Their Mothers to Construct Male Gender Identity," *The International Journal of Psychoanalysis* 85, no. 2 (2004): 359–379.

[35] Chodorow, *The Reproduction of Mothering.*

[36] Julia Kristeva, *Powers of Horror: An Essay on Abjection*, trans. L.S. Roudiez (New York: Columbia University Press, 1980).

experiences of pregnancy, and how the environment, family, and existing children's reactions, (including gender), may be processed in relation to the mother's own physicality.[37] Nonetheless the field would benefit from further knowledge.[38]

Chodorow helped open the intriguing question of how heterosexuality actually happened. That provided a template for the same readers of the now classic second-wave feminist health book *Our Bodies Ourselves*[39] to be able to think and reflect about how their sexual feelings were being directed and toward whom and for what purposes. It was startling too many to be introduced to a notion that it was the feelings for her *mother* that became transformed and available to court men's love. Chodorow helped explained Freud's idea of human "bisexuality." As Metzl puts it, "The girl's resolution of her Oedipal complex creates a leitmotif with vestiges of her primary identification with her mother realized throughout her life".[40]

Chodorow asks difficult questions that follow on from what she has laid down. She also writes a wonderful critique of Freud's early views of sex and gender development. So what about the girl who does not take that path? Girls can profoundly reject their mothers too. "Girls" she says,

> ...for many over-determined reasons, do develop penis envy and may repress knowledge of their vagina because they cannot otherwise win the heterosexual mother...because the penis symbolizes independence from the

[37] See for example: Kleeman, "The Establishment of Core Gender Identity," 1971; Kulish and Holzman, *A Story of Her Own*, 2008; Rosemary Balsam, *Womens' Bodies in* Psychoanalysis (London: Routledge, 2012); Galit Atlas, *The Enigma of Desire: Sex, Longing, and Belonging in Psychoanalysis* (London: Routledge, 2015); Joan Raphael-Leff, *Pregnancy: The Inside Story* (London: Karnac, 2001); Joan Raphael-Leff, *The Dark Side of the Womb: Pregnancy, Parenting, and Persecutory Anxieties* (London: Anna Freud Centre, 2015); Ingrid Moeslein-Teising and Frances Thomson Salo, *The Female Body: Inside and Outside* (London: Karnac, 2013).

[38] I believe that Chodorow importantly put in place a need to support, accept and investigate "differences" between females and males. Hopefully new investigation can be even freer of "less than or more than" comparative interpretations than the older investigations, holding open and fulfilling the promise of this early work for continuing productive understanding of our sexed and gendered lot and our gender variance.

[39] Boston Womens' Health Group Collective, *Our Bodies, Ourselves: A Book by and for Women* (Cambridge: Touchstone, 1976).

[40] Metzl, "From Sociology to Psychoanalysis," 56.

> (internalized) powerful mother; as a defense against fantasies of acting on sexual desires for their father ... etc.[41]

This style echoes how Freud asked why a person manifests one neurosis rather than another. Chodorow wonders about which features of the mother's thinking and habits she takes on as hers, and which she bypasses. What of her mother will she herself pass to her own daughter? She considers the aggression in dynamics of competition, say, with second generation daughters who can be perceived unconsciously as siblings, still competing over their own mother. One can see intimations of the future psychotherapist and psychoanalyst here in these psychodynamic elaborations, even in her eleventh chapter on "The Sexual Sociology of Adult Life"[42] where she focuses on patterns of development. Her commitment however is to try to think about individuals, as well as to attempt to apply such knowledge to large group behaviors. I am not enough of a sociologist to have a sense of how some of the last chapters stand up to time, or how time-bound they were. I can imagine her readers—especially at that time in the United States, female readers who grew up in a domestically idealized atmosphere in the post-war years who had a great hunger in college to have "a ring by Spring" and to settle down with a family. They would have been pleased to have a psychological way of understanding difficult perceptions male dominance, and having a named sense of male capacities to repress personal feelings and to deny dependence, that Chodorow and others described as propelling men into the "nonfamilial competitive world",[43] a world that was so closed to women. She expresses a final idealized sense of how sharing domestic life and child rearing could mitigate some of the gendered agony of everyday life by diluting the woman's power and omnipotence as *the* mother. This would (in theory) make men less afraid of her, and women less bound to her. Chodorow is realistic though in her dubiety about how slowly she believes that change might be effected.

The part of Nancy Chodorow's theory that is groundbreaking and still vital and contemporary is her recognition of the power of these *processes of internalization* for the same-sex family duo of mother and daughter,

[41] Chodorow, *The Reproduction of Mothering*, 164.

[42] Ibid., Chapter 11.

[43] Ibid., 191.

where dependency and attuned caretaking are the basic ego building interactional exchanges that will be woven into the girl's and, later, woman's wider abilities to socialize and become intimate. From the sociological point of view, the newness of Chodorow's proposal was that the phenomenon of mothering had little to do with conscious will. Agentic choices may of course emanate from such knowledge, but Chodorow's reformulation took the idea of motherhood away from purely willful purpose, intention or blame, and thus also purely willful opposition. Neither could people rest easy with motherhood's sole biological predetermination. It was a case of emotional knowledge leading to the possibility of thoughtful liberation and an empowering agency of women.

Chodorow's ideas were less liable to be dismissed in the academic and feminist worlds, I believe, than had they been put forward solely as psychoanalytic ideas, due to the phallocentic rigidity of the psychoanalysis of that era. Apart from the excellent title of the book—with its brand value of the double entendre *Reproduction* alongside "Mothering" in its active participle form—Chodorow gave to the conceptualization the weight of her position as a sociologist and scholarly feminist writing from the West Coast of the United States, from the most socially progressive and respected institutions in the American academy at the heart of the women's movement. Hers was a stunningly successful book right from its birth, in its impact on those tumultuous times. It was an idea offered in the right place at the right time by the right person, and Chodorow commanded an audience that was open to learning her valuable lessons.[44] We are still learning eagerly from her, and her example of scholarship, teaching, mentoring, her excitement about ideas, and her capacity to live life so fully.

Chodorow's Self-Reflection

From time to time in this paper I have compared Chodorow to Freud. I believe that there are few scientists or humanists who have the flexibility and vision to be able to assess their work retrospectively, and with

[44] She does not actually agree with this very positive opinion, speaking from her personal experiences rather than as here, looking back with the possibly rosier spectacles of the broad social impressions of an outsider to academic life in the United States of that era. The reader will no doubt judge this impression about the reception of her early ideas, for her- or himself.

hindsight describe which of their previous paths may have been less well conceived than they thought at the time they were published. Freud had a talent for that self-assessment. He famously shifted elements in his developing theories over the course of his career (except his basics about females!) Nancy Chodorow too shares her own evolving ideas over time, and looks back. This is not only very interesting for her readers, but the quality represents an ability to make use of her further experiences, and then helpfully embed them into her analyses. She has done this in various papers. The following example showcases this scholarly asset.

Contemporary Clinical Application

Chodorow's 2003 clinical paper "Too Late: Ambivalence about Motherhood, Place and Time"[45] is one of my favorite papers, and is a clinically most useful and apt contemplation of time and the female body. Always the master (or mistress) of the opening line, she writes: "This paper delineates a particular manifestation of the nonreproduction of mothering."

Chodorow is struck by her clinical experiences of women who act as if time stands still for them, in the aftermath of the cultural revolution that she was a part of in the 1970s: "...women who have used various feminist-or career-derived reasons for delaying motherhood and then find themselves up against the fertility clock, ...[and]... women who have more actively sabotaged their fertility and for whom time plays a particularly potent role in their psychology and the progress of their treatment—hence, too late".[46] Courageously and movingly she states: "[T]hey and I have both had to recognize that although they now very much want to bear children, they will never do so, and to recognize also how this not having children was due to their own psychic realities and the behaviors that these realities generated".[47] Thinking of her *Reproduction* that spoke to the interrelation of mother and daughter, anticipating

[45] Nancy Chodorow, "'Too Late': Ambivalence About Motherhood, Choice, and Time," *Journal of the American Psychoanalytic Association* 51, no. 4 (2003): 1181–1198.

[46] Ibid., 1181.

[47] Ibid.

the later *Individualizing Gender*,[48] and *Power of Feelings*[49] that told how culture became internalized psychically, Chodorow says (prophetically for her work to come), "Although we can separate out the intrapsychic from the cultural as theoretical categories, we cannot do so in individual, lived clinical reality".[50] Here she shows how the element of time, that is not centrally gender-driven per se, enters the inner world to weave in and animate some women's gendered constellations. Time, though, even in this dimension, can also be subjected to reflective scrutiny. With hindsight, Chodorow criticizes *Reproduction* because in stressing the object relational components, she says she shortchanged there the physical experience and dimension of mothering.[51] Twenty years later in this paper, Chodorow also shows how scholars from each specialty that she bridged in her early book had complaints that she did not somehow take it far enough into their own sphere. She writes,

> ...the grand theory of the sex-gender system in *The Reproduction of Mothering* is not as elaborated or complex as the account of development and psychological life. Its grand theoretical strengths lie in its articulation of psychological, cultural, and social analysis and ... [their combined necessity] to understand gender adequately. It is therefore not surprising that so many of the people who draw upon the account are interested in subjectivity or the psyche-culture nexus. Those whose professional or personal identity comes from arguing for the primacy of society and culture, and the autonomy from psychology of these, find it less appealing. Accordingly, it has from the beginning been viewed with some ambivalence among feminist sociologists and within my academic home discipline of sociology".[52]

This is one of the inevitable vicissitudes of an interdisciplinary work. Her own in-depth immersion in this world had been as a very well-read academic in her early thirties. As a psychoanalyst and sociologist she

[48] Nancy Chodorow, *Individualizing Gender and Sexuality: Theory and Practice* (London: Routledge, 2011).

[49] Nancy Chodorow, *The Power of Feelings: Personal Meaning in Psychoanalysis, Gender and Culture* (New Haven: Yale University Press, 1994).

[50] Chodorow, "Too Late," 1182.

[51] Nancy Chodorow, "Reflections on *The Reproduction of Mothering*—Twenty Years Later," *Studies in Gender and Sexuality* 1, no. 4 (2000): 337–348.

[52] Ibid., 341.

now says in 2003, "Pregnancy, childbirth, the felt reproductive drive [are] filtered through the prism of the intrapsychic and intersubjective reproduction of mothering."[53] In defense of the early Chodorow, even if she had been fully immersed in the practice of psychoanalysis as well as the theory of all of her points of view back then, it is notoriously difficult to try to render multiple influences together conceptually in a satisfactory form on paper.[54] Chodorow's "Too Late" paper and her current renderings of these simultaneously occurring phenomena are now, I believe, among the best in the psychoanalytic field.[55]

From there, Chodorow, at times lyrically, contemplates how these patients showed her that unconsciously they could operate as if they could cause time to stand still. As examples she chooses two women in their late forties—where in both the cases they needed to protect themselves from less consciously developed destructiveness toward both themselves and their internalized mothers that had coalesced around the centrality of their shared female bodies and had become fraught in the battle with their possibilities for procreation. Many previous abortions for potential pregnancies that these women were unprepared for from earlier in their lives became a source of bitter self castigation when they desperately wanted to become pregnant at a late reproductive age. They were convinced they had damaged their reproductive organs. In analyses they found out how enmeshed that could be with ragefully damaging their mothers within. Chodorow movingly writes that the culture of feminist liberation of the time when these women were coming of age was one that was dichotomized—pregnancy and motherhood were seen very negatively as *the* ways to remain tied and oppressed as an earth mother. At the time, the way to grow and prosper in the "outside" culture seemed to be to relinquish becoming a mother. Chodorow says "I regrettably

[53] Chodorow, "Too Late," 1183.

[54] I have tried myself just from within medicine and psychoanalysis. I have found myself favoring the psycho-physical dimension over other and also relevant aspects of the social, historical or intrapsychic world (see for example, Balsam, "The Vanished Pregnant Body in Psychoanalytic Developmental Theory," *Journal of the American Psychoanalytic Association* 51, no. 4 [2003]: 1153–1179). Limitations are nearly inevitable, alas.

[55] Joan Raphael-Leff, a contemporary analyst of the London Middle Group, also displays similar conceptual openness in her own associative and rich metaphoric writing about pregnancy, birth and parenting, e.g., "[A]ny woman's desire for children, whether immediately fulfilled, fulfilled belatedly, or never fulfilled, contains layers of affect and meaning" (*The Dark Side of the Womb*, 1183).

was a contributor." But of course one needs to grasp what a hold "biological essentialism" held in the 1970s—in short, the idea that the only way to fulfillment in womanhood was to have a baby, just because one happened to possess the anatomical ability; or that because men were physically stronger, it was "natural" that they should dominate society and women should be compliant with that arrangement. It was thus vital to counter such erroneous beliefs and their accompanying value systems. Chodorow did so forcefully in 1978—and then subsequently she took these arguments much further into the individual sphere.

Chodorow points out with insight how those forces of genuine social liberation were consciously and also unconsciously used by some women like those she encountered clinically later who described experiences of self-sabotage. It was a tragic coming together of a need for social approval at their own expense. Their way of coping and procrastinating facing up to their own decisions, was to make time stop internally and act as if it would still all be possible. Advances in medicine can support this possibility of course. Women in their fifties now exist with little children they have physically carried and delivered. For example, Melissa Willetts reports, "[A]ccording to the Centers for Disease Control and Prevention, births by women between the ages of 50 and 54 increased by more than 165 percent from 2000 to 2013."[56] However, this is still rare. For many women, coming to terms with the limits of technically assisted reproduction becomes a sad aspect of their evolving maturation. Chodorow resists the classical psychoanalytic story of the patient with the happy ending. I note with admiration that every attitude woven into Chodorow's presentation here is a writing enactment of understanding the very medicine that she is giving to her patients—the resistance and working through of omnipotence and its transformation into agency, empathy for oneself and others, and action as tempered self-preservative choices. For one patient this step toward maturity represents too much internal loss and she drifts away from analysis; for the other it represents a renewed liveliness of choosing in marriage a widow with grown children with whom she gains the expression of her loving ambition to be generative, while not denying her regrets about life events and time having passed.

[56] Melissa Willetts, "More and More Women are Getting Pregnant after 50 Years Old," *Parenting Magazine* (Meredith Women's Network Corporation), http://www.parenting.com/.

Coda

There is no "conclusion" that I can come to here. Nor do I want to. We can never do enough to keep these explorations open and on the forefront of our own disciplines. I have supremely enjoyed the companionship in spirit of Nancy Chodorow, this extraordinary feminist, sociologist and psychoanalyst scholar who is so generative to others, and so immensely capable of drawing all these theoretical maps and possibilities on behalf of the gendered sexual, environmentally absorbing and object-seeking mind; not to mention all of her contributions to women.

Bibliography

Atlas, Galit, *The Enigma of Desire: Sex, Longing, and Belonging in Psychoanalysis* (Relational Perspectives Book Series). London: Routledge, 2015.

Balsam, Rosemary H., "Freud, Females, Childbirth, and Dissidence: Margarete Hilferding, Karen Horney and Otto Rank." *The Psychoanalytic Review* 100, no. 5 (2013): 695–716.

———, "Oedipus Rex: Where Are We Going, Especially with Females?" *The Psychoanalytic Quarterly* 84 (2015): 555–588.

———, "The Vanished Pregnant Body in Psychoanalytic Developmental Theory." *Journal of the American Psychoanalytic Association* 51, no. 4 (2003): 1153–1179.

———, "The War on Women in Psychoanalytic Theory Building: Past to Present." *The Psychoanalytic Study of the Child* 69 (2015): 83–107.

———, "Women of the Wednesday Society: The Presentations of Drs. Hilferding, Spielrein and Hug-Hellmuth." *American Imago* 60, no. 3 (2003): 303–343.

———, *Womens' Bodies in Psychoanalysis*. London: Routledge, 2012.

Boston Womens' Health Group Collective, eds., *Our Bodies, Ourselves: A Book by and for Women*. Cambridge: Touchstone, 2nd edition, 1976.

Chiang, Mengchun, "'You Just Know It's the Only Thing You Can Think': A Conversation with Chodorow." *Women & Therapy* 40, nos. 3–4 (2017): 308–322.

Chodorow, Nancy, "Family Structure and Feminine Personality." In *The Homeric Hymn to Demeter: Translation, Commentary, and Interpretive Essays*, ed. Helene P. Foley. Princeton: Princeton University Press, 1994, 243–264.

———, *Femininities, Masculinities and Sexualities: Freud and Beyond*. Lexington: University Press of Kentucky, 1994.

———, *Individualizing Gender and Sexuality: Theory and Practice* (Relational Perspectives Book Series). London: Routledge, 2011.

———, "Reflections on *The Reproduction of Mothering*—Twenty Years Later." *Studies in Gender and Sexuality* 1, no. 4 (2000): 337–348.

———, "The American Independent Tradition: Loewald, Erikson, and the (Possible) Rise of Intersubjective Ego Psychology." *Psychoanalytic Dialogues* 14, no. 2 (2004): 207–232.

———, *The Power of Feelings: Personal Meaning in Psychoanalysis, Gender and Culture*. New Haven: Yale University Press, 1994.

———. *The Reproduction of Mothering*. Oakland: University of California Press, 1978/1999 (with a new preface).

———, "'Too Late': Ambivalence About Motherhood, Choice, and Time." *Journal of the American Psychoanalytic Association* 51, no. 4 (2003): 1181–1198.

Diamond, Michael J., "The Shaping of Masculinity: Revisioning Boys Turning away from Their Mothers to Construct Male Gender Identity." *The International Journal of Psychoanalysis* 85, no. 2 (2004): 359–379.

Greenacre, Phyllis, "Early Physical Determinants in the Development of a Sense of Identity." *Journal of the American Psychoanalytic Association* 6 (1958): 612–627.

Greenson, Ralph, "Disidentifying from Mother: Its Special Importance for the Boy." *The International Journal of Psychoanalysis* 49 (1968): 370–374.

Harris, Adrienne, *Gender as Soft Assembly*. Hillsdale: Analytic Press, 2005.

Kleeman, James, "The Establishment of Core Gender Identity in Normal Girls. II: How Meanings are Conveyed between Parent and Child in the First 3 Years." *Archives of Sexual Behavior* 1, no. 2 (1971): 117–129.

Kristeva, Julia, *Powers of Horror: An Essay on Abjection*, trans. L.S. Roudiez. New York: Columbia University Press, 1980.

Kulish, Nancy and Deanna Hotzman, *A Story of Her Own: The Female Oedipus Complex Re-examined and Renamed*. Hillsdale: Jason Aronson Inc., 2008.

Loewald, Hans W., "On the Therapeutic Action of Psycho-Analysis." *The International Journal of Psychoanalysis* 41 (1960): 16–33.

Makari, George, *Revolution in Mind: The Creation of Psychoanalysis*. New York: Harper/HarperCollins, 2008.

Metzl, Marilyn, "From Sociology to Psychoanalysis: The Works of Nancy J. Chodorow." *Psychoanalytic Psychology: The Journal of the American Psychological Association Division* 39 (2003): 55–60.

Mitchell, Juliet, *Psychoanalysis and Feminism: Freud, Reich, Laing and Women*. London: Vintage Books, 1974.

Moeslein-Teising, Ingrid and Frances Thomson Salo, eds., *The Female Body: Inside and Outside* (International Psychoanalytical Association Psychoanalytic Ideas and Applications Book Series). London: Karnac, 2013.

Raphael-Leff, Joan, *Pregnancy: The Inside Story*. London: Karnac, 2001.

———, *The Dark Side of the Womb: Pregnancy, Parenting, and Persecutory Anxieties.* London: Anna Freud Centre, 2015.

Willetts, Melissa, "More and More Women Are Getting Pregnant after 50 Years Old." *Parenting Magazine* (Meredith Women's Network Corporation). www.parenting.com.

Young-Bruehl, Elisabeth, *Freud on Women: A Reader*. New York: W. W. Norton, 1992.

CHAPTER 5

Thinking Back Through Our Mothers: The Legacies of Nancy Chodorow

Elizabeth Abel

Nancy Chodorow's writings about mothers and daughters opened our eyes to a narrative current that has coursed through literary history. The narrative features of her theory spoke forcefully to feminist literary critics who felt empowered to recognize patterns of merger and separation that diverged from traditional novelistic arcs. The result was an outpouring of Chodorow-inspired literary criticism in the 1980s and '90s. This essay starts by mapping that critical field but turns, in keeping with the pattern Chodorow identified, to the less familiar separations exacted by a different kind of object relations from a later chapter of the mother–daughter story. What happens when a mother lingers after death in objects whose fate must be determined by the daughter? How might Chodorow guide us through this material object world? Since stories are my site and mode of intervention, I begin each portion of this essay by setting the stage for the analysis that follows.

E. Abel (✉)
University of California, Berkeley, Berkeley, CA, USA
e-mail: eabel@berkeley.edu

P. Bueskens (ed.), *Nancy Chodorow and* The Reproduction of Mothering,
https://doi.org/10.1007/978-3-030-55590-0_5

Maternal Subjects

The scene: a crowded lecture room in 142 Dwinelle Hall at the University of California, Berkeley in the fall of 1982. We had assembled to hear the Austrian philosopher and social critic Ivan Illich deliver a lecture on his new (and uncomfortably retrograde) book, *Gender*. Since the room was packed, I perched in the aisle; glancing up to my right, I recognized a face from a book jacket prominently displayed on my shelves. Could this be Nancy Chodorow? Indeed, above a very pregnant body sat the head of the author of *The Reproduction of Mothering*.[1] As I summoned the courage to initiate a conversation, I realized that the exchange emerging in the aisles formed a countercurrent to the ideology of complementary gender spheres that was promoted from the stage. Mothering was being symbolically reproduced on the ground as that embryonic conversation grew into a long and sustaining relationship that encompassed my inheritance of Nancy's stylish maternity clothes along with her compelling conceptual universe. But the terms of that transmission straddled and disrupted the gender-divided spheres of intellect and body, public and private, sociology and psychology, objectivity and subjectivity, individuality and community.

It is this straddling of boundaries that has made Nancy Chodorow's work so impactful in literary study (as well, of course, as elsewhere). By bringing psychoanalysis into conversation with the sociology of gender, while foregrounding intersubjectivity rather than static states of being, she offered a narrative of gendered subjectivity that was ripe for feminist literary adaptation. The critical *agon* with Freudian theory (whose most compelling manifestation at that time was Harold Bloom's oedipal model in *The Anxiety of Influence* of a literary inheritance wrested by "strong" masculine poets from their paternal precursors), yielded to the rich new genealogies of a paradigm shift to maternal figures of origin. In tandem with a broad-based second-wave feminist recuperation of the maternal, an exploration of what it means to be, in Adrienne Rich's resonant title (borrowed from Shakespeare) *Of Woman Born*, Chodorow both consolidated and complicated a new intersection among feminism, psychoanalysis, and literature. As a primary conduit of object relations theory into the humanities—for although several outstanding second-wave feminist theorists resurrected this theoretical discourse in the 1970s

[1] Nancy Chodorow, *The Reproduction of Mothering: Psychoanalysis and the Sociology of Gender* (Berkeley, CA: University of California Press, 1978).

and '80s, none mapped its internal faultlines as comprehensively—*The Reproduction of Mothering* had a ripple effect that traversed the traditional boundaries within literary study as well as across the disciplines.

To begin with the most canonical: Shakespeare quickly emerged as a rich node of inquiry into the psychic formation of gender, especially of masculinity, translocated through the lens of object relations theory from a struggle for authority in the political theater to a struggle for autonomy in a psychological theater staged by the maternal body. Beyond the insight into the tangled interior worlds of individual characters, rendered newly legible in relation to the phantasmatic presence of the mother, object relations enabled a new interpretation of the arc of Shakespeare's career. As Janet Adelman argues in *Suffocating Mothers*, a title that captures the ambivalence of the infantile relation to a pre-oedipal mother who figures as both an imaginary agent and object of suffocation, the Oedipal framework that mapped onto the historical drama of royal succession yields with *Hamlet* to the ambivalent confrontation with maternal origins that catalyzes Shakespeare's greatest tragedies.[2] Through the 1980s and '90s, feminist psychoanalytic criticism, under the aegis of object relations, was the cutting edge of Shakespeare studies.[3]

But it was Chodorow's signature insight into the developmental arc of the mother–daughter bond that has arguably been her most enduring legacy for literary critics, at least for critics of the novel genre. By refocusing attention on what Adrienne Rich called "the cathexis between daughter and mother … the great unwritten story,"[4] Chodorow opened up a novelistic terrain that had been submerged, like Freud's Minoan-Mycenean civilization, beneath a more linear Oedipal trajectory.[5] Her contention that mothering by women engenders more fluid ego boundaries in the same-sex child, whose gendered task is to identify with, rather than differentiate from, her primary caregiver brought to light the fluctuating rhythms of merger and separation that Marianne Hirsch

[2] Janet Adelman, *Suffocating Mothers: Fantasies of Maternal Origin in Shakespeare's Plays, Hamlet to the Tempest* (London: Routlege, 1991).

[3] See, for example, Murray M. Schwartz and Coppélia Kahn, *Representing Shakespeare: New Psychoanalytic Essays* (Baltimore: Johns Hopkins University Press, 1980).

[4] Adrienne Rich, *Of Woman Born* (New York: Norton, 1976), 226.

[5] Sigmund Freud, "Female Sexuality" (1931), in *Women & Analysis: Dialogues on Psychoanalytic Views of Femininity*, ed. Jean Strouse (New York: Grossman Publishers, 1974), 40.

has charted in *The Mother/Daughter Plot*: a transhistorical narrative that wends its way across centuries and cultures, from classical mythology through nineteenth- and twentieth-century British and French novelists to contemporary writers of color such as Toni Morrison, Alice Walker, and Cherrie Moraga.[6] Although emerging from the mother–daughter nexus, this plot extends to the stories of female friendships and communities, including the communities of writers and editors that have generated multiply authored, generically fluid feminist anthologies.[7]

It is the generativity of Chodorow's model that differentiates it from many of those presented by her object relational peers. For theorists such as Jane Flax, Dorothy Dinnerstein, and Jessica Benjamin, who draw from a similar tradition, fluid mother–daughter boundaries are freighted with more burdens than opportunities. Entangled in conflicting desires for autonomy and nurturance, the daughter in Jane Flax's rendition finds her path to an autonomous adulthood impeded.[8] For Dorothy Dinnerstein, the daughter risks engulfment with a mother from whom she inherits a culturally devalued gender identity and a culturally appointed stigma as the bearer of mortality.[9] The cross-generational affiliations between women, as Jessica Benjamin signals in her title *The Bonds of Love: Psychoanalysis, Feminism, and the Problem of Domination* (1988), are not exclusively loving; they also bind the daughter to the system of male domination in which the mother is inscribed. As Judith Kegan Gardiner

[6] Marianne Hirsch, *The Mother/Daughter Plot: Narrative, Psychoanalysis, Feminism* (Bloomington: Indiana University Press, 1989). See also Marianne Hirsch, "Mothers and Daughters," *Signs: Journal of Women in Culture and Society* 7, no. 1 (Autumn, 1981): 200–222.

[7] The exemplary instance is *This Bridge Called My Back: Writings By Radical Women of Color*, eds. Cherrie Moraga and Gloria Anzaldua (New York: Kitchen Table: Women of Color Press, 1981); for an analysis of this and other variants, see Cynthia G. Franklin, *Writing Women's Communities: The Politics and Poetics of Contemporary Multi-Genre Anthologies* (Madison: University of Wisconsin, 1997).

[8] See especially the implicit conversation between Nancy Chodorow in "Gender, Relation, and Difference in Psychoanalytic Perspective" and Jane Flax in "Mother-Daughter Relationships: Psychodynamics, Politics, and Philosophy," both included in *The Future of Difference*, eds. Hester Eisenstein and Alice Jardine (Boston: G. K. Hall, 1980), 3–19, 20–40. See also Jane Flax, "The Conflict between Nurturance and Autonomy in Mother-Daughter Relationships and Within Feminism," *Feminist Studies* 4, no. 2 (June, 1978): 171–189.

[9] Dorothy Dinnerstein, *The Mermaid and the Minotaur: Sexual Arrangements and Human Malaise* (New York: Harper and Row, 1976).

points out in "A Wake for Mother," twentieth-century fiction by women often stages the matricidal wishes this contaminated inheritance provokes: "In the Oedipus myth, the son murders his father to take his place. Contrastingly, in the new woman's myth, the daughter 'kills' her mother in order *not* to have to take her place."[10] Against this somber backdrop, Chodorow's more expansive vision of the capacities conferred by the mother–daughter bond offers an enticing genealogy to trace within and between books authored by women.

Several feminist literary critics of the 1970s and '80s embraced this literary genealogy as a way to "think back through our mothers," as Virginia Woolf first put it in *A Room of One's Own* (1929). Echoing Woolf's title in *A Literature of Their Own: British Women Novelists from Bronte to Lessing*, Elaine Showalter's landmark 1977 study traced successive generations of British women's writing. Published the year before Chodorow's landmark work, *A Literature of Their Own* presents its own version of generational succession from "feminine" (1840s–1880s) to "feminist" (1880–1920) to "female" (1920-present), but Chodorow's influence is manifest in a subsequent essay whose title, "A Criticism of Our Own," reclaims the ownership hedged by the third-person pronoun in the previous book title. Showalter now pays tribute to the "enormously influential study, *The Reproduction of Mothering*, [which] revised Freudian psychoanalysis and British object relations psychology to emphasize the pre-Oedipal phase," yielding a feminist literary criticism "in which intergenerational conflict is replaced by female literary intimacy, generosity, and continuity."[11] The consequences are manifested in what Sandra Gilbert and Susan Gubar call the "female affiliation complex" that (always in fraught dialogue with a conflictual patrilineal inheritance) subtends their monumental three-volume study, *No Man's Land: The Woman Writer in the Twentieth Century*.[12]

[10] Judith Kegan Gardiner, "A Wake for Mother: The Maternal Deathbed in Women's Fiction," *Feminist Studies* 4, no. 2 (June, 1978): 146–165.

[11] Elaine Showalter, "A Criticism of Our Own: Autonomy and Assimilation in Afro-American and Feminist Literary Theory," in *Feminisms: An Anthology of Literary Theory and Criticism*, eds. Robyn R. Warhol and Diane Price Herndl, 226.

[12] See especially Sandra Gilbert and Susan Gubar, "'Forward into the Past': The Female Affiliation Complex," in *No Man's Land: The Place of the Woman Writer in the Twentieth Century*, eds. Sandra M. Gilbert and Susan Gubar (New Haven: Yale, 1988), 165–226.

It would not be entirely fanciful to propose that *The Reproduction of Mothering* fulfils Virginia Woolf's wistful desire for a theoretical (in both senses) daughter who could produce "that elaborate study of the psychology of women by a woman" that would illuminate the elusive "question of women and fiction."[13] Certainly, Chodorow's account of women's fluid boundaries affords new insights into what Joan Lidoff characterizes as the "hidden maternal presence in the narrative voice" of late twentieth-century women writers: a presence rendered less in overt plots or characters than in the nuanced tonal and formal shifts that bespeak a distinctively feminine poetics propelled by a "less absolute separation of self from other."[14] Lidoff discerns this poetics in the short fiction of Tillie Olsen and Grace Paley; Judith Kegan Gardiner uncovers a related expression of "mothering theory" in what she calls a "politics of empathy" that (along with matricidal fantasies) binds the authors, characters, and readers of fiction by Jean Rhys, Christina Stead, and Doris Lessing.[15]

The flowering of women's writing in the twentieth century, fueled by the evolution of feminist discourse and politics in the early decades of the century, arguably begins with Virginia Woolf. In *Virginia Woolf and the Fictions of Psychoanalysis* (1989), I explore the interpretive reach of Chodorow's account of women's fluid ego boundaries by focusing on the painting of Mrs. Ramsay by Woolf's aesthetic surrogate, Lily Briscoe, whose imaginary composition traces the course of the autobiographical novel *To the Lighthouse* (1927). At the end of the novel, Lily "drew a line there in the centre" of her canvas: concluding with that indeterminate gesture (is it vertical or horizontal? divisive or connective?) the process through which Woolf "ceased to be obsessed by [her] mother" by accomplishing "what psycho-analysts do for their patients" through a symbolic resolution of the tug of war between autonomy and merger in

[13] Virginia Woolf, *A Room of One's Own* (1929) (New York: Harcourt Brace, 1975), 81.

[14] Joan Lidoff, "Fluid Boundaries: The Mother-Daughter Story, the Story-Reader Matrix," *Texas Studies in Literature and Language* 35, no. 4 (Winter, 1993): 398–399. The essay is drawn from a manuscript, *Fluid Boundaries: Maternal Echoes in Women's Literary Voices,* that was unfinished at Lidoff's death in 1989.

[15] Judith Kegan Gardiner, *Rhys, Stead, Lessing, and the Politics of Empathy* (Bloomington: Indiana University Press, 1989). Other twentieth-century writers who explore these fluid boundaries include Marilynne Robinson, Rosellen Brown, Jamaica Kincaid, Toni Morrison, Maxine Hong Kingston, and Kim Chernin.

the mother–daughter nexus.[16] *The Reproduction of Mothering*, however, also brings into focus (and is refocused by) the historical inflection of the mother–daughter bond that is enacted in the longer arc of Woolf's career. Turning from the matrilineal narratives that flourished in the 1920s (encouraged by a wave of anthropological speculation about early matriarchal civilizations) to the more circumspect perspective induced by the fascist conscription of the maternal to the reproductive needs of the patriarchal state in the 1930s, Woolf brings psychoanalysis and history into a mutually informing conversation.

That conversation has been unfolding culturally as well as historically as women from marginalized traditions have brought into play their distinctive matrilineal traditions. Their intervention has been especially strong in the literary curriculum, where multicultural courses on mother–daughter narratives have constituted a common ground during a time at which inequities have threatened to divide us. My own course on "Mother-Daughter Fictions in Late Twentieth-Century American Cultures" uses *The Reproduction of Mothering* as a springboard for exploring cultural inflections of the mother–daughter story across African-American, Chicana/Latina, and Asian-American contexts. From Alice Walker, Toni Morrison, and Jamaica Kincaid; to Cherrie Moraga, Cristina Garcia, and Sandra Cisneros; to Maxine Hong Kingston, Joy Kogawa, and Amy Tan: we mapped the fluctuating contours of the mother–daughter plot.

The early 1980s were a high point in this exploration that was crystalized for me by an unwitting performance of fluid boundaries at the landmark SUNY, Buffalo, conference on Feminism and the Creative Use of Difference, in 1980 (itself a sequel to "The Scholar and the Feminist VI: The Future of Difference" Conference at Barnard College the previous year). Three of us aspiring assistant professors of English showed up for a panel on "Pre–Oedipal Psychology in Fiction by Women" in almost identical outfits (burgundy jackets and black pants) to deliver papers whose cascading resonances created the impression that our collective paradigm could travel anywhere. By the century's end, however, we had reached a saturation point. There were no more mother–daughter

[16]Virginia Woolf, *To the Lighthouse* (1927) (New York: Harvest/HBJ, 1981), 209. Virginia Woolf, "A Sketch of the Past," In Jeanne Schulkind (ed.), *Moments of Being: Unpublished Autobiographical Writings* (New York: Harvest/HBJ, 1985), 81.

plots to uncover and literary criticism had moved on from psychoanalysis to a spectrum of materialisms (historical, social, theoretical, physical), while we, the daughter generation, had become adults negotiating the material as well as emotional landscape of a final separation from our mothers. It was time for another chapter in the narrative of women's object relations.

Orphaned Objects

The scene: I sit on the floor of the living room in the home in which I grew up; I had played here with similar absorption as a child. But now, instead of toys, the transitional objects through which children learn to negotiate between the objectively real and the subjectively perceived, I am surrounded by piles of books, letters, photographs, and old clothing. A dumpster squats in the driveway. I have come, a year after my mother's death, to dismantle the family home. It has fallen to me, the daughter, to take apart the object world that has been sleeping peacefully here for almost a century.

Nancy Chodorow no longer sits by my side, but I conjure her guidance to help me navigate this passage through the entanglement of female subjects and objects. This will be an improvisatory collaboration in which I seek to extend her narrative by asking how the daughter negotiates a separation from her mother through the objects in which the maternal now resides. There are few guidelines here, for although virtually every human culture has created rituals for handling the dead to safeguard the human body from casual disposal, we have no rituals for disposing of the objects of the dead. "Take as much as you can," some friends advise; "Walk away from it all," others propose: either regress into some undifferentiated maternal matrix or cut the umbilical cord once and for all.

Emptied of its inhabitants, the family home is full of what Mark Twain called "not unsentient matter," quickened from both ends of the generational spectrum.[17] Now that the mother is irrevocably gone, we confront transitional objects once again as the psychological object of our earliest

[17] Mark Twain, Letter to Rev. J.H. Twichell, January 19, 1897. *The Letters of Mark Twain*, 4, 1886–1900. Project Gutenberg, 2006. http://www.gutenberg.org/files/3196/3196-h/3196-h.htm.

attachment intersects with the material objects in which she still inheres. For as they age, our mothers recede into the object world they have assembled and on which they increasingly rely as their universe shrinks to the home; the holding environment they created for their children has become the environment in which they are held. Which objects to keep, which to give away, which to exile to the second-hand stores, which to carry in our own hands to the dumpster: these choices re-engage us in the tangible process of picking things up and putting them down, trying to derive from sensory experience where and in what modes maternal presence now resides in objects that must be relinquished at the moment at which they are full of presence once again.

This challenge has been obscured by a focus on classic memory objects; lockets, jewelry, photographs, things that are small, intact, hard-edged, and portable. Sanitizing the problem, they seem to make it vanish, but they only mask the challenge of memorializing the permeable boundaries of an intersubjective world, boundaries materialized in the frayed borders of disintegrating objects. Unlike things that are well preserved, which are relatively easy to keep or sell or give away, those whose deteriorated state renders them worthless in the eyes of the world embody a maternal materiality that seems impossible either to dispose of or to hold onto. *Shmattes*—frayed nightgowns, discolored dresses, threadbare sweaters, stained bathrobes, mold-flecked hats, unraveling shawls: fabrics onto which the maternal body has spilled over, intimate second skins and outer borders of a self with which we have been psychically and physically merged. How could we consign these to the dumpster? But how can we safeguard all this dusty stuff that will clutter our lives, for which we don't have room, and which, like the bodies they have rubbed against, will continue to disintegrate?

The dilemma began generations ago in a gendered relation to the object world that W.H. Auden (anticipating Chodorow in another vein) renders in his poem "Up There."[18]

[18] "Up There" from COLLECTED POEMS by W.H. Auden, edited by Edward Mendelson, copyright c. 1976 by Edward Mendelson, William Meredith and Monroe K. Spears, Executors of the Estate of W.H. Auden. Used by permission of Random House, an imprint and division of Penguin Random House LLC.

Men would never have come to need an attic.
Keen collectors of glass or Roman coins build
Special cabinets for them, date on, index
Each new specimen: only women cling to
Items out of their past they have no use for,
Can't name now what they couldn't bear to part with.

Up there, under the eaves, in bulging boxes,
Hats, veils, ribbons, galoshes, programs, letters
Wait unworshipped (a starving spider spins for
The occasional fly): no clock recalls it
Once an hour to the household it's a part of,
No Saint's Day is devoted to its function.

All it knows of a changing world it has to
Guess from children, who conjure in its plenum,
Now an eyrie for two excited sisters,
Where, when Mother is bad, her rage can't reach them,
Now a schooner on which a lonely only
Boy sails north or approaches coral islands.

Maternal inheritance for Auden is an attic full of inconsequential objects waiting to be transformed in the play world of children. But what will those grown children do when the house must be sold and the attic emptied of its objects?

Or rather, what will the daughter do? Since sons, as Chodorow argues, develop their gender identity through a process of differentiation from the maternal body and psyche, diffuse modes of attachment and enmeshment in an object world (psychological or material) are transmitted across the generations through the mother–daughter relationship. This was certainly true for me. My brother's contribution to the dismantling of our parents' home was limited to our father's books, which he meticulously catalogued, packed and shipped to the site he had diligently researched. As a keepsake, he selected a pair of solid glass bookends. For the rest: the dumpster would suffice.

A similar perspective is offered by the theorist of domestic affect James Krasner. "After two days," he writes about cleaning out his parents' home, "we fled, overwhelmed by the number and intensity of unexpected ghosts raised by these soiled and useless items. We hired a cleaning company:

people to whom such speaking objects were mute, people who could disinterestedly claw through and dispose of them without being touched by the memories they carried. The challenge we all face cleaning out basements and attics is primarily one of being disarmed by materialized memory." As the holding environment devolves into a battlefield, touch—elsewhere embraced as the sustaining "medium of domestic experience"—becomes both a threat and a weapon. Hands must transform into claws. "We" must resurrect our infantile rage, summon our inner kicking, biting, clawing, unsocialized childhood selves—or hire a cleaning company—in order to avoid being "disarmed by materialized memory." But do we *all* experience this threat in the same way? Might daughters be more able to embrace these "soiled and useless items" along with the ghosts that inhabit them? But where, then, do we put them?

These are questions rather than answers, but I have confidence that Nancy Chodorow's work will help us to resolve them. For me, she offered a beginning. I was able to separate from the "soiled and useless" objects in which I was invested but which I could not keep by picking each one up individually, holding it in my arms for a while, and placing it carefully in the dumpster as if it were a burial site rather than a garbage heap. I acknowledged the intimate memories these objects held before saying goodbye to them. By making a connection before each dispossession, I felt I was enacting a Chodorowian ritual of merger and separation that continued to bind me to my mother in a rhythm that extended backwards to my birth and forwards through her death and the dismantling of her object world. It wasn't necessary after all to summon infantile rage; one could enter a more benign object relational world of recurring attachment and detachment. Mothering was being reproduced once more on the ground, this time in the family home instead of the lecture hall. I had internalized Chodorow's model in ways I hadn't fully recognized. That her model could travel so widely, across the realms of theory and practice and the course of a lifetime from birth to death, points toward the rich legacies still to unfold.

Works Cited

Abel, Elizabeth, *Virginia Woolf and the Fictions of Psychoanalysis.* Chicago: University of Chicago Press, 1989.

Benjamin, Jessica, *The Bonds of Love: Psychoanalysis, Feminism, and the Problem of Domination.* New York: Pantheon, 1988.

Bloom, Harold, *The Anxiety of Influence*. New York: Oxford, 1973.
Chodorow, Nancy, *The Reproduction of Mothering: Psychoanalysis and the Sociology of Gender*. Berkeley: University of California Press, 1978.
———, "Gender, Relation, and Difference in Psychoanalytic Perspective." In *The Future of Difference*, eds. Hester Eisenstein and Alice Jardine. Boston: G. K. Hall, 1980, 3–19.
Dinnerstein, Dorothy, *The Mermaid and the Minotaur: Sexual Arrangements and Human Malaise*. New York: Harper and Row, 1976.
Flax, Jane, "The Conflict between Nurturance and Autonomy in Mother-Daughter Relationships and Within Feminism." *Feminist Studies* 4, no. 2 (June, 1978): 171–189.
———, "Mother-Daughter Relationships: Psychodynamics, Politics, and Philosophy." In *The Future of Difference*, eds. Hester Eisenstein and Alice Jardine. Boston: G. K. Hall, 1980, 20–40.
Franklin, Cynthia G., *Writing Women's Communities: The Politics and Poetics of Contemporary Multi-Genre Anthologies*. Madison: University of Wisconsin, 1997.
Freud, Sigmund, "Female Sexuality" (1931). In *Women & Analysis: Dialogues on Psychoanalytic Views of Femininity*, ed. Jean Strouse. New York: Grossman Publishers, 1974, 40.
Gardiner, Judith Kegan, "A Wake for Mother: The Maternal Deathbed in Women's Fiction." *Feminist Studies* 4, no. 2 (June, 1978): 146–165.
———, *Rhys, Stead, Lessing, and the Politics of Empathy*. Bloomington: Indiana University Press, 1989.
Gilbert, Sandra M., and Susan Gubar, "'Forward into the Past': The Female Affiliation Complex." *No Man's Land: The Place of the Woman Writer in the Twentieth Century*. New Haven: Yale University Press, 1988, 165–226.
Hirsch, Marianne, "Mothers and Daughters." *Signs: Journal of Women in Culture and Society* 7, no. 1 (Autumn, 1981): 200–222.
———, *The Mother/Daughter Plot: Narrative, Psychoanalysis, Feminism*. Bloomington: Indiana University Press, 1989.
Lidoff, Joan, "Fluid Boundaries: The Mother-Daughter Story, the Story-Reader Matrix." *Texas Studies in Literature and Language* 35, no. 4 (Winter, 1993): 398–420.
Moraga, Cherrie and Gloria Anzaldua, eds. *This Bridge Called My Back: Writings by Radical Women of Color*. New York: Kitchen Table: Women of Color Press, 1981.
Rich, Adrienne. *Of Woman Born*. New York: Norton, 1976.
Schwartz, Murray and Coppélia Kahn, eds. *Representing Shakespeare: New Psychoanalytic Essays*. Baltimore: Johns Hopkins University Press, 1980.
Showalter, Elaine, *A Literature of Their Own: British Women Novelists from Bronte to Lessing*. Princeton: Princeton University Press, 1977.

———, "A Criticism of Our Own: Autonomy and Assimilation in Afro-American and Feminist Literary Theory." In *Feminisms: An Anthology of Literary Theory and Criticism*, eds. Robyn R. Warhol and Diane Price Herndl. New Brunswick: Rutgers University Press, 1997, 213–233.

Twain, Marc, *The Letters of Mark Twain*, 4, 1886–1900. Project Gutenberg, 2006. http://www.gutenberg.org/files/3196/3196-h/3196-h.htm.

Woolf, Virginia, *A Room of One's Own* (1929). New York: HBJ, 1957.

———, *To the Lighthouse* (1927). New York: Harvest/HBJ, 1981.

———, "A Sketch of the Past." In *Moments of Being: Unpublished Autobiographical Writings*, ed. Jeanne Schulkind. New York: Harvest/HBJ, 1985.

CHAPTER 6

The Impact of Nancy Chodorow's *The Reproduction of Mothering* and Its Implications for the Future

Madelon Sprengnether

The impact of Nancy Chodorow's *The Reproduction of Mothering*[1] on the field of feminism and psychoanalysis is enormous. Most importantly, it linked the discipline of sociology to that of psychoanalysis, which opened new ways of thinking about women at a crucial moment in the development of second-wave feminism. The argument Chodorow introduced, making use of Anglo-American object relations theory to describe the course of female development in patriarchal society, liberated feminist discourse from bitter and futile attacks on Freud, while opening avenues for literary, social, and philosophical theories of women's cultural roles and subjectivities.

[1] Nancy Chodorow, *The Reproduction of Mothering: Psychoanalysis and the Sociology of Gender* (Berkeley: University of California Press, 1978).

M. Sprengnether (✉)
University of Minnesota, Minneapolis, MN, USA
e-mail: spren001@umn.edu

P. Bueskens (ed.), *Nancy Chodorow and* The Reproduction of Mothering,
https://doi.org/10.1007/978-3-030-55590-0_6

Her work, along with that of Carol Gilligan's *In a Different Voice*,[2] offered new ways of thinking about girls and women: how we are shaped by our environment, not only socially and culturally but also psychologically. Together, they helped to shift the focus from an exclusive emphasis on men (with women as an afterthought) to women ourselves as the center of inquiry.

I felt this change in my own field of literary studies as a paradigm shift—from the assumption that men and masculinity provide the norms of human development and humanity itself, to the uncharted territory of womanhood, given that our lives, writings, and self-understandings had been historically suppressed or ignored. Major changes in academia ensued from Chodorow's work and that of other groundbreaking feminists.

As women writers began to enter college and university curricula, they also broke through into mainstream publishing. Women established their own literary magazines and presses, while Women's Studies Programs, and national women's organizations sprang up.[3] This was a time in which women began to take power into our own hands, not only theoretically but also sociopolitically. Second-wave feminism in the social sphere intersected with and stimulated academic feminism to include the voices of lesbians, women of color, and working-class women. For any of these developments to take place, the cultural assumption that men are at the center of social, political, and cultural life had to be challenged and subverted. So engrained was this idea in the history of Western civilization that it was regarded as both natural and inevitable. My own education (undergraduate and graduate) was based on this premise.

[2] Carol Gilligan, *In a Different Voice: Psychological Theory and Women's Development* (Cambridge, MA: Harvard University Press, 1982).

[3] I am thinking of NOW, the national political movement sparked by Betty Friedan, founded in 1966, and the National Women's Studies Association (NWSA), created in 1977 to foster women's studies within and outside of the academy. Another landmark moment was the publication of *MS Magazine* (1972), which helped to establish and popularize the term "Ms." over the standard "Miss" or "Mrs." Grass roots movements, of course, preceded, supported, and sustained these developments. I recall, for instance, the creation of women's bookstores, domestic violence centers, lesbian resource centers, coffeehouses, writing retreats, and alternative learning institutes in the Twin Cities, beginning in the early 1970s and continuing to this day. Women my age will also remember the establishment of the journals *Women's Studies* (1971), *Frontiers* (1975), *Signs* (1975), and *Sinister Wisdom* (1976), in addition to the founding of feminist presses such as Virago (1973), Calyx (1980), Kitchen Table (1980), and Cleis (1980).

Psychoanalysis, as it was practiced in 1950s' America, did nothing to alter this view. By shifting the focus from Freud's Oedipus complex and his contorted theories of femininity to the conceptual basis of object relations theory, which posits the mother/infant relationship as central to psychological development, Chodorow and others who followed her altered the terms of discourse regarding women and femininity. Quite simply, the figure of the mother displaced that of the father. Such a massive change did not, of course, occur overnight, and it is ongoing. In the field of psychoanalytic studies, however, the shift of emphasis from the oedipal to the preoedipal period is well-established by now and unlikely to revert.[4]

While object relations theory overtook classic Freudian theory in the United States and Britain, Lacanian theory arose in France and altered the field of psychoanalysis on the continent. While claiming his ideas as a radical return to Freud and as an opposition to American ego psychology, Lacan performed his own transformation on Freud's body of theory by renaming the major periods of development as the Imaginary and the Symbolic.[5] While maintaining fidelity to Freud's emphasis on the oedipal phase as crucial to patriarchal social structure, Lacan provided a rich vocabulary for the preoedipal period, re-baptized as the Imaginary. French feminists were quick to take advantage of this new conceptual framework to claim the space of the Imaginary as the ground for women's voices and writings.[6]

However you might describe the differences between object relations theory and Lacanian theory, it is obvious that both displace the figure of the father in favor of the mother as the center of interest. I would suggest that second-wave feminism furthered the movement in psychoanalysis away from Freud's vision of a commanding father as central to family structure (and by extension to the development of civilization)

[4] I discuss the preoedipal turn in psychoanalytic theory in Madelon Sprengnether, *Mourning Freud* (New York: Bloomsbury, 2018). See also Joel Whitebook, *Freud: An Intellectual Biography* (New York: Cambridge University Press, 2017).

[5] Jacques Lacan, *Écrits*, trans. Alan Sheridan (London: Tavistock, 1977).

[6] This is a very highly condensed summary of my views on Lacan and French feminism. For more nuanced accounts see Madelon Sprengnether, *The Spectral Mother: Freud, Feminism and Psychoanalysis* (Ithaca, NY: Cornell University Press, 1990), and my article Madelon Sprengnether, "Feminist Criticism and Psychoanalysis," in *A History of Feminist Literary Criticism*, eds. Gill Plain and Susan Sellars (Cambridge, UK: Cambridge University Press, 2007), 235–263.

in favor of a woman-centered focus of inquiry. Chodorow grasped this connection and explicated it in *The Reproduction of Mothering*.

Her thesis is at once simple and revolutionary. In a patriarchal society, women raise daughters to replicate themselves in their roles as women and mothers. This process is as much psychological as social, that is to say, prescribed and sustained by the culture at large. Object relations theory, which focuses on the care-giving functions of the mother and the process by which the infant undergoes separation and individuation from her, explains how girls remain more attached to their mothers than boys, who are encouraged to differentiate themselves from the primordial maternal matrix. In this complex and continually evolving body of thought, we enter the world in a condition of attachment, even symbiosis, with the body/psyche of the mother, from which we must all detach in order to achieve individual selfhood.[7] This process is more fraught, in its early stages, for boys who must also struggle to define themselves as masculine and male. For girls, separation is offset and muted by the fact of their

[7] Object relations theory presumes that infants do not thrive outside of the context of relationship. The work of John Bowlby, based on infant and early childhood observation, demonstrated how children in orphanages whose physical needs are attended to but neglected in terms of loving interaction, fail to develop normally. It would seem that we need a loving, or at least attentive, caregiver in order to invest in life. The British school of object relations theory absorbed this primary understanding, while focusing on specific aspects of the mother/infant relationship and creating a body of theory based on the assumption that infants' first attachments are to their mothers. Margaret Mahler elaborated the theory of an original mother/infant symbiosis, from which the child must slowly disengage in order to create an independent selfhood. The assumption that boys, because of their gender difference from the body of the mother, struggle harder than girls to differentiate from their mothers flows from this concept. Given how little we know about infants and how strong the cultural biases are in favor of relegating the functions of early infant caretaking to women and mothers, I think that the idea of mother/infant symbiosis should be held in suspension. See John Bowlby, *Attachment and Loss* (London: Hogarth Press, 1959); Margaret Mahler, *On Human Symbiosis and the Vicissitudes of Individuation* (New York: International Universities Press, 1968).

It is true (to date) that human gestation requires the body of a woman in order to come to fruition. Yet we remain in the dark about the possible meanings of this experience. For the mother, the act of giving birth is a profound but also disruptive experience, separating her from the fetus she has carried for nine months. Perhaps the infant registers its expulsion as equally disruptive? How can we know? Otto Rank, one of Freud's closest colleagues, thought so, describing this event as a trauma. If Rank was right, perhaps our first experience of being in the world is separation, rather than fusion. The myth of birth we choose to embrace is significant in my view because it affects how we conceptualize the drama of human development. Otto Rank, *The Trauma of Birth* (New York: Robert Brunner, 1952 [1924]).

primary gender identification with their mothers. Girls, in this view, value their relational ties as a positive reinforcement of their gender identity. Boys, in contrast, value their identities as separate individuals over their relational bonds.

I am aware that I am presenting this argument in a streamlined form. Yet it helps to capture the liberation of Chodorow's argument. She made a cogent case for how patriarchy perpetuates itself through the father-dominant, mother-nurturant structure of the family, while also suggesting new ways of thinking about women's relational abilities and pointing towards new social-psychological formations that might alter this seemingly fixed set of dichotomies. Altering the parenting structure of patriarchal society, she maintained, would similarly alter the psychological profiles of masculinity and femininity.

Not everyone grasped the revolutionary impact of her position. Trained in anthropology and sociology, Chodorow understood that social structures are human constructs and hence subject to change. She regarded patriarchy as rooted in the realm of social relations as opposed to biology. She viewed psychoanalytic theories through the same lens. To change the structure of parenting that we have come to view as normal (and universal) will also alter the gender profiles and relations that flow from them.

At the time of the publication of *The Reproduction of Mothering*, binary modes of thinking dominated the field of gender and sexuality. So obvious did this way of thinking appear that few could imagine the need to establish new areas of research or to define new disciplines. It was hard enough to convince one's academic colleagues of the need to create a program focused on the study of women. Once these initial obstacles had been overcome, rapid changes ensued.

Women activists within and outside of the academy opened up the category of "woman" to the myriad forms of expression within it. A virtual kaleidoscope of possibilities emerged as a result. Women's Studies Programs quickly evolved into GLBTQ or Gender, Women, and Sexualities Programs (as they did at my home institution). In the meantime, binary structures of categorizing human experience (theoretically at least) lost sway. The rise of ethnic studies departments coincided roughly with the establishment of gender-based disciplines. Each emphasized diversity and equality among ways of being over the binary systems of thinking that prioritize one over the other. Think, for instance, of the dichotomies west/east, up/down, reason/emotion, civilized/primitive, light/dark, white/black, or male/female.[8]

Psychoanalysis, in my view, has been slower to follow this lead. While the oedipal/preoedipal paradigm has shifted from an emphasis on the oedipal father/son model to the preoedipal mother/infant pair, it has not seriously challenged the social structures that continue to privilege male power over female authority. In this respect, social change may be leading psychoanalysis, theoretically at least, at this moment in time.

* * *

I discovered Chodorow's work in the early 1980s, as I began to feel its impact among my feminist peers in the study of women writers, both contemporary and premodern. While continuing my study of Shakespeare and his portrayals of tragic masculinity, I went on a reading spree that included women writers I'd heard of but never studied and ones whose names were entirely new to me, while venturing to write poetry and personal essays drawn from my own experience. My strongest motivation at that time came from the realization that I did not see my subjectivity represented in the canonical texts I had been trained to analyze, venerate, and promulgate through teaching. How do women view the world and our own experiences, I asked myself? Forty plus years later, I am still asking the same question.

In this period of intellectual ferment, I noticed the virtual absence of the figure of the mother in Freud's body of work. This absence seemed glaring and also key to developments in post-Freudian theory, as Chodorow's work makes clear. Object relations theory begins with the assumption that we are born into relationship and develop as a result of our interactions with our primary caregivers, most often our mothers or a female nurturing figure.

Freud refers obliquely to this period of life but does not dwell on it, skipping quickly to the role of the father, who fosters male development through the threat of castration, which leads to sublimation and the

[8] Deconstruction, a strategy of reading and interpretation introduced by Jacques Derrida, holds that binary categories automatically privilege one term over the other. See Jacques Derrida, *Of Grammatology*, trans. Gayatri Chakravorty Spivack (Baltimore: Johns Hopkins University Press, 1976). Luce Irigaray's influential work applies this axiom to the categories man/woman and masculine/feminine. See Luce Irigaray, *Speculum of the Other Woman*, trans. Gillian C. Gill (Ithaca: Cornell University Press, 1985).

boy's capacity to contribute to culture. In *The Spectral Mother* I analyzed Freud's texts for their suppression of the figure of the mother and forms of interpretation that might include her as a shaping force in the child's development. I also traced the consequences of this suppression in his theories of female sexuality and femininity—widely regarded by now as erroneous.

At the same time, I did not view object relations theory as a feminist alternative to the sexism embedded in Freud's thinking, as it does nothing to disturb the binary structure that informs the oedipal/preoedipal hierarchy. Chodorow herself pointed to this problem, by making clear that her analysis of femininity within patriarchy was an explanation of how women come to see themselves primarily as mothers who encourage their daughters to adopt the same role, while men regard themselves as creators of culture.

I did not see that French feminism offered a viable alternative, as it reinstates the oedipal/preoedipal structure, while shifting focus to the preoedipal, much as Anglo-American psychoanalytic feminism does. On a sociopolitical level, I'm not sure that the debates within and between object relations theory and Lacanian theory have had much impact, although each may have benefited individual women seeking psychoanalytic treatment, which is far more personal, varied and unpredictable than either of these theories can capture in analytic prose.

Juliet Mitchell, in her book *Psychoanalysis and Feminism*[9] published four years prior to Chodorow's *The Reproduction of Mothering*, made a similar case, but from the point of view of continental theory. Both Freud and Lacan, she argued, describe the internal, psychological structure of patriarchy, rather than affirming or prescribing it. Her point, as well as Chodorow's, that social structures create the psychic structures that serve to perpetuate them, has been lost since then. Both Freud's and Lacan's assumptions about male dominance and the natural or inevitable status of patriarchy, prevented them from thinking seriously about maternity and how women exist in multiple dimensions over the course of their lives, not limited to their roles as mothers.

In *The Spectral Mother*, I argued that neither object relations theory nor Lacanian theory displaced Freud's oedipal construct as the linchpin of patriarchy. I suggested separation rather than fusion as a point of

[9] Juliet Mitchell, *Psychoanalysis and Feminism* (New York: Pantheon, 1974).

departure for thinking about psychological development. Much of object relations theory, as I understood it then, rests on the assumption of an original state of symbiosis between mother and infant. Such an assumption can be posited but not proven, as we have no way of testing the mind of an infant, and the experiences of mothers are largely undocumented. This assumption acts, rather, as a founding myth, like the Garden of Eden in *Genesis*. Changing this founding myth from one of original plenitude to original loss, opens other possibilities for theorizing development. From this perspective, the differences between boys and girls seem less of a given and more of a matter of individual histories and circumstances of parenting.

* * *

In the course of researching *The Spectral Mother*, I read Ernest Jones' classic three volume biography of Freud *The Life and Work of Sigmund Freud*,[10] along with Peter Gay's learned update, *Freud: A Life for Our Time*.[11] These led me deeper into the field of biography, not only of Freud but also of his immediate associates, family members, and followers. From these, I began to construct a different portrait of him from the one presented by Jones and Gay, both of whom affirm Freud's own self-conception and the oedipal theory based on it. While Jones and Gay take on faith Freud's claim that he arrived at his central theory through a process of self-analysis that was unique, rigorous, and accurate, I began to have doubts. I saw flaws in this assumption as well as gaps in Freud's self-understanding, especially in regard to the earliest period of his life, which (as I had argued) he was unable to theorize.

I began, as a result, to measure Freud's theoretical labors against the circumstances of his life, as documented by Jones and Gay and subsequent

[10] Ernest Jones, *The Life and Work of Sigmund Freud*, 3 Vols. (New York: Basic Books, 1953, 1955, 1957).

[11] Peter Gay, *Freud: A Life for Our Time* (New York: W. W. Norton, 1988).

historians. Benefiting from the emerging field of trauma studies,[12] I speculated about the multiple losses of Freud's own preoedipal period and how they might have affected his thinking. Although he was his mother's favored, firstborn son, he soon had a rival in the birth of his brother Julius, who died at the age of seven months. In addition, his mother Amalia was in mourning for her own brother's death, after whom Julius had been named. To add to this complexity, Freud's beloved nanny was dismissed (on charges of stealing) not long afterwards.

Freud's mother Amalia had losses of her own to deal with, compounded by the rapid succession of births of Freud's five other siblings (Anna, Rosa, Marie, Adolfine, Pauline, and Alexander). Given that his family originally occupied a one-room apartment on the second floor of a building owned by the Zajic family, Freud as an infant and toddler must have witnessed a fair amount of emotional drama well before he was able to speak. Lastly, his family (apparently due to financial stresses) left his birthplace Freiburg for Vienna when he was about four years old. Freud himself relates his lifelong phobia of train journeys to this seemingly irrevocable loss. The traumas of Freud's early life, I argued, contributed to his inability to revisit, much less theorize, the preoedipal period. I viewed many of Freud's key texts through this lens of interpretation.

In the "Dream of Irma's Injection," for instance, I argued that Freud imposed a phallic interpretation on oral material, which in turn displaced his underlying identification with Irma. I also examined the instances of mourning in Freud's life in relation to his construction of the Oedipus complex. Ostensibly the result of the self-interpretation undertaken in the aftermath of his father's death, this achievement seems to occlude as much as it illuminates.

Avoiding the feelings of uprootedness and vulnerability that accompany this loss, Freud elaborates a theory of masculine lust, aggression, deferred ambition, and ultimate power. Such a concept owes little to Freud's actual family structure, which included two half-brothers (from his father's first marriage) and their children, who were Freud's childhood

[12] The literature on trauma, from a psychoanalytic perspective as well as from personal testimony, is too vast to cite here. That said, I want to call attention to an excellent history of the use of this term/concept. See Bessel van der Kolk, Lars Weisaeth, and Onno van der Hart, "History of Trauma in Psychiatry," in *Traumatic Stress: The Effects of Overwhelming Experience on Mind, Body and Society* (New York: Guilford Press, 1996), 47–74.

companions, although he was technically their uncle. His mother, twenty years younger than his father, may also have been attracted to his older brother Philipp, whose role in his mother's pregnancies Freud puzzled over. Such a complex family system bears little resemblance to the nuclear (father/mother/son) model that he posited as central to his oedipal theory. Finally, Freud's father, by all accounts, was a mild-mannered, easy-going man, rather than a commanding patriarch. It is hard to imagine him threatening to castrate his small son for demonstrating illicit desire for his mother.

As intrepid as Freud was in exploring his own unconscious, there is one area that he avoided, that of helplessness or vulnerability, which he associated with women, femininity, and castration. The Oedipus complex insulated him, theoretically at least, from occupying this position. At the same time, there are undercurrents in his writing that suggest other, more radical possibilities. For me as a reader, the endurance of Freud's writing owes more to its suggestiveness than to its authority. Like great works of literature, it opens itself to multiple (and sometimes conflicting) interpretations. As a result, each text contains within itself the seeds of its own unraveling, or deconstruction.

Despite his avoidance of the preoedipal period in his theorizing, Freud alluded to it often enough to open prospects for his followers, most immediately his daughter Anna Freud (analyzed by none other than her father) and Melanie Klein (analyzed by Freud's close colleague Karl Abraham). Both transformed the discipline they inherited by focusing on children and the unique challenges and demands of their treatment. Anna Freud, with her partner Dorothy Burlingham (also analyzed by Freud) established the Hampstead War Nursery in 1947, where they observed and treated children affected by war. Melanie Klein, who proclaimed her fidelity to Freud, created a new body of theory to map the territory of the infant's preverbal existence and fostered the practice of play therapy, which focuses on the creative and symbolic aspects of children's undirected, and seemingly nonsensical, play. Both must have felt authorized by Freud's acute observations on the fort-da game played by his grandson Ernst and reported to him by his parents, his daughter Sophie and son-in-law Max Halberstadt.[13]

[13] Sigmund Freud, *Beyond the Pleasure Principle*, *Standard Edition*, Vol. 18 (London: Hogarth Press, 1920), 1–64.

In this repeated game, Ernst throws a spool out of his cot and then reels it back again. Freud saw how this simple action represented the child's complex feelings about the absence of his father (recruited to the front in the Great War) and that of his mother (when she left him alone for whatever reason). At the heart of this game is a child's understanding of how parents may depart, but also return, including the possibility of control over their otherwise unpredictable actions. In this way, we might imagine, Ernst sought to manage his anxiety about losing them permanently. Freud relates this game to the phenomenon of repetition compulsion, as a means of mastering a situation of vulnerability and loss. This line of thinking, prompted by Freud's meditation on the condition of "shell shock," as revealed in the recurring flashbacks and nightmares of soldiers returning from war, led him toward one of his most controversial theories: the death instinct.[14] It might also have induced him to explore further the mental life of small children and the symbolic meanings of their play, but he left this area of inquiry to his daughter Anna and others who followed her lead.

In *Mourning Freud*,[15] I collected my thoughts about the discrepancies between the actual circumstances of Freud's life and his body of theory to subsequent developments in psychoanalytic theory (virtually all focused on preoedipal aspects of development) in order to make the case that loss, trauma, and mourning are the dominant subjects of investigation for our time.[16] This emphasis, in turn, alters the ways that we are able to think

[14] The starting point for most contemporary theorists of trauma is this famous study, induced by Freud's connection between his grandson's game and the phenomenon of "repetition compulsion," witnessed in some soldiers returning from the Front. It remained for others to elaborate on his speculations in order to articulate a full-fledged theory of trauma and how it affects the brain, body, and psyche. Freud, *Beyond the Pleasure Principle*.

[15] Sprengnether, *Mourning Freud*.

[16] I would add nonverbal or unrepresented states of being to this list, as this area of psychoanalytic theory is relatively new, hence unexplored. The preoedipal turn in psychoanalysis, with its emphasis on early childhood development naturally leads in this direction as infants only gradually become speaking subjects, and much of what they remember from their early lives is lost as they mature. Also, the concept of the suppression of memory formation in trauma theory raises the question of how traumatic experience is registered in the psyche. Lastly, Lacan's focus on the Imaginary has inspired many of his followers to emphasize aspects of the unconscious that are inaccessible, or only indirectly accessible, to language. See Nicolas Abraham and Maria Torok *The Shell and the Kernel* (1994) for an explication of how trauma enigmatically inscribes itself in language and Annie Rogers'

about masculinity, femininity, gender, and the social structures that flow from them.

Indeed, we live in a world vastly different from the one that Freud was born into and experienced over the course of his life. As a young man, he suffered the repressions of a bourgeois culture that denied the varieties of sexual expression yet permitted them through subcultures of prostitution, and "perversion." In addition, he experienced the devastation of the Great War, the collapse of the Austro-Hungarian and Russian empires, the dizzying social changes of the 1920s, including the Women's Suffrage movement, the Great Depression, and the rise of National Socialism. How could we expect him to imagine the challenges of our own era, much less the psycho-social realignments that we struggle with today?

Structures of binary thinking have been rigorously critiqued as new communities of gay, lesbian, bisexual, transgender, and queer identities have emerged and claimed their own space. Marriage as a privilege available only to heterosexual couples has opened (in some countries, including the United States) to include same sex partners. Children (male or female) may grow up in arrangements that include traditional and nontraditional families. Many find themselves in single-parent homes or in foster families. The structure of the nuclear family was not universal in Freud's time nor in his own experience and is even less so now. How do we know what constitutes masculinity or femininity, male or female sexual development, or the proper social roles of men and women in these circumstances?

I support a less rigidly theoretical and more inquiring stance towards these questions going forward. Most of us will address them through the troubled lens of our own experiences, personal, social, cultural, and historical. What I wished to demonstrate in *Mourning Freud* is how deeply embedded Freud's thinking was in the cultural assumptions of his time, as well as how we are all shaped and warped by the individual circumstances of our lives. As influential and revolutionary as Freud was in dismantling the Victorian world he had been born into and contributing to the modernist sensibility of the twentieth century, he also suffered from some of the problems of self-knowledge he aimed to dispel. In particular, he could not see past his assumptions about women as wounded

A Shining Affliction (1995) and *The Unsayable* (2006) for examples of the clinical uses of Lacanian theory in the treatment of traumatized children.

(by virtue of their castration) and femininity as a condition of helplessness and vulnerability. Maleness and masculinity, in contrast, signaled independence, aggression, power, and authority.

Many have challenged this bias in Freud's body of theory, pointing not only to its blind spots but also to the inconsistencies in his actual behavior towards women, many of whom he included in his personal circle of friends and whose careers and ambitions he fostered.[17] That is not the point I wish to make. Rather, I want to suggest that theory should not proceed too far in advance of the available evidence, and we know far too little about girls,' women's, and mothers' knowledge and experience to theorize or prescribe it.

What would happen if we continued to explore the diversity of our gender, cultural, class, racial, and historical experiences before attempting to categorize them? I see this happening in non-totalitarian governments and societies, but I also see more virulent attempts in some countries and parts of the world to impose strictures on how to behave (sexually as well as socially and culturally) and what can publicly be said.

The work of second-wave of feminism, far from being over, has only just begun.[18] From my (admittedly limited) vantage point, I would say

[17] For a useful overview of Freud's relationships with women, see Lisa Appignanesi and John Forester, *Freud's Women* (New York: Basic/HarperCollins, 1992); Elisabeth Young-Bruehl, *Freud on Women: A Reader* (New York: W. W. Norton, 1990). This includes citations from his texts on girls and women, with commentary provided by the author (1990). For views of Freud provided by two of his significant women admirers, see Hilda Doolittle [H.D.], *A Tribute to Freud* (New York: New Directions, 1974 [1956]); and Ernst Pfeiffer, ed. *Sigmund Freud and Lou Andreas Salomé Letters* (New York: W. W. Norton, 1966 [1985]).

[18] I am speaking of feminism both in the United States and in the world at large. There was a period of time during the 1990s when US feminism seemed to lose momentum, as younger women, having gained ground in the professions, preferred not to call themselves feminists. The next generation has brought new life and energy to the movement, especially around issues of sexual harassment, equal pay, domestic violence, and rape. I was personally moved to read Nicholas Kristof and Cheryl WuDunn's book *Half the Sky*, which demonstrates the degree to which women in developing countries lack the basic rights and freedoms that US feminists have long taken for granted. Nicholas Kristof and Cheryl WuDunn, *Half the Sky: Turning Oppression into Opportunity for Women Worldwide* (New York: Knopf, 2009). Their documentation of the practices of forced prostitution, honor killing, genital cutting, female infanticide, and the denial of education to girls reminded me of Mary Daly's early feminist work which called attention to similar historical atrocities (Indian bride burning, Chinese foot-binding, African genital mutilation, and European witch burning). Daly was a lesbian feminist philosopher and theologian, and her argument focuses on patriarchy as a system that oppresses women. See Mary Daly,

that women have made significant advances in challenging the social norms and expectations that confined us to prescribed roles and occupations. At the same time, the world as a whole is governed by men and reflects their priorities. If the goal of second-wave feminism was not only to question patriarchy but also to replace it with a more egalitarian form of social organization, that goal has not been attained. In order for such a transformation to occur, an underlying set of assumptions about the inherent superiority of men over women and their innate, gender-based, differences needs to dissipate, if not completely dissolve.

Psychoanalysis, which I regard as an evolving discipline, has contributed to this process in significant ways over time—first by welcoming women analysts into its exclusive male club, then by opening itself to the development of new ideas not specifically anticipated or authorized by Freud, and finally by relaxing its boundaries to include the work of psychoanalytic social workers, historians, and literary scholars such as myself.[19] It is the expansiveness and inclusiveness of psychoanalysis and psychoanalytically informed thinking, in my view, that assures its vitality and legacy long after the death of its lonely (and sometimes beleaguered) founder.

That said, I want to draw attention to the innovative work of women analysts over the course of the last half-century, who have furthered our exploration and understanding of women's lives and subjectivities—not as they are biologically ordained but as they have been lived and experienced in real time. I don't have the leisure here to refer to the vast body of literature that has appeared or been excavated since the early 1970s when I found it nearly impossible to include a woman writer in one of my standard syllabi. My point, rather, is that women are now a part of the culture that I inhabit and visible within it, whereas fifty years ago when I first entered my profession we were not.

Chodorow's career began but did not end with *The Reproduction of Mothering*, as demonstrated by the titles of her subsequent books:

Gyn/Ecology: The Metaethics of Radical Feminism (Boston: Beacon Press, 1978), Kristof and WuDunn are investigative reporters, who ground their position in research, individual interviews, and statistics. Despite these differences, Daly, Kristof and WuDunn, in their emphases on specific instances of women's oppression, have much in common.

[19] For an overview of the intersections between literary and psychoanalytic feminism over the course of the last half-century, see Sprengnether, "Feminist Criticism and Psychoanalysis".

Feminism and Psychoanalytic Theory (1991); *Femininities, Masculinities, Sexualities: Freud and Beyond* (1994); *The Power of Feelings: Personal Meaning in Psychoanalysis, Gender, and Culture* (1999); *Individualizing Gender and Sexuality: Theory and Practice* (2012); and her most recent book *The Psychoanalytic Ear and the Sociological Eye: Towards an American Independent Tradition* (2019). Chodorow's training as a psychoanalyst and years of experience in private practice inform all of these books, which explore the diversity of women's conscious and unconscious wishes, choices, conflicts, and desires in the context of contemporary theory and culture. She, along with women analysts such as Jessica Benjamin,[20] Muriel Dimen,[21] and Adrienne Harris[22] brought nuance and complexity to the subject of gender identity.

Other women clinicians and analysts have called for attention to the specifics of maternity including the range of possible responses to conception, pregnancy, miscarriage, abortion, childbirth, and parenting. It is important to understand the significance of this work. For instance, when I was a girl, motherhood was regarded as a woman's destiny, a product of nature and instinct rather than choice. Analysts such as Barbara Almond[23] and Rosemary Balsam (*Women's Bodies in Psychoanalysis* 2012), by listening to actual women patients describe their physical and emotional responses to maternity, query these assumptions and call them into question.

I began this essay by describing the paradigm shift within psychoanalysis and feminism from a focus on men (the Oedipus complex as an organizing principle of the male psyche) to women (as mothers but also as the point of departure for thinking about psychological and cultural development). Over the course of the last half-century, the discourses of feminism and psychoanalysis have taken different, but also intersecting, paths. Both have altered our ways of thinking about women, gender, and sexuality. But neither has succeeded in overturning the patriarchal status quo. Can we even imagine that?[24]

[20] Benjamin, *The Bonds of Love*.

[21] Muriel Dimen, *Sexuality, Intimacy, Power* (New York: Routledge, 2014).

[22] Adrienne Harris, *Gender as Soft Assembly* (Hillsdale, NJ: Analytic Press, 2005).

[23] Barbara Almond, *The Monster Within: The Hidden Side of Motherhood* (Berkeley: University of California Press, 2010).

[24] In their recent book *Why Does Patriarchy Persist?* Carol Gilligan and Naomi Snider answer this question by "connecting the persistence of patriarchy to the psychology of

* * *

A major obstacle to thinking about women from a psychoanalytic perspective is the Oedipus complex: the outcome of Freud's self-analysis and the cornerstone of his theories of gender, sexuality, and social organization. The fact that he drew from ancient myth (the story of Oedipus, his father Laius, and his mother Jocasta) has inspired women to consider alternate myths to represent the complexity of female experience. Many have turned to the Demeter/Persephone story to counter the oedipal view of women as lacking or deficient.[25] The most recent and fully developed version of this argument, which seeks to replace the term "female Oedipus complex" with the Persephone myth, is titled *A Story of Her Own: The Female Oedipus Complex Reexamined and Renamed* (1998). The authors Nancy Kulish and Deanna Holtzman begin by stating:

> Throughout his formulations of the female triangular phase, Freud emphasized what the female lacks. Nowhere were there ideas—now falling under the umbrella of 'primary femininity'—about the *role played by the female body in the triadic phase in terms of what it has*, and not what it lacks [italics in the original].[26]

loss" (143). They argue that the onset of puberty involves a psychic sacrifice for both boys and girls, although in an asymmetrical fashion. While boys suppress the awareness of feelings of tenderness and affection in the service of assuming a prescribed masculine identity, girls begin to lose confidence in their ability to voice their own thoughts and feelings in the service of sustaining their relational ties to others. This bifurcation exaggerates and reifies the culture's perceptions of sexual difference, hence also perpetuating the structure of patriarchy. The implication of this argument is that an acknowledgement or realization of this process offers the means to end it. Carol Gilligan and Naomi Snider, *Why Does Patriarchy Persist?* (Cambridge, MA: Polity Press, 2018).

[25]The turn to ancient myth offers other possibilities than the myth of Demeter and Persephone, although this option remains relatively unexplored. Carol Gilligan, in *The Birth of Pleasure* offers an alternative by exploring the Greek myth of Amor and Psyche. Her reading of Psyche's violation of the taboo on looking directly at the face of her (nighttime) lover offers an interpretation of female self-assertion that has an unusually positive outcome: the birth of their child, named Pleasure. Carol Gilligan, *The Birth of Pleasure* (New York: Knopf, 2002).

[26]Nancy Kulish and Deanna Holtzman, *A Story of Her Own: The Female Oedipus Complex Reexamined and Renamed* (Lanham, MD: Rowman and Littlefield, 2008).

Kulish and Holtzman find support in the myth of Demeter and Persephone to validate their account of the preoedipal phase of girls' development and the ways in which they both separate from and retain ties to their mothers over the course of their lives. In this account, there is no need for a girl to perceive herself as "castrated," much less to blame her mother for her lack in order to adapt to her role in heterosexual relations. One obvious flaw in this argument is its assumption that the normal path to maturity is heterosexual. Yet it avoids the assumption in Freud's paradigm that women are maimed, both physically and psychologically due to their lack of a male organ, while also acknowledging women's continuing bonds with their mothers. I see their work as part of a long trajectory within feminism and psychoanalysis to reclaim women's experience in its own terms instead of maintaining a priori assumptions.

That said, I found the most appealing aspect of Kulish and Holtzman's argument to be their restoration of the figure of Baubo to this myth. I was familiar with the story of how Kore (later named Persephone) wandered in a field from which she was rapt into the underworld by Hades. I also knew the part about her mother Demeter's desperate mourning and attempts to bargain with Hades for her release. So deep was Demeter's grief that the above world suffered from the loss of her grace, causing widespread famine. The deal that permitted Persephone to return from the underworld to reside with her mother for a part of each year not only restored the earth's fertility but also established the rotation of the seasons.

Many feminists (including Chodorow) have understood this myth as a recognition of how girls love and remain attached to their mothers throughout their lives. The surprise for me in Kulish and Holtzman's rereading of this myth was their restoration of the figure of Baubo, whom I'd never encountered before.

Among the various accounts of this ancient myth, Baubo figures prominently—as an older woman, or servant, in the household where Demeter offers herself as a caretaker for a boy named Demophoon. But so depressed is Demeter at the loss of her daughter that she refuses to eat or drink. Baubo, perceiving her distress lifts her skirts to show her genitals. This transgressive act causes Demeter to laugh and begin to recover herself.

Images of Baubo were common in the ancient world. Even Freud knew of them.[27] Yet Baubo has not figured large in the imagination of western culture, ancient or modern. Why not? I venture to guess that it is because she is a blatantly sexual (older) woman, beholden to no one, hence unfettered by patriarchy. Her act of lifting her skirts to expose her naked genitals suggests that she is proud of her own body and revels in her sexuality. She does not perceive herself as deficient, envious, guilty, or ashamed.

I fell in love with the figure of Baubo, because of the enigmatic nature of her representation, which allows us to project our own meanings onto her bawdy image.[28]

Chodorow's *The Reproduction of Mothering* sparked a revolution in thinking about women from a simultaneously social and psychological perspective and contributed to a profound paradigm shift from an emphasis on maleness as the norm and femaleness as a maimed variation thereof. This revolution, far from having ended, is still in an early developmental stage and far from maturity. But my point is this: women now have a say in how we imagine and theorize our own lives, possibilities, and subjectivities.

I picture Baubo gleefully raising her skirts and laughing.[29]

[27] Sigmund Freud, "A Mythological Parallel to a Visual Obsession," in *Standard Edition*, Vol. 4 (London: Hogarth Press, 1916), 337–338.

[28] For an exploration of the figure of Baubo, in myth and in art, see Winifred Milius Lubell, *The Metamorphosis of Baubo: Myths of Woman's Sexual Energy* (Nashville: Vanderbilt University Press, 1994).

[29] Baubo's gesture of lifting her skirts and provoking Demeter's laughing response resonates in my memory with Hélène Cixous' essay "The Laugh of the Medusa," where she makes the case for a liberated form of women's writing. In *The Spectral Mother*, I expressed skepticism about the possibility of a gender-based form of writing with the power to subvert, if not overthrow patriarchy. Cixous herself implied that the subversive practice she advocated could also be embraced by men, although she was not entirely consistent in this. Rereading her essay now, I am struck by the extraordinary lyricism and energy of this piece, which induces in the reader an almost hypnotic state. Rhetorically, it is a tour de force, including the now famous lines: "You only have to look at the Medusa straight on to see her. And she's not deadly. She's beautiful and she's laughing." Hélène Cixous, "The Laugh of the Medusa," trans. Keith Cohen and Paula Cohen. *Signs* 1, no. 4 (1976): 875–893. In Lubell's account, Medusa, a separate character from Baubo in mythological terms, nevertheless has ties to her in the manner of her representation: a woman's head surrounded by writhing snakes. Baubo figurines often show a woman's face in the place of her pudendum, hence perhaps inspiring Freud's assumption that the sight of an adult woman's genitals strikes a paralyzing fear in men, who regard women as castrated.

References

Abraham, Nicolas and Maria Torok, *The Shell and the Kernel*, Vol. 1, ed. and trans. Nicholas T. Rand. Chicago: Chicago University Press, 1994.

Almond, Barbara, *The Monster Within: The Hidden Side of Motherhood*. Berkeley: University of California Press, 2010.

Appignanesi, Lisa and John Forester, *Freud's Women*. New York: Basic/HarperCollins, 1992.

Balsam, Rosemary, *Women's Bodies in Psychoanalysis*. New York: Routledge, 2012.

Benjamin, Jessica, *The Bonds of Love: Psychoanalysis, Feminism and the Problem of Domination*. New York: Pantheon, 1988.

Bowlby, John, *Attachment and Loss*. London: Hogarth Press, 1959.

Chodorow, Nancy, *Femininities, Masculinities, Sexualities: Freud and Beyond*. Lexington, KY: University Press of Kentucky, 1994.

———, *Feminism and Psychoanalytic Theory*. New Haven: Yale University Press, 1991.

———, *Individualizing Gender and Sexuality: Theory and Practice*. New York: Routledge, 2012.

———, *The Power of Feelings: Personal Meaning in Psychoanalysis Gender, and Culture*. New Haven: Yale University Press, 1999.

———, *The Psychoanalytic Ear and the Sociological Eye: Towards an American Independent Tradition*. New York: Routledge, 2019.

———, *The Reproduction of Mothering: Psychoanalysis and the Sociology of Gender*. Berkeley: University of California Press, 1978.

Cixous, Hélène, "The Laugh of the Medusa," trans. Keith Cohen and Paula Cohen. *Signs* 1, no. 4 (1976): 875–893.

Daly, Mary, *Gyn/Ecology: The Metaphysics of Radical Feminism*. Boston: Beacon Press, 1978.

Derrida, Jacques, *Of Grammatology*, trans. Gayatri Chakravorty Spivack. Baltimore: Johns Hopkins University Press, 1976.

Dimen, Muriel, *Sexuality, Intimacy, Power*. New York: Routledge, 2014.

Doolittle, Hilda [H.D.], *A Tribute to Freud*. New York: New Directions, 1956 [1974].

Freud, Sigmund, *Beyond the Pleasure Principle, S.E.* 18 (1920): 1–64.

———, *The Interpretation of Dreams, S.E.* 4 (1900): 1–338.

———, "A Mythological Parallel to a Visual Obsession." *S.E.* 14 (1916): 337–338.

Friedan, Betty, *The Feminine Mystique*. New York: W. W. Norton, 1963.

Gay, Peter, *Freud: A Life for Our Time*. New York: W. W. Norton, 1988.

Gilligan, Carol, *The Birth of Pleasure*. New York: Knopf, 2002.

———, *In a Different Voice: Psychological Theory and Women's Development*. Cambridge, MA: Harvard University Press, 1982.
——— and Naomi Snider, *Why Does Patriarchy Persist?* Cambridge, MA: Polity Press, 2018.
Harris, Adrienne, *Gender as Soft Assembly*. Hillsdale, NJ: Analytic Press, 2005.
Irigaray, Luce, *Speculum of the Other Woman*, trans. Gillian C. Gill. Ithaca: Cornell University Press, 1985.
Jones, Ernest, *The Life and Work of Sigmund Freud*, 3 Vols. New York: Basic Books, 1953, 1955, 1957.
Kristof, Nicholas and Cheryl WuDunn, *Half the Sky: Turning Oppression into Opportunity for Women Worldwide*. New York: Knopf, 2007.
Kulish, Nancy and Deanna Holtzman, *A Story of Her Own: The Female Oedipus Complex Reexamined and Renamed*. Lanham, MD: Rowman and Littlefield, 2008.
Lacan, Jacques, *Écrits*, trans. Alan Sheridan. London: Tavistock, 1977.
Levine, Howard B., Gail S. Reed, and Dominique Scarfone, eds., *Unrepresented States and the Construction of Meaning: Clinical and Theoretical Contributions*. London: Karnac Books, 2013.
Lubell, Winifred Milius, *The Metamorphosis of Baubo: Myths of Women's Sexual Energy*. Nashville: Vanderbilt University Press, 1994.
Mahler, Margaret, *On Human Symbiosis and the Vicissitudes of Individuation*. New York: International Universities Press, 1968.
Mitchell, Juliet, *Psychoanalysis and Feminism*. New York: Pantheon, 1974.
Pfeiffer, Ernst, ed., *Sigmund Freud and Lou Andreas Salomé Letters*. New York: W. W. Norton, 1966 [1985].
Rank, Otto, *The Trauma of Birth* [no trans. listed]. New York: Robert Brunner, 1952 [1924].
Rogers, Annie, *A Shining Affliction: A Story of Harm and Healing in Psychotherapy*. New York: Penguin, 1995.
———, *The Unsayable: The Hidden Language of Trauma*. New York: Ballantine, 2006.
Sprengnether, Madelon, "Feminist Criticism and Psychoanalysis." In *A History of Feminist Literary Criticism*, eds. Gill Plain and Susan Sellars, Cambridge: Cambridge University Press, 2007, 235–263.
———, *Mourning Freud*. New York: Bloomsbury Academic, 2018.
———, *The Spectral Mother: Freud, Feminism, and Psychoanalysis*. Ithaca, NY: Cornell University Press, 1990.
Van der Kolk, Bessel, Lars Weisaeth, and Onno van der Hart eds., "History of Trauma in Psychiatry." In *Traumatic Stress: The Effects of Overwhelming Experience on Mind, Body and Society*, eds. Bessel van der Kolk, Alexander McFarlane, and Lars Weisaeth. New York: Guilford Press, 47–74.

Whitebook, Joel, *Freud: An Intellectual Biography*. New York: Cambridge University Press, 2017.
Young-Bruehl, Elisabeth, *Anna Freud: A Biography*. New York: Summit/Simon and Schuster, 1988.
———, *Freud on Women: A Reader*. New York: W. W. Norton, 1990.

PART II

Daughters

CHAPTER 7

The Reproduction of Mothering: A Love Story

Ilene Philipson

I fell in love with *The Reproduction of Mothering* when I read it in manuscript form as a graduate student in 1977, and if I'm honest, I confess that I love it to this day. I recognize it has been extolled and critiqued, lauded and dismissed over the past 40 years. But there is something about young love that endures. This is my love story.

The Context

It is difficult to describe the thrill of being an undergraduate at the dawn of Second-Wave Feminism. When I entered UC Berkeley as a freshman in 1970, there seemed to me that there was a seamless connection between academic and intellectual pursuit and the advancement of the feminist revolution. In my women's consciousness raising group and in conversation with my girlfriends, we shared the latest book, article, pamphlet, or manifesto we had read that illuminated aspects of life previously unexamined or unknown. The most popular feminist writers were those who unsettled and provoked the most, who spoke to those of us who, in our late teens, were open to the most radical ideas, often taking drugs and having sex for the first time. Could it be possible, as psychiatrist Mary

I. Philipson (✉)
Institute of Contemporary Psychoanalysis, Los Angeles, CA, USA

P. Bueskens (ed.), *Nancy Chodorow and* The Reproduction of Mothering,
https://doi.org/10.1007/978-3-030-55590-0_7

Jane Sherfey argued in *The Nature and Evolution of Female Sexuality in Relation*, that women's insatiable sex drive had been suppressed in order to maintain civilization?[1] Did we agree with Shulamith Firestone in *The Dialectic of Sex* when she called for women to take control of the means of *re*production and destroy the nuclear family?[2] Certainly no one could deny Kate Millett's warning in *Sexual Politics:* "Sex is deep at the heart of our troubles… and unless we eliminate the most pernicious of our systems of oppression, unless we go to the very center of the sexual politic and its sick delirium of power and violence, all our efforts at liberation will but land us again in the primordial stews."[3]

Over the course of my four years at Berkeley, feminist dialogue increasingly moved from our apartments, collective households, and cafes into the classroom. Academic departments in the humanities and social sciences began offering courses that emerged from the feminist movement for the first time: gender, sex differences, sex roles, and women became subjects of entire courses in history, economics, sociology, anthropology, English, psychology, political science, and rhetoric. As I took many of these classes, I also was engaged in my first, serious relationship, as were many of my friends. While we all were smart, ambitious feminists, increasingly we seemed to be confronting deeply engrained, rather shameful personal problems in both our romantic relationships and in school. Many of us found ourselves to be more emotional, more insecure and labile than our boyfriends. We hated ourselves for the ways we felt needy and dependent on the men with whom we were involved. Some of us appeared to evince what Matina Horner had recently termed "the fear of success."[4] We questioned our abilities, failed to write papers, and didn't speak up in class. How, I wondered, could this be? We had had our consciousness raised; we were well-read in feminist thinking, and yet…

I believe it is at this point, somewhere in my senior year, that I began to question the adequacy of the socialization model that had become hegemonic in explaining women's second sex status. This questioning largely

[1] Mary Jane Sherfey, *The Nature and Evolution of Female Sexuality* (New York: Random House, 1972).

[2] Shulamith Firestone, *The Dialectic of Sex: The Case for Feminist Revolution* (London: Paladin, 1972).

[3] Kate Millett, *Sexual Politics* (New York: Doubleday and Co., 1970), 334.

[4] Matina Horner, "Toward an Understanding of Achievement-Related Conflicts in Women," *Journal of Social Issues* 28, no. 2 (1972): 157–175.

emanated from my own internal turmoil. While I consciously and cognitively understood "my oppression as a woman," somehow my awareness, my intellect, appeared puny indeed in the face of the emotions and negative thinking I was experiencing. I was having difficulty completing term papers, had taken four incompletes, and seemed to be spending inordinate amounts of time worrying about my relationships with men. With varying degrees of distress, I found myself turning to a feminist literature that was in its infancy but that somehow was taking root in 1974. It is in that year that three books were published that spoke to a psychoanalytic underpinning for feminist theorizing.

Juliet Mitchell's *Psychoanalysis and Feminism* sought to recuperate Freud from feminist criticism, arguing that "psychoanalysis is not a recommendation *for* a patriarchal society, but an analysis *of* one."[5] Mitchell explains and defends Freud, claiming that psychoanalysis provides a means of understanding ideology and sexuality commensurate with Marxism's explanation of history and political economy. What was illuminating for me at that time was Mitchell's critique of feminism. She asserted that feminist thinking:

> ...denies any attribute of the mind other than rationality. As a result it must also end up denying the importance of childhood experiences. The feminist's children are born directly into the reality principle, not so Freud's.[6]

It was this observation that began to make sense of my personal experience, that is, that which felt irrational and not subject to conscious control. There was something more, something hidden that Mitchell found in Freud's theory of the unconscious that resonated.

Jean Strouse in the anthology she edited that year, *Women and Analysis*, echoed Mitchell in her desire to reanimate Freud's work in a feminist context.[7] However, she allowed for greater acknowledgment of Freud's shortcomings in the 11 chapters in which she paired a contemporary commentator with the work of a well-known psychoanalyst, beginning

[5] Juliet Mitchell, *Psychoanalysis and Feminism: Freud, Reich, Laing and Women* (New York: Pantheon Books, 1974), xv.

[6] Mitchell, *Psychoanalysis and Feminism*, 354.

[7] Jean Strouse, *Women and Analysis: Dialogues on Psychoanalytic Views of Femininity* (New York: Grossman Publishers, 1974).

with Juliet Mitchell on Freud. Many of these commentators either repeated what was then well-known criticisms of Freud—his biological determinism, his culture-bound ideas, his lack of attention to women's reproductive capacities—or celebrated his underlying and implicit analysis of "interactions between social organization and the deepest levels of human sexuality".[8] The volume seemed to me repetitive and uninventive, that is, until the last chapter by a UCLA psychoanalyst whom I had never read, Robert Stoller. In "Facts and Fancies: An Examination of Freud's Concept of Bisexuality,"[9] Stoller, who, unbeknownst to me, had already published two books, *Sex and Gender: On the Development of Masculinity and Femininity*, and *Splitting*, analyzed the consequences of what he termed the initial symbiosis with the mother for the development of gender identity in boys and girls.[10] I was arrested by his argument and particularly affected by a passage that I would use over and over in years to come in my own teaching and writing. He states:

> Thus the whole process of becoming masculine is at risk in the little boy from the day of birth on; his still-to-be created masculinity is endangered by the primary, profound, primeval oneness with mother, a blissful experience that serves, buried but active in the core of one's identity, as a focus which, throughout life, can attract one to regress back to that primitive oneness. That is the threat lying latent in masculinity, and I suggest that the need to fight it off is what energizes some of what we are familiar with when we call a piece of behavior masculine.[11]

I found this insight astounding for it suddenly illuminated an inchoate understanding I had been developing all my life and particularly in my current relationship, namely, that the posturing, assertion of superiority, competitiveness, and fear of commitment that often characterized normal masculinity was fundamentally defensive and compensatory. How I and many of my women friends negotiated what we called the "male ego"

[8] Strouse, *Women and Analysis*, 3.

[9] Robert Stoller, "Facts and Fancies: An Examination of Freud's Concept of Bisexuality," in *Women and Analysis: Dialogues on Psychoanalytic Views of Femininity*, ed. Jean Strouse (New York: Grossman Publishers, 1974), 343–364

[10] Robert J. Stoller, *Sex and Gender: On the Development of Masculinity and Femininity* (London: Karnac, 1984); Robert J. Stoller, *Splitting: A Case of Female Masculinity* (New York: Quadrangle, 1973).

[11] Stoller, "Facts and Fancies," 358.

now stood revealed as founded in the early, universal relationship to the mother. To me, Stoller's insight demonstrated that psychoanalytic thinking could be used as an enormously important tool for understanding gender relations in a meaningful way that Juliet Mitchell's and Jean Strouse's contributors did not. Stoller was building something new rather than simply asserting the importance of appreciating the unconscious and the Oedipus complex.

The third book that I read in my senior year turned out to be the most important. It was an anthology edited by two anthropologists, Michelle Rosaldo and Louise Lamphere, entitled *Women, Culture and Society.*[12] The third chapter was written by a graduate student in sociology at Brandeis University by the name of Nancy Chodorow and was entitled "Family Structure and Feminine Personality." In an uncanny manner, the first paragraph of the chapter spoke directly to what I had been intellectually yearning for; it was a key that fit precisely into what I felt was locked inside:

> I propose here a model to account for the reproduction within each generation of certain general and nearly universal differences that characterize masculine and feminine personality and roles... [E]xplanations based on patterns of deliberate socialization are in themselves insufficient to account for the extent to which psychological and value commitments to sex differences are so emotionally laden and tenaciously maintained, for the way gender identity and expectations about sex roles and gender consistency are so deeply central to a person's sense of self.[13]

To my ear, the author's tone was remarkably, shockingly confident and certain that she could supply—at last—a structural model for understanding the differences between men and women, differences reproduced cross culturally and across time. Additionally, she spoke to the affect that undergirded those differences, the tenacity and emotional nature of our gendered sense of self. That this self-assured voice of hope and certitude emanated from a graduate student, that is, a status I now wished to inhabit, was truly stunning to me.

[12] Michelle Rosaldo and Louise Lamphere, *Women, Culture and Society* (Stanford: Stanford University Press, 1974).

[13] Nancy Chodorow, "Family Structure and Feminine Personality," in *Women, Culture and Society*, eds. Rosaldo and Lamphere, 43.

In the Spring of 1976, a sociology professor told me of another article that had just been published in the journal *Social Problems* by Nancy Chodorow. "Oedipal Asymmetries and Heterosexual Knots," set out to demonstrate how women's mothering gives rise to women and men with discordant relational needs that ultimately undermine heterosexual unions.[14] The same bold voice that I had encountered before now revealed a fundamental contradiction that lies at the heart of contemporary, heterosexual family life. Its use of psychoanalytic theory was similar to that of Stoller's, but Chodorow moved what to Stoller had been inevitable and unchanging, that is women's mothering, onto a sociological plane and hence subject to change.

Right around the time I was reading this new offering, I discovered that the University of California, Santa Cruz was starting a new doctoral program in sociology. Santa Cruz was 75 miles away from where I was living in Berkeley, and the sociology department had just hired a new assistant professor, Nancy Chodorow. In short order, I was accepted into this program and would become Nancy's first PhD student, a remarkable confluence that would forever shape my interest and career.

The Reproduction of Mothering

Shortly after being admitted to the doctoral program, I became a teaching assistant for Nancy's undergraduate courses on the "Sociology of Women" and then "Family and Society." I was part of a small seminar she taught on psychoanalytic drive theory and object relations, and it is there that I became conversant with the fundamentals of comparative thinking that I utilize to this day in teaching theory courses at the Institute of Contemporary Psychoanalysis where I am a Training and Supervising Analyst.[15] But the most gratifying and, to me, impressive event of my first year in graduate school occurred when Nancy gave me a copy of *The Reproduction of Mothering* in manuscript form shortly before the end of the Spring quarter 1977.

As with most young loves, it is somewhat embarrassing to acknowledge how flattered and thrilled I was by this gesture. I regarded this work,

[14] Nancy Chodorow, "Oedipal Asymmetries and Heterosexual Knots," *Social Problems* 23, no. 4, (1976): 454–468.

[15] Ilene Philipson, Institute of Contemporary Psychoanalysis, https://icpla.edu/member-search/ilene-philipson-ph-d/.

which contained and then expanded upon all the insights I had encountered in the two articles I had previously read, as an almost sacred text, a book that I imagined would revolutionize feminist theory. And so it was with great reverence that I carefully—extremely carefully—read the manuscript over the summer. Each day I would study just three or four pages. I would sit in the mornings, the book on my dining room table, and with ruler and green ink pen in hand (for some reason I used only green ink in those days), I would carefully underline what I deemed the most important sentences. Needless to say, I utilized a lot of green ink.

I was captivated, enthralled, in love that summer. And unlike many loves from early in one's life, I have no regrets. In assessing *The Reproduction of Mothering* from a distance of 40 years, I fully understand the awe, respect, and excitement I experienced. While many of the insights of the book were dependent on the historical context in which it was written, a context that has transformed dramatically since 1978 in terms of both work and family life, there are many of its features that endure, that stand the test of time.

I think *The Reproduction of Mothering* continues to serve as a model for how much fresh insight and innovative thinking derive from an interdisciplinary perspective. The book draws on sociology, psychoanalysis, anthropology, feminist theory, the history of the family, and an understanding of the workings of capitalism that together form a dynamic way of understanding the world and the place of gender within it.

Its particular, Chodorow's reading of psychoanalysis allowed for a paradigm shift in how feminists could use psychoanalysis to deconstruct gender relations. In 1978 virtually no one within either academia or organized psychoanalysis was even aware of Object Relations. By introducing her audience to Fairbairn, Guntrip, Balint, Winnicott, and John Bowlby, the Attachment Theory creator, Nancy made an enormous and lasting contribution. These theorists are really theorists of the pre-Oedipal period, the period in life when mothers are salient. This move from Oedipal to pre-Oedipal, from the father to the mother provided us with a whole new way of viewing gender development and development in general. It anticipates the relational turn in psychoanalysis and the rise of Attachment Theory as the prevailing means of understanding how children grow and mature. And it has at its foundation a different conception of human nature than Freud's. Early on in the book, Nancy pinpoints what she sees as the foundational difference between traditional Freudianism and Object Relations:

> [E]ach position reflects a fundamentally different conception of human nature—whether human connection and sociality or human isolation and self-centeredness are more in need of psychological and social explanation. Each affects arguments about the basis for human selfishness and human connection.[16]

In its reliance on Object Relations theory, *The Reproduction of Mothering* moved much of feminist theorizing at the time away from that of authors who extolled Freud, and hence away from his view of human nature as being founded in drive discharge and drive satisfaction.

Finally, my encounter that summer with *The Reproduction of Mothering* convinced me that gender relations as we knew them were not immutable, biological, and inevitable. Simultaneously it acknowledged that the differences between men and women, heterosexual antagonisms, and women's second sex status were deeply and persistently rooted in the unconscious mind; thus not open to easy, superficial alteration. The message that I heard was that change will be very, very hard to effect, but there is hope, a form of hope that emanates from serious reflection, well-grounded and open intellectual inquiry, and the capacity to see the world anew. I believe I have held that message in mind throughout my life, and I owe much of that fundamental thinking to being introduced at a young and impressionable age to *The Reproduction of Mothering*.

Bibliography

Chodorow, Nancy, "Family Structure and Feminine Personality." In *Women, Culture and Society in Women, Culture and Society*, eds. Rosaldo and Lamphere. Stanford: Stanford University Press, 1974, 43–66.

———, "Oedipal Asymmetries and Heterosexual Knots." *Social Problems* 23, no. 4 (1976): 454–468.

———, *The Reproduction of Mothering: Psychoanalysis and the Sociology of Gender*. Berkeley: University of California Press, 1978.

Firestone, Shulamith, *The Dialectic of Sex: The Case for Feminist Revolution*. London: Paladin, 1972.

Horner, Matina, "Toward an Understanding of Achievement-Related Conflicts in Women." *Journal of Social Issues* 28, no. 2 (1972): 157–175.

Millett, Kate, *Sexual Politics*. New York: Doubleday and Co., 1970.

[16] Nancy Chodorow, *The Reproduction of Mothering: Psychoanalysis and the Sociology of Gender* (Berkeley: University of California Press, 1978), 67.

Mitchell, Juliet, *Psychoanalysis and Feminism: Freud, Reich, Laing and Women*. New York: Pantheon Books, 1974.
Philipson, Ilene, Institute of Contemporary Psychoanalysis. https://icpla.edu/member-search/ilene-philipson-ph-d/.
Rosaldo, Michelle, and Louise Lamphere, *Women, Culture and Society*. Stanford: Stanford University Press, 1974.
Sherfey, Mary Jane, *The Nature and Evolution of Female Sexuality*. New York: Random House, 1972.
Stoller, Robert J., "Facts and Fancies: An Examination of Freud's Concept of Bisexuality." In *Women and Analysis: Dialogues on Psychoanalytic Views of Femininity*, ed. Jean Strouse. New York: Grossman Publishers, 1974, 343–364.
———, *Sex and Gender: On the Development of Masculinity and Femininity*. London: Karnac, 1984.
———, *Splitting: A Case of Female Masculinity*. New York: Quadrangle, 1973.
Strouse, Jean, ed., *Women and Analysis: Dialogues on Psychoanalytic Views of Femininity*. New York: Grossman Publishers, 1974.

CHAPTER 8

Mothering in Life and Therapy: An Appreciation of Chodorow's Lifelong Contribution

Daphne de Marneffe

In the Spring of 1980, I encountered Nancy Chodorow's *The Reproduction of Mothering*—in its Sixties-style, yellow-covered incarnation—for the first time. I was a junior at Harvard, majoring in Psychology and Social Relations, and I had signed up for a class on adult development. On the printed syllabus, my gaze instantly gravitated to the readings on women, which, true to the times, were squeezed into one week of a semester-long course: Nancy Chodorow's *The Reproduction of Mothering*,[1] Irene de Castillejo's *Knowing Woman*,[2] and Carol Gilligan's essay "Woman's Place in Man's Life Cycle."[3]

[1]Nancy Chodorow, *The Reproduction of Mothering: Psychoanalysis and the Sociology of Gender* (Berkeley and Los Angeles: University of California Press, 1978).

[2]Irene de Castillejo, *Knowing Woman: A Feminine Psychology* (Boston: Harper Colophon, 1973).

[3]Carol Gilligan, *In a Different Voice* (Cambridge: Harvard University Press, 1982).

D. de Marneffe (✉)
Corte Madera, CA, USA

P. Bueskens (ed.), *Nancy Chodorow and* The Reproduction of Mothering,
https://doi.org/10.1007/978-3-030-55590-0_8

To me such readings were like sacred texts, offering a form of guidance about what mattered most deeply to me as a young woman wrestling with intellectual, sexual, emotional, and one day (I hoped) maternal identity. The course led me to write an undergraduate psychology thesis under the advisorship of Gilligan and, after graduation, I wrote letters (by snail mail of course) to my other two "goddesses," Dorothy Dinnerstein and Nancy Chodorow, asking them for their advice about the kind of graduate studies that would train me to write in the feminist-psychological tradition they had pioneered. Both kindly replied. A few years later I was studying clinical psychology at UC Berkeley where Nancy, a sociology professor, became my dissertation advisor for a study on children's understanding of genital difference and gender categorization.[4]

Recently I thought back to my first encounter with *The Reproduction of Mothering* and the feeling of high-stakes emotional immediacy that it produced, when I read the closing essay of Nancy's latest book, entitled "Could you direct me to the Individuology Department?"[5] She opens the essay with an anecdote: a male undergraduate in her "Psychoanalysis and Feminism" class at UC Berkeley leans across the cafe table and says to her "Do you know that we are reading and talking about what *every one of us* thinks about 24/7?"[6] This student and I, though separated by age, era, background, and gender, both felt that Nancy's interests engaged the most urgent issues in life—love, sex, relationships, family, gender, desire, identity, and all the complexities of our passions and how to make sense of them. This bit of history provides my jumping-off point to celebrate *The Reproduction of Mothering* not only as a founding document in the psychoanalytic study of maternal subjectivity, but also as the work that introduced Nancy's lifelong contribution to psychoanalytic thinking in general, through which she has deepened, illuminated, and contextualized her earlier prescient and brilliant insights.

I don't think it's an exaggeration to say that *The Reproduction of Mothering* established the study of maternal subjectivity as a field within psychoanalysis. The book provided a developmental account of women's subjective experiences of mothering daughters and sons, and analyzed

[4] Daphne de Marneffe, "Bodies and Words: A Study of Young Children's Genital and Gender Knowledge," *Gender and Psychoanalysis* 2, no. 1 (1997): 3–33.

[5] Nancy Chodorow, *Psychoanalytic Ear and the Sociological Eye: Toward an American Independent Tradition* (New York: Routledge, 2020), 245–262.

[6] Chodorow, *Psychoanalytic Ear and the Sociological Eye*, 245.

how these experiences shaped children's gendered construction of self. The argument relied on the empirical grounding of psychoanalytic case history to elucidate inner experience. It moved from this psychoanalytic frame to a social scientific one in describing how patterns of maternal experience contribute to the constructions of identity, which in turn become codified and expressed in gendered parenting arrangements. Nancy's effort to map, in a theoretically rigorous way, the connections between subjective experience and social structure would become a unique hallmark of her method.

At the time Nancy wrote *The Reproduction of Mothering*, the psychoanalytic resources available to chart maternal subjectivity were scant. For decades the baby was at the center of psychoanalytic description, and the field had a rich, if highly conjectural, trove of inferences about the baby's mental state and experience of the mother. The description of the mother's experience leaned on a developmental model that focused on the mother as the facilitator of the baby's growth rather than a person in her own right. To the extent that the mother's experience was considered, it was largely inferred from, and analogized to, the baby's own. For example, the psychoanalyst Alice Balint wrote, "just as the child does not recognize the separate identity of the mother, so does the mother look upon her child as a part of herself whose interests are identical with her own."[7] Nancy offered a psychoanalytic-feminist critique of the idea of perfect symmetry in the mother–infant bond and emphasized the mother's individuality and adult personhood apart from her baby. Simultaneously she recognized and centralized experiences of oneness and merger as a powerful, if transient, aspect of mothers' experience with their babies, and held that there were important subjective differences in how mothers experience such feelings with daughters and sons.

In my view, certain aspects of this psychoanalytic framework joined with second-wave feminist sensibilities to obscure and diminish mothers' affirmative desire to care for children, and the value of mothering activity to a woman's sense of identity and autonomy. In my book *Maternal Desire*, I described the ways that *both* mother and child derive meaning, pleasure, and growth from their shared emotional experiences.[8] I drew

[7] Chodorow, *Reproduction of Mothering*, 85.

[8] Daphne de Marneffe, *Maternal Desire: On Children, Love, and the Inner Life*, 2nd ed. (New York: Scribner, 2019 [2004]).

on a range of psychoanalytic and developmental findings to capture what makes these experiences so subjectively meaningful to mothers themselves, including the work of Stern on affect attunement, Main and Slade on attachment, Target and Fonagy on mentalization, Csikszentmihalyi on flow states, and Loewald and Kristeva on the immersive, embodied experience of language between child and parent. I also analyzed the social and historical forces that inclined women to accept the ideology that the embodied and integrative relational experiences of mothering were somehow passive, infantile, or self-sacrificial.

As Nancy writes (this volume), second-wave feminism was suspicious of the personal. It was also suspicious—not coincidentally—of motherhood, specifically of motherhood as a positive expression of women's agency and desire. I observed in *Maternal Desire* that for many women, second-wave feminism appeared tone deaf and even suspicious of a central feature of their subjective reality, "namely that caring for their children *matters* deeply to them. What if we were to take this mattering seriously," I asked, "to put it at the core of our exploration? Even to pose the question is to invite almost instant misconstrual. It's as if this would recommend to women to live through others, forsake equality, or relax into the joys of subsidized homemaking. But that reflexive misinterpretation is itself evidence of how difficult it is to think about maternal desire as a positive aspect of self."[9]

In her Introduction to the second edition of *The Reproduction of Mothering*, Nancy alluded indirectly to this dilemma when she reflected on the era in which she wrote the book. She commented on the pressure she'd felt "to choose between one position that seemed biologically determinist and entrapping of women" and another that claimed women's feelings about mothering were the product of "social structure and cultural mandate." She continued "On a more personal level. . . I, along with many feminists of my generation, did not in our twenties and early thirties adequately understand how mothering is actually experienced. . . and many of us were ourselves not prepared for the powerful transformative claims that motherhood would make upon our identities and senses of self."[10]

[9] de Marneffe, *Maternal Desire*, 16.

[10] Chodorow, *The Reproduction of Mothering*.

1999 might be seen as the starting point of the second half of Nancy's prolific career, in which she turned her focus to a deeper study of individual subjectivity through both her psychoanalytic practice and psychoanalytic writing. This was the year she wrote the Introduction for *The Reproduction of Motherhood's* second edition; it was also the year of publication for her book *The Power of Feelings: Personal Meaning in Psychoanalysis, Gender, and Culture*. Her Introduction to *The Power of Feelings* began this way: "This book is a contribution to our understanding of individual subjectivity. It is an argument for the existence of an irreducible realm of psychological life in which we create unconscious personal meaning in the experiential immediacy of the present."[11]

These themes, emergent in *The Reproduction of Mothering*, have taken center stage in Nancy's work in the subsequent two decades. For those of us who are clinicians working with patients every day, Nancy's developmental account of the individual, and her humane and humanistic concern for the complexity of the individual, are the defining values of her later body of work. These values are animated most deeply by her long-standing engagement with—and lifelong love of—the writings of the psychoanalyst Hans Loewald. Nancy, like her other intellectual hero Erik Erikson, shares Loewald's "great respect for a developmental view that goes from birth throughout life."[12]

In Loewald's developmental view, a person's current reality is endowed with meaning and a sense of aliveness through an open and fluid transfer between levels of experience—unconscious and conscious, fantasy and reality, individuation and merger, memory and present perception. Only by being infused with intensity of early ways of experiencing and unconscious fantasy are present-day relationships felt to be alive and meaningful. Development does not proceed via progression and regression, but rather through a constant oscillation between developmental periods and levels.

Maturity is a personal and creative developmental process undertaken by each individual, a key feature of which is "recognizing and taking responsibility for our lives as our own."[13] Culture complicates and

[11] Nancy Chodorow, *The Power of Feelings: Personal Meaning in Psychoanalysis, Gender, and Culture* (New Haven, CT: Yale University Press, 1999), 1.

[12] Chodorow, *Psychoanalytic Ear and the Sociological Eye*, 96.

[13] Chodorow, *Psychoanalytic Ear and the Sociological Eye*, 108.

obstructs that process, particularly for the marginalized and disempowered. But it is a profoundly hopeful aspect of Loewald's psychoanalytic vision that each of us has the freedom and the necessity to "to experience ourselves as agents, notwithstanding the fact that we are born without our informed consent and did not pick our parents."[14]

These aspects of Loewald's developmental thinking (movingly represented in Nancy's articles explicating his ideas)[15] offer extremely relevant, even essential, elaborations of Nancy's earlier themes in her model of mothering. When a given mother experiences a sense of meaning in caring for children, it likely derives from her access to feeling and memory from multiple registers of her experience. Agentic and engaged participation in mothering (or anything else) rests on assuming responsibility for trying to know and accept who one is—including knowing and expressing one's desire. In describing Loewald's impact on her, Nancy wrote, "It is a challenge to turn this private passion – experienced, as Loewald himself might describe it, in undifferentiated magical-evocative, primary-process form – into public secondary-process reasoning."[16] This statement could also be applied to the challenge of articulating (and writing about) what is most deeply meaningful about caring for and relating to children.

Nancy's post-*Reproduction of Mothering* writings are devoted to creating a discourse—even a field—that holds in productive tension, and addresses with sufficient complexity, the individual and culture. In this project, she writes, "psychoanalysis is a refuge and a wonder, the most complex theory and practice for studying and changing individuality from within, even as many ingredients of this individuality are drawn from the social, cultural, and historical surround."[17] She is continually drawn to the "flicker of the other" in psychoanalyst James McLaughlin's beautiful phrase, the irreducible precious core of the individual in her

[14] Hans Loewald, "The Waning of the Oedipus Complex," in *The Essential Loewald* (Hagerstown, MD: University Publishing Group, 1979 [2000]), 392. For Chodorow's description and analysis of these ideas, see Chodorow, "The Psychoanalytic Vision of Hans Loewald," in *Psychoanalytic Ear and the Sociological Eye*, 93–112.

[15] See Chodorow, *Psychoanalytic Ear and the Sociological Eye*, especially Chapters 5, 6, and 7.

[16] Ibid., 96.

[17] Ibid., xiv.

essential private otherness.[18] In the clinical encounter, as in the mothering encounter, this sensibility is of ultimate importance.

Therapy offers the opportunity for a new experience with a new "object," the therapist, catalyzing a subjective sense of emotional receptivity and loosening the grip of psychic compromises.[19] The therapist's optimal attitude is a feeling-full, robust investment in the developmental unfolding of each patient, wherein emotions are of central interest and concern. The psychological activities involved, which Loewald so evocatively described, are not fundamentally different in kind from those involved in mothering: a fluid interplay of conscious and unconscious, a poetic use of language, an intense and embodied emotional participation joined with reflectivity. I've called this latter combination "feeling with and thinking about," and in psychology it is called "reflective function" or "mentalization."[20] A good therapist, like a good parent, needs both empathy *and* the capacity to think. As Nancy puts it, the patient "needs to be bathed in the flow of affect and the music of words from the analyst, recalling the global features of early experiencing, but she also needs interpretation."[21] Being able to offer both, and to move between them as needed, is the crucial characteristic of a responsive relationship of any kind, the necessary ingredient if a child or patient is to flourish and grow.

Beginning decades ago and continuing to the present, the arc of Nancy's contribution has taken us into a rich and subtle exploration of personal and cultural meaning. I have a fortunate vantage from which to view this trajectory in that my life has intertwined with Nancy's in different ways. We both crisscrossed the continent—she the Bay Area Californian who found her home in Cambridge, me the girl from Cambridge who found my home in Bay Area California. From her first

18 Ibid., 18.

19 Hans Loewald, "On the Therapeutic Action of Psychoanalysis," in *The Essential Loewald* (Hagerstown, MD: University Publishing Group, 1960 [2000]), 221–256. See also, Chodorow, *Psychoanalytic Ear and the Sociological Eye*, Chapter 7.

20 For a clinically relevant discussion of "feeling with and thinking about," see Daphne de Marneffe, *The Rough Patch: Marriage and the Art of Living Together* (New York: Scribner, 2018), Chapters 3 and 4. For fuller clinical discussions of reflective function and mentalization, see Jeremy Holmes and Arietta Slade, *Attachment in Psychotherapeutic Practice* (Thousand Oaks, CA: Sage, 2018).

21 Chodorow, *Psychoanalytic Ear and the Sociological Eye*, 110.

letter to me as an eager and unknown student, through her academic teaching and mentorship, through her engaged interest and helpful challenge when I have sought her perspective on my written work, I have experienced firsthand the value Nancy places on individual development.

My mother's name is also Nancy, and over the years, my email autofill has occasionally replaced one Nancy with the other. As I live my ongoing relationship to my mother, now 86, and my daughter, now 26, I think about mothering across the lifespan, and that our need for a mother never really ends. I feel deep gratitude for those mothers, including my own, who have the capacity to love their children in their otherness, to delight in them, to think about them, and to both fiercely protect and appropriately challenge. Nancy has been an intellectual mother to me, as she has been to many. In her own evolution as a thinker, in her investment in the development of others, and—not least—in her revolutionary rethinking of mothering, she has modeled continual growth and searching. In all spheres of her life and work she has put into practice—in Loewald's well-known words—the "objectivity and neutrality the essence of which is love and respect for the individual and individual development."[22]

Bibliography

Chodorow, Nancy J., *The Reproduction of Mothering*. Berkeley: University of California Press, 1978; second edition 1999.

Chodorow, Nancy J., *The Power of Feelings: Personal Meaning in Psychoanalysis, Gender, and Culture*. New Haven, CT: Yale University Press, 1999.

Chodorow, Nancy J., *The Psychoanalytic Ear and the Sociological Eye: Toward an American Independent Tradition*. New York: Routledge, 2020.

Chodorow, Nancy J., and Terrence Becker, "SFCP Dialogues: The Loewaldian Legacy." San Francisco Center for Psychoanalysis, March 21, 2009.

Csikszentmihalyi, Mihaly, *Flow: The Psychology of Optimal Experience*. New York: Harper Perennial, 1990.

de Castillejo, Irene C., *Knowing Woman: A Feminine Psychology*. Boston: Harper Colophon, 1973.

de Marneffe, Daphne, "Bodies and Words: A Study of Young Children's Genital and Gender Knowledge." *Gender and Psychoanalysis* 2, no. 1 (1997): 3–33.

[22] Loewald, "Therapeutic Action," 229. Love in the clinical encounter, as understood in Loewald's terms, was discussed by Chodorow and Becker. See Nancy Chodorow and Terrence Becker, "SFCP Dialogues: The Loewaldian Legacy," San Francisco Center for Psychoanalysis, March 21, 2009.

de Marneffe, Daphne, *Maternal Desire: On Children, Love, and the Inner Life*, 2nd ed. New York: Scribner, 2019 [2004].
de Marneffe, Daphne, *The Rough Patch: Marriage and the Art of Living Together*. New York: Scribner, 2018.
Fonagy, Peter, Gyorgy Gergely, Elliot L. Jurist, and Mary Target, *Affect Regulation, Mentalization, and the Development of the Self*. New York: Other Press, 2002.
Fonagy, Peter and Mary Target, "Mentalization and the Changing Aims of Psychoanalysis." *Psychoanalytic Dialogues* 8 (1998): 87–114.
Gilligan, Carol, *In a Different Voice*. Cambridge: Harvard University Press, 1982.
Holmes, Jeremy and Arietta Slade, *Attachment in Psychotherapeutic Practice*. Thousand Oaks, CA: Sage, 2018.
Kristeva, Julia, "Stabat Mater," trans. Leon S. Roudiez. In *The Kristeva Reader*, ed. Toril Moi. New York: Columbia University Press, 1986, 161–186.
Kristeva, Julia, "Women's Time." In *The Kristeva Reader*, ed. Toril Moi. New York: Columbia University Press, 1986, 187–213.
Loewald, Hans W., "On the Therapeutic Action of Psychoanalysis" (1960). In *The Essential Loewald*. Hagerstown, MD: University Publishing Group, 2000, 221–256.
Loewald, Hans W., "Primary Process, Secondary Process, and Language" (1978). In *The Essential Loewald*. Hagerstown, MD: University Publishing Group, 2000, 178–206.
Loewald, Hans W., "The Waning of the Oedipus Complex" (1979). In *The Essential Loewald*. Hagerstown, MD: University Publishing Group, 2000, 384–404.
Main, Mary, "The Organized Categories of Infant, Child, and Adult Attachment: Flexible vs. Inflexible Attention Under Attachment-Related Stress." *Journal of the American Psychoanalytic Association* 48, no. 4 (2000): 1055–1096.
Slade, Arietta, Jay Belsky, J. Lawrence Aber, and June L Phelps, "Mothers' Representations of Their Relationships with Their Toddlers: Links to Adult Attachment and Observed Mothering." *Developmental Psychology* 35, no. 3 (1999): 611–619.
Stern, Daniel, *The Interpersonal World of the Infant: A View from Psychoanalysis and Developmental Psychology*. New York: Basic Books, 1985.
———, *The Motherhood Constellation: A Unified View of Parent-Infant Psychotherapy*. New York: Basic Books, 1995.

CHAPTER 9

Mother Figures: On Becoming the Mother One Wishes One Had

Meg Jay

In 1997, I wrote a letter to Nancy Chodorow. I had stumbled upon a copy of *The Reproduction of Mothering* in the stacks of the library at the University of Colorado, back when internet use was not widespread and one did still regularly stumble upon books. I was in the process of applying to graduate school in clinical psychology and was in search of faculty who were interested in the same areas that interested me: clinical work, psychoanalytic theory, gender. Nancy, it seemed, was just the person I was looking for. Email was not yet the customary way to introduce oneself so, in a move I can only describe as more naive than brave, I typed out a few paragraphs and sent them to Nancy—to Dr. Chodorow at the University of California, Berkeley, that is—by way of U.S. Mail. Looking back, I can only imagine what those paragraphs said as I am

This material has been adapted from *Supernormal: The Secret World of the Family Hero* by Meg Jay (Twelve, 2017).

M. Jay (✉)
University of Virginia, Charlottesville, VA, USA

P. Bueskens (ed.), *Nancy Chodorow and* The Reproduction of Mothering,
https://doi.org/10.1007/978-3-030-55590-0_9

certain that, even though I read *The Reproduction of Mothering*, at the time I could not possibly have understood it.

When Nancy wrote back, I was elated. She had taken the time to type up a few paragraphs, and to stamp and address an envelope, too. First and foremost, her letter was kind: she explained she was on faculty in the Department of Sociology and if I was admitted to the clinical psychology program I should get in touch; she taught classes on psychoanalytic theory and, as a practicing psychoanalyst, served as a clinical supervisor for psychology graduate students.

Maybe more importantly, her letter was encouraging—literally: it gave me the courage to see graduate school as more than just a fantasy, and she gave me the courage to see myself as a student at Cal who could knock on her door. I packed my car and headed to California before I was even admitted. Berkeley, I thought, here I come.

I did indeed become a student at Cal, one who knocked on Nancy's door. And, true to her word, Nancy served first as my clinical supervisor and then later as my dissertation co-chair. What follows, however, is not a summary of the work I did under Nancy. Rather it is a glimpse of—even a tribute to—how Nancy taught me to stand up for mothering, in my own life and, as a result, in the lives of my clients even years down the line. One of those clients is a woman I'll call Jennifer.

* * *

Jennifer came to my office after she quit treatment with another clinician. Some might take this to be a bad sign, that she was one of those clients who would never be satisfied or whose therapist could not do anything right. Perhaps. But, I realized, it might also be true that, either consciously or unconsciously, Jennifer knew what she wanted out of therapy, and she also knew that, thus far, she had not gotten it. This, in fact, can be a very good sign.[1]

Jennifer could point to the time her previous therapy ended, which was months before she actually stopped attending sessions. The defining moment took place when Jennifer told her therapist about a picnic she had attended with friends, many of whom had young children running about. Jennifer was a married woman in her early thirties who was trying

[1] Joseph Weiss, *How Psychotherapy Works: Process and Technique* (New York: Guilford Press, 1993), 131.

to decide whether she wanted to have children herself, a question she had never before felt "good enough" or "normal enough" to consider. At the picnic, Jennifer worried that the children there would intuit it somehow, that there was something wrong with her, that she was not fit to be around them.

Then, a few days later, in a therapy session, came this: "I told [my previous therapist] I should have been somebody's second wife so I could have skipped all that," Jennifer remembered. "Looking back, I'm not sure why I said that or what I even meant by that second wife comment. I guess I'll never know because she didn't ask me about it or challenge it in any way. She just nodded and I'm not sure if she seemed relieved I wasn't having kids, or I took it to mean she was relieved I wasn't having kids. Either way I felt like she let this view I had of myself stand, that I was not good enough or normal enough to have a family."

After that session, Jennifer dutifully kept her appointments, although she began to take more notice in the parking lot of her previous therapist's car, the one outfitted with children-sized booster seats. Now, it seemed to Jennifer, her therapist was the doctor, and she was the patient. Her therapist was sane, and Jennifer was crazy. Her therapist was normal, and Jennifer was not normal. Her therapist was a have, and Jennifer was a have not.

Sometime later, Jennifer gave the woman a fresh opportunity to take up her fears; in other words, she tested her therapist once again.[2] She mentioned another social event, this one a kid-friendly work function when Jennifer noticed herself just feeling at ease, surprising herself by frolicking with the sons and daughters of colleagues; one co-worker even asked if she was interested in babysitting. "Maybe I *could* be somebody's mother..." Jennifer said tentatively in a session soon after. Rather than seeing the hope that might have been building within Jennifer, her therapist saw the contradiction: "I thought you didn't want to have children," she said.

"I kind of hated her for that," Jennifer recalled, "and I never went back to see her again. I didn't know it at the time, but now I realize I wanted her to doubt my fear that I could never be a parent. I guess it was a useful therapy in a way because I walked away thinking that I wasn't going to be sold short like that. It made me realize she was wrong about me. I was wrong about me."

[2] Weiss, *How Psychotherapy Works*, 108.

* * *

When Jennifer was a child, her father backhanded her mother so often that, all her life in her mind's eye, she could see that particular crab-colored pinky-red hue, the look of flesh that had been slapped hard. When she was a little girl, she could not understand why her parents had married one another, although to hear her mother tell it, "Everything was fine until we had you. The day you were born your father stopped getting his way." This was puzzling to Jennifer because all she had ever known was his getting almost nothing but his way. The family ate his favorite foods and watched his favorite television shows. They tiptoed around his early bedtimes and pretended not to be bothered when he banged out of the house for his early predawn shifts at work.

Later, Jennifer would come to understand that, after twenty years in the military, Jennifer's father was more of a confirmed bachelor than an eligible one when he met Jennifer's mother, a vision-impaired woman with a high-school education. Jennifer's mother may have thought that being married was a bargain that would bring security, but Jennifer's father hated spending money he worked for on other people, so he often left his wife's and daughter's bills unpaid. Jennifer knew this because more than once she sat in the waiting room of her pediatrician's office, while the receptionist explained that, unless Jennifer's mother had cash, the girl could not be seen. After Jennifer had braces put on her teeth, her orthodontist refused to take them off until he was paid in full, which for a long time he was not. When Jennifer got her first period and told her mother she needed sanitary pads, her mother shrieked in a panic, "We can't ask your father for anymore money this week!"

On one unusual afternoon, Jennifer's mother declared she could sit on a threadbare couch not one more day and, with Jennifer's help, she dragged the hulking piece of furniture through the family room and hoisted it off of the railing of their back deck. When Jennifer saw it crash to the cement below with a thud, she felt hopeful, like something was going to change. When her father came home, he broke Jennifer's mother's arm, and now it was Jennifer who was shrieking in a panic, begging him to stop.

"Marriage is for better or worse," was all Jennifer's mother would say later.

* * *

In the middle of the twentieth century, Heinz Hartmann suggested that normal development takes place in what he called an "average, expectable" environment.[3] Something like what pediatrician and psychoanalyst Donald Winnicott referred to as a "good-enough" upbringing, the average, expectable environment is a home—or a school or a neighborhood—where there is enough safety, enough food, enough affection, enough peace, enough discipline, enough supervision, enough role modeling, enough attention, enough love, and at least one good enough parent or adult who cares.[4] In the good enough childhood, life need not be without problems as moderate, age-appropriate challenges are good for us. Still, according to Hartmann and Winnicott, those problems ought to be predictable and they ought to feel normal, whatever we as a culture think that might be.

Yet, ironically, the average, expectable environment that Hartmann envisioned maybe neither average nor expectable. Many more children than we might like to think wake up to what Hartmann called "above-average environmental burdens."[5] These are the most common adversities that children and teens face before the age of 20 (CDC):

Death of a parent or sibling
Divorce
Alcoholism or drug abuse in the home
Emotional abuse
Physical Abuse
Sexual Abuse
Having a parent who is mentally ill
Neglect
Having a parent in jail
Witnessing domestic violence

[3] Heinz Hartmann, *Ego Psychology and the Problem of Adaptation* (New York: International University Press, 1939), 23.

[4] Donald Winnicott, "Transitional Objects and Transitional Phenomena: A Study of the First Not-Me Possession," *International Journal of Psychoanalysis* 34 (1953): 93.

[5] Hartmann, *Ego Psychology and the Problem of Adaptation*, 23.

Considered individually, each of these experiences may affect only a minority of families, but considered together under the umbrella of childhood adversity, multiple studies in the United States and around the world suggest that up to 75 percent of children and teens are exposed to one of these events—or more—as one hardship often leads to another and another.[6]

Still, these might sound like problems that "other people" have, or ones that reside only below the poverty line, yet, the landmark study that stunned the medical community with just how prevalent and harmful these early stressors are—the Adverse Childhood Experiences (ACE) Study, begun in the late 1990s and sponsored by the CDC and Kaiser Permanente and conducted by co-principal investigators Vincent J. Felitti and Robert F. Anda—was an examination of nearly 18,000 mostly middle-class families. Of these, nearly two-thirds reported at least one of the aforementioned adversities, and almost half reported two or more.[7]

What this means is that, for too many children and teens, rather than a source of safety or security, home is the most dangerous place there is. For some, family is something to be survived and ultimately escaped, and escaping is what, as a teen, Jennifer ultimately did. "I tried to save my mom but she wouldn't listen so I had to save myself," Jennifer explained about the day when, not long after she turned 18, she fled her house and rushed toward the waiting car of a friend. "You'll understand one day when you have children!" Jennifer's mother shouted after her, like Jennifer was going to make the same choices, like her life was going to turn out just the same way.

[6] See Centers for Disease Control and Prevention (CDC), *Behavioral Risk Factor Surveillance System Survey Questionnaire, 2010* (Atlanta: U.S. Department of Health and Human Services, CDC.gov, 27 August 2017); Maxia Dong et al. "The Interrelatedness of Multiple Forms of Childhood Abuse, Neglect, and Household Dysfunction," *Child Abuse and Neglect* 28, no. 7 (2004): 771.

[7] Centers for Disease Control and Prevention (CDC) and Kaiser Permanente, *The ACE Study Survey Data* [Unpublished Data] (Atlanta: U.S. Department of Health and Human Services, CDC.gov, 2016); Vincent Felitti, et al., "Relationship of Childhood Abuse and Household Dysfunction to Many of the Leading Causes of Death in Adults: The Adverse Childhood Experiences (ACE) Study," *American Journal of Preventive Medicine* 14, no. 4 (1998): 249.

* * *

"Women mother," as Chodorow begins *The Reproduction of Mothering*, it is true (3); and, of course, it is also true that some women mother better than others. For those who were fortunate enough to have been raised in average, expectable homes by the good enough mothers out there, the notion of reproduction—and of the reproduction of mothering—may seem like a special form of empowerment. As Chodorow makes clear, "people's experience of their early relationship to their mother provides a foundation for expectations of women as mothers,"[8] so girls who were brought up by mothers who were able to enjoy mothering, and be good at it and gratified by it, have every reason to expect similar experiences for themselves. For other women, though, those who were not fortunate enough to be raised in average, expectable homes by good enough mothers, the notion of reproduction can be terrifying. Women like Jennifer are afraid to become mothers or, to be more accurate, they are afraid to become *their* mothers.

From what Jennifer's mother shouted on the day the girl left home—"You'll understand one day when you have children!"—Jennifer could expect to find herself similarly stuck one day, trapped in an unhappy marriage with a child she could not protect. Maybe—her mother seemed to be suggesting—she would even be a victim of domestic violence herself, or perhaps an abuser.

It does seem to almost go without saying that children who are raised in unhappy families are in grave danger of becoming like the adults with whom they live. But maybe worse than its going without saying is that there are countless everyday expressions to remind us that this is supposedly true. The apple does not fall far from the tree. Like father, like son. Like mother, like daughter. Violence begets violence. Water seeks its level. Monkey see, monkey do.

To be sure, children learn by observing others, and they often imitate—they reproduce—what they see. Among the best-known studies of observational learning are the groundbreaking experiments by Albert Bandura, a psychology researcher at Stanford University, involving the Bobo doll. A Bobo doll is an adult-sized blow-up doll, in the shape of a bowling pin and usually painted to look like a clown; it is weighted on

[8] Nancy Chodorow, *The Reproduction of Mothering: Psychoanalysis and the Sociology of Gender* (Berkeley: University of California Press, 1999 [1978]), 57.

the bottom such that if it is knocked over it will bounce back up again. In 1961, Bandura's subjects were preschoolers at the Stanford University Nursery School, some of whom were shown an adult physically abusing the Bobo doll—punching it, hitting it in the face with a mallet, and kicking it high into the air. Later, when these same preschoolers were able to interact with the Bobo doll, those who had seen an adult beat-up the Bobo doll were more likely to do the same.[9] The Bobo doll study is iconic in that it famously provided powerful data and imagery—photos of the adults and children beating up Bobo can be found in almost any introductory psychology text—to support the commonsense notion of "money see, monkey do."

Bandura's seminal work provided the theoretical foundation for what is commonly known as the "cycle of violence," or the widely held view that those who are exposed to some sort of abuse will become abusers or victims themselves.[10] The problem with the notion of the cycle of violence, or what is more formally known as the intergenerational transmission of abuse, is that it makes dysfunction sound like an infinite loop that one cannot get out of when, in fact, the evidence for the cycle of violence is rather sparse.[11]

Studies of the cycle of violence are rife with methodological problems, including being unable able to rule out other contributing factors such as poverty or alcohol or education, and relying too heavily on isolated case studies or extreme clinical samples such as families living in shelters. In one review that examined every study of the intergenerational transmission of abuse published between 1975 and 2000, only 10 out of 200 studies were adequately designed to make statements about causality and only one used a nationally representative sample; from these data, authors concluded that the evidence for the cycle of violence was inconsistent at best.[12] Similarly, a meta-analysis of intergenerational

[9] Albert Bandura, Dorothea Ross, and Sheila Ross, "Transmission of Aggression Through Imitation of Aggressive Models," *Journal of Abnormal and Social Psychology* 63, no. 3 (1961): 577.

[10] Cathy Widom, "Does Violence Beget Violence? A Critical Examination of the Literature," *Psychological Bulletin* 106, no. 1 (1989): 3.

[11] Ilgi Ozturk Ertem, John Leventhal, and Sara Dobbs, "Intergenerational Continuity of Child Physical Abuse: How Good is the Evidence?" *The Lancet* 356, no. 9232 (2000): 814.

[12] Ibid.

intimate partner violence conducted in the year 2000 concluded that a family history of violence had only a small-to-moderate effect on whether one would become involved in an abusive relationship in adulthood.[13] Further studies conducted since the year 2000 have found the relationship between family violence in childhood and adulthood to be weak, except in the severest of cases.[14]

What this means is that while a cycle of violence exists in a minority of families it does not exist in most. The majority of children exposed to violence will not themselves become involved in violent relationships, as too many other variables—individual strengths, positive aspects of their surroundings, other influential relationships—matter at least as much.[15] Importantly, this holds true for other types of abuse as well—whether that abuse is physical, emotional, sexual, or related to alcohol or drugs—and for other adversities that many fear might be handed down from parent to child. Although some who are sexually abused in childhood will go onto to become perpetrators, most will not (Salter et al. 2003).[16] Parenting style has not been shown to be passed cleanly like a baton from generation to generation[17] and neither has divorce.[18] Even for problems in which

[13] Sandra Stith, "The Intergenerational Transmission of Spouse Abuse: A Meta-Analysis," *Journal of Marriage and Family* 62, no. 3 (2000): 640.

[14] David Fergusson, Joseph Boden, and L. John Horwood, "Examining the Intergenerational Transmission of Violence in a New Zealand Birth Cohort," *Child Abuse and Neglect* 30, no. 2 (2006): 89; Timothy Ireland and Carolyn Smith, "Living in Partner-Violent Families: Developmental Links to Antisocial Behavior and Relationship Violence," *Journal of Youth and Adolescence* 38, no. 3 (2009): 323.

[15] Widom, "Does Violence Beget Violence?" 3.0.

[16] Ashley Jespersen, Martin Lalumière, and Michael Seto, "Sexual Abuse History Among Adult Sex Offenders and Non-Sex Offenders: A Meta-Analysis," *Child Abuse and Neglect* 33, no. 3 (2009): 179.

[17] Marinus Van IJzendoorn, "Intergenerational Transmission of Parenting: A Review of Studies in Nonclinical Populations," *Developmental Review* 12, no. 1 (1992): 76.

[18] Jaap Dronkers and Juho Härkönen, "The Intergenerational Transmission of Divorce in Cross-National Perspective: Results from the Fertility and Family Surveys," *Population Studies* 62, no. 3 (2008): 273.

heredity is known to play a role—such as depression[19] and alcoholism[20]—it is estimated that genes are only responsible for about half of the variance in the outcomes; the rest can be attributed to other factors within the person and the environment.

Taken together, the evidence for the "cycle of" of just about any kind of adversity is thin. It is far more accurate to say that what is passed down from father to son or mother to daughter is a risk for such problems, but being at risk for something is not the same thing as being destined for—or doomed to—any particular outcome. Like a family history of breast cancer or heart disease may increase by some margin the likelihood that we will experience similar health problems, in no way does it guarantee that we will suffer from these ills. In fact, awareness of the risks may even spur us toward making intentional, conscious, healthy, protective choices, and a family history of unhappiness can do the same.

Consider this parable that a minister shared with me; a tale about a father and sons that could be about a mother and daughters instead: Two brothers are raised in a home in which the father is an abuser and an alcoholic. One brother grows up to be a heavy drinker and a terror of a parent, while the other becomes an abstinent and gentleman who cares deeply for his partner and children. When asked by the minister how they think they came to be who they were, both brothers gave the same answer: "Given who my father was, how could I not?"

Where some see the inevitability of sameness, others see an imperative to be different.

* * *

Children do learn a lot from their parents—many do reproduce what they grow up with—but learning goes beyond imitation. In 1963, Bandura conducted a follow-up study to his famous Bobo doll experiment in which preschoolers witnessed an adult being aggressive against the Bobo doll, only this time the aggression was rewarded with praise and treats in one condition of the experiment, and in another condition the aggression was reprimanded and punished. Preschoolers who saw that aggression

[19] Falk Lohoff, "Overview of the Genetics of Major Depressive Disorder," *Current Psychiatry Reports* 12, no. 6 (2010): 539.

[20] Justine Campbell and Tian Oei, "A Cognitive Model for the Intergenerational Transference of Alcohol Use Behavior," *Addictive Behaviors* 35, no. 2 (2010): 73.

led to bad things were less likely to copy what they saw than those who saw that aggression led to rewards.[21] Though unfortunately lesser known that the original Bobo doll study, this experiment showed that even preschoolers pay attention not only to the actions of others but also to the consequences of those actions.

"A wise man learns from the mistakes of others,"[22] it is said. Although we tend to think of role models as those who show us the way forward, some of our most influential models serve as cautionary tales. We watch them go down paths that we decidedly do not follow. They are people we vow never to be. In one qualitative study of youth who had been exposed to domestic violence some, like Jennifer, worried that they too would wind up trapped in unhappy relationships yet even more said that they had learned from their parents' misdeeds.[23] They paid close attention to how their suitors conducted themselves, choosing to stay far away from those who reminded them of a troubled mother or father. Because they did not take good relationships for granted, some even felt particularly poised to make good and careful choices.

"To see the parent is not to be the parent," wrote Leonard Shengold in *Soul Murder*.[24] So it went for New York City mayor, Bill de Blasio, a man whose father returned from World War II a hero, only to become a distant alcoholic, before ultimately committing suicide when de Blasio was eighteen. By his twenties, de Blasio had changed his last name to the family name on his mother's side and, though he said there was a time when he questioned his ability to have a family himself, he went on to become a man for whom his partner and children are central. Looking back, de Blasio credits his father for his military service and with teaching him some "very, very powerful personal lessons in terms of how to live

[21] Bandura, Ross, and Ross, "Transmission of Aggression Through Imitation of Aggressive Models," 601

[22] Otto Von Bismarck, "Quotes by Otto von Bismarck." *GoodReads*. n.d.

[23] Hadass Goldblatt, "Strategies of Coping Among Adolescents Experiencing Inter-parental Violence," *Journal of Interpersonal Violence* 18, no. 5 (2003): 532.

[24] Leonard Shengold, *Soul Murder: The Effects of Childhood Abuse and Deprivation* (New Haven: Yale University Press, 1989), 315.

life."[25] From his father, Mr. de Blasio says, "I learned primarily negative lessons. I learned what not to do."[26]

Without question, the primary negative lesson, the most powerful "what-not-to-do" that those like Jennifer learn, is simply not to be a parent at all. Having a child is a choice, and one sure way to do life differently than one's parents is never to become a mother or a father. Knowing all too well that marriage may not work, that childhood may not be happy and that not all parents are up to the task, being a parent may seem especially risky to those like Jennifer. Some decide not to have children because they are tired of taking care of others—"I just want finally to live for me," said one client of mine—and this is a good thing to know about yourself.

But all too often, women—and men—who do not have good enough parents decide that the only way to "break the cycle" or "do things differently" is to opt out of parenting altogether. They feel abnormal, as if they are carrying a defective gene, and the only way to stop their sickness from being passed down to the next generation is not to reproduce. "Probably for the best that the family line ended with me," said one—quite depressed, excruciatingly lonely—woman in her 60s, a client of mine who, back when she was about Jennifer's age, decided not to have children because her own mother had been "a monster." From where I sat, across the room from her decades later, I was not sure that not having children had been "for the best" at all. Her mother had robbed her of her chance to be a child and then of her chance to be a mother. As a result, my client had never been able to discover—to experience—that she was not a monster too.

For Jennifer, there had indeed been something melancholy about the solution of remaining childless—the one she had floated like a trial balloon in her previous therapy several years before. It had never been so much that she did not *want* children as much as she thought that, because of the way she was parented, she may not be cut out to have them. And she worried that by having children she might become trapped somehow in a life like her mother's, and the cycle of abuse and unhappiness would go around again.

[25] Ana Sale, "Exclusive: Bill de Blasio Speaks with WNYC About His Father's Suicide," *WNYC*, 20 September 2013.

[26] Javier Hernandez, "From His Father's Decline, de Blasio 'Learned What Not to Do'," *New York Times*, 13 October 2013.

What Jennifer could not quite see—or trust—was that having a family of one's own is as much an opportunity to break with the past as to repeat it. She felt haunted by the words her mother shouted after her on the day she left home—"You'll understand when you have children!"—and this, Jennifer said, was what she feared most. "I don't want to understand my mother. To me, understanding her means excusing her. It means having a life so much like hers that I might do the same things. Nothing is more terrifying than the thought that I would have worked so hard to get away from how I grew up but then just wind up in the same place. If having a baby means that I have to be more understanding ... then I cannot do it."

When I suggested to Jennifer that, once she had children, rather than being more understanding of her mother, she might find she is even *less* understanding of the choices her mother made, she began to cry with relief. "When you told me that," Jennifer would say later, "all of a sudden, I felt freed up to be a mother—to be a *good* mother—like I didn't have to understand my mother and it didn't have to be the way she said."

* * *

One afternoon in Nancy's office—about two years before I was due to graduate and several years before I would meet Jennifer—Nancy and I sat and discussed the timeline of my dissertation and clinical internship. I had recently married so I mentioned—offhandedly, probably quite tentatively—something about finding time to have a baby too. Shuffling through some forms I had handed her, Nancy asked me how old I was, and when I said I was 34, she abruptly put the papers down in her lap—she stopped everything—and looked right at me: "You'd better get going!" she said.

I was stunned.

In the clinical psychology program at Berkeley, perhaps like at many graduate programs, having a baby was something that was seldom discussed and rarely encouraged. A short time after the aforementioned meeting with Nancy, I had a similar meeting with a male advisor who would be writing internship recommendations for me, too. I mentioned seeking a top-tier site, one that set me up to live in a town with good schools where I might like to raise children. Without even asking my age, he responded this way: "Aren't you a little young to be worrying about all that?" Children, it seemed, could—and should—be postponed.

Maybe the advisors I worked with—most of them male—were unaccustomed to thinking about one's biological clock, or maybe they were thinking about my professional clock instead. In academia, as in many careers, one's thirties are a "make-or-break" decade, a time when one moves "up or out." And, at least for women, children can be obstacles to moving up. Indeed, more than a decade of research at Berkeley by law professor Mary Ann Mason and colleagues has shown that there is a "baby penalty" for women but not for men.[27] Women lose time, money, and advancement for every child they have while sons and daughters have no such effect on men's careers. Too often, Mason says, children are "career killers" for women (Chronicle).

It should be noted that I did have one male faculty advisor with a new baby who was openly enthusiastic about having children—he recommended the joys of parenting to all who would listen—yet I observed it was his wife who did most of the caretaking (and who packed his sandwiches every day). In its details, this exception seemed to prove the rule. Having children was something that was sure to be an impediment to one's progress—or, to be more precise, as something that was sure to be an impediment to a female student's progress: there would be infants to care for and sandwiches to make. Or, at the very least, colleagues would *perceive* that, as a mother, one was now preoccupied by such tasks.

Maybe for this reason, when one of my fellow graduate students eloped, she never informed her (unmarried) male advisor. Like many female students, she worried about being "written off" when she announced she was married. When she became pregnant, she was too afraid to disclose this news too, certain her mentor would be angry, now seeing her as a waste of grant money and a waste of time. With no guidance on how to pursue both her professional and personal desires, she left the state and then the field.

Women mother, as Chodorow writes, and women mentor too; and it is also probably true that, on the average, women mentor differently than men. Maybe for the reasons that Chodorow outlines in *The Reproduction of Mothering*—that, for women, romantic relationships are often not enough, that women tend to cast a wider relational net—women are likely to enjoy meaningful, rewarding relationships with multiple others,

[27] Mary Ann Mason, "The Baby Penalty," *Chronicle of Higher Education*, 5 August 2013; Mary Ann Mason, Nicholas Wolfinger, and Marc Goulden, *Do Babies Matter? Gender and Family in the Ivory Tower* (New Brunswick: Rutgers University Press, 2013).

such as children, relatives, friends, clients, and even students (viii).[28] The result is that those who are mentored by women may be more likely to receive a certain, crucial, connected kind of help—help that makes room for professional ambitions and for relationships too.

Indeed, in a 2001 study researchers examined the mentoring relationships of nearly 200 graduate students at a University of California school, and divided the help these students received from their mentors into two categories: instrumental and psychosocial.[29] As the names suggest, instrumental help is practical in nature and includes professional coaching, and offering up opportunities to excel or advance; psychosocial help includes role modeling, empathizing, and counseling. While instrumental help was associated with publishing more papers, psychosocial help was associated with greater satisfaction in graduate school (338). Perhaps not surprisingly, female faculty were more likely to offer psychosocial support to their students than were male faculty (328).

To be sure, Nancy provided unparalleled instrumental help: She wrote countless recommendations; she introduced me to my writing group; she sponsored my attendance at conferences; she tested the rigor of my thinking; she offered up chance after chance. I can hardly think of a publication, grant, fellowship, or book contract that would have come to be without her. But, just as important, her mentoring was psychosocial too. She not only dared to be a woman who stood up for mothering as a concept; she dared to be a woman who stood up for *my* being a mother.

To some, Nancy's comment, "You'd better get going!" may seem presumptuous, but she was, of course, simply asserting one of *The Reproduction of Mothering*'s foundational claims: that "women by and large want to mother, and get gratification from their mothering" (7). To Nancy, becoming a mother was not about what one had to lose but about what one had to gain. With Nancy, there was no talk of baby penalties or career killers. There was just the clear and confident conviction that mothering was something worth doing. It was something *I* could do. It was something I should not miss.

[28] Chodorow, *The Reproduction of Mothering*, viii.

[29] Harriet Tenenbaum, Faye Crosby, and Melissa Gliner, "Mentoring Relationships in Graduate School," *Journal of Vocational Behavior* 59, no. 3 (2001): 330.

* * *

Some say children are like little scientists. They are born with a drive to make sense of the world in order to adapt to it, and in the process they develop theories about how things work. Cars go zoom. Cats go meow. Stoves can be hot, but are not all the time. When theories are proven again and again, they become beliefs that can be resistant to change. Although much of what we think of as learning involves getting to know the material world—or how things work—children form theories and beliefs about how people work too. Children who are abused learn that adults can be dangerous. Children of alcoholics learn that tempers may flare at any time. Those whose siblings have problems learn that babies can be born with devastating illnesses. Teens who are sexually abused conclude that relationships are not safe.

By the time they reach adulthood, children have made up their minds not only about the world but about themselves too, at least for the time being. One of the most common beliefs of this sort that those like Jennifer wrestle with is that, having not been raised in average, expectable, good enough homes, they are not good enough or normal enough to have families or homes of their own. "I'd not only never been in love, but I hadn't ever dreamed of it. It was something that existed for other people—people who had families and homes," said Marilyn Monroe in *My Story*, her memoir about growing up in foster homes after being orphaned by a mentally ill mother (89). Like a child who is raised in poverty learns that warm coats and shiny toys are for other kids, those who go without love or care learn that these are things that other people get to have, luxuries they may never know.

Sociologist and psychotherapist Lillian Rubin, whose father died when she was five years old, made a career out of studying children who transcended trauma.[30] One thing she found was that those who triumph over hardship do so, at least in part, because they have a quality she called "adoptability," or a knack for being taken in by others (11).[31] When life is difficult at home, or parents are not there, many children and teens find surrogate mothers or substitute caregivers.

[30] Paul Vitello, "Lillian B. Rubin, 90, Is Dead; Wrote of Crippling Effects of Gender and Class Norms." *New York Times*, 1 July 2014.

[31] Ibid., 11.

Yet, let's be honest. Lillian Rubin's term "adoptability" is a misnomer. In truth, most orphans, like Marilyn Monroe, never are adopted, and neither are most children or teens like Jennifer. Most, if they are lucky, are fostered by a variety of good people. They piece together good enough mothering—a weekend with this friend, a holiday with that relative, a week on this couch, a word of encouragement from that teacher, some advice from this mentor, a smile from that neighbor—like bricolage. They fashion better lives out of the scraps of the lives of others.

This pathway to mothering gets just one explicit mention in *The Reproduction of Mothering*: "A mother identifies with her own mother [or with the mother she wishes she had] and tries to provide nurturant care for the child," writes Chodorow.[32] But more often than we might realize, identifying with the mother one wishes one had is precisely the way—is the *only* way for some—that good enough mothering can be reproduced at all. It is through the good enough mother figures out there who are, those who are wittingly, and often unwittingly, fostering children not their own.

Jennifer said she felt like she came to therapy to be mothered in 45-minute increments. And, outside of therapy, she noticed herself watching older women and the things they did like tiny miracles. When her mother-in-law placed a wooden spoon across the top of a boiling pot of pasta, to keep the water from boiling over. Or when her boss at work said simply, offhandedly, "Don't drive in the snow, Jennifer. It's not safe." Or when a woman on an airplane quieted a young mother's crying baby, holding the squirming bundle up to her shoulder: "You're good at that," the young woman said; "I've had a lot of practice," the woman said back generously, taking care not to undermine the new mother's confidence. Jennifer said she felt like she was stealing moments of mothering like breadcrumbs to nourish her, or maybe she was saving them up to give to her child.

Moments like these may not seem like much to go on but, writes Maya Angelou in *I Know Why the Caged Bird Sings*, "the hero is that man who is offered only the crumbs from his country's table but by ingenuity and courage is able to take for himself a Lucullan feast."[33] Sometimes the hero is that woman, too, the one who dares to make a lot out of a little, who

[32] Chodorow, *The Reproduction of Mothering*, 90.

[33] Maya Angelou, *I Know Why the Caged Bird Sings* (New York: Random House, 2015), 120.

takes the bits mothering and the pieces of encouragement she receives and, from this, becomes a mother herself.

* * *

"Whenever people ask me about having children or not having children, I never tell them what to do. I simply say, 'There is no experience like having children.' That's all. There is no substitute for it. You cannot do it with a friend. You cannot do it with a lover. If you want the experience of having complete responsibility for another human being, and to learn how to love and bond in the deepest way, then you should have children."[34] These are the words not of Nancy Chodorow but of Morris Schwartz, the sociology professor who is the subject of the memoir by Mitch Albom, *Tuesdays with Morrie*, published in 1997. Some twenty years after *The Reproduction of Mothering*, Chodorow may have been glad to see that men, too, are touting the special power of parental love and care.

These are also some of the words I find myself wanting to say to every client or student who ponders having children of their own, even and especially those who, like Jennifer, did not grow up in average, expectable homes. When I first met Jennifer, women with children were the "haves" and she was a "have not." She had been a "have not" all her life, of course, deprived of even the most basic necessities from love and protection to medical care to sanitary pads. It seemed almost extravagant to imagine herself as a mother, not to mention as a good enough one. Especially for those who have lived with trauma, the ordinary can seem extraordinary.

In an interview on National Public Radio, author Jonathan Safran Foer recalled how his grandmother, a Holocaust survivor, spoke about what having children and grandchildren meant to her: "She would say, 'like other people have diamonds and pearls, you're my diamonds and pearls."[35] Jennifer's children—she went on to have two—were her diamonds and pearls as well, and she treasured moments she once could not imagine would be hers: when her son brought her handfuls of rocks like they were the most precious of gems, which, of course, they were; when she watched both children hop off the school bus and run headlong

[34] Mitch Albom, *Tuesdays with Morrie: An Old Man, a Young Man, and Life's Greatest Lesson* (New York: Broadway Books, 1997), 93.

[35] National Public Radio, "Jonathan Safran Foer on Marriage, Religion and Universal Balances," *Fresh Air*, 11 October (2016).

toward the house in stark contrast to the way she had once run away from her own; when she heard them racing to the dinner table as if every night was Christmas morning, excited with anticipation about whether their favorite foods might be served. "I don't remember having any favorite foods," Jennifer said, "much less having any hope that I might get them."

There were simple pleasures she had never known, like when her daughter returned from kindergarten with an "All About Me" worksheet on which in response to the prompt "I feel...." she wrote in her 6-year-old scrawl "peaceful at home." Seeing the world through the eyes of a happy child was something she had never done before. "I used to think because of the way I grew up I was less cut out than other people to be a parent. Now I think I may actually be more cut out for it than other people," Jennifer said about her experience of treasuring being a mother. "In the smallest ways, every day, I cannot believe this is my life."

I remember feeling something like that too, back in 2005, the year I graduated from Cal and the year Nancy retired from the sociology department. There was a celebration in her honor and, not surprisingly, it was attended by a rich and varied group of academics, clinicians, analysts, and children. Two of her students gave remarks while those in the audience held their infants. I spoke wearing my first baby in a Baby Bjorn.

As with the letter I wrote to Nancy so many years ago, I do not recall what I said when I stood up there that day. But I am pretty certain that I did not say what I now wish I had: that, whether she meant to be or not, Nancy was a mother figure who encouraged me to become a mother; and she and her work have given me permission to embolden my clients and students—even and especially those who did not have good enough mothers—to do the same. And, quite fortunately, this is how mothering reproduces itself too.

Bibliography

Albom, Mitch, *Tuesdays with Morrie: An Old Man, a Young Man, and Life's Greatest Lesson*. New York: Broadway Books, 1997.

Angelou, Maya, *I Know Why the Caged Bird Sings*. New York: Random House, 2015.

Bandura, Albert, Dorothea Ross, and Sheila A. Ross, "Transmission of Aggression through Imitation of Aggressive Models." *Journal of Abnormal and Social Psychology* 63, no. 3 (1961): 575–582.

———, "Vicarious Reinforcement and Imitative Learning." *Journal of Abnormal and Social Psychology* 67, no. 6 (1963): 601–607.

Campbell, Justine M., and Tian P. Oei, "A Cognitive Model for the Intergenerational Transference of Alcohol Use Behavior." *Addictive Behaviors* 35, no. 2 (2010): 73–83.

Centers for Disease Control and Prevention (CDC), *Behavioral Risk Factor Surveillance System Survey Questionnaire, 2010*. Atlanta: U.S. Department of Health and Human Services, CDC.gov, 27 August 2017.

Centers for Disease Control and Prevention (CDC) and Kaiser Permanente, *The ACE Study Survey Data* [Unpublished Data]. Atlanta: U.S. Department of Health and Human Services, CDC.gov, 2016.

Chodorow, Nancy J, *The Reproduction of Mothering: Psychoanalysis and the Sociology of Gender*. Berkeley: University of California Press, 1999 [1978].

Dong, Maxia et al., "The Interrelatedness of Multiple Forms of Childhood Abuse, Neglect, and Household Dysfunction." *Child Abuse and Neglect* 28, no. 7 (2004): 771–784.

Dronkers, Jaap, and Juho Härkönen, "The Intergenerational Transmission of Divorce in Cross-National Perspective: Results from the Fertility and Family Surveys." *Population Studies* 62, no. 3 (2008): 273–288.

Ertem, Ilgi Ozturk, John M. Leventhal, and Sara Dobbs, "Intergenerational Continuity of Child Physical Abuse: How Good Is the Evidence?" *The Lancet* 356, no. 9232 (2000): 814–819.

Felitti, Vincent J. et al., "Relationship of Childhood Abuse and Household Dysfunction to Many of the Leading Causes of Death in Adults: The Adverse Childhood Experiences (ACE) Study." *American Journal of Preventive Medicine* 14, no. 4 (1998): 245–258.

Fergusson, David M., Joseph M. Boden, and L. John Horwood, "Examining the Intergenerational Transmission of Violence in a New Zealand Birth Cohort." *Child Abuse and Neglect* 30, no. 2 (2006): 89–108.

Goldblatt, Hadass, "Strategies of Coping among Adolescents Experiencing Interparental Violence." *Journal of Interpersonal Violence* 18, no. 5 (2003): 532–552.

Hartmann, Heinz, *Ego Psychology and the Problem of Adaptation*. New York: International University Press, 1939.

Hernandez, Javier C, "From His Father's Decline, de Blasio 'Learned What Not to Do'." *New York Times*, 13 October 2013.

Ireland, Timothy O., and Carolyn A. Smith, "Living in Partner-Violent Families: Developmental Links to Antisocial Behavior and Relationship Violence," *Journal of Youth and Adolescence* 38, no. 3 (2009): 323–339.

Jespersen, Ashley F., Martin L. Lalumière, and Michael C. Seto, "Sexual Abuse History Among Adult Sex Offenders and Non-Sex Offenders: A Meta-Analysis." *Child Abuse and Neglect* 33, no. 3 (2009): 179–192.

Lohoff, Falk W, "Overview of the Genetics of Major Depressive Disorder." *Current Psychiatry Reports* 12, no. 6 (2010): 539–546.

Mason, Mary Ann, "The Baby Penalty." *Chronicle of Higher Education*, 5 August 2013.

Mason, Mary Ann, Nicholas H. Wolfinger, and Marc Goulden, *Do Babies Matter? Gender and Family in the Ivory Tower*. New Brunswick: Rutgers University Press, 2013.

Monroe, Marilyn and Ben Hecht, *My Story*. Lanham, MD: Taylor Trade, 2007.

National Public Radio, "Jonathan Safran Foer On Marriage, Religion and Universal Balances," *Fresh Air*, 11 October 2016.

Rubin, Lillian B, *The Transcendent Child: Tales of Triumph Over the Past*. New York: Basic Books, 1996.

Sale, Ana, "Exclusive: Bill de Blasio Speaks with WNYC About His Father's Suicide." *WNYC*, 20 September 2013.

Salter, Daniel, Dean McMillan, Mark Richards, Tiffany Talbot, Jill Hodges, Arnon Bentovim, Richard Hastings, Jim Stevenson, and David Skuse. "Development of Sexually Abusive Behaviour in Sexually Victimised Males: A Longitudinal Study." *The Lancet* 361, no. 9356 (2003): 471–476.

Shengold, Leonard, *Soul Murder: The Effects of Childhood Abuse and Deprivation*. New Haven: Yale University Press, 1989.

Stith, Sandra M. et al., "The Intergenerational Transmission of Spouse Abuse: A Meta-Analysis." *Journal of Marriage and Family* 62, no. 3 (2000): 640–654.

Tenenbaum, Harriet R., Faye J. Crosby, and Melissa D. Gliner, "Mentoring Relationships in Graduate School." *Journal of Vocational Behavior* 59, no. 3 (2001): 326–341.

Van IJzendoorn, Marinus H., "Intergenerational Transmission of Parenting: A Review of Studies in Nonclinical Populations." *Developmental Review* 12, no. 1 (1992): 76–99.

Vitello, Paul, "Lillian B. Rubin, 90, Is Dead; Wrote of Crippling Effects of Gender and Class Norms." *New York Times*, 1 July 2014.

Von Bismarck, Otto, "Quotes by Otto von Bismarck." *GoodReads*. n.d.

Weiss, Joseph, *How Psychotherapy Works: Process and Technique*. New York: Guilford Press, 1993.

Widom, Cathy S., "The Cycle of Violence." *Science* 244, no. 4901 (1989): 160–166.

———, "Does Violence Beget Violence? A Critical Examination of the Literature." *Psychological Bulletin* 106, no. 1 (1989): 3–28.

Winnicott, Donald, "Transitional Objects and Transitional Phenomena: A Study of the First Not-Me Possession." *International Journal of Psychoanalysis* 34 (1953): 89–97.

CHAPTER 10

The Production of Male Mothering

Leslie C. Bell

Mark greets me at the door with his ten-month-old daughter in his arms. She was supposed to be down for a nap but they are running late after preschool drop-off for his son earlier in the day. He apologizes that he needs to feed her a bit before she goes down. The table is piled with the detritus of young children—books, toys, and breakfast dishes. Plopping her in the high chair, he readies some food for her while she and I play with blocks. We start the interview and Mark seamlessly tends to his daughter while answering my questions. When she starts to fuss, Mark takes her upstairs for a nap. He comes back downstairs and we move to the living room where we carry out the rest of our interview.

What was so remarkable for me about this exchange was how unremarkable it is in the lives of the fathers I have interviewed who are full-time caregivers to their children. These fathers do not make jokes about being "Mr. Mom" or comment on their incompetence at changing a diaper. They also do not overplay their domestic skills, talking as though they deserve a medal for preparing a bottle and putting a baby to sleep. They talk in much the same way that mothers who are primary carers do—about the pleasure they take in spending time with their children,

L. C. Bell (✉)
The Psychotherapy Institute, Berkeley, CA, USA

P. Bueskens (ed.), *Nancy Chodorow and* The Reproduction of Mothering,
https://doi.org/10.1007/978-3-030-55590-0_10

the exhaustion they feel at the end of the day, the meaning they find in having significant and primary relationships with their children, and the tedium that can accompany the experience of caring for children.

And what is still noteworthy in this exchange is that I had it with a man. Mark had decided to be a "stay-at-home dad." No one had forced him to take on this role. He did not consider himself less of a man for doing it and he was not bitter or resentful about his choice. It was not the model that he grew up with—he had a stay-at-home mother and his father was the primary breadwinner. He had a successful career before having children. He was not just biding his time until his career prospects picked up. His wife was not domineering or controlling.

At the particular historical moment during which Chodorow wrote *The Reproduction of Mothering*, full-time mothering was at once idealized, expected, and reviled. It was also quite isolating. I believe that Chodorow (at the time) could not conceive of full-time mothering as freely chosen because it was so often imposed upon women who had few choices. Since Chodorow's writing in 1978, we have seen a proliferation of writing and thinking in both the academic and the popular press about the why's and how's of mothering—Why would lesbians want to mother?[1] Why do some women not want to mother?[2] How does the desire to mother look different depending upon race, class, and culture?[3] And how else might we understand the desire to mother under different economic and cultural conditions?

For my purposes, the question posed by another of Chodorow's students, Daphne de Marneffe,[4] is particularly apt. She asks: Might some women desire to mother not because of their unsatisfying relationships to men and their propensity for intimacy, but because attachment to,

[1] See, for example, Beverley Burch, *Other Women: Psychoanalytic Views of Women* (New York: Columbia University Press, 1997); Gibson Margaret, ed., *Queering Motherhood: Narrative and Theoretical Perspectives* (Bradford, Ontario: Demeter Press, 2014); Maureen Sullivan, *The Family of Woman: Lesbian Mothers, Their Children, and the Undoing of Gender* (Berkeley, CA: University of California Press, 2004).

[2] Meghan Daum, ed., *Selfish, Shallow, and Self-Absorbed: Writers on the Decision Not to Have Kids* (New York: Picador, 2016).

[3] Kathryn Edin and Maria Kefalas, *Promises I Can Keep: Why Poor Women put Motherhood Before Marriage* (Berkeley, CA: University of California Press, 2005).

[4] Daphne de Marneffe, *Maternal Desire: On Children, Love, and the Inner Life* (New York: Little, Brown, and Co., 2004).

nurturing of, and being depended upon by children is a rewarding, challenging, and satisfying experience? The men I have spoken with who serve as primary parent to their children would emphatically answer yes, and might argue that the question could easily be posed to both men and women. This is not to say that the psychoanalytic themes underlying Chodorow's argument in *Reproduction of Mothering* are misguided or incorrect. Merely that as the culture and society have changed in terms of the organization of work and family (to some degree), so too have the psychological explanations for serving as primary parent changed.

Reproduction of Mothering

I first read *Reproduction of Mothering*[5] in 1989 when I was 19 years old. At the time, I remember understanding about half of it but nonetheless feeling profoundly excited and understood as I read it. Like all great writing, the arguments seemed both basic and profound. I read it closely in graduate school as a student of Nancy Chodorow's at age 26, and I primarily engaged with it as a daughter and not a mother. Now at 48, I am a mother to thirteen and nine-year-old daughters and read it as a mother, a daughter, a psychotherapist, and a sociologist.

Now that I have done some research and writing myself, I am struck by the simplicity and brilliance of Chodorow's premise—that the reproduction of mothering needs to be explained. It is not natural. It is not just socialization. There is something else at the intersection of the psyche and culture that is needed to explain why mothering by women gets reproduced over and over.

Chodorow posed the original question that made possible subsequent explorations and understandings of the role of mothering in perpetuating gender. How is it that women come to want to be mothers, over and over again? Previously women's mothering had been described as natural because they give birth and lactate, but Chodorow sought to understand the psychology of mothering, under particular social, economic, and cultural conditions, beyond the biologically determinist view. Particularly if mothering is often a fundamental basis of gender inequality, why would women desire it?

[5] Nancy Chodorow, *The Reproduction of Mothering: Psychoanalysis and the Sociology of Gender* (Berkeley, CA: University of California Press, 1978).

Of central importance to the issue of women's desire to mother is the question of boys' and girls' connection to and separation from their mothers. Chodorow argues that parenting arrangements in the late twentieth century, in which women were primarily responsible for parenting and men went out to work in the public sphere and had limited parenting responsibilities, produced different personality structures in girls and boys. For both boys and girls, Chodorow argued that while mothers may be socially devalued, they are extremely powerful in children's eyes and experiences. The mother is the primary attachment figure in boys' and girls' early lives, and is therefore the person that both boys and girls most profoundly need in their early lives. The puzzle for Chodorow then became, how do boys and girls manage to connect to and separate from their own mothers, and how does this connection and separation look different in boys and girls?

Girls, in Chodorow's model, grow up with an experience of sameness and continuity with their mothers. Girls then must struggle intensely to attain a sense of separateness and individuation from their mothers. Heterosexual relationships for women are unlikely to be satisfying because of women's conflicts over closeness and separateness (based on their relationships with their mothers) and because of men's unavailability for connection and intimacy (based on their resolution of the Oedipal conflict). Women then have a need for attachment beyond heterosexual relations with men even if they are heterosexual, and Chodorow argued that they therefore mother and develop close attachments to their children, and the cycle continues.

Boys, on the other hand, grow up with an early experience of continuity with their mothers and a later experience of difference from their mothers once they come to recognize gender difference. Because of boys' experience of difference, they are more easily able to separate and individuate from their mothers. They identify with their fathers who occupy the public sphere and turn toward material achievement in the outside world both as a means of achieving gender identity and as a means of freeing themselves from their mothers' power. Later in life, men will desire to love and be close to women, grounded in the safe position in the public sphere that they have occupied. Heterosexual activity and relationships for men will likely be a satisfying return to the primary oneness originally experienced with their mothers.

When *Reproduction of Mothering* was first published, my mother was a full-time mother to me and my sister. She had been a superior student to my father in college, but there was no question that he would be the breadwinner and she the primary parent. In 1978, theirs was a typical arrangement. 47 percent of US couples who lived with children at the time looked like ours—a married heterosexual couple with children in which the father was the primary breadwinner and the mother the primary parent. Families in which women were the primary breadwinner and men the primary parent were rare and comprised only 2 percent of married couples with children living at home. By 2017, families with arrangements such as mine had in 1978 comprised only 27 percent of US married couples with children living at home. And families in which women are the primary breadwinner and men the primary parent, while still rare, now constitute 5 percent of married couples with children living at home. While most stay-at-home parents are mothers, fathers represent a growing share of all at-home parents—16 percent in 2012, up from 10 percent in 1989.[6] At the same time, the largest share of stay-at-home fathers (35 percent) is at home due to illness or disability. This is in sharp contrast to stay-at-home mothers, most of whom (73 percent) report that they are home specifically to care for their home or family; just 11 percent are home due to their own illness or disability.[7]

Much has changed since Chodorow first wrote *The Reproduction of Mothering* (1978). Women in the US participate in the workforce (and the public sphere in general) in much larger numbers and with far greater investment than they did in 1978. The intact nuclear and heterosexual family with a male breadwinner and female stay-at-home parent is no longer the primary family structure in which children are raised in the US. Men in the US participate in the parenting of their children with somewhat greater hours and investment than they did in 1978. And yet, men's participation in parenting has come much more slowly and with

[6] Gretchen Livingston, "Growing Number of Dads Home with the Kids: Biggest Increase Among Those Caring for Family" (Pew Research Center, 2014). Retrieved from http://www.pewsocialtrends.org/2014/06/05/growing-number-of-dads-home-with-the-kids/#fn-19605-4, June 5.

[7] D'Vera Cohn, Gretchen Livingston, and Wendy Wang, "After Decades of Decline, a Rise in Stay at Home Mothers" (Pew Research Center, 2014). Retrieved from http://www.pewsocialtrends.org/2014/04/08/after-decades-of-decline-a-rise-in-stay-at-home-mothers/, April 8.

more resistance than the other changes mentioned, and has been variously termed the stalled revolution (Hochschild, 1989), the unfinished revolution,[8] and the uneven revolution.[9]

The understanding of gender in the academy and in the public discourse has also exploded since 1978. Some people now describe themselves as along a gender continuum and often do not see gender as a binary system at all. The idea of requiring identification with a same-sex parent in order to develop "healthy" gender identification is now up for question. Could not a boy primarily identify with his female parent and still develop a masculine gender identification? Could not a girl primarily identify with her male parent and still develop a feminine gender identification? These are questions that Chodorow herself has subsequently explored in her later work.[10] And could not children of any sex identify with parents of any sex and develop a non-binary or fluid gender identification? Or a transgender identification? Some have developed the notion that gender fluidity and flexibility, not the rigid identification with one gender or another, is actually the ultimate developmental goal.[11,12,13]

The economy has changed, society has changed, and politics have changed. I am interested in the ways in which women's and men's identities have shifted in response to these changes wrought by the feminist movement, the LGBTQ movement, and changes in the economy. Has it happened, as Chodorow suggested that it would, that women's participation in the public sphere and men's participation in the private sphere have resulted in an end to the cycle of the reproduction of mothering? Are men just as likely to become and be invested in being the primary parent

[8] Kathleen Gerson, *The Unfinished Revolution: Coming of Age in a New Era of Gender, Work, and Family* (New York: Oxford University Press, 2009).

[9] Paula England, "The Gender Revolution: Uneven and Stalled," *Gender and Society* 4, no. 2 (2010): 149–166.

[10] Nancy Chodorow, *The Power of Feelings: Personal Meaning in Psychoanalysis, Gender, and Culture* (New Haven, CT: Yale University Press, 1999).

[11] Jessica Benjamin, *Like Subjects, Love Objects: Essays on Recognition and Sexual Difference* (New Haven: Yale University Press, 1995); *Shadow of the Other: Intersubjectivity and Gender in Psychoanalysis* (New York: Routledge, 1998).

[12] Ken Corbett, *Boyhoods: Rethinking Masculinity* (New Haven: Yale University Press, 2011).

[13] Virginia Goldner, "Toward a Critical Relational Theory of Gender," *Psychoanalytic Dialogues* 1, no. 3 (1991): 249–272; Virginia Goldner, "Ironic Gender/Authentic Sex," *Studies in Gender and Sexuality* 4, no. 2 (2003): 113–139.

of children as are women? Are women just as likely to work outside the home and be invested in their identities in the public sphere such that they do not turn toward their children and mothering as their primary source of identity and intimacy?

The Production of Men Who Mother

I am currently researching professional heterosexual couples in which the woman is the primary breadwinner and the man is the primary caregiver. Given that we have seen slower and less radical changes in men's participation in parenting than we have in women's participation in the workforce, I am curious to understand both the structural and the psychological factors that make some men more likely to take on a significant role in parenting. I am looking at professional couples with college degrees because I want to understand what makes it possible for men to freely *choose* to be primary parents—not because they are unemployed or disabled or have poorer job prospects than their partners but because they want to do the work of caring for their children.

At this preliminary stage, I have interviewed ten couples and intend to interview a total of fifty couples. I have found the couples using snowball sampling in the San Francisco Bay area, a unique region of the US in terms of its progressive gender politics, its booming tech economy, and its high cost of living. While these factors make the couples I am speaking with unusual in some respects—surrounded by people who do not view being a stay-at-home dad as an anomaly; earning higher than average salaries in their professions; and paying higher than average housing costs—they also arguably make these couples more likely to choose unconventional arrangements in terms of organizing work and family life. I conducted separate interviews with each member of the couple and used a semi-structured interview guide to ask about their history as a couple, their work history, their decision to organize work and family in the ways they have, their families of origin, their division of labor and their feelings about it, their decision-making as a couple and their feelings about it, their areas of conflict and compromise in their couple relationship, their experiences of gender, and what they want for their children in terms of work, family, and gender.

We have some quantitative data about the structural factors that matter in determining whether men share in parenting. Yarovsky et al. have found that the following six factors are significant in predicting that men will share in parenting: (1) higher education; (2) men's beliefs about gender roles (but not women's beliefs); (3) being financially dependent on a female spouse; (4) having a female spouse who works long hours, has spent many years getting an education, and has a higher income than the man; (5) men working in female-dominated fields; and (6) mismatch of schedules such that both parents are not home at the same time.[14]

While this quantitative data is informative, it does not tell us the psychological factors that are relevant in men deciding to be primary parents. If we apply Chodorow's explanation for the reproduction of mothering to men, in order to want to be a primary parent, a man would need to have the following psychological characteristics: (1) a capacity for empathy; (2) tolerance for attachment and dependency; and (3) a desire for intimacy.

The men I have spoken with who were most satisfied with their arrangement (they were not universally satisfied), did indeed have a capacity for empathy that they enjoyed exercising in the care of their children. There is a pleasure that many of the men took in understanding and being attuned to their children. Sometimes men described themselves as better suited to being the primary parent than their partner because of their greater empathy and patience than their partner. They also sometimes cited their higher capacity (than their female partners) to tolerate the frustration, boredom, and endless repetition that often characterize empathic parenting. This capacity for and desire to express empathy in the care of their children sometimes was born of identification with a parent who provided empathy for them, and sometimes originated in a determination to do things differently than their own parents, who did not provide adequate empathy when they were children.

All of the men I spoke with acknowledged that the needs of children were high and could feel overwhelming at times. These men had developed the capacity to tolerate the intense dependency and attachment that accompany being a primary parent. For many men this capacity was bolstered by a value they placed on care. Several men spoke of their desire to have a parent at home who could provide individualized care for their children and who could meet their children's intensive needs.

[14] Jill Yavorsky, Claire Dush, and Sarah Schoppe-Sullivan, "Production of Inequality: Gender Division of Labor Across the Transition to Parenthood," *Journal of Marriage and Family* 77, no. 3 (2015): 662–679.

The pleasure at having close relationships with their children came up in all of my interviews with men. They expressed pride and pleasure at being so closely involved in their children's lives, and at being a crucial part of their development. Some contrasted this with their own experience growing up with parents who were not physically or emotionally available to them—sometimes fathers, sometimes mothers. Others related this to their experience as children of parents who were close to them and were actively involved in their care.

In addition to these capacities, I have found a few other qualities that men need in order to want to serve as primary parent in their families. Gender flexibility characterizes all of the men I have spoken with. By flexibility I mean a different version of masculinity than the traditional one—financial provider, emotionally removed, powerful and domineering, intolerant of vulnerability, radically independent, sexually aggressive. Given the challenges to masculinity that primary parenting as a father presents, the men I spoke with often saw their version of masculinity as countercultural, as going against the capitalist grain with its focus on earnings and acquisitions, and as bucking expectations of what men can and should do. The men I spoke with generally admired and respected their successful female partners, whose accomplishments were a source of pride for their male partners. The men also saw their own contributions to the household as important and valuable—both for the care they provided their children and for the support they provided their female partners. While it felt complicated for many of the men I spoke with, they all managed to tolerate being financially dependent on a woman.

Given their female partners' relative success in the public sphere, it is not surprising that the men I spoke with also needed a strong sense of self and secure identity that could match their professionally successful female partners. These men often held primary responsibility for the domestic sphere and needed to maintain a strong sense of self without as large a public/work identity as their female partners had. In partnerships in which the woman had a very demanding work schedule of more than forty hours per week, female partners tended to look more like "traditional fathers" in their contributions to and knowledge of household labor. Partnerships in which the woman had a more contained work schedule of forty hours per week or less tended to look more egalitarian, with men and women contributing more equally to household labor. These men were not, as the social conservative movement in the

US would have us believe, weak in relation to their powerful female partners. They had often moved across the country for their female partners' work, and had continued to adapt themselves to the realities and limitations of her work schedule. And yet, many of them would explain these adaptations using functional language—their arrangement "works" and is "logical" for all involved, they are part of a "well-functioning machine." These men are generally involved in the major decisions in the family—financial, educational, and household. And they described feeling respected by their female partners.

In order for these arrangements to be successful, the men I spoke with described needing a secure relationship with a partner who values and appreciates the work they are doing as primary parents. When both forms of work—wage earning work and the work of caring for children—were valued by both members of the couple, men felt themselves to be making an important contribution to the family. When either or both members of the couple did not value the work of caring for children, men tended to feel more ambivalent about their role as primary parent.

These desires and capacities to be a primary parent did not seem to come from the same sources as they did for Chodorow's archetypal mother. What was striking about the men I spoke with is the degree to which they were not seeking to return to an experience of merger and closeness from their own early childhoods. If anything, they were often looking to have more intimacy and closeness with their children than they had with their own parents. They also seemed to have emotionally satisfying relationships with their female partners. While my data is still limited, it does suggest that if men who are primary parents do not have a solid sense of self with firm ego boundaries, and if their partner is not emotionally available, they could look similar to Chodorow's description of typical mothers from the 1970s—and become fathers who are overinvested in their relationships with children. If, on the other hand, men who are primary parents do have a solid sense of self with firm ego boundaries, and they have their emotional and relational needs met elsewhere, then their children will get their needs met, and will likely grow up not feeling the need for release from an early intense relationship with their father of need and dependency. In the arrangement Chodorow describes, mothering is about an exclusive relationship, socially isolated, in a context in which women's relational and intellectual competency needs are not met elsewhere, so mothering is their only recourse. The fathers I have spoken with do not fit this pattern.

In their relationships with their children, the men I spoke with who had sons were hoping to develop a more intimate relationship with them than they had with their own fathers. They were also hoping to raise boys who would be feminists, who would develop flexible versions of masculinity and appreciation for flexible versions of femininity. The men I spoke with who had daughters expressed pride at showing their daughters that men could be nurturing, relational, and supportive of strong and powerful women. They looked forward to raising girls who would be comfortable with ambition, power, and drive and who would expect the men in their lives to be comfortable with and supportive of them.

Chodorow's Enduring Contributions

In many ways my current study is an outgrowth of Chodorow's original contribution. The men I am studying were born in the late 1970s and early 1980s and are the products of the work/family arrangements and psychological development outlined by Chodorow. As adults, these men are still outliers, the men on the margins who are pushing the boundaries of traditional masculinity. But they are interesting precisely because they are *not* the norm. They show us how enduring are the patterns of reproduction that Chodorow outlines, and they show us what it takes, both structurally and psychologically, to interrupt the reproduction of mothering.

As we attempt to make sense of the versions of toxic masculinity that continue to permeate the culture, we need Chodorow's formulation now more than ever. Masculinity that denies and eschews dependency, vulnerability, relatedness, and need is at the core of a masculinity that grounds itself in violence, aggression, domination, and radical independence. Masculinity that defines itself in opposition to care, relatedness, and emotion keeps men tone deaf about the impact of violence, aggression, and domination.

One of Chodorow's primary contributions is providing us a way to think about how cultural, social, economic, and psychological forces interact in producing different versions of masculinity and femininity, and identity in general. Her insistence that the social and the psychological can never be isolated, that they always need to be considered together, has encouraged me and countless others to ask questions that probe deeper and more completely than we otherwise might.

Bibliography

Benjamin, Jessica, *Like Subjects, Love Objects: Essays on Recognition and Sexual Difference*. New Haven: Yale University Press, 1995.

———, *Shadow of the Other: Intersubjectivity and Gender in Psychoanalysis*. New York: Routledge, 1998.

Burch, Beverley, *Other Women: Psychoanalytic Views of Women*. New York: Columbia University Press, 1997.

Chodorow, Nancy, *The Reproduction of Mothering: Psychoanalysis and the Sociology of Gender*. Berkeley, CA: University of California Press, 1978.

———, *The Power of Feelings: Personal Meaning in Psychoanalysis, Gender, and Culture*. New Haven, CT: Yale University Press, 1999.

Cohn, D'Vera, "Gretchen Livingston, and Wendy Wang, After Decades of Decline, a Rise in Stay at Home Mothers." *Pew Research Center*. Retrieved from http://www.pewsocialtrends.org/2014/04/08/after-decades-of-decline-a-rise-in-stay-at-home-mothers/. April 8, 2014.

Corbett, Ken, *Boyhoods: Rethinking*. New Haven: Yale University Press, 2011.

Daum, Meghan, ed., *Selfish, Shallow, and Self-Absorbed: Writers on the Decision Not to Have Kids*. New York: Picador, 2016.

De Marneffe, Daphne, *Maternal Desire: On Children, Love, and the Inner Life*. New York: Little, Brown, and Co., 2004.

Edin, Kathryn, and Maria Kefalas, *Promises I Can Keep: Why Poor Women put Motherhood Before Marriage*. Berkeley, CA: University of California Press, 2005.

England, Paula, "The Gender Revolution: Uneven and Stalled." *Gender and Society* 4, no. 2 (2010): 149–166.

Gerson, Kathleen, *The Unfinished Revolution: Coming of Age in a New Era of Gender, Work, and Family*. New York: Oxford University Press, 2009.

Gibson, Margaret, ed., *Queering Motherhood: Narrative and Theoretical Perspectives*. Ontario: Demeter Press, 2014.

Goldner, Virginia, "Toward a Critical Relational Theory of Gender." *Psychoanalytic Dialogues* 1, no. 3 (1991): 249–272.

———, "Ironic Gender/Authentic Sex." *Studies in Gender and Sexuality* 4 (2003): 113–139.

Hochschild, Arlie, *The Second Shift: Working Parents and the Revolution at Home*. New York: Avon Books, 1989.

Livingston, Gretchen, "Growing Number of Dads Home with the Kids: Biggest Increase Among Those Caring for Family." *Pew Research Center*. Retrieved from http://www.pewsocialtrends.org/2014/06/05/growing-number-of-dads-home-with-the-kids/#fn-19605-4. June 5, 2014.

Sullivan, Maureen, *The Family of Woman: Lesbian Mothers, Their Children, and the Undoing of Gender*. Berkeley, CA: University of California Press, 2004.
Yavorsky, Jill, Claire Dush, and Schoppe-Sullivan, Sarah, "Production of Inequality: Gender Division of Labor Across the Transition to Parenthood." *Journal of Marriage and Family* 77, no. 3 (2015): 662–679.

CHAPTER 11

Full Circle with Chodorow: Reflections on Women's Desire and Lesbian Sexuality

Jade McGleughlin

The editor of this important volume honoring Nancy Chodorow asked me as a lesbian and mother to comment on what *The Reproduction of Mothering*[1] has said to me and how it has shaped my thinking over time. In 1986, I used Chodorow's foundational theorizing about women's development and the role of the mother–daughter relationship to think about the failure of the current psychological theory to shed light on women's sexual desire and to understand lesbian sexuality. Now, forty years later, I am still thinking about queer sexuality. I have departed from Chodorow in significant ways and would not rely on the language I used then, or its binary framing of gender, yet I realize that Chodorow's early thinking has remained the ground on which I, even unconsciously, play, negate, refuse, and embrace.

This essay will be organized in three sections: The first reviews my early work using Chodorow to trace difficulties in articulating women's desire. The second reviews issues of lesbian sexuality as they emerged in

[1] Nancy J. Chodorow, *The Reproduction of Mothering: Psychoanalysis and the Sociology of Gender* (Berkeley, CA: University of California Press, 1978).

J. McGleughlin (✉)
Massachusetts Institute for Psychoanalysis, Brookline, MA, USA

P. Bueskens (ed.), *Nancy Chodorow and* The Reproduction of Mothering,
https://doi.org/10.1007/978-3-030-55590-0_11

the Women's Liberation movement. Both were largely written in 1986. The third section, written 40 years later, is an unconscious tribute to Chodorow, highlighting the centrality of the mother–daughter bond. But it also includes a personal story, looking at how queer theory has contributed to my ideas about that bond and how my own mother's sense of sexual subjectivity potentially influenced my development both as a sexual subject and a psychoanalyst intent on understanding desire. My ideas are informed by Chodorow's ideas of the "reproduction of mothering," even as I ponder the value of the break from such generational inheritance.

Part One: Early Engagement with Chodorow

In 1986, I began a project called "The Freedom to Want Passionately: A Theoretical Exploration of Women's Desire." It revealed a gap between practical literature that addressed problems with sexual frequency in lesbian couples and theoretical literature that had not yet imagined women as having their own sexual desire. Although desire and sexuality constitute a major part of individual development, desire had been consistently constructed as male, and women's desire was seen in its shadow. Few authors at the time examined the sexual rather than the emotional component of lesbian relationships. If they did, they began with the problem of the *infrequency* of genital sexual contact for lesbians in long-term couples and suggested that relationships between women were not sexual enough because lesbians get caught in a never-ending Möbius strip of too close/too much alike.[2] Heterosexual couples, by implication, do not have the same propensity for fused relationships, remain differentiated, and have frequent sexual contact. What was a lesbian to do? Using a heterosexual model with gender bias, these theorists, though theoretically disparate, all proposed that lesbians needed more boundaries and greater

[2] John Gagnon and William Simon, *Sexual Conduct: The Social Sources of Human Sexuality* (Chicago: Aldine, 1973); Karla Jaye and Allen Young, *The Gay Report: Lesbians and Gay Men Speak Out about Sexual Experiences and Lifestyles* (New York: Summit Books, 1979); Letitia Anne Peplau and Hortensia Amaro, "Understanding Lesbian Relationships," in *Homosexuality: Social, Psychological, and Biological Issues*, eds. William Paul, James D. Weinrich, John C. Gonsiorek, and Mary E. Hotvedt (Beverly Hills, CA: Sage, 1982), 233–247; Victoria A. Vetere, "The Role of Friendship in the Development and Maintenance of Lesbian Love Relationships," *Journal of Homosexuality* 8, no. 2 (1983): 51–65.

individual autonomy; in doing so, they bypassed Chodorow's important work in *The Reproduction of Mothering*[3] about how women develop their sense of self in relationships. By equating ***differentiation*** with ***autonomy***, the fusion theorists defined autonomy in a way that is incompatible with women's development. They failed to theorize women's sexual desire and ignored the reality of male power to define and dictate women's sexuality.

I argued that this explanation for the desexualization of lesbian relationships was inadequate. It assumed that desire would not be a problem for women if fusion did not occur in relationships, yet this literature could not account for the frequently documented problem of desire in heterosexual women. When studies looked at women's desire in heterosexual relations with frequent sexual contact between partners, satisfaction among women was quite low. Heterosexual women often felt they had to adapt to male sexuality (focused on genital contact) when what they wanted was a feeling of closeness better expressed in cuddling and other forms of foreplay. When women were assigned sexual initiative, both frequency and satisfaction suffered.[4] These data raise fundamental questions about women's desire in the absence of male power. The problem of desire for heterosexual women did not appear to be one of fusion with their sexual partners. Therefore differentiation, as expressed in heterosexual relationships, was not the key to missing desire among lesbians.

By looking at frequency rates as the measure of satisfaction in lesbian relationships, I argued, fusion authors confused what Jessica Benjamin[5] calls "alienated desire" with sexual subjectivity for women and disregarded the problem of desire. The solution had to start with a deeper exploration of women's desire, not in a theory of lack. A theory of women's desire necessarily starts with a theory that examines gender difference in the formation of adult personality, which Chodorow aptly provided. My project became an inquiry into the character of women's desire (whether in heterosexual or lesbian relationships), in an attempt to illuminate the deeper factors that may underlie women's lack of sexual subjectivity.

[3] Chodorow, *The Reproduction of Mothering*.

[4] Philip Blumstein and Pepper Schwartz, *American Couples: Money, Work, Sex* (New York: William Morrow, 1983).

[5] Jessica Benjamin, "A Desire of One's Own: Psychodynamic Feminism and Intersubjective Space," in *Feminist Studies/Critical Studies*, ed. Teresa de Lauretis. Bloomington, IN: Indiana University Press, 1986, 78–101.

The work of Chodorow,[6] both sociologically and psychoanalytically, was seminal to my 1986 project.

By now we are familiar with how Chodorow importantly reimagined the preoedipal period as crucial for both men's and women's development and her placing the mother at the center of such development. Her work[7] exposed that our culture's celebration of individuality was a gender-related project. She did this by critiquing the way men's developmental pathway, resulting in the capacity for autonomy (and individuation), is valued over the development of relational capacities in women. In doing so, she turned norms of health and pathology on their heads. Chodorow redeemed what had been devalued in women's domain—qualities of relatedness, connection, and attachment. She told us that crucial differences in development occur for girls and boys as a result of parenting arrangements, and that this development gives women and men dissimilar, even conflicting, needs. Ultimately, it also leaves women unsatisfied in heterosexual relationships. For Chodorow, the girl's identification with her mother and the relational capacities that engenders means that women's relational needs may not feel met by heterosexuality and they will turn to mothering their children to fulfill their desire for connection.

Chodorow's original impulse to show that women do not fail to desire appropriately but instead have different relational needs, detoured into an examination of men's inability to meet women's relational rather than sexual needs. While Chodorow's theory of development *explains* women's lack of sexual agency, it does not *challenge* it. She saw that women, without agency and in the shadow of male-defined sexuality, took up empathy and connection as their counterpart in the sexual schema. But by focusing on generational inheritance—how women develop the intrapsychic desire to mother in part to compensate for their unmet relational needs—Chodorow unwittingly left us without a model of how a girl might develop sexual agency. The subject of female desire, defined always by its phallic or mothering organization, was muted in importance. This critique was first put forward by another psychoanalytic feminist, Jessica Benjamin. Benjamin questioned whether identification with a largely desexualized mother as a source of femininity undermines the

[6] Chodorow, *The Reproduction of Mothering*.

[7] Nancy J. Chodorow, "Oedipal Asymmetries and Heterosexual Knots," *Social Problems* 23, no. 4 (1976): 454–468; Chodorow, *The Reproduction of Mothering*.

possibility of women's agency and accepts the deprivations of subjectivity, and particularly loss of sexual agency.

Benjamin's 1985 manuscript, on which I based my 1986 thesis, turned out to be her groundbreaking *Bonds of Love*.[8] It traced how women's desire had been alienated through splitting, in which contradictory strivings are assigned to different objects. The mother becomes the *object of desire* and the father the *subject of desire* in whom one recognizes oneself. Men hold desire and women hold relationships in a power-divided society both materially and symbolically. A critique of splitting was used to explore the division between desire and relationship and to explain why women have been relegated to being objects of desire rather than subjects or agents of their own desire. Benjamin suggested that desire has only been expressed by women through alien offshoots of idealization, submission, and envy.[9] Denied access to being the hero, or subject of desire, women become subsumed in winning the love of the idealized other, in being desirable to him; ideal love, then, consists of worshipping a powerful male as a way to have access to the qualities a hero possesses.

Benjamin conceptualized women as coming to have desire of their own through the then-novel and now widely recognized idea of *intersubjectivity*. In her model of intersubjectivity, women need a place to both experience their own desire *and* have it recognized by another as theirs, but because women had largely been desexualized and disempowered, mothers are unable to recognize their daughters as subjects of desire. Only fathers have the power to recognize. Fathers, defined as subjects and the carriers of desire, will, agency, freedom, excitement, and engagement in the world, deny their daughters the possibility of identificatory love. For Benjamin, a girl's turn to her father reflected more than a solution to the crisis of separation with the mother, as suggested by Chodorow; it reflected the genuine wish to identify with and be recognized by the figure who represents power. If denied that recognition, she like her mother, can only be the object of desire.

[8] Jessica Benjamin, *The Bonds of Love* (New York, Toronto: Pantheon Press, 1988).

[9] Benjamin, "A Desire of One's Own: Psychodynamic Feminism and Intersubjective Space".

Identification with the father could allow the developing girl a sense of agency, but it would be a stolen agency bought at the price of culturally defined "secure" gender identification, which, for Benjamin,[10] is the second way women are alienated from desire. Much of the psychoanalytic theory, before feminist and queer revisions, saw male-identified women as "the third sex" who had wrong gender identification and, subsequently, faulty object choice.[11] While the path of male identification might be possible, Benjamin argued it maintains splitting by allowing women to identify with only one gender.

How might a woman develop as a sexual subject who experiences desire and has agency? For Benjamin, an intersubjective mode challenged "the differential meanings of mother and father, rooted in the early acquisition of gender, shaped by the earliest splitting of the psyche."[12] In development, ideally, the mother creates a holding space that Benjamin saw as akin to Winnicott's transitional space, an intermediate or potential space existing between inner and outer worlds.[13] Here, given safety without intrusion, the infant can be in a state of relaxation…where its own impulses or drives are experienced as real and coming from within. However, the experience of having a sense of self, of knowing who I am, requires a second step: a subject powerful enough to name their desire as theirs.[14] Benjamin described the boy who is able to discover his desire because the mother provided the holding space and the father provided the recognition. For the girl, however, desire is foreclosed because she only had access to the holding mother, and no one to recognize her desire, since the mother was not a subject in her own right and father rejects her identification. Identification with the mother means a *loss* of subjectivity.

[10] Ibid.

[11] Joyce McDougall, *A Plea for the Measure of Abnormality* (New York: International Universities Press, 1980).

[12] Benjamin, "A Desire of One's Own," 99.

[13] Donald W. Winnicott, *The Maturational Process and the Facilitating Environment: Studies in the Theory of Emotional Development* (New York: International Universities Press, 1965), 41.

[14] Benjamin, "A Desire of One's Own."

Benjamin's intersubjective formulation contrasts with Chodorow's formulation of development of subjectivity in which the infant uses the Other as a need-gratifying object to construct "an internal set of unconscious affectively laden representations of others in relation to itself" and an internal sense of self in relationship.[15] Chodorow argued that the child learns to perceive herself as separate through a process of fusion, separation, and refusion with the mother. Benjamin, instead, emphasized the real experience of interacting with another *subject* in which autonomy is rooted in relationship, and differentiation and connection are held in tension. Benjamin explained that if two people recognize each other as subjects an "autonomous selfhood develops and is later confirmed chiefly by the sense of being able to affect others by one's own actions and be recognized as such."[16] Having a sense of self, being a subject, allows the possibility of owning desire.

While Chodorow believed that changing parenting arrangements could crucially refigure development, ultimately her theory did not grapple adequately with the psychic reproduction of symbolic meaning as Benjamin's had begun to (which is beyond this paper to describe). Neither theorist could conceive of the impending explosion of categories of sex and gender and the potential for revolutionary change that would follow.

My 1986 work argued that if it is only in recognition from the Other that one develops a sense of self and agency, the solution for women to problems of desire would not be located in greater differentiation outside of relationship, as Chodorow's work helped underscore, but in the development of greater subjectivity within relationship, in which a woman may become the subject of desire. Psychoanalysis, Benjamin offered, creates the possibility of an intersubjective space. It provides both the safe holding environment in which desire is allowed to emerge freely and a recognizing Other (the analyst) to allow one to experience those desires as one's own.[17] My project emphasized a second kind of intersubjective space—one that I believed allowed both Chodorow and Benjamin to postulate their new models: the transformational possibilities of collective

[15] Nancy J. Chodorow, "Gender, Relation and Difference in Psychoanalytic Perspective," in *The Future of Difference* (Newark: Rutgers University Press, 1985), 11.

[16] Jessica Benjamin, "The Bonds of Love: Erotic Domination and Rational Violence," *Feminist Studies* 6 (1980): 47.

[17] Benjamin, "A Desire of One's Own: Psychodynamic Feminism and Intersubjective Space."

movements. Because my 1986 project suggested that the Women's Liberation Movement was an important place where subjectivity, agency, and desire could develop, I examined changes and also tensions that stymied a feminist-defined sexuality. My project sought to highlight the presence of lesbians, lesbian desire, and lesbian sexuality in that Movement.

Part Two: The Power of a Movement to Transform Sexuality

A project in 1982[18] had led me to read hundreds of Women's Liberation, Gay Liberation, and Black Liberation newspapers, which sharpened my understanding of the power of social movements to produce radical change. But I had not yet tied social movements to the development of personal agency and sexual subjectivity. In the 1986[19] project, through the lens of intersubjectivity, I came to see that the Women's Liberation Movement allowed the blooming of not just political transformation but personal agency and desire as well. Interestingly, the work of both Chodorow[20] and Benjamin (1980, 1986)[21] grew out of the existence of the modern Women's Liberation Movement. Not only did that movement bring a critical discussion of gender and sexuality into the public sphere, but it radically transformed women's relationships with one another in a way that allowed women to develop at least partial subjectivity and agency. Those critical discussions, the value placed on women's relationships, and the burgeoning sense of women's agency (including sexual subjectivity) that accompanied the movement, I argued, meant that a collective movement could and should be considered an intersubjective space akin to Benjamin's model.

That work documented that the movement offered women a safe space, a transitional space, relatively free from male presence and traditional mores. In this space women had the freedom to create, imagine,

[18] Jade McGleughlin, "Power, Liberation and Sexuality" (Division Three thesis, Hampshire College, 1982, Amherst, MA).

[19] Jade McGleughlin, "The Freedom to Want Passionately: A Theoretical Exploration of Women's Desire" (thesis, Smith College School for Social Work, 1987).

[20] Chodorow, "Oedipal Asymmetries and Heterosexual Knots," in *The Reproduction of Mothering*.

[21] Benjamin, "A Desire of One's Own," in *The Bonds of Love* (New York: Pantheon, 1986).

and discover themselves. Without men to establish the value of women, their work, and their sexuality, women within this movement became subjects with the power to recognize each other. Women's relationships to each other were radically transformed, and in that transformation, subject met subject. With subjectivity came agency, the ability to act on erotic urges in the world rather than submitting to an imposed ideal.

In fact, the movement emerged partially in response to a crisis of sexuality and what some women were calling oppressive institutions: the family and heterosexuality.[22] The impulse and energy of the early movement shifted the ground, creating the possibility of refusal, and opened new possibilities for women's desire. A space opened for imagining a sexual practice that disrupted cultural codes. This explosive discussion generated whole new ways for women to disrupt the passive reproduction of oppressive sexual lives and to transform the intimate terrains where sexuality is lived out.[23] The possibilities for sexual agency and satisfaction beckoned. While the terrain was deeply personal and private, it was also part of larger political struggle for liberation. The early movement, then, provided a glimpse of intersubjectivity, which gave feminist theorists like Chodorow and Benjamin a different context from which to challenge the norms of the culture. Feminism elevated women to subject status and allowed them to know and assert the power of female desire in a myriad of forms.

However, as the cultural, political, and interpersonal contexts shifted, so did discussions around sex. For a variety of complicated reasons that have been written about extensively,[24] a paralysis set in when it came to developing a feminist politics of sexuality. The early Women's Liberation Movement started by addressing the most oppressive aspects of heterosexuality, and many women's liberationists came out of a Civil Rights and New Left tradition where what passed for sexual freedom was actually

[22] Betty Friedan, *The Feminine Mystique* (New York: W. W. Norton, 1963). See also Germaine Greer, *The Female Eunuch* (London: MacGibbon & Kee, 1970).

[23] Jill Lewis and Gloria Joseph, *Common Differences: Conflicts in Black and White Feminist Perspectives* (Garden City, NY: Anchor Books, 1981).

[24] Alice Echols, "The Taming of the Id: Feminist Sexual Politics, 1968–83," in *Pleasure and Danger: Exploring Female Sexuality*, ed. Carol S. Vance (Boston: Routledge & Kegan Paul, 1984), 50–72; Lewis and Joseph, *Common Differences*; McGleughlin, "Power, Liberation and Sexuality"; Carole S. Vance, ed., *Pleasure and Danger: Exploring Female Sexuality* (Boston: Routledge & Kegan Paul, 1984).

another set of demands to accommodate male sexuality.[25] Consciousness-raising groups revealed not private or random difficulties individual women had with sexuality but rather showed that sexual oppression was built into the fabric of white American culture.[26] The responses to the movement's analysis of institutionalized and personal heterosexuality varied.

Importantly, a trend had developed during the 1970s in which a definition of lesbianism was based on political ideals as much as on women's sexual desire for one another. There was a curiosity about the new bonds between women that were being created, including an exploration of women's desire for one another. Many women experimented with erotic relationships. (Both Chodorow and Benjamin seemed to ignore this aspect of the movement.) A tension emerged. For some, the movement provided a context in which they could acknowledge their sexual desire for other women. Some of these women ultimately identified themselves as gay and began developing a new lesbian identity on the margins of both the feminist and gay liberation movements. For other women, these same-sex relationships emerged out of the valuing of female bonding within a feminist political and social context.[27]

They felt the need, in an effort to combat an idea of sex that had been based on male demand, to constitute something other than what had been oppressing them. As the poet, political theorist, and radical feminist Robin Morgan wrote in 1974:

> Every woman knows in her heart the vast differences between her sexuality and that of any patriarchal-trained male or straight. That has always been a source of pride in the lesbian community that the emphasis on genital sexuality, objectification, promiscuity, non-emotional and tough invulnerability were the male style and we as women placed greater trust in love, sensuality, humor, tenderness, strength, and commitment.[28]

[25] Marge Piercy, "The Grand Coolie Damn," in *Sisterhood Is Powerful: An Anthology of Writings from the Women's Liberation Movement*, ed. Robin Morgan (New York: Vintage Books, 1970), 473–492. See also Germaine Greer, *The Female Eunuch.*

[26] Lewis and Joseph, *Common Differences.*

[27] Echols, "The Taming of the Id"; Joan Nestle, "Butch-Fem Relationships: Sexual Courage in the 1950s," *Heresies* 3, no. 4, 12 (1981): 21–24.

[28] Morgan, "The Taming of the Id," 59.

Lesbianism and lesbian sex got constituted as an ideal sexuality. This vision of lesbianism imagined women engaging in egalitarian, struggle-free relationships with diffuse sex.[29] Women who entered into lesbian feminism entered into a certain set of "feminist" norms and ways of being. What part these values played in the actual sexual life of lesbians at that historical juncture is unknown but many of the studies on lesbian sexuality, including Blumstein and Schwartz's,[30] retain an ideal of egalitarian, power-free lesbian sex. Their view of women's desire clashed with those of women whose sexual desire for other women was a deeply rooted part of their identity.[31]

In particular, there was tension with lesbians in communities that predated feminism. The 1970s conflation of lesbianism and feminism was anathema to 1950s lesbians, many of whom lived and socialized in erotic communities structured primarily around sexual desire. Further, the feminist critique of male/female gender roles was extended to butch–femme relationships, which insulted many lesbians for whom butch–femme relations had been a way of life, especially working-class lesbians in large urban areas.[32] Some believed that ideological roots of lesbian identity that emerged from the Women's Movement often overshadowed the importance of sexual desire[33] and marginalized gay women within the Women's Movement.[34] Sexual desire became a contested arena as the Women's Movement attempted to define a "women's sexuality."

Such tensions were accompanied by class and racial tensions. Working-class lesbians articulated a feeling of erasure by middle-class lesbians. By the late 1970s, Black women were articulating the way the (white) Women's Liberation movement did not always speak to them. Black women's liberation would always be tied to Black Liberation radically

[29] Echols, "The Taming of the Id."

[30] Blumstein and Schwartz, *American Couples*.

[31] McGleughlin, "Power, Liberation and Sexuality."

[32] Madeline Davis and Elizabeth Kennedy, "Oral History and the Study of Sexuality in the Lesbian Community, Buffalo, New York, 1940–1960." *Feminist Studies* 12, no. 1 (1986).

[33] McGleughlin, "Power, Liberation and Sexuality."

[34] Nestle, "Butch-Fem Relationships: Sexual Courage in the 1950s."

shifting the terms of sexual oppression and necessarily rejecting the separatism some white feminists espoused.[35] Black feminism also highlighted the role of structures in constituting the conditions of life for racially and economically marginalized women.[36] Those actual structural differences were radically different across race, shaped sexual identities, influenced women's access to power and exclusion, and informed how those identities could be used for political change.[37] Powerful work by women of color opened the movement to ideas of intersectionality. The Combahee River Collective[38] taught that identities are not distinct but always permeated by other categories, fluid and changing, in the process of creating and being created by dynamics of power. They urged intersectional analysis about "the problem of sameness and difference and its relation to power" (2013).[39] This framing, as Crenshaw et al write, emphasizes what intersectionality does rather than what intersectionality is.[40] Some women of color prioritized multi-issue organizing over an autonomous women's movement.

While internal divisions over race and sexuality were very much alive, shifts in perception in mainstream culture precipitated by feminist thought and activism were soon challenged by ideas of the New Right which quickly laid the groundwork for a regressive sexual agenda and the valorization of the heterosexual nuclear family throughout the 1980s. Opposition to abortion was their most widely publicized effort, but they also opposed, and gained ground against, sex education, contraceptive access for young people, premarital sex, easy divorce, and gay and lesbian liberation. Their campaign was explicitly anti-feminist, countering the

[35] Lewis and Joseph, *Common Differences*.

[36] Bell Hooks, *Feminist Theory: From Margin to Center* (Boston, MA: South End Press, 1984).

[37] Kimberlé Crenshaw, "Mapping the Margins: Intersectionality, Identity Politics, and Violence against Women of Color," *Stanford Law Review* 43, no. 6 (July 1991): 1241–1299.

[38] Combahee River Collective, "The Combahee River Collective Statement," in *Home Girls: A Black Feminist Anthology*, ed. Barbara Smith (New York: Kitchen Table Women of Color Press, Inc., 1983).

[39] Sumi Cho, Kimberlé Williams Crenshaw, and Leslie McCall, "Toward a Field of Intersectionality Studies: Theory, Application and Praxis," *Signs* 38, no. 4 (2013): 795.

[40] Cho et al., "Toward a Field of Intersectionality Studies: Theory, Application and Praxis," *Signs* 38, no. 4 (2013).

notion of women as sexual beings and framing women's sexuality as limited to reproduction functions.

Fissures within the Women's Movement, in combination with attacks by the New Right, meant that issues like abortion, once understood marginally in terms of the right to have sex, was diluted to a legalistic "right to choose." Similarly, if new eros allowed women to explore their own sexuality and their own relationship to desire, fantasy, and violence, the anti-pornography movement refocused attention on women's relationship to male power and violence, further questioning women's agency. The 1986 project,[41] noted that the possibility for intersubjective space was less and less in women's lives, as intimate relationships were once more privatized amid a shrinking sense of community. Conversations that once took place in consciousness-raising groups about sexual practice and desire were relegated again to private discussions to be had by the individual woman, or couple, with her/their therapist.

For some feminists, works such as Chodorow's, once radical, in this new context seemed to symbolize a privatization of women's struggles. Housman[42] wrote that Chodorow's work, offered as a partial explanation for the social creation of men and women, now became a formula for change through altered family structures. "Women's ability to act for changed relationships between the sexes was seen to lie in their role as mothers and within individual struggles with men concerning parenting. Absent was the acknowledgement of the powerful political meaning that female bonding had taken on in the context of the Women's Liberation Movement."[43]

At the same time that women in the 1980s confronted the diminishing possibilities of what the Women's Movement had represented about the hope of a transformed relationship to desire, to other women and to community, a growing public discussion about issues of desire began to reemerge. Fresh discussions of sexuality, particularly within gay, progressive feminist, and leftist circles aimed at uprooting an idea of women's sexuality that prioritized women's relational needs over their sexual desires, and contesting the idea that sexuality was dangerous terrain

[41] McGleughlin, "The Freedom to Want Passionately".

[42] Judith Housman, "Mothering, the Unconscious and Feminism," *Radical America* 16, no. 6 (1982): 47–62.

[43] Ibid., 49.

for women, rather than a site of pleasure.[44] These discussions countered Chodorow's schema, which saw women's unmet needs as primarily relational; they also questioned whether Benjamin's assertion that desire had only been expressed in alienated forms held true for lesbians.

Increasing dialogue in gay, feminist, and leftist journals and conferences on the subject of sex and desire contributed to new language to describe sexual encounters that never fit comfortably within the lesbian feminist ideal of soft, diffuse, friendly, mutual, egalitarian sex, and were left out of psychological lesbian literature. One such exploration into the realm of lesbian desire was the embracing of butch–femme relationships as a model of sexual subjectivity for lesbians. "Old world" lesbians were sexual agents who took responsibility for their own sexual desire prior to feminism. Nestle[45] wrote that these relationships were not phony replicas of heterosexual couples but complex erotic statements that had everything to do with an exclusively lesbian language of stance, dress, gesture, loving, courage, and autonomy; "an erotic partnership serving both as a conspicuous flag of rebellion and as an intimate exploration of women's sexuality. In the 50s this courage to feel comfortable with arousing another woman became a political act."[46] A foray into pre-Stonewall lesbian culture altered the collective understanding of the sexual boundaries, pleasures, and desires possible for women. The exploration of butch–femme relationships asserted a challenge to the idea that women do not have very real and sexual desire for one another. Further, it challenged the fusion literature that makes lesbians into a one-dimensional category and does not account for gender differences much less class or race differences among lesbians. Explorations into butch–femme sexuality, a sexuality in which women were not suffering from too much sameness, or lack of differentiation, revealed relationship dynamics beyond the scope of what could be measured in frequency rates.

At the same time, explorations of lesbians in the 1930s, 1940s, and 1950s revealed that a discussion of private, intimate sexual life could not be separated from a discussion of public life, social life, and community. Sexual mores changed as resistance to homophobia and oppression

[44] Gayle Rubin, "Thinking Sex: Notes for a Radical Theory of the Politics of Sexuality," In *Pleasure and Danger: Exploring Female Sexuality*, ed. Carol S. Vance (Boston: Routledge & Kegan Paul, 1984), 267–319.

[45] Nestle, "Butch-Fem Relationships."

[46] Ibid., 21.

evolved. There was an inextricable relationship between desire, sexual life, and community.[47] Lesbians shaped their sexual experience, as that experience was shaped by the subculture and larger culture. It might be argued that to the extent women had a sense of sexual agency and subjectivity, it flourished from a community, albeit underground, that provided a space of intersubjectivity.

Lesbians claiming the importance of women's pleasure found themselves in conflict with anti-porn feminists focused on sexual violence and the oppressive aspects of male-imposed sexuality but were joined by other outlaw pro-sex communities. Conversations about sexual liberation developed into "the sex wars" defining the feminist politics of the 1980s.[48]

It is clear now that a public gay/lesbian movement for sexual freedom was nearly brought to standstill by the HIV/AIDS epidemic all across the United States. Community spaces such as gay bathhouses, sites of sexual exploration, were shut down as the specter of men infecting other men via sex acts dominated the media. Gay and lesbian communities were consumed with responding to the sick and dying. The right-wing movement poured resources into ballot initiatives and legislative proposals to segregate HIV positive individuals from the "general" (read: straight) population. Less draconian but still lethal proposals deprived AIDS services organizations of public funding. AIDS activism, and the pleasures of collective movement-building, provided a new way to become politically involved in public conversations about sexuality and mirrored the transformative possibilities of the Women's Movement's intersubjective space. But it would be decades before ever more effective treatments were developed (for those with money and access to health care) allowing enough of a calming of the anxieties of (predominately white) gay and lesbian communities to restore previous levels of public experimentation with sexuality.

The queer experimentations and conversations were also complicated when the 2000s brought the possibility of legal marriage to same-sex couples and then when legislative and electoral battles began over the right to marry. Pro-marriage movement organizations crafted messages

[47] Davis and Kennedy, "Oral History and the Study of Sexuality in the Lesbian Community, Buffalo, New York, 1940–1960."

[48] McGleughlin, "The Freedom to Want Passionately."

that emphasized love, family relationships, and children, messages that were ultimately successful. What followed was a distancing of the pro-marriage movement from the pro-sexuality aspects of the LGBTQ liberation movement. "Good gays" got married, had kids, and lived behind a white picket fence; "bad gays" eschewed marriage, had sex, and talked about it. If both the HIV epidemic and the pro-marriage campaigns had stultifying effects on a burgeoning sexual liberation movement, though, neither entirely shut it down.

The last two decades have brought a new shift: an increasing focus on gender. Entire categories of gender are transforming and being transformed by people whose gender assigned at birth does not conform with the gender they feel themselves to be. Similar to the Women's Liberation Movement of the 1980s, this new movement to free people from constraining definitions of gender is lively and vigorous. For the past 20 years and continuing today, transgender and gender nonbinary people are creating an intersubjective movement/community space for themselves. Many of us no longer assume that gender is constituted by two differentiated definitions of "woman" and "man" or that gender is a destination rather than a shifting configuration of desire or identity.[49] A social and political movement aims to expand our notions of gender to include transgender women, transgender men, nonbinary gendered people, and gender expressions that do not conform to traditional ideals and do not even have or seek labels. This movement seeks to liberate humans from the idea that biology must necessarily define us; the definition-changing is happening, in significant part, through personal transformations but also in public conversations in the media, in social media, in support groups both online and in real time, and in the political and legal spheres. Just as was true for women who sought freedom from male definitions of gender and sexuality through mutual recognitions of their own subjectivities in consciousness-raising groups, transgender and nonbinary people offer the same holding spaces and recognitions to each other.

Reading backward and summarizing my early projects for this tribute is jarring. I take note of my own binary thinking and use of fixed categories. Though gender was certainly already "soft assembly"[50] and genderqueers were at the forefront of gay liberation struggles before and

[49] Jack Halberstam, *Trans** (California: University of California Press, 2018).

[50] Adrienne Harris, *Gender as Soft Assembly* (New York: Analytic Press, 2005).

after Stonewall, gender categories were not yet explored in mainstream culture and were either flattened or in continual tension within lesbian feminist communities. As issues of gender are once again catapulted into public conversation, some of the tensions that were emblematic of the Women's Liberation struggles around gender and sexuality are reemerging in the contemporary debate where people identified with gender liberationists are in struggle with those feminists who adhere to the binary gender categories of woman and man, often citing threats to civil rights protections and issues of personal safety for women and girls.[51] As happened when radical lesbians joined new right antifeminists to oppose pornography, some contemporary feminists are joining with conservative organizations to try to obstruct those making claims for recognition of their new genders and a public backlash is developing against increasing recognition for the rights and freedoms of transgender people.[52] Contemporary tensions about gender and sexuality among feminists retain many of the tensions and some of the binaries that have been present in public and private conversations juxtaposing pleasure and danger, safety and risk, rights and liberation. There remain deep divides in any feminist constructions of women's sexuality. And while it might seem I have gotten far away from Chodorow's brilliant *Reproduction of Mothering*, I remain cognizant of Davis and Kennedy's lesson in studying lesbian life before Stonewall, that discussions of private, intimate sexual life cannot be separated from a discussion of public life, social life, and community, and that sexual mores change as resistance to homophobia and oppression evolved. We know there is an inextricable relationship between desire, sexual life, and community.[53]

Part Three: The Broken Link of Unbeing

In the 1970s and 1980s, both Chodorow and Benjamin, each first a sociologist and then a psychoanalyst, deepened our understanding of women's desire and enhanced our understanding of women's lack of

[51] Abigail Shrier, "The Transgender War on Women," New York: *The Wall Street Journal* (March 26, 2019).

[52] Katelyn Burns, "The Rise of Anti-trans 'Radical' Feminists, Explained," Vox Media (September 5, 2019).

[53] Davis and Kennedy, "Oral History and the Study of Sexuality in the Lesbian Community, Buffalo, New York, 1940–1960."

sexual agency and potential to become sexual subjects. Like them, I went on to be a psychoanalyst interested in issues of subjectivity and sexuality. The previous two sections of this chapter were written before I became a psychoanalyst when I was an undergraduate and then a graduate student in social work. I wanted to show my engagement with Chodorow's ideas as I discovered her then and in proximity to the time her work was written and gaining wide influence. And by placing the two already written projects next to each other in this chapter and adding a current section about a way I think now, I wanted to suggest the ways I have come full circle with Chodorow but at the same time I depart from her.

Ironically, at the time I was asked to write about Chodorow's *Reproduction of Mothering* for this book, I was completing a paper for a panel on mothering that is abridged here for section three of this chapter. I employed Jack Halberstam's *Queer Art of Failure*[54] as a way to play with and articulate a version of my mother's life that took her "failures" and "forgettings" and reimagined them to re-vision the possibilities of her life outside of a normative developmental story. I stake this "story" of my mother's sexual subjectivity on her break from identification with her (largely desexualized) mother that allowed her to forge a different kind of mothering in which she privileged her own sexual subjectivity and her desire. I argue, with hindsight, that my identification with her as sexual subject was a strand that allowed my own queerness to grow, both because she unwittingly made space for wrongness, and because she claimed other kinds of kinship even as she longed for conventional living. But my mother did not recognize me as like her in the way Chodorow narrated. And while I maintained a lifelong psychic relationship with her, as Chodorow suggests is typical, the qualities Chodorow describes as part of a daughter's maternal inheritance were not necessarily mine. Nor did my mother, a sexual subject in her own right, with the power to recognize me as like her, supply recognition of my own sexual agency as Benjamin thought might be possible when mothers were not desexualized but rather sexual agents. That would have meant recognizing my queerness. Instead, I sought recognition outside the family in queer worlds and collectives, and I argue it was there that real agency developed for me.

In psychoanalytic terms, my mother was not Winnicott's "good enough mother," and yet borrowing from queer theory and knowing the

[54] Jack Halberstam, *The Queer Art of Failure* (Durham: Duke University Press, 2011).

violence of norms and the power of social exclusions, I wanted to claim something of her failed mothering as having a generative aspect allowing me to forge a different path of sexual subjectivity. Consciously using Halberstam's ideas of "the importance of the disruption of lineage rather than its continuation, and the undoing of self rather than its activation,"[55] I thought I was departing from Chodorow's frame of the reproduction of mothering.

I don't mean this story as a true object relational version of anything like what really happened. I don't want to draw linear connections about my mother and a theory of agency, identification, separation, or subjectivity. I don't believe in tracing the etiology of sexuality and don't think it's possible to know. Efforts to sort instinct against drive against need against object are potentially useful, on a meta psychological level, but as a clinician rooted in Laplanche and the ethics of the unknowability of our sexuality, I live with my otherness, my strangeness to myself. I cannot know what enigmatic messages she passed on to me or what kind of libidinized object I was for her or how she touched me or how my efforts to translate her messages really map or create the basis of my sexuality, of my unconscious. Or how body and language shape the unconscious. Further, I don't imagine the family as the only site of subject formation, nor its reformation as the site of liberation.

In the intervening decades since I first read Chodorow, my own understanding of sexuality has been influenced not just by Laplanche but by queer theory and an abiding belief in the need to refigure our discussions of desire outside of a frame of identifications/failed identifications and outside of an Oedipal family drama, in order to imagine new ways to live and love.

And yet, as you will see, we don't know what we show. It is with some irony that I note that unconsciously I have returned to Chodorow's object relational frame and theories of identification to tell the story of my mother's anti-Oedipal desire even as I don't want to. Conscious wishes are undermined by the unknowability of ourselves and the other. In tribute to Chodorow, I have unwittingly returned to her. She is one of the mothers implanted inside me, powerful, strange, and disruptive.

Queer theory urges us away from linear connections of development toward progress; it invites us to live in the chaos of a different kind of

[55] Ibid., 126.

temporality[56] which I attempted in grouping the projects in this chapter together without a linear argument. But I see I am still my mother's daughter, wanting to make good her bad, and mine. Take the story below as the kind of conclusion I can offer, not one at all.

A Story

My mother practiced the art of not knowing, forgetting and lying. She wanted to break from the Judaism she feared would doom her. Because she wouldn't be Jewish, she couldn't interact with her family. So, she broke from them, too. Her father, dead when she was 17, disappeared from stories; she voluntarily lost her sexless mother. Without contact with her family, she felt free to create other narratives. In the habit of not knowing, forgetting, and lying, she persisted. Like the lies she told about my father's death. He, too, disappeared from our narrative. She was lying and forgetting about *origin*, hers and ours.

Because I am her daughter, loss and not knowing are my inheritance. Of course, there are many other inheritances (or "reproductions," to use Chodorow's important language). These are internal, unconscious, drive-inflected experiences as well as relational and intersubjective knowings. But here I focus on sexuality. The biggest shame I felt in the private girls' school I attended on full scholarship was not being fatherless or less privileged, but having not once or twice, but three times, a different last name than my mother. Everyone could see it on the class list. Marriage shame. I was humiliated by her wrongness made public and exemplified not only by being a failed woman—a divorcée—but by the obviousness of her sexual life. She must have been having sex. A lot of it. Her low-cut clothes, big breasts and bad rental address coded us "the wrong side of the tracks," not upper-east-side WASPs, even as her own aspirations had everything to do with feigning respectability. She structured her life around a series of "omissions" that would help her belong, and yet she remains an unwilling outlier. No matter how many times she married, how relentless her effort or how performative, the family form failed her, and she failed the family. And no matter the failures, she clung to normative family ideology.

The verboten struggle with the complexity of who she was, our unconscious identifications, meant that I sought out other "wrong" girls: two

[56] Halberstam, *The Queer Art of Failure.*

Jews, one African American, and one Puerto Rican in the school. Later, I lived queer lives with them. In her appall, and my abjection, I also had to lose my mother before I could take her back. That is my inheritance.

But I didn't lose my mother's lessons about sexuality and identity. I learned the lies behind "right living," the failures of desire, the fragility of heterosexuality and respectability. But that's not all. In the break from Oedipal rivalries (to remain within a psychoanalytic frame) my mother was my lover, though I was not hers. She didn't like women—certainly not as lovers, even friends. She was a man's man. But my mother had real sexual subjectivity. And her desire couldn't be policed. This marked her as gender non-conforming and family-busting. Hungry for her own pleasure, embodied, she was the first powerful woman with a desire of her own whom I ever loved, jazzy with sexual subjectivity. I'll call that mixture of sexual power and gender wrongness "butch" for now. And so, to her implied butch, I became her declared femme. And I have done what femmes do: try to make the wrongness of the other right. I thought, before I came out, "I will never be like my mother. No bad men for me." But I wanted nothing more than her happiness. My mother named my queerness defiance, but it might have been about achieving respectability for her (the worst kind of substitution): I wouldn't do it with a man exactly, but I did manage three things my mother longed for but didn't have: a lifelong partner, a "real" job, and a mortgage. I wanted her to fit. All the things she and I were ashamed of—her not choosing between a sexual life and motherhood, her matriarchal insistence that her children were hers and that men were peripheral, her hidden ethnicity—I claim them. I queered the family, but I am still my mother's daughter. And, she is still not performing "mother."

Halberstam tells us that women are often the repository for the "generational logics of being and becoming" and transmit that logic to the next generation.[57] Who was my mother becoming when she sought a place unfettered by memory, tradition or a usable past? Forgoing a mother, she did not receive the logics of her becoming.

Psychoanalysis frowns on severing the temporal link, disrupting the continuity of what has come before. Our bodies link us indelibly to our parents, theory tells us, and if we sever ourselves from what came before, we are at grave risk, masochistic. Instead, psychoanalysis offers

[57] Halberstam, *The Queer Art of Failure*, 70.

us mourning—remembering, repeating, working through. In my own psychoanalysis, I dutifully reach for her pathology, her badness, and I dwell in what it means to be without a family, history, religion, or culture. I know intimately what it means to form around another, I know the disorientation of not knowing who you are when you break from those that form you.[58]

Is my mother's choice masochistic to cut herself off from history and origin? Or does the effort to live in some other way interrupt a familiar Oedipal story that is bound to reproduce exactly what has come before?[59] Bersani names masochism as the counternarrative of sexuality that undergirds the propulsive maturational and linear story installed by psychoanalysis; he suggests that the heroic organizing narrative defines sexuality as an exchange of intensities between individuals. But the masochistic version constitutes a "condition of broken negotiations with the world, a condition in which others merely set off the self-shattering masochism of jouissance."[60]

If my mother's masochism, to use Bersani's language, constitutes a "condition of broken negotiations with the world," then her "self-shattering masochism of jouissance" opens possibility. In this broken line of unbeing, my mother is forging a way out of an endlessly repeating story. She is rejecting generational inheritance. She is refusing to merely transmit a set idea of who a woman can become.

Of course, Halberstam writes, "the model of passing down knowledge from parent to child is quite clearly invested in white, gendered, heteronormativity; indeed, the system inevitably stalls in the face of scenes of difference."[61] Stockton[62] employing Edelman writes, "The figure of the child as the emblem of parents (impossible) continuity spawns delusional visions … of the seamless reproduction of oneself whose future is always represented by (one's) children. Thus, the future and our children are bound together in a kind of frightening and (hermetically sealed)

[58] Judith Butler, *Giving an Account of One's Self* (New York: Fordham University Press, 2005).

[59] Bersani, *The Freudian Body*.

[60] Ibid., 41.

[61] Halberstam, *The Queer Art of Failure*, 124.

[62] Kathryn Bond Stockton, *The Queer Child, or Growing Sideways in the Twentieth Century* (Durham and London: Duke University Press, 2009).

reproductive futurism."[63] For Edelman, like Bersani, the death drive, "its energetic jouissance," is an "open-eyed denial of a person's continuance."[64] My mother's choice to cut herself off from connections might be seen as a self-preservative death drive—an unconscious choice to live in the break, toward pleasure albeit with unbearable pain.

The idea of the break[65] is made infamous in the wake of slavery when children were routinely separated from their families. Halberstam reads Saidiya Hartman, who writes "the only sure inheritance passed from one generation to the next was this loss and it defined the tribe... an identity produced by negation."[66] Hartman's book, *Lose Your Mother*, indicates a loss that has always already happened for African Americans. Using her text, Halberstam argues against a simple genealogical account of history that stretches back in time through the family line. It is the colonized mind, he argues, that is passed down Oedipally from generation to generation.[67]

Halberstam asks, are there other models of generation, temporality, and politics available to worldmaking? He urges us to think "in terms of the negation of the subject rather than formation, the disruption of lineage rather than its continuation, the undoing of self rather than its activation."[68] Losing one's mother, Halberstam suggests, frees us from the Oedipal model and allows us other models of time, space, place, and connection.

What I have been naming as my mother's unknowing, forgetting, and lying, in Halberstam's hands, is not pathology, but radical edge; a potent intervention. Of course, my mother didn't "choose" as I imply here. And this revisioning story leaves out her pain and suffering and mine. As kids we wanted to be "normal," and we wanted her to be normal too. But in this inflected translation my mother is forging a way out of the reproduction of mothering, of the generational transmission of who she can

[63] Stockton, *The Queer Child*, 13.

[64] Ibid., 12.

[65] Fred Moten, *In the Break: The Aesthetics of the Black Radical Tradition* (Minneapolis: University of Minnesota Press, 2003).

[66] Saidiya Hartman, *Lose Your Mother: A Journey along the Atlantic Slave Route* (New York: Farrar, Straus and Giroux, 2008), 103.

[67] Jack Halberstam, *The Queer Art of Failure*, 132.

[68] Ibid., 126.

become. Women and queers, Halberstam says, *should* forget, *should* lose our mothers: "Delinking the process of generational inheritance from the force of historical progress is a queer project."[69] In fact, if the queer project seeks to uncouple becoming from the supposedly organic and immutable forms of family identity and inheritance,[70] we might say my mother was the first queer I ever knew. Her own break from stultifying forms of family life came not from mourning, but from refusal. In refusing her origin, culture, and identity, and in unwittingly disrupting normative heterosexual life stories, she uncoupled motherhood from right living, wedging open space for new forms of kinship, creating room for my queerness to grow.

Without my mother's welcome, without a history or culture, my own opening to women—to "our sharp jester's tongues, our cartwheels of pleasure, the queen's own pearl at our fingertips"[71]—was everything. I found home in other queer minds and theirs in mine, the basis of one psychoanalytic story of subjectivity. Coming into lesbian identity, finding community with other women, living collectively, being recognized and wanted, being eroticized,[72] saved me. It was about pleasure and it was about survival and it was about developing agency and of course, critique. Queer lives in turn create potential for different world making.

And so, we raised our children queerly with other families where queer has meant not just the consolidation of normative identity with two same gendered people but an effort to live alternatively. We belonged to a tribe. We tried for loose collectivity, for no nuclear, no simple two. And so we rub up against and disrupt the symbolic order. And sometimes, we fall into queer heteronormativity. In fact, the struggle for recognition as queer families can get argued in the language of legal rights and relationship recognition ("Our relationships are just like yours"), but those claims are often covers for a deeper set of longings to be seen as whole, as full citizens.[73] The longing to be included in a society that is organized

[69] Ibid., 70.

[70] Ibid.

[71] Olga Broumas, *Beginning with O* (New Haven: Yale University Press, 1977).

[72] Eve Kosofsky Sedgwick, *Epistemology of the Closet* (Los Angeles: University of California Press, 1990).

[73] Jade McGleughlin, "Can a Diamond Ever Be Gay?" *Studies in Gender and Sexuality* 9, no. 2 (2008): 184–205.

not just by one's origin story but by a place in its primary institutions—like family, even if we critique them—is powerful. The underbelly of these longings, of course, is the way we remain psychologically tied to *belonging* in the very culture we eschew. The psychic reproduction of certain desires is not a matter of individual wish or personal alienation but is inculcated into our hearts and minds and lives in the symbolic realm. This is how ideology is reproduced. It hails us to become a certain kind of subject. To be outside the proper story of it is to be a mistake, a deviation.[74] Still we risk it. Like my mother, but with intention. Like Benjamin, but with queers. Like Chodorow, but with desire forward. And with gratitude, for we wouldn't have gotten here without all of them.

Our kids are actively living other forms of world making. They are neither spared the longings to belong nor do they escape the symbolic meanings of mother or father or origin despite having a very different "nuclear family" and forms of kinship. But being queer is also a difference that matters. And they wouldn't give up our queer world, or queer worldmaking, for anything. As Sara Ahmed[75] tells us, bodies are shaped by pleasures and pleasures open bodies to new worlds.

Max, our now grown son is rethinking origins. As the child of more than a few queers, Oedipal narratives fail him. He writes that while origins have by their nature a singular starting point, for him origin scenes, such as the primal scene in his dreams and the scene of physical conception, invariably raise questions that cannot be satisfied by a singular symbol that marks a first point of causation. He writes,

> These two scenes must be held in tension. ... Without a marking point for my beginning, a congruency between my mothers' creative act and biological reproduction, and in the absence of a knowable legacy, projected into the future, I began my translation [of origin] empathetically, focusing on those messages contained in affect, in the unseen, with little regard for the visually discernable origin of a birth father or the physical reality of a family history, about which I knew little.[76]

[74] Jade McGleughlin, "The Analyst's Necessary Vertigo," *Psychoanalytic Dialogues* 21, no. 5 (2011): 630–642.

[75] Sara Ahmed, *The Cultural Politics of Emotion* (Edinburgh, Scotland: Edinburgh University Press, 2004).

[76] Maxwell McGleughlin, "Two Way Reaching" (undergraduate graduation paper, Wesleyan University, 2017).

Origin is rooted in affect, in longing. "[History is] a thing which is not yet there" Munoz says.[77]

We rework origin, make new models, disrupt. But Max and his sister are his mothers' son and daughter. The enigmatic messages[78] we pass to the children, like our mothers passed to us, seek new translation. Certain recurring aspects of ourselves return again and again, and no narrative story can contain them. Because we cannot translate these messages, they remain as the unconscious core of our subjectivity, signifying something important but enigmatic and eroticized, disrupting psychological life. Subjectivity—interiority and unconscious fantasy—are built from the labor of translation but they alert us to the implantation of the other, the inevitable unknowableness of the other inside us. The repetitive presence of these messages breaches our continuity of being (already a fantasy) and suggests the non-sovereignty of the self.[79] Identity is always disrupted, nonsovereign, fractal.

Identity matters. My queer patients come because they need my susceptibility. They feel crushed by norms that produce a them that feels strange to themselves. They are trying to make a break—with an atmosphere, an expectation, an insistence on a way to be. Sometimes they want a mother, like my mother, cut off from the weight of history without being cut off from desire. They don't want to be their mother; they don't want me to be their mother or any parent. (If I am the same mother, only better than the mother they already have, there is little affective future that can be very different.) They want other ways to live and love they can and can't imagine. They think I might belong to the same tribe that they do, that we might share, in Eyal Rozmarin's words, a notion of an unconscious that is not within subjects but between them.[80] With Butler they believe, "I am not formed once and definitively, but continuously

[77] Jose Esteban Munoz, *Cruising Utopia: The Then and There of Queer Futurity* (New York: New York University Press, 2010).

[78] Jean Laplanche, *Essays on Otherness* (New York: Routledge, 1999).

[79] Jade McGleughlin, "The Analyst's Necessary Non-Sovereignty and the Generative Power of the Negative," *Psychanalytic Dialogues* (2020).

[80] Eyal Rozmarin, *Identity In-Formation*, Talk for The International Psychoanalytic Association (London, England, July 26, 2019). Is there a date, location and link for this talk?

or repeatedly. I am still being formed as I form myself in the here and now,"[81] as I form myself (queerly) with you.

My mother lived in an imagined future in which emotions circulate between bodies,[82] and there is emergence and potentiality in relation to the body[83] and to the way it links with other bodies.

There is the push to collectives and the pull to their undoing. There is affect, and desire, and it connects us. It is the animating condition of our lives. This is how we open up a livable future.

Chodorow was an innovator. She broke from sociology to become a psychoanalyst and from psychoanalysis to include the social and political. Her own constructions created a new body of work powerful and resonate. Genealogical breaks create space for new assemblages that are sometimes continuous with the history from which they broke but also radical departures that change the meaning of what came before. We need full circles, mobius strips and broken lines of being.

Bibliography

Ahmed, Sara, *The Cultural Politics of Emotion*. Edinburgh, Scotland: Edinburgh University Press, 2004.

Barthes, Roland, *Camera Lucida: Reflections on Photography*. New York, NY: Hill and Wang, A Division of Farrar, Straus, and Giroux, 1980.

Bell, Alan M. and Martin Weinberg, *Homosexualities: A Study of Diversity among Men and Women*. New York: Simon & Schuster, 1978.

Benjamin, Jessica, "Beyond Doer and Done to: An Intersubjective View of Thirdness." *Psychoanalytic Quarterly* 73 (2004): 5–46.

———, "The Bonds of Love: Erotic Domination and Rational Violence." *Feminist Studies* 6 (1980): 144–174.

———, *The Bonds of Love*. New York and Toronto: Pantheon Press, 1988.

———, "A Desire of One's Own: Psychodynamic Feminism and Intersubjective Space." In *Feminist Studies/Critical Studies*, ed. T. de Lauritis. Bloomington, IN: Indiana University Press, 1986, 78–101.

———, "Recognition: The Matrix of the Self." In *The Bonds of Love*. New York: Pantheon, 1986.

[81] Butler, *Giving an Account of One's Self*.

[82] Ahmed, *The Cultural Politics of Emotion*.

[83] Brian Massumi, "The Autonomy of Affect," in *Cultural Critique* (Minneapolis: University of Minnesota Press, 1995).

Berlant, Lauren and Lee Edelman, *Sex, or the Unbearable*. Durham NC and London: Duke University Press, 2014.

Bersani, Leo, *The Freudian Body: Psychoanalysis and Art*. New York: Columbia University Press, 1986.

Blair, Ralph, "Gay Couple Counseling: Proceedings of a Conference." *Homosexual Counseling Journal* 1, no. 3 (1974): 88–139.

Blumstein, Philip and Pepper Schwartz, *American Couples: Money, Work, Sex*. New York: William Morrow, 1983.

Bollas, Christopher, *The Shadow of the Object: Psychoanalysis of the Unthought Known*. New York: Columbia University Press, 1987.

Broumas, Olga, *Beginning with O*. New Haven: Yale University Press, 1977.

Burch, Beverly, "Psychological Merger in Lesbian Couples: A Joint Ego Psychological and Systems Approach." In *Family Therapy* 9, no. 3 (1982): 201–208.

Butler, Judith, *Giving an Account of One's Self*. New York: Fordham University Press, 2005.

———, "Melancholy Gender—Refused Identification." *Psychoanalytic Dialogues* 5 (1995): 165–180.

———, *Senses of the Subject*. New York: Fordham University Press, 2015.

Cho, Sumi, Kimberlé Williams Crenshaw, and Leslie McCall, "Toward a Field of Intersectionality Studies: Theory, Application and Praxis." *Signs* 38, no. 4 (2013): 785–810. Chicago University Press Journals.

Chodorow, Nancy J., "Gender, Relation and Difference in Psychoanalytic Perspective." In *The Future of Difference*. Newark: Rutgers University Press, 1985.

———, "Oedipal Asymmetries and Heterosexual Knots." *Social Problems* 23, no. 4 (1976): 454–468.

———, *The Reproduction of Mothering: Psychoanalysis and the Sociology of Gender*. Berkeley, CA: University of California Press, 1978.

Combahee River Collective, "The Combahee River Collective Statement." In *Home Girls: A Black Feminist Anthology*, ed. Barbara Smith. New York: Kitchen Table Women of Color Press, Inc., 1983.

Crenshaw, Kimberlé, "Mapping the Margins: Intersectionality, Identity Politics, and Violence against Women of Color." *Stanford Law Review* 43, no. 6 (July 1991): 1241–1299.

Davis, Madeline, and Elizabeth Kennedy, "Oral History and the Study of Sexuality in the Lesbian Community, Buffalo, New York, 1940–1960." *Feminist Studies* 12, no. 1 (1986): 7–26.

Densmore, Dana, "On Sex: No More Fun and Games" (Available at Amherst College Archives), 1968.

Echols, Alice, "The Taming of the Id: Feminist Sexual Politics, 1968–83." In *Pleasure and Danger*. Boston: Routledge & Kegan Paul, 1984.

Edelman, Lee, *No Future: Queer Theory and the Death Drive*. Durham: Duke University Press, 2005.
Freud, Sigmund, *New Introductory Lectures on Psychoanalysis*. New York: W. W. Norton, 1933.
Friedan, Betty, *The Feminine Mystique*. New York: W. W. Norton, 1963.
Gagnon, John, and William Simon, *Sexual Conduct: The Social Sources of Human Sexuality*. Chicago: Aldine, 1973.
Gilligan, Carol, *In a Different Voice: Psychological Theory and Women's Development*. Cambridge: Harvard University Press, 1982.
Greer, Germaine, *The Female Eunuch*. London: MacGibbon & Kee, 1970.
Halberstam, Jack, *The Queer Art of Failure*. Durham: Duke University Press, 2011.
———, *Trans**. Oakland, CA: California University Press, 2018.
Hall, Marny, "Lesbians, Limerance and Longterm Relationships." In *Lesbian Sex*, ed. J. Loulan. San Francisco: Spinsters, Inc., 1984.
Harris, Adrienne, *Gender as Soft Assembly*. New York: Analytic Press, 2005.
Hartman, Saidiya, *Lose Your Mother: A Journey along the Atlantic Slave Route*. New York: Farrar, Straus and Giroux, 2008.
———, *Scenes of Subjection: Terror, Slavery, and the Self-Making in Nineteenth Century America*. Oxford: Oxford University Press, 1977.
Hollibaugh, Amber and Cherrie Moraga, "What We're Rollin' Around in Bed with: Sexual Silences in Feminism: A Conversation Toward Ending Them." *Heresies* 3#4, no. #12 (1981): 58–62.
Hooks, Bell, *Feminist Theory: From Margin to Center*. Boston, MA: South End Press, 1984.
Housman, Judith, "Mothering, the Unconscious and Feminism." *Radical America* 16, no. 6 (1982): 47–62.
Jaye, Karla and Allen Young, *The Gay Report: Lesbians and Gay Men Speak Out about Sexual Experiences and Lifestyles*. New York: Summit Books, 1979.
Karpel, Mark, "Individuation: From Fusion to Dialogue." *Family Process* 15, no. 1 (1976): 65–82.
Kauffman, Phyllis, Elizabeth Harrison, and Mary Lou Hyde, "Distancing for Intimacy in Lesbian Relationships." *American Journal of Psychiatry* 141, no. 4 (April 1983): 530–533.
Krestan, Jo-Ann, and Claudia S. Bepko, "The Problem of Fusion in the Lesbian Relationship." *Family Process* 19, no. 3 (1980): 277–289.
Laplanche, Jean, *Essays on Otherness*. New York: Routledge, 1999.
Lewis, Jill, and Gloria Joseph, *Common Differences: Conflicts in Black and White Feminist Perspectives*. Garden City, NY: Anchor Books, 1981.
Lindenbaum, Joyce P., "The Shattering of an Illusion: The Problem of Competition in Lesbian Relationships." *Feminist Studies* 11, no. 1 (Spring 1985): 86–103.

Lowenstein, S.F., "Understanding Lesbian Women." *Social Casework* 61, no. 1 (1980): 29–38.
Massumi, Brian, "The Autonomy of Affect." In *Cultural Critique*. Minneapolis: University of Minnesota Press, 1995.
McDougall, Joyce, *A Plea for the Measure of Abnormality*. New York: International Universities Press, 1980.
McGleughlin, Jade, "The Analyst's Necessary Non-Sovereignty and the Generative Power of the Negative."*Psychoanalytic Dialogues* 30, no. 2 (2020): 123–138.
———, "The Analyst's Necessary Vertigo." *Psychoanalytic Dialogues* 21, no. 5 (2011): 630–642.
———, "Answering Gestures." *Psychoanalytic Dialogues* 25, no. 2 (2015): 256–264.
———, "Can a Diamond Ever Be Gay?" *Studies in Gender and Sexuality* 9, no. 2 (2008): 184–205.
———, "Do We Find or Lose Ourselves in the Negative?" *Psychoanalytic Dialogues* 25, no. 2 (2015): 214–236.
———, "The Freedom to Want Passionately: A Theoretical Exploration of Women's Desire" (Thesis, Smith College School for Social Work, 1987).
———, "Power, Liberation and Sexuality" (Unpublished manuscript, Hampshire College, 1982).
McGleughlin, Maxwell, "Two Way Reaching" (Undergraduate graduation paper, Wesleyan University, 2017).
Mencher, Julie, "Changing the Lens on Female Personality Development: A Feminist Vision of Fusion in Lesbian Relations" (Unpublished master's thesis, Smith College School for Social Work, 1984).
Mendola, Mary, *The Mendola Report*. New York: Crown, 1980.
Miller, Jean Baker, *Toward a New Psychology of Women*. Boston: Beacon Press, 1976.
Moraga, Cherrie, *Loving in the War Years*. Boston: South End Press, 1983.
Morgan, Robin, ed., *Sisterhood Is Powerful: An Anthology of Writings from the Women's Liberation Movement*. New York: Vintage Books, 1970.
Morgan, Robin, "Theory and Practice: Pornography and Rape." *Going Too Far: The Personal Chronicle of a Feminist*. New York: Vintage, 1977.
Moten, Fred, *In the Break: The Aesthetics of the Black Radical Tradition*. Minneapolis: University of Minnesota Press, 2003.
Munoz, Jose Esteban, *Cruising Utopia: The Then and There of Queer Futurity*. New York: New York University Press, 2010.
Nestle, Joan, "Butch-Fem Relationships: Sexual Courage in the 1950s." *Heresies* 3 (#4, no. #12) (1981): 21–24.
Nichols, Margaret, "The Treatment of Inhibited Sexual Desire in Lesbian Couples." *Women & Therapy* 1, no. 4 (1982): 12–17.

Peplau, Letitia Anne, "Research on Homosexual Couples: An Overview." *Journal of Homosexuality* 8, no. 2 (1982): 3–8.

———, Christine Padesky, and Marie Hamilton, "Satisfaction in Lesbian Relationships." *Journal of Homosexuality* 8, no. 2 (1982): 23–35.

——— and Hortensia Amaro, "Understanding Lesbian Relationships." In *Homosexuality: Social, Psychological, and Biological Issues*, eds. William Paul, James D. Weinrich, John C. Gonsiorek, and Mary E. Hotvedt. Beverly Hills, CA: Sage, 1982, 233–247.

———, Susan Cochrane, Karen Rook, and Christine Padesky, "Loving Women: Attachment and Autonomy in Lesbian Relationships." *Journal of Social Issues* 34, no. 3 (1978): 7–27.

Piercy, Marge, "The Grand Coolie Damn." In *Sisterhood Is Powerful: An Anthology of Writings from the Women's Liberation Movement*, ed. Robin Morgan. New York: Vintage Books, 1970.

Roth, Sallyann, "Psychotherapy with Lesbian Couples: Individual Issues, Female Socialization, and the Social Context." In *Innovations in Psychotherapy with Homosexuals*, eds. Emery S. Hetrick and Terry S. Stein. Washington, DC: American Psychiatric Press, 1984.

———, "Psychotherapy with Lesbian Couples: Individual Issues, Female Socialization and the Social Context." *Journal of Marital and Family Therapy* 11, no. 3 (July 1985): 273–286.

Rozmarin, Eyal, *Identity In-Formation*. Presentation for The International Psychoanalytic Association. London, England, July 2019.

Rubin, Gayle, "Thinking Sex: Notes for a Radical Theory of the Politics of Sexuality." *Pleasure and Danger: Exploring Female Sexuality*, ed. Carol S. Vance. Boston: Routledge & Kegan Paul, 1984.

Sedgwick, Eve Kosofsky, *Epistemology of the Closet*. Los Angeles: University of California Press, 1990.

Snitow, Ann, Christine Stansell, and Sharon Thompson, *Powers of Desire*. New York: Monthly Review Press, 1983.

Stern, Donnell, *The First Relationship: Mother and Infant*. Cambridge: Harvard University Press, 1977.

Stockton, Kathryn Bond, *The Queer Child or Growing Sideways in the Twentieth Century*. Durham and London: Duke University Press, 2009.

Tanner, Donna M., *The Lesbian Couple*. Lexington, MA: D. C. Heath, 1978.

Toder, Nancy, "Lesbian Couples: Special Issues." In *Positively Gay*, eds. Betty Berzon and Robert Leighton. Millbrae, CA: Celestial Arts, 1978.

Tuller, Neil R., "Couples: The Hidden Segment of the Gay World." *Journal of Homosexuality* 3, no. 4 (1978): 331–343.

Vance, Carole S., *Pleasure and Danger: Exploring Female Sexuality*. Boston: Routledge & Kegan Paul, 1984.

Vetere, Victoria A., "The Role of Friendship in the Development and Maintenance of Lesbian Love Relationships." *Journal of Homosexuality* 8, no. 2 (1983): 51–65.

Winnicott, Donald W., *The Maturational Process and the Facilitating Environment: Studies in the Theory of Emotional Development*. New York: International Universities Press, 1965.

———, "The Use of an Object." *International Journal of Psycho-Analysis* 50 (1969): 711–716.

PART III

Grand Daughters

CHAPTER 12

Mother–Daughter Relations and the Maternal in Irigaray and Chodorow

Alison Stone

God the Father and Jesus the Son; Abraham and Isaac; Uranus, Cronus, and Zeus; Zeus and Dionysus; Hamlet and his father; Fyodor Karamazov and his three sons—representations of and fantasies about father–son relationships are central to Western culture and philosophy. Within philosophy, one thinks of Hegel's conception of the dialectic in terms of the divine trinity, Nietzsche's preoccupation with Christ and Dionysus, or Kierkegaard's meditations on Abraham's near-murder of Isaac. In contrast, mother–daughter relationships have been shrouded in near-universal silence—much more so than representations of either mothers and sons (Oedipus and Jocasta; Mary and Jesus) or fathers and daughters (Agamemnon and Iphigenia; Lear and Cordelia). Female and feminist

Originally published in *philoSOPHIA: A Journal of Continental Feminism* 1, no. 1 (2011): 45–64, reprinted with permission.

A. Stone (✉)
Department of Politics, Philosophy and Religion, Lancaster University, Lancashire, UK
e-mail: a.stone@lancaster.ac.uk

P. Bueskens (ed.), *Nancy Chodorow and* The Reproduction of Mothering,
https://doi.org/10.1007/978-3-030-55590-0_12

theorists, writers, and artists have done much to bring mother–daughter relationships into representation and to reimagine the maternal beyond its traditional subservience to father–son dynasties. Among continental feminists, Luce Irigaray and Julia Kristeva have, of course, made major contributions to this task. Within Anglophone feminism, too, feminist psychoanalytic thinkers have sought to rectify Freud's overemphasis on the paternal and father–son relations. Nancy Chodorow's important work in this area paints a portrait of contemporary mother–daughter relations which seems, at first sight, strikingly similar to Irigaray's. Both thinkers suggest that mothers and their infant daughters experience a unique level of mutual identification. But under patriarchy—specifically, given exclusively female childrearing for Chodorow and given the absence of any symbolization of female subjectivity for Irigaray—daughters are forced to turn to the father to achieve any psychical independence from their mothers. The independence that daughters thus attain coexists with ongoing psychical identification with their mothers, so that women oscillate endlessly between separation from and mergence with their mothers. If the dominant template for father–son relations involves violent rivalry followed by guilt-ridden father-worship as the cement of fraternal society, as Freud described in *Totem and Taboo*,[1] the template for mother–daughter relations involves hostile separation constantly undone by ongoing fusion. This difference in templates maps the social–symbolic difference between the paternal position of power/authority/law and the maternal position of powerlessness/silence/body. However, the manifest similarities between Irigaray's and Chodorow's pictures are embedded in deep theoretical differences. The details of their descriptions of mother–daughter relations differ, and they give different explanations for why these relations follow a logic of separation and fusion: female mothering for Chodorow, the paternal symbolic order for Irigaray. They make different proposals for how to change these relations: shared parenting for Chodorow versus symbolic transformation for Irigaray. They hold conflicting conceptions of the self and of language, reflecting their heterogeneous psychoanalytic backgrounds in Anglo-American object relations versus French Lacanianism and poststructuralism. These deep differences raise questions about whether Chodorow and Irigaray are discussing mother–daughter relations in the same sense at all. Bringing Irigaray

[1] Sigmund Freud, *Totem and Taboo and Other Works*, ed. James Strachey (New York: Vintage, 2001).

and Chodorow together across their different intellectual contexts, this article compares and partially synthesizes their visions of the maternal and mother-daughter relations. By integrating their perspectives, we can move beyond the "impasse" between Lacanian and object-relations feminisms that dominated psychoanalytic feminist debates in the 1980s and 1990s[2]—debates that have crucially shaped continental feminists' orientation toward questions of sexual difference, language and representation, and the embodied psyche.

The impasse in question has at least two strands. First, for object-relations feminists such as Chodorow, our pre-Oedipal relations with our mothers shape us so that we acquire "core" selves with a fairly stable gender. This approach elevates the mother in importance (compared to classical psychoanalysis with its emphasis on the father), but it loses sight of psychic and gender instability. This can make Chodorow's views seem rather dated given the impact of Judith Butler's work and her emphasis on the unstable, shifting nature of gender. Lacanian feminists such as Jacquelyn Rose reemphasize psychic instability, but they do so by stressing that the subject is split between paternal language and the pre-Oedipal maternal realm, which means that these theorists also restore the father's power over the mother.[3]

Second, object-relations feminists such as Chodorow think in terms of the concept of gender. For them, our masculine/feminine identities are shaped by our early social relations in the family, which reflect the broader gender division of labor; *qua* social, these can be changed, and our gender-divided personalities with them. On the positive side, then, for object-relations feminists, patriarchy can be undone; but problematically, as Lacanians have noted, the psyche is reduced to the social: Children's psychical reality is reduced to an effect of their mothers' empirical and socially determined behavior.[4] This reduction is problematic, not

[2] Teresa Brennan, "An Impasse in Psychoanalysis and Feminism," in *A Reader in Feminist Knowledge*, ed. Sneja Gunew (New York: Routledge, 1991), 114–138.

[3] Jacquelyn Rose, *Sexuality in the Field of Vision* (London: Verso, 1986).

[4] Nancy Chodorow concedes that there is this problem with her earlier work. Nancy Chodorow, *Feminism and Psychoanalytic Theory* (Cambridge, UK: Polity Press, 1989), 7. Her later work increasingly recognizes the importance of culture and language. See Nancy Chodorow, *Feminism and Psychoanalytic Theory* (Cambridge, UK: Polity Press, 1989); Nancy Chodorow, *Femininities, Masculinities, Sexualities: Freud and Beyond* (London: Free Association Books, 1994); Nancy Chodorow, *The Power of Feelings* (New Haven: Yale University Press, 1999).

least because it makes feminist object relations (despite itself) worryingly continuous with oppressive discourses of the "good-enough" mother and her supposed all-importance to the child's well-being.[5] Yet in reemphasizing the irreducibility of psyche and language to the social, Lacanians make them resistant, if not immune, to sociopolitical change, which threatens to make patriarchy immutable.[6]

Irigaray takes us some way past this impasse by retaining a concept of the symbolic but rethinking the symbolic as open to change. Thus, she retains the strengths of Lacanian positions (the subject's instability and the irreducibility of the psyche to the social) while losing the disadvantages of these positions (the impossibility of change and the privileging of father over mother). But an Irigarayan perspective still has something to learn from Chodorow. In particular, Chodorow gives us important insights into (1) the importance and vitality of *actually existing*—not merely possible future—mother–daughter bonds, and (2) the need for social change of family and parenting arrangements, not simply in addition to symbolic change, but as a necessary co-condition *of* symbolic change. In this essay, I attempt to integrate these insights of Chodorow's into Irigaray's philosophy of sexual difference.

I begin by returning to Chodorow's *The Reproduction of Mothering*[7] (hereafter *Reproduction*), where she sets out her key account of mother–daughter relations and her psychoanalytic reappraisal of the maternal. My discussion of Chodorow will be focused mainly on this work, although she has since revised her views. I will focus on *Reproduction* because it remains Chodorow's most important and influential work and gives her richest account of the daughter's relation to her mother.

For Chodorow, all infants begin life as "matrisexual,"[8] erotically loving the mothers who tend them; they are psychically undifferentiated from

[5] For some now-classic feminist criticisms of these discourses, see Parveen Adams, "Mothering," *m/f* 8 (1983): 40–52; Janice Doane and Devon Hodges, *From Klein to Kristeva: Psychoanalytic Feminism and the Search for the "Good Enough" Mother* (Ann Arbor: University of Michigan Press, 1992); Denise Riley, *War in the Nursery: Theories of the Child and Mother* (London: Virago, 1983).

[6] For this objection to Lacanianism, see Brennan, "An Impasse in Psychoanalysis and Feminism," 114–127.

[7] Nancy Chodorow, *The Reproduction of Mothering: Psychoanalysis and the Sociology of Gender* (Berkeley: University of California Press, 1978).

[8] Ibid., 95.

their mothers, experiencing her feelings as theirs and vice versa. Gradually, by age three, children achieve individuation, becoming aware of their own bodily boundaries and feelings as distinct from those of others and from the outer world. During this period, gender differences are also formed in Chodorow's view—contrary to Freud, for whom these become established only via the castration and Oedipus complexes.

Because their daughters are the same sex as they are, mothers unconsciously identify with them, projecting their interests, desires, beliefs, and feelings onto them. Daughters come to feel like extensions of their mothers, with little sense of psychical difference from their mothers, in this sense remaining "identified" with their mothers. Conversely, mothers unconsciously push their sons toward separation, and—being heterosexual but cloistered at home with little contact with adult men, who are out at paid work for much of the time—mothers "sexualize" and act seductively toward their sons.[9] Then, in the boy's Oedipal phase, Chodorow says that he fully sexualizes his mother and competes for her against his father, finally resolving this crisis by identifying with his father in his abstract role and rejecting his own early identity with his mother. The boy's "core" masculine self centers on separateness from the mother, the body, emotions, and relations with others.

Girls also turn to their fathers to break from their suffocating lack of differentiation from their mothers. As breadwinners, fathers count as "symbols of freedom"[10] from the mother. The penis in particular comes to symbolize this freedom; its idealization forms the basis of female heterosexuality,[11] reinforced by seductive paternal behavior toward daughters. But crucially, for Chodorow, a girl's turn to her father reflects not only her urge to escape her mother, but also her ongoing preoccupation with and love of her mother.[12] The mother's sexualized treatment of men has conveyed that the mother prefers men. So the girl turns to men in hope of finding a successor love who will not reject her as her mother has done, and of winning her mother's love by being or trying to be like a man. Being thus partly rooted *in* love of the mother, love of the father cannot conclusively supplant it. Chodorow therefore describes

[9] Ibid., 104.

[10] Ibid., 121.

[11] Ibid., 113.

[12] Ibid., 124–125.

the girl's/woman's emotional world as triangular: It always involves both sexual/genital love of the father/men and a deeper identificatory love for the mother/women.[13] But from this psychoanalytic perspective, women's love for their mothers/women is also erotic. So, although the family structure that Chodorow describes rests on institutionalized heterosexuality, it also places heterosexuality under considerable "strain".[14,15] And ultimately, because women can rarely fulfill with men their needs for love of a deep, intimate, identificatory kind, women come to want children with whom they can regain that kind of intimacy.[16] Chodorow thus finds a "place … for the little girl's love for her mother,"[17] describing that love as the overarching, constant factor in each woman's psyche. In saying this, she corrects Freud's claim[18] that girls repudiate their mothers totally on discovering their mothers' and their own castration—a claim that he himself eventually acknowledged to be false.[19] Chodorow accounts much better than Freud for the strong, lifelong bonds that exist between many mothers and daughters, and for how these bonds often persist despite considerable hostility and animosity, since those negative effects rest on ongoing love in the first place.

How does this picture of mother–daughter relations compare to Irigaray's? First, we must ask how legitimately these two thinkers can even be compared. After all, Chodorow aims to "get psychoanalytic

[13] Ibid., 127.

[14] Ibid., 78.

[15] This can be obscured by the desexualized view of love-relations that Chodorow inherits from object-relations theory. Despite saying that infants are matrisexual, she in fact tends to describe them as mother-*loving* but says little about sexual drives, which she regards merely as "vehicles for personal contact" (Chodorow, *The Reproduction of Mothering*, 47–48). I take it, though, that infants do relate erotically to their mothers, in the broad psychoanalytic sense of the erotic, as involving fantasy, bodily drives, and corporeal energies, as Chodorow also at times says (e.g., Nancy Chodorow, *Femininities, Masculinities, Sexualities: Freud and Beyond* [London: Free Association Books, 1994], 39).

[16] Chodorow, *The Reproduction of Mothering*, 201–204.

[17] Ibid., 124.

[18] Sigmund Freud, "Some Psychical Consequences of the Anatomical Distinction Between the Sexes," in *On Sexuality*, ed. James Strachey (Harmondsworth: Penguin, 1977b), 331–343.

[19] Sigmund Freud, "Female Sexuality," in *On Sexuality*, ed. James Strachey (Harmondsworth: Penguin, 1977a), 366–392.

theory right—to make it accurately represent the facts of psychic development."[20] In contrast, Irigaray's fullest portrayal of a mother–daughter relationship, in "And the One Doesn't Stir Without the Other,"[21] is poetic, not intended to describe empirical facts but to unearth and rewrite Western culture's prescribed script for mother–daughter relations, a script of separation undercut by fusion. As a post-Lacanian, Irigaray thinks that "empirical" life is always mediated through such scripts. This seems a crucial difference from Chodorow. But we should not overstate this difference. For Irigaray, Western culture's prescriptions shape us psychically: Our public, social imaginary becomes individual fantasy. Cultural scripts structure how we live and construct our relations with one another. Thus, in excavating the separation/fusion template, Irigaray does equally mean to excavate a pattern in actual, lived mother–daughter relations. So Irigaray's picture of the lived grain of mother–daughter relations can productively be compared with Chodorow's.

Irigaray sees these relations as more negative, more conflictual, than Chodorow does. Irigaray suggests that mother and infant daughter undergo a paralyzing fusion—"With your milk, Mother, I swallowed ice."[22] The milk of maternal kindness freezes, stifles the daughter. This forces her to break away toward her father—idealizing him as a beacon of individuation, then settling for having him as a sexual object, acceding to his individuation vicariously. But the daughter cannot really abandon her early love for her mother, so deeply has it constituted her; she can only repress it. Meanwhile the mother, abandoned by the daughter with whom she identified so utterly, is left bereft. Despite regretting this situation, the daughter feels powerless to alter it. To abandon her fixation on the father/men would mean plunging back into the fusion she has escaped/repressed, since her feelings for her mother, confined in her unconscious, have been paralyzed, frozen, as feelings of fusion. For Irigaray, then, the daughter's love for her mother persists only unconsciously as psychical fusion, and consciously as anger, frustration, and

[20] Diana Tietjens Meyers, *Subjection and Subjectivity: Psychoanalytic Feminism and Moral Philosophy* (London: Routledge, 1994), 78.

[21] Luce Irigaray, "And the One Doesn't Stir without the Other," trans. Helene Vivienne Wenzel in *Signs* 7, no. 1 (1981): 60–67.

[22] Ibid., 60.

regret. The unconscious fusion goes on to structure the daughter's feelings toward any daughter(s) of her own, reproducing between them another stifling merger that the new daughter(s) will flee.

In subsequent writings, notably *Sexes and Genealogies*,[23] Irigaray seems to see mother–daughter relations more positively. Although the childhood process of differentiation from the mother is always painful,[24] daughters can accept this pain and can self-differentiate more easily than sons. This is because daughters can identify themselves as being of the same sex as their mothers, as potential mothers,[25] who, though distinct from their own mothers as individuals, have the potential to recreate and return to the early mother–child proximity. They can carry a child in their own bodies and can undergo a mother's bodily and affective closeness with her young child(ren).

This reasoning seems to invert Irigaray's earlier thinking. Now, the *son* finds it hard to self-differentiate (as he can never give birth), and so he oscillates between saying "yes" and "no" to his mother, between unconscious fusion with and conscious rejection of her.[26] Yet individuation is easier for daughters than sons only in principle; in practice, patriarchy passes the burden of difficulty on to daughters. Boys/men resolve their difficulties in individuating by arrogating subjectivity to themselves and denying it to the mother, construing the maternal figure as a mere speechless, passive body. In this way, the son overcomes his difficulties by denying that he had anything to lose by differentiating himself, since he now casts closeness with the mother as a fusion embodying all that is negative (silence; passivity; body) and casts differentiation as a separation that is the repository of all value. The son splits bad (the maternal/female) from good (the paternal/male).

This patriarchal denial of maternal subjectivity makes it impossible for the daughter to individuate by identifying herself as a potential mother

[23] Luce Irigaray, *Sexes and Genealogies*, trans. Gillian C. Gill (New York: Columbia University Press, 1993b).

[24] Ibid., 16.

[25] Irigaray, *Sexes and Geanealogies*, 18; Luce Irigaray, "'Je—Luce Irigaray': A Meeting with Luce Irigaray," interview with Elizabeth Hirsh and Gary A. Olson, *Hypatia* 10, no. 2 (1995): 107–108; Luce Irigaray, "Thinking Life as Relation: An Interview with Stephen Pluhacek and Heidi Bostic," *Man and World* 29 (1996b): 353.

[26] Irigaray, *Sexes and Genealogies*, 195.

like her mother. In this situation, to be mother is to be a formless, speechless, boundless body; this is not a position that confers individuation. Only the paternal/male subject-position allows individuation vis-à-vis the mother. So, the daughter becomes split—insofar as she identifies herself as a speaking subject, she must position herself as male. Insofar as she nonetheless identifies herself as female, she feels herself to be a formless, devalued body, and thus an impure, defective kind of rational subject.

Irigaray thus continues to see actually existing mother–daughter relations more negatively than Chodorow, as involving an enforced split between women's rejection of the maternal, female, and bodily and women's ongoing immersion in maternal qualities, an immersion felt as overwhelming, threatening, and bad. Thus, women's relations to their mothers threaten to drag them down into a netherworld, ruining the dream of assimilating to male standards of value. Irigaray seems not to recognize the positive—empathetic, intimate—character that Chodorow finds in many existing mother-daughter bonds.[27] But Chodorow is surely right that even if these bonds become mired in female feelings of antagonism and (self-)hatred, these bonds often retain positive value for women as well. We need to integrate this insight into Irigaray's perspective on sexual difference. Doing so is not straightforward because Irigaray and Chodorow's disagreement about those bonds is linked to their divergent approaches to difference itself. Irigaray seeks to create an as-yet-nonexistent sexual difference and to create mother–daughter bonds that she thinks patriarchy has fairly comprehensively broken. Chodorow wishes to revalue women's already existing "different," feminine traits—relationality, empathy—including empathetic mother–daughter bonds that, she thinks, persist despite patriarchy. If Chodorow is right that these bonds do persist, then does it follow, contrary to Irigaray, that we need to revalue women's already existing difference and bonds? But wouldn't this constitute an uncritical celebration of pre-Oedipal mother–daughter fusion?

[27] This criticism of Irigaray may seem uncharitable. After all, she speaks of girls trying through doll play and whirling games to situate themselves in relation to their mothers, and trying to speak with their mothers as female-to-female. Irigaray, *Sexes and Genealogies*, 97–99. Nonetheless, for Irigaray, the symbolic allows girls no resources to fulfill these attempts. When she says "Neither the little girl nor the woman needs to give up the love for her mother" she means that while in principle they need not do so, in practice they must. Ibid., 20.

Let us explore this problem. Lacanian feminists such as Jacqueline Rose accuse Chodorow of just such a celebration.[28] Lacanians argue that Chodorow neglects the negative, overpowering, alienating aspects of pre-Oedipal mother-daughter fusion, and also neglects the universal requirement and the liberatory value of entering the symbolic order via castration from the mother. Rose makes similar criticisms of Irigaray—unfairly.[29] Irigaray is emphatic that women's identification with their mothers is damaging. It involves a bodily mergence that engulfs and dissolves women's individuality and flings women into a vortex of primitive passions and terrors associated with their once venerated, now radically devalued, mothers. This complex of feelings underlies patterns of female-to-female hostility.[30] Rather than stressing this hostility, Chodorow focuses on how women's ongoing identification with their mothers motivates them to bear and raise children and makes women psychically capable of mothering by giving them the fluid ego boundaries that enable them to identify and empathize with their child(ren)'s needs. For Chodorow, a woman's preoccupation with her child does not—as Irigaray would have it—plunge her back into the dreaded, devalued symbolic position of mother; rather, this preoccupation reflects and confirms a (relatively) unproblematic feminine identity premised on identification with one's mother. Chodorow's more benign view of mothering reflects her view that women always feel grounded in (even if ambivalent about) identificatory ties with their mothers.

Does this mean that Chodorow does indeed celebrate pre-Oedipal fusion? No, for she is not uncritical of women's relational selfhood. She thinks that this form of selfhood makes women prone to excessive absorption in others' needs, to caring for others at their own expense. It makes women insufficiently autonomous and overly deferential to goals given them by others. Chodorow is less negative about existing mother-daughter relations than Irigaray, but she is not entirely positive either. Chodorow's criticisms of feminine selfhood do not imply that she endorses masculine autonomous selfhood, which for her rests on denigration of mothers and women, involves an inability to care for and empathize with others and to connect with one's own emotions, and

[28] Jacquelyn Rose, *Sexuality in the Field of Vision* (London: Verso, 1986), 52.

[29] Ibid., 78.

[30] Irigaray, *Sexes and Genealogies*, 85.

involves a self-deceiving belief in one's freedom from ties to others (self-deceiving because that very posture of freedom has been constructed out of a history of object-relations). Nevertheless, Chodorow thinks that feminine relational selfhood should be transformed to include more autonomy and masculine selfhood to include more relationality: ideally, all individuals would be relationally autonomous. Chodorow thus sees traits of care and empathy in women's relational selfhood that are worth preserving. As Diana Meyers says, Chodorow sees feminine relationality as an underappreciated good.[31]

For Irigaray, however, mother–daughter identification as it currently exists is pathological. The positive mother–daughter bonds that Irigaray envisages as a future possibility would be bonds allowing the daughter to differentiate herself from her mother, not identificatory/fusional bonds. Identity/fusion is not Irigaray's goal (on this, at least, she agrees with Lacanians such as Rose). Yet perhaps Chodorow too agrees with Irigaray here. After all, for Chodorow, women would ideally be autonomous as well as relational, having their needs, wishes, and feelings differ from, although still related to, those of their mothers. However, Chodorow's ideal is a mixture of (currently masculine) autonomy and (currently feminine) relationality, where the latter is conceived *in terms of empathetic identification*, whereas for Irigaray, the ideal is a mixture of individuation and connection where the latter is *not* identification/fusion.

Admittedly, Chodorow thinks that ideally, relationality would be transformed by its combination with autonomy into something more like interconnection than identification.[32] Even so, she conceptualizes relationality in terms of identification, ego-fluidity, and lack of psychical boundaries.[33] This marks a vital difference from Irigaray, for whom, again, identificatory mother–daughter bonds are bad, an oppressive extension of the pre-Oedipal (as Lacanians would agree), and not a source of positive, potentially post-patriarchal value (as for Chodorow). For Irigaray, the problem is that under patriarchy, the maternal lacks symbolic articulation, and mother–daughter fusion cannot be transformed into connection.

[31] Meyers, *Subjection and Subjectivity*, 81.

[32] Chodorow, *The Reproduction of Mothering*, 108.

[33] Ibid., 167.

This difference between Irigaray and Chodorow rests on their different reconstructions of female psychosexual development. For Irigaray, the daughter first aspires to the male position of individuation and then falls from this aspiration back onto an identification with the female and maternal to which she now relates as one construed and valorized *negatively*, in negative contrast to the male subject-position.[34] For Chodorow, however, the daughter's aspirations toward her father are significantly rooted in her prior identificatory love for her mother. So, however ambivalent the daughter subsequently becomes about her mother, that ambivalence is rooted in prior love, a love that must therefore remain at base positive, whatever qualifications it takes on as overwhelming, oppressive, etc. (By "positive," I mean that this love exists in its own right and that it is felt as constitutive of and a source of good in the daughter's/woman's self.)

Whose reconstruction should we prefer? We cannot answer this question without appreciating that the difference between Irigaray's and Chodorow's reconstructions rests on a still deeper divergence—namely, whether or not they recognize the existence of the symbolic order. We can explore this divergence by seeing how it shapes their different explanations of the separation/fusion logic of mother–daughter relations.

Irigaray, as we have seen, explains this logic as stemming from the symbolic denial of maternal subjectivity. Chodorow's explanation is sociological. As industrial capitalism was developed and production moved outside the home, women's work contracted into child care at home, while men worked elsewhere as breadwinners. This empirical social arrangement made all infants originally matrisexual and made children feel overpowered by their mothers and see their fathers as symbols of freedom. But equally, girls retained the feminine identification that gave them fluid ego-boundaries, disposing them to prefer mothering to paid work; whereas men's suppression of their early relational selves made them unwilling and more or less unable to parent. Thus, the gendered private/public split was reproduced: Social division wrote itself into the psyche through early relationships in the family (not through conscious role learning). Individuals' gendered psyches then led them to make the choices that recreated that social division.

[34] Luce Irigaray, *This Sex Which Is Not One*, trans. Catherine Porter and Carolyn Burke (Ithaca: Cornell University Press, 1985), 69.

Chodorow's sociological explanation has a problem that Irigaray's symbolic explanation avoids: the increasing diversity of family practices in contemporary Western societies—single-parent families, post-divorce families, stepfamilies, same-sex families, and increasing involvement of fathers in child care, along with an ever-expanding participation of women and mothers in paid work. For Chodorow, this diversification in family practices should correlate with a decline in male domination. For example, a single-mother family has no empirical father figure onto whom sons or daughters can latch as the bastion of individuation. If fathers are increasingly involved in childcare and mothers in paid work, then the connection of mothers with relationships and fathers with autonomy should be disintegrating. Yet the diversification of the family has not dislodged the notion of the "traditional" family or the ideology that families should adhere to a traditional, gender-based division of labor.[35]

One way to understand this is if fantasies about maternal and paternal roles stem from the symbolic order as a horizon of meaning that endures across changes in empirical family structure, as Irigaray holds. From Irigaray's perspective, these fantasies structure our psyches, whatever forms of family we come from, because we all must individuate within the terms the symbolic provides. Given the cultural denial of maternal subjectivity, a girl raised by a lone mother must still locate separate subjectivity with the paternal position, even if she has no empirical father who instantiates this position. A girl raised by gay men will still be forced to locate in the maternal the corporeal fusion from which she must escape, even though empirically, men have been her caregivers. Chodorow does not recognize this because, in *Reproduction*, she does not acknowledge the symbolic level of existence. She overlooks "the relation between gender as she describes it and representation, ... the effect of a preexisting system of representation on the emergence of gender."[36] Chodorow's account of family dynamics in *Reproduction* makes no reference to any idea of a shared cultural horizon of meaning and representation. Admittedly, the meaning of the symbolic order is not unaffected by empirical changes in family practices. "Nontraditional" family practices create a dissonance

[35] Elizabeth B. Silva and Carol Smart, "The 'New' Practices and Politics of Family Life," in *The New Family?* (London: Sage, 1999), 1–12.

[36] Shirley Nelson Garner, Claire Kahane, and Madelon Sprengnether, eds., *The (M)Other Tongue: Essays in Feminist Psychoanalytic Interpretation* (Ithaca: Cornell University Press, 1985), 20.

with the symbolic, and this dissonance can prompt individuals to place new interpretations on and to reimagine symbolic constructions.

Unless new family practices introduced this dissonance, it is hard to see why the conservative right wing would find them threatening. But once we admit that individuals can and constantly do impose conflicting interpretations on symbolic constructions, we have to acknowledge that the symbolic must be internally heterogeneous. It is not a monolithic bloc; rather, it contains uneven layers of dominant and subordinated elements, all coexisting uneasily with one another. (Indeed, Chodorow herself argues this in her more recent work, *The Power of Feelings,* in which she has paid increasing attention to the level of culture and representation.[37] She argues that the symbolic does not provide a fixed set of positions into which individuals must fit. Rather, she says, individuals constantly attribute new meanings to the symbolic in light of their context-specific experiences.)

How, then, does Irigaray's and (the earlier) Chodorow's divergence on the symbolic relate to their different reconstructions of female development? For Irigaray, to individuate from the mother is to enter the symbolic order, to position oneself within the available field of meaning. Necessarily, this field of meaning colors everything; therefore, once a woman has entered a symbolic order that defines the maternal–female position in pejorative contrast to the male, then, necessarily, this fundamentally alters her experience of her mother and her relations to her mother. However much the woman loved her mother in infancy, and however much that love fuels her very aspiration to the paternal male position, on entering the patriarchal symbolic, her love for her mother will become qualified as pathological and threatening. Once we accept that there is a symbolic dimension of existence, this conclusion of Irigaray's seems unavoidable. But this creates a puzzle. If the symbolic indeed exists, but if (as I suggested) Chodorow is right that many mothers and daughters do retain positive bonds despite patriarchy, then how are these positive bonds possible? An answer emerges once we recognize the heterogeneity of the symbolic, as Irigaray does not do sufficiently. For her, the Western symbolic has constantly and unequivocally reduced the female to the "other of the same." In saying this, she overlooks

[37] Chodorow, *The Power of Feelings.*

how female (and some male) thinkers, writers, and artists have continually contested and reimagined symbolic schemes. Christine Battersby[38] notes how Irigaray[39] treats Unica Zürn—one of the very few female artists whom Irigaray discusses—as a tragic failure, victimized by patriarchal aesthetic practices. But not all female artists have been tragic failures; many of them have engaged in highly successful projects of reimagining, the female/maternal in particular. These reimaginings may be a subordinate element in the Western symbolic, but they are not nonexistent.[40]

Because Irigaray over-homogenizes the symbolic, she thinks that entering the symbolic means coming to experience the maternal wholly negatively. Daughters, for Irigaray, have no symbolic resources that they can consciously and unconsciously appropriate so as to re-envision the maternal, the bodily, and the passional as positive qualities to be embraced. But resources *do* exist, and they enable women to value (to at least some extent) and to hold onto their ties with their mothers as the source of these positive qualities. Consider an example of Battersby's, a poem by the Early German Romantic Karoline Günderode. Having been flitting about like an insubstantial shadow, the narrator suddenly feels:

> And it was if once I had
> torn myself away from a sweet body,
> and now for the first time
> the wounds of this ancient agony bled.
> … I had to cry,
> dripping with tears
> I sank down
> into the lap of the mother …
> to the hidden place
> from which life springs.[41]

[38] Christine Battersby, *The Sublime, Terror, and Human Difference* (London: Routledge, 2008), 159.

[39] Luce Irigaray, "A Natal Lacuna," *Women's Art Magazine* 58 (May/June, 1994): 11–13.

[40] Irigaray's strategy of mimesis presupposes that such reimagining is possible, but she seems reluctant to concede that writers and thinkers other than herself have ever engaged in it.

[41] Karoline Günderode, cited in Battersby, *The Sublime, Terror, and Human Difference*, 123.

The narrator first admits the pain of having separated from her mother, and then reconnects with her mother ("[sinks] down" into her lap) by recognizing that she has sprung from her mother and that their shared power to generate life gives them a lasting connection. Of course, this particular poem is hardly well known, but it is one of many striking similar themes. Imagery and ideas of this kind and their traces and reverberations in culture and language enable women, to some degree at least, to embrace their mothers and their closeness to their mothers—although, given the overall dominance of the patriarchal image of mother-as-mere-body, women also continue to have grounds to repudiate their mothers and to find their ongoing imbrication with their mothers threatening and bad. Thus arise the mingled hostility *and* enduring love that many women feel toward their mothers, which Chodorow rightly identifies. These mixed emotions are how women respond to their mothers given a heterogeneous and uneven symbolic.

Chodorow and Irigaray make different proposals for how to restructure mother–daughter relations to defuse their hostility. Irigaray proposes that the mother be symbolically recognized as a subject. To recognize maternal subjectivity is to recognize mothers as subjects of desire, individuals not wholly absorbed in or exhaustively fulfilled by their children, who maintain other interests, activities, and relationships outside motherhood.[42] But what is required is not just to recognize mothers as individual, desiring subjects like any other. Mothers and women qua potential mothers are to be reimagined as subjects of a specific kind given their maternal or potentially maternal bodies: as subjects with shifting, porous bodily boundaries. Maternal subjects are not sharply separated from others but in constant osmotic, fluid exchange with the world and with others (e.g., in breastfeeding) and with others inside their bodies during pregnancy.[43]

Symbolizing maternal subjectivity would enable the daughter to identify herself as a potential future mother and just to that extent a (specific kind of) subject, hence a subject distinct from her mother. At the same time, she would remain connected to her mother: First, in having the potential to recover early mother–infant intimacy with any child(ren) of

[42] Irigaray, *Sexes and Genealogies*, 18.

[43] Luce Irigaray, *An Ethics of Sexual Difference*, trans. Carolyn Burke (London: Athlone, 1993a).

her own, and, second, in that she has that potential because she is of the same sex as her mother, thus being connected to her mother in this way. This is not a matter simply of having shared biological features but of being the same ***kind*** of subject, a member of the same sexuate kind, a kind marked out by shared maternal potential.

The idea that all women could individuate by identifying with a maternal subject-position may seem to reinforce a conservative woman–mother equation.

But women, Irigaray claims, “are always mothers just by being women.”[44] Women can symbolically “mother” whenever they exercise any form of creativity, “birthing” their creations in a fluid process, as their mothers bore them. Thus, to identify as a potential maternal subject is to see oneself as having potentials for creativity and porous exchange that one can actualize in many other contexts besides literal birth-giving, contexts in all of which one would remain connected to one’s mother.

For Chodorow, on the other hand, the precondition of restructured mother–daughter relations is that parenting is shared equally between men and women.[45] With both parents fully involved in childcare, no parent would be overpoweringly close, as the mother now is, or a distant ideal, as the father now is. Thus, neither girls nor boys would have to react against their mothers to individuate but could acknowledge their early bonds with their mothers as compatible with, not stifling, their autonomy. Consequently, boys/men would cease to denigrate women; girls/women would cease to overvalue men. In turn, women would not convey to their own daughters that boys/men are superior, which would take away daughters’ second motivation—thwarted love—for rejecting their mothers. Women could then remain related to their mothers while being autonomous rather than oscillating between rejection of their mothers and ongoing (but dependency-inducing) attachment.

Surely, though, shared parenting would not suffice to undo existing gendered personality structures. Given the patriarchal symbolic, shared parenting would disrupt but not undo the dominant equations man-subject, woman-body. Symbolic change, to challenge and rework dominant representations, is also necessary. Yet on its own, symbolic change would not suffice to undo patriarchy either; without a diversification in

[44] Irigaray, *Sexes and Genealogies*, 18.

[45] Chodorow, *The Reproduction of Mothering*, 215, 218.

family practices (or rather, without political and ideological support for their already occurring diversification), our gender-divided family lives will reinforce and reinstall dominant symbolic codes.

Admittedly, "diversification in family practices" is not quite the same as "shared parenting." The latter notion has the connotation of exclusively heterosexual families, as does Chodorow's model of how children raised under shared parenting would relate autonomously and relationally to parents of both sexes.[46] Chodorow's key point, though, is just that whatever the empirical makeup of particular families, men generally should be as involved in (private and public) childcare as women. Otherwise, aside from women's continuing to bear an unjustly heavy burden of the hard physical and emotional labor of parenting and to be disadvantaged and marginalized outside the home, women's role as primary caregivers will foster and reinforce equations between women and body, emotions and selflessness. The projects of symbolic change and social change intersect.

In a second way, too, shared parenting would not in itself suffice to transform gendered personalities, as Chodorow hopes. She sharply distinguishes biological sex from social/psychical gender,[47] holding that biological sex differences do not cause women's childcare responsibilities. She notes, though, that inevitably breastfeeding (if children are breastfed) must fall to women.[48] She seems to think that this qualification is unimportant. But a breastfed child will almost always attach most strongly to, and initially love and identify with, the breastfeeding parent—namely, the (usually biological) mother.[49] So in a breastfeeding family, whatever jobs the parent(s) empirically undertake, the feeding mother is very likely to become the child's first love, obliging the child to turn to some person who is not-mother—let's assume for now, the father—to individuate. Breastfeeding aside, plausibly further biological factors push the child to attach principally to its biological mother: the child's recognition of her smell, voice, and the rhythm of her heartbeat; her body's special continuity with the intra-uterine environment. And plausibly, a social mother's female smell, voice, and body, too, will tend to have

[46] Doane and Hodges, *From Klein to Kristeva*, 85.

[47] Chodorow, *The Reproduction of Mothering*, Chapter 2.

[48] Ibid., 28.

[49] It may be objected that men can share in breastfeeding if the mother expresses her breast milk. Even so, the baby will still attach principally to the person who feeds him or her skin-to-skin; few mothers exclusively express except for medical reasons.

similar resonance for the child and provoke a similar principal attachment of child to mother. Even given shared parenting, then, biological factors would apparently still press our *psyches* toward the dichotomy mother-body-fusion, father-subjectivity separation—unless we reject Chodorow's claim that the developing child turns to some nonmaternal empirical person for an instantiation of individual subjectivity. If, instead, the developing child identified with a position of individual subjectivity as defined by the symbolic, and if that symbolic did not attach individual subjectivity exclusively to the male position, then the child would not necessarily have to turn away from its mother to individuate.

The problem with Chodorow's proposals for change is that she thinks that social change to parental roles would suffice to produce psychical change. But, as Lacanians have rightly argued against Chodorow,[50] the psyche—and, I am specifying, the significance of the mother in each child's psyche—is not reducible to social arrangements. Plausibly, a working mother will still be the primary attachment-figure and bearer of emotional significance to the young child, even if the father is that child's main caregiver. Chodorow cannot admit this because for her, it would entail that the child's subsequent reaction against the mother, and hence a male-dominant division of labor, are unalterably fixed. This entailment follows for Chodorow because she does not recognize the symbolic level of existence or, therefore, the possibility of ending male domination and the child's propensity to react against the mother by transforming how the symbolic structures the child's developing psyche, specifically by introducing a conception of maternal subjectivity.

If, though, our psyches came to be structured by a symbolic that recognizes maternal subjectivity, then boys/men could no longer resolve their individuation difficulties by splitting the good father from the bad mother, who embodies corporeal fusion. How, then, would men be able to resolve those difficulties? Irigaray suggests that boys/men could instead identify as male subjects, distinct from female subjects.[51] Apparently, men could accept loss of their early closeness with their mothers by becoming reconciled to occupying their own specific subject-position, belonging to their own sexuate genre.

[50] For example, Adams, *Mothering*.

[51] Luce Irigaray, *I Love to You*, trans. Alison Martin (London: Routledge, 1996a), 27, 41.

In claiming that men, unlike women, must become reconciled to leaving altogether their early closeness with their mothers, Irigaray seems to assume that men, unlike women, cannot ever hope to recapture that early closeness through parenting. Seemingly, she assumes that men's role in parenting must be relatively impersonal and abstract. Effectively, this reserves the primary role in parenting to women. As such, her proposals appear to imply that in the symbolic order to come, women would remain the main parent both psychically and socially. Here, her perspective actually discourages changing the division of parental labor. So, just as Chodorow neglects the symbolic and the need for symbolic change, Irigaray neglects the need to support change to empirical parenting patterns. But this change *does* require support, not least because otherwise, gender-divided parenting will undermine our efforts to resymbolize sexed positions.

Therefore, we should revise Irigaray's position. We should say that, even if biological constraints prevent men from recapturing their early closeness to their mothers as deeply as women can, men can potentially recapture much of that closeness, by (bottle-)feeding, bathing, cleaning, holding, soothing, and babbling to their babies. Men, like women, can potentially return to the early phase of corporeal proximity by parenting. For boys/men to accept becoming distinct from their mothers, they need to be able to access a symbolic identity as a male subject who can potentially return to that early proximity. The paternal figure needs to be reimagined as loving, caring, and nurturing; one who holds and stays near, not merely enforcing the law or introducing rough-and-tumble play. The correlate of imagining maternal subjectivity is imagining paternal nurturance. Moreover, to provide men with their own symbolic identity, this nurturance must be imagined as specifically male, related to distinctively male biological powers. In part, this means recognizing that women can relate to children in biologically specific ways—via breastfeeding and rhythms of touch and speech continuous with the intra-uterine world—and that paternal nurturance involves supporting and nurturing mothers, at work and home, in exercising these capacities. If this reimagining of the paternal is not to be undermined by our empirical family lives, it requires a move away from gender-divided parenting. Again, symbolic and social change must support one another.

I have argued that Chodorow is right about the need for "shared parenting," in the sense of equal participation by men and women in private and public childcare. Shared parenting is actually a co-condition of the symbolic change that Irigaray advocates. But how can the projects of social and symbolic change intersect, when for Chodorow, the aim in changing the family is to revalue mother-daughter bonds that already exist, whereas for Irigaray, the goal of symbolic change is to create *not* yet-existent mother-daughter bonds? I have tried to move beyond these alternatives by insisting on the internal heterogeneity of the symbolic. Being unstable, the symbolic already contains glimmerings and fragments of a positive conception of the maternal alongside the dominant negative image of the mother-as-mere-body. The partial presence of this positive conception makes it possible for many women to value and retain positive bonds with their mothers (despite having hostile and negative feelings, too).

So these positive bonds do already exist, as Chodorow rightly says—but they exist because of the (heterogeneity of the) symbolic, as Chodorow does not say. The goal of symbolic change is to move the fragments of a positive image of the maternal from the margins to the center: to represent a maternal-female difference that has only a fleeting, tenuous status in the symbolic at present. Thus, the aim of symbolic change is not only to revalue existing mother-daughter bonds, but also to deepen them and transform their significance by enabling them to be lived in light of a fully positive symbolization of the maternal. Yet for Chodorow, already existing mother–daughter bonds are identificatory; whereas for Irigaray, already existing mother–daughter relations are qua identificatory toxic and need replacing by non-identificatory bonds of difference and connection. So in arguing that there are existing bonds worth valuing, am I suggesting that these are identificatory and hence that (as Chodorow thinks) identificatory bonds are valuable? On the contrary: I think that to the extent that existing mother–daughter bonds are positive, these are already bonds of difference and connection of the kind that Irigaray envisages (but wrongly restricts to a possible future). For, insofar as positive symbolic images of the maternal exist, these images position the maternal as a subject-position that women can embrace. These images position the maternal body not as a site of pathological fusion but as the source of connection, of osmotic exchange between two entities, and of embodied care for the other. This enables women to identify themselves, to some extent, as subjects, distinct from their mothers, and yet as maternal subjects, connected to their mothers.

Irigaray is right, then, about the value of mother–daughter bonds structured by connection, not by relationality as identification. But, contrary to Irigaray, many such bonds already exist. And this brings me to a crucial issue that I want to consider in conclusion: whether mother-daughter bonds ought ideally to be gender-neutral (as Chodorow argues) or sexually specific (as Irigaray argues). For Chodorow, under shared parenting, girls/women would acknowledge and retain their constitutive bonds with their mothers while also, as autonomous individuals, being fully aware of being distinct from their mothers.

Daughters would be acknowledging their autonomy to have been forged *in*, not against, their early bonds with their mothers. Equally, daughters would be acknowledging and retaining their dependency on their fathers, as the latter would have been equally involved as parents. Sons, too, would adopt the same attitude of relational autonomy vis-à-vis both parents. Women and men would relate in identical ways to both parents: our personalities would have ceased to be structured by gender. In this sense, Chodorow advocates a "non-gender world,"[52] although she believes that it may take a long time to get there.

In contrast, for Irigaray, daughters' possible relations in difference with their mothers would take a sexually specific form. With maternal subjectivity represented, daughters could accept being different from their mothers despite the painfulness of exiting their early proximity. This is because daughters would be aware that they retain the possibility of returning to a similar closeness with their own child(ren); and because in their awareness of being the kind of subject who can do this, they retain a connection to their mothers—not an identity but a connection between *two* maternal–female subjects. This thought underlies Irigaray's well-known proposal for public images of and rediscovery of mythic and religious narratives about mother–daughter couples: a couple being two people who are distinct yet connected.[53] Moreover, because daughters could bear the painfulness of individuating, they could acknowledge that pain and what they have lost. Thus, they could acknowledge that they are constituted by a primary corporeal and emotional proximity to their

[52] Nancy Chodorow, *Feminism and Psychoanalytic Theory* (Cambridge, UK: Polity Press, 1989), 101.

[53] Irigaray, *Sexes and Genealogies*, 189–191.

mothers that exceeds their grasp as individuated subjects, who qua individuated, necessarily stand outside that proximity. Daughters would be identifying not only as individual subjects but also as subjects constituted, birthed, from a matrix of maternal relations.

Chodorow's picture of mother–daughter relations in terms of autonomy and relationality goes along with her idea that, ultimately, these relations should be gender-neutral. Irigaray's picture of these relations in terms of difference and connection goes along with her idea that they should be sexually specific, with daughters identifying as potential mothers and as remaining connected to their mothers along that distinctively female axis. This disagreement entwines with Chodorow's and Irigaray's different conceptions of the self. For Chodorow, the ideal is for ourselves to be whole.[54]

A person's self is whole if he or she acknowledges and embraces constitutive relations, admitting these relations into the conscious self and thus retaining autonomy (in and through relations), rather than being controlled by those relations as if by an outer force.[55] For Irigaray, in contrast, assuming individuation should ideally mean acknowledging one's finitude, one's not-wholeness. This is, first, because one would be assuming a sexually specific position to which the other-sexed position stands as an inaccessible limit. Second, one would be admitting that a prehistory of maternal relations has constituted one's self, a prehistory that, as an individuated self, one can no longer consciously access or narrate. One can regain that prehistory only by undergoing it anew in mothering (I would add: mothering biologically or socially, or by fathering); or through forms of writing and creativity that express this buried stratum of the self. The sexually specific selves of the (possible) future would, then, be finite sexually and generationally vis-à-vis their own infantile prehistories.[56]

My arguments imply that we should endorse Irigaray's vision of the sexually differentiated and finite self, not Chodorow's vision of the gender-neutral and unified self. Biological constraints mean that, even given equal involvement of both sexes in childcare, the mother

[54] Chodorow, *Feminism and Psychoanalytic Theory*, 155; Chodorow, *The Power of Feelings*, 274.

[55] Chodorow, *The Power of Feelings*, 271.

[56] Luce Irigaray, *To Be Two*, trans. Monique M. Rhodes and Marco F. Cocito-Monoc (London: Athlone, 2000), Chapter 3.

(if available) will generally be a child's first great love. Early-infantile experience can never be gender-neutral; it involves a felt priority of the maternal/female. So, under any symbolic order that defines individual subjectivity gender-neutrally, subjectivity will in practice become understood in antithesis to the maternal and the early period of overwhelming maternal presence, and hence will become positioned as paternal/male. This can be avoided only if subjectivity is explicitly defined as sexually differentiated, as female–maternal or male–paternal, so that we can conceive of female–maternal subjectivity as distinct from—but still connected to—the early time of overwhelming intimacy with the mother. In sum, once we recognize the irreducibility of psyche to social, and specifically that the psychical significance of the mother is irreducible to the social role of institutionalized motherhood, then we must also recognize the need for symbolic transformation toward a culture of sexual difference in particular. A culture of neutral subjectivity will always, de facto, be a male culture.

Consequently, symbolic transformation must also be toward an acknowledgment that our selves are finite: sexually limited, and limited also by their (sexually differentiated prehistories in a) matrix of maternal relations that can never be fully recuperated into consciousness. The self can be "split" without this having to mean breaking from the mother and subjection to the law of the father. Instead, the self might be "split," internally folded away from itself, in being constituted by a maternal prehistory that that self can never access consciously; and yet, for all that, a prehistory that need not be totally lost, with which we could retain (sexually different modes of) connection, and which we could recover, to varying degrees, in mothering, fathering, nurturing, art-working, writing—creating.

Bibliography

Adams, Parveen, "Mothering." *m/f* 8 (1983): 40–52.

Battersby, Christine, *The Sublime, Terror, and Human Difference*. London: Routledge, 2008.

Brennan, Teresa, "An Impasse in Psychoanalysis and Feminism." In *A Reader in Feminist Knowledge*, ed. Sneja Gunew. New York: Routledge, 1991, 114–138.

Chodorow, Nancy, *Feminism and Psychoanalytic Theory*. Cambridge, UK: Polity Press, 1989.

———, *Femininities, Masculinities, Sexualities: Freud and Beyond*. London: Free Association Books, 1994.

———, *The Power of Feelings*. New Haven: Yale University Press, 1999.

———, *The Reproduction of Mothering: Psychoanalysis and the Sociology of Gender.* Berkeley: University of California Press, 1978.

Doane, Janice and Devon Hodges, *From Klein to Kristeva: Psychoanalytic Feminism and the Search for the "Good Enough" Mother.* Ann Arbor: University of Michigan Press, 1992.

Freud, Sigmund, "Female Sexuality." In *On Sexuality*, ed. James Strachey. Harmondsworth: Penguin, 1977a, 366–392.

———, "Some Psychical Consequences of the Anatomical Distinction Between the Sexes." In *On Sexuality*, ed. James Strachey. Harmondsworth: Penguin, 1977b, 331–343.

———, *"Totem and Taboo" and Other Works*, ed. James Strachey. New York: Vintage, 2001.

Garner, Shirley Nelson, Claire Kahane, and Madelon Sprengnether, eds., *The (M)Other Tongue: Essays in Feminist Psychoanalytic Interpretation.* Ithaca: Cornell University Press, 1985.

Irigaray, Luce, "A Natal Lacuna." *Women's Art Magazine* 58 (May/June, 1994): 11–13.

———, *An Ethics of Sexual Difference*, trans. Carolyn Burke. London: Athlone, 1993a.

———, "And the One Doesn't Stir without the Other." Translated by Helene Vivienne Wenzel. *Signs* 7, no. 1 (1981): 60–67.

———, *I Love to You*, trans. Alison Martin. London: Routledge, 1996a.

———, "'Je—Luce Irigaray': A Meeting with Luce Irigaray." Interview with Elizabeth Hirsh and Gary A. Olson. *Hypatia* 10, no. 2 (1995): 93–114.

———, *Sexes and Genealogies*, trans. Gillian C. Gill. New York: Columbia University Press, 1993b.

———. "Thinking Life as Relation: An Interview with Stephen Pluhacek and Heidi Bostic." *Man and World* 29 (1996b): 343–360.

———, *This Sex Which Is Not One*, trans. Catherine Porter with Carolyn Burke. Ithaca: Cornell University Press, 1985.

———, *To Be Two*, trans. Monique M. Rhodes and Marco F. Cocito-Monoc. London: Athlone, 2000.

Meyers, Diana Tietjens, *Subjection and Subjectivity: Psychoanalytic Feminism and Moral Philosophy.* London: Routledge, 1994.

Riley, Denise, *War in the Nursery: Theories of the Child and Mother.* London: Virago, 1983.

Rose, Jacquelyn, *Sexuality in the Field of Vision.* London: Verso, 1986.

Silva, Elizabeth B. and Carol Smart, "The 'New' Practices and Politics of Family Life." In *The New Family?* eds. Silva and Smart. London: Sage, 1999, 1–12.

CHAPTER 13

Mothers Reproducing the Social: Chodorow and Beyond

Petra Bueskens

In *The Reproduction of Mothering* Nancy Chodorow laid the blue print for understanding mothers and daughters in their intricate psychosexual identification. Synthesizing object relations theory with feminist sociological concerns regarding gender equality Chodorow brought together complex psychoanalytic theory with feminist utopian projects. This weaving of the social and the psychic hearkened back to earlier work by Karen Horney and Eric Fromm (Mitchell and Black 1995), while also connecting with contemporary progressive politics of the 1970s. While speaking to many issues relevant in her own day, particularly a growing theoretical divide in psychoanalysis between object relations and drive theories, and the parallel rise of second-wave feminism, *The Reproduction of Mothering* endures

Originally published in *Journal of Psychosocial Studies, Volume 13, Number 1, March 2020, pp. 65–86(22).* Re-published with permission of Policy Press (an imprint of Bristol University Press, UK).

P. Bueskens (✉)
University of Melbourne, Melbourne, VIC, Australia
e-mail: petra.bueskens@unimelb.edu.au

P. Bueskens (ed.), *Nancy Chodorow and* The Reproduction of Mothering,
https://doi.org/10.1007/978-3-030-55590-0_13

precisely because of its emphasis on the mother-daughter relationship. This relationship had been hitherto dismissed in orthodox psychoanalysis as irrelevant to the central Oedipal drama. In situating mother-daughter relations both within the classic "family romance," and also prior to and constitutive of it, Chodorow bequeathed a critically important legacy. She literally provided a new psychoanalytic language for understanding female subjectivity, inclusive of yet differentiating the mother's and the daughter's subjectivity. As she said, "it is a cyclical process that I break into at the daughter's birth, but developmental outcomes in the mother already situate that birth...."[1] It is the dynamic quality of the mother-daughter relationship across time—that is, its capacity to both reproduce and recreate itself—that helps us grasp generational continuity and change.[2]

This chapter will review Chodorow's classic work *The Reproduction of Mothering* while also extending her original formulation to a contemporary understanding of changing gendered social relations. Drawing on the recent work of Alison Stone, I elucidate the process of not only reproducing but also reinventing mothering. From here, I tentatively explore how mothers are symbolically and actually "reproducing the social". Citizen mothers, I argue, have the potential to transform human relations, economies and polities, integrating an "ethic of care"[3] with an "ethic of justice"[4] in turn transforming the gendered split of public and private personae—men as rational and defensively individuated public actors; women as emotional and enmeshed wives and mothers undertaking unpaid care in the home. The challenge in extending Chodorow's thesis at the socio-political level is to examine the emergence of "autonomous mothers" as more psychosocially integrated personae begin to emerge (including more emotionally connected fathers involved in the day-to-day care of children—see Bell, Chapter 10, this volume). The last section of this paper shall tentatively explore the emergence of "autonomous mothers."

[1] Nancy Chodorow, *The Reproduction of Mothering: Psychoanalysis and the Sociology of Gender* (Berkeley: University of California Press, 1999 [1978]), vii.

[2] See Chodorow, Chapter 2, this volume.

[3] Carol Gilligan, *In a Different Voice: Psychological Theory and Women's Development* (Cambridge, MA: Harvard University Press, 1993 [1982]).

[4] Lawrence Kohlberg, *Essays on Moral Development, Vol. I: The Philosophy of Moral Development* (San Francisco, California: Harper & Row, 1981).

Chodorow's Feminist Object Relations

Nancy Chodorow shifted the tone of object relations theory from a child-centered discourse focused on male infants to the interrelationship between mothers (as subjects) and their male and female infants, with an emphasis on the mother-daughter relationship. By gendering the object and subject under discussion and putting them into dynamic interplay *The Reproduction of Mothering*[5] mapped a rich account of psychosexual identity formation. In addition, Chodorow asked the seemingly straightforward but actually radical question: *why do women mother?*[6] Refusing common sense understandings, she sought to understand women's desire to become mothers using the tools of psychoanalysis. If sociology is the art of making the familiar strange, arguably this is what Chodorow did for maternal subjectivity. While her theoretical workings were informed by and closely aligned with object relations theory, she nonetheless brought a sociological and feminist eye to her subject matter, which dramatically altered her analysis. Here I will trace a thumb nail sketch of her key argument regarding gendered identity formation, bearing in mind that Chodorow's account is elucidating the normal developmental pattern of gender identity corresponding with biological sex, and the concomitant development of heterosexuality. As she qualifies, this is a "…statistically prevalent rather than a morally normative model …".[7]

To begin with, Chodorow identified the peculiar context of mothering in the late twentieth century in a family structure she aptly identified as the "male dominant but father-absent family"[8] in which early mothering was undertaken by women at home alone. Here she opened up space for a sociology of the psychoanalytic subject; that is, for asking questions not only about the psychic but also the social constitution of the subject.[9] Mid to late twentieth century maternal subjectivity was forged in an historically specific context and this was relevant to its intra-psychic formation

[5] Chodorow, *Reproduction of Mothering*.

[6] Ibid., 47.

[7] Chodorow, "Preface to the Second Edition," xi–xii.

[8] Ibid., 40.

[9] These questions were asked by earlier analysts too, notably Karen Horney and Erich Fromm, but never entered the core of orthodox psychoanalysis. See Petra Bueskens, *Mothering and Psychoanalysis: Clinical, Sociological and Feminist Perspectives* (Bradford, Ontario: Demeter Press, 2014), 10.

and contours. In this view, psyche and society are mutually constitutive and dynamic, which means that both are amenable to reciprocal influence and change. This constitutes the political core of the book in her call for shared parenting.[10] Chodorow's call for greater equality was underscored with an analysis of the intra-psychic formation of the mother. The focus was still on the infant however this too was expanded; the infant was a paradigmatic daughter as well as son.[11]

For Chodorow both the male and the female child begin life "matri-sexual" (*not* bisexual, as Freud contended), experiencing themselves as physically and psychically contiguous with the mother.[12] Gradually infants come to see themselves as separate beings however for Chodorow (as with Freud) this has a different psychosexual quality for boys and girls. The mother has a stronger identification with her daughter given the conscious and unconscious activation of her own (female) infancy and girlhood. Mothers typically project their thoughts, feelings, and desires onto daughters and are more inclined to see daughters narcissistically as extensions of themselves.[13] In turn, daughters often experience themselves as psychically continuous with their mothers. This creates a mutual identification for both mother and daughter at the dual and interconnected levels of subjectivity and gender, which makes it harder for the daughter—and thus, of course, for women in general—to individuate. Instead, they have a tendency to oscillate, between fusion and separation.

By contrast, Chodorow argued, the mother treats her male infant as a separate Other from the outset, as both sexually and psychically different.[14] While the boy identifies with his mother initially, he typically moves to a sexualised rivalry with his father in the Oedipal phase (4–7 years) before accepting defeat and identifying with his father and the abstract masculine realm of work and participation outside the home.[15] His masculine identity is thereafter founded in *separation from the mother*

[10] Chodorow, *Reproduction of Mothering*, 211–219.

[11] While Chodorow was not the first woman analyst to engage with the question of maternal subjectivity (Helen Deutsche, Karen Horney and Melanie Klein among others came before her), she was the first to adopt an explicitly feminist lens.

[12] Chodorow, *Reproduction of Mothering*, 95.

[13] Ibid., 95, 102.

[14] Ibid., 105.

[15] Ibid., 94.

and from the embodied, emotional realm she inhabits and represents. In this sense, the male child differentiates twice over: first, as an "object"—or, more properly, a subject!—and second, in terms of his sexed-gender identity, in turn, producing stronger ego-boundaries. For Chodorow, strongly differentiated ego-boundaries are well suited to participation in civil society while being less suited to interpersonal care, intimacy, and empathy.[16] Boys' sense of identification shifts from mother (as primary carer) to father who, under prevailing conditions of industrial-capitalism, is often absent in the abstract realm of paid work and therefore less emotionally available or in tune with the child's embodied rhythms. This identification with absent, emotionally remote fathers means boys and men in industrial-capitalist societies typically have a less secure gender identity.[17] This generates a vigilance around slippage: boys, and the men they become, do not want to psychically fold back into the mother (or her adult replacement: the wife or partner) and thus take great pains to remain emotionally contained.[18] Later, this manifests as resistance to intimacy and the desire for space from (hetero)sexual partners.

For Chodorow, women do not need to *prove* their femininity in the way that (many) men feel the need to prove their masculinity. This is because it is built on a solid core of continuous and tangible same-sex/same-gender identification. This produces, in turn, more porous ego boundaries and a greater capacity for intimacy and empathy; however, the shadow side is it also predisposes women to self-sacrifice (potentially leading to resentment), and greater difficulty differentiating between self and other. It is this psychological disposition that leads to the traditional assumption, from antiquity to the present, articulated by Freud[19] (and

[16] Ibid., 169.

[17] Chodorow, The *Reproduction of Mothering*. Obviously, the extent to which fathers are present and engaged with sons and daughters varies across families, but broad outlines are garnered from national statistics in western nations. It is still mothers (women) who perform most of the childcare. See, Petra Bueskens, *Modern Mothering and Women's Dual Identities: Rewriting the Sexual Contract* (London: Routledge, 2018). Interestingly, the pre-industrial family where fathers worked at home offered much more paternal contact with, and mentoring of, sons.

[18] Chodorow, *The Reproduction of Mothering*, 213. This of course refers to the overwhelming majority who are both masculine in gender presentation and heterosexual in object choice.

[19] Sigmund Freud, "Femininity," *New Introductory Lectures on Psychoanalysis*, Standard Edition, Vol. 22 (London: Hogarth Press, 1964), 112–135.

other developmental psychologists, including Erik Erickson and Lawrence Kohlberg), that women are more parochial and biased with a narrower range of interests, in turn, deeming them less suited to public life (a self-fulfilling prophecy if ever there was one!). For Chodorow, then, women mother from a complex psychosexual inheritance of identification, and at times destructive fusion, with their own mothers; a pattern of intimacy and ambivalence that typically persists in adult mother-daughter relations and in female-female relations more generally.

In Chodorow's re-reading the girl has a considerably longer pre-Oedipal period (something Freud also arrived at in his later work). She remains primarily attached to her mother into her fourth or fifth year and, even then, only *partially* transfers her affections to her father.[20] The resolution of her Oedipus complex is therefore never complete and remains permanently defined by a deep identification with her mother that is lived and re-lived in key lifecycle transitions (including: menarche, coitus, pregnancy, parturition, lactation and menopause). For Chodorow, like Freud, the daughter remains triangulated between her mother and father in her internal and external object-world—a situation that persists into adulthood when she transfers this triangulation onto her primary love relationships. In a perspicacious analysis, Chodorow updates Freud's schema in her contention that most women end up "genitally heterosexual" while remaining emotionally oriented to women (mothers, sisters, daughters, friends) and to the recreation of the dyadic mother-child bond, albeit set within, and triangulated through, heterosexual love.[21]

For Chodorow, it is women's need to recreate primary dyadic intimacy, so often missing in their heterosexual relationships (with men who are defended against intimacy), that predisposes them to become mothers. Women mother to recreate the primary union they once experienced in the arms and at the breast of their own mothers and also, as adults, to inhabit the central emotional role of the mother. To this end, Chodorow argues, girls retain their "matrisexual" core through which their heterosexual object choice—should they follow the majority path—emerges.[22]

[20] Chodorow, *Reproduction of Mothering*, 128.

[21] Ibid., 128–129.

[22] Ibid., 95. By contrast being lesbian is a continuous object choice for women.

In this sense, she concurs with Freud that there are essentially two psychosexual positions: *to have the mother or to be the mother*.[23] Most, though not all, women make the complex (and likely only partial) transition from having to being.[24] Intimate, albeit non-sexual, relations with other women and with children provide (heterosexual) women with a core sense of satisfaction and self, alongside—and indeed undergirding—their relations with men. This recreates the emotional layering of female baby and girlhood in which relations with fathers always come after, and remain mediated by, a primary, embodied dyad with the mother. In this sense, Chodorow argues insightfully, women's heterosexuality is always underscored with, and indeed depends upon, a primary relationship with a woman. This creates an imperative for heterosexual women to triangulate since this was the original familial template. Or, to put it somewhat more provocatively: every straight woman has a lesbian on the inside. As she says,

> Given the triangular situation and emotional asymmetry of her own parenting, a woman's relation to a man *requires* on the level of psychic structure a third person, since it was originally established in a triangle. A man's relation to women does not. His relation to his mother was originally established first as an identity, then as a dual identity, then as a two-person relationship, before his father ever entered the picture.[25]

Chodorow explains an important dimension of women's generationally contiguous and sexually layered subjectivity here: the internalization of the mother-daughter relationship in every woman (mothered by a woman). She conceives of the mother as developmentally inside the daughter and so placed the egg neither before nor after the chicken, but where it belonged: inside! Women are like babushka dolls: daughter-mothers inside mother-daughters. This "reproduction of mothering" is embedded in the embodied psyches of women. However, she tells us less about the mother on her own—a heuristic distinction to be sure, since maternal subjectivity is a crowded theatre. In Chodorow we remain more in the territory of the mother as the desired object (for the daughter)

[23] Ibid., 194–195.

[24] Ibid., 194.

[25] Ibid., 201.

rather than the desiring subject (for herself). Of course, she is both simultaneously but it is the latter that remains opaque in our analyses of maternal subjectivity as more recent work by Lisa Baraitser[26] and Alison Stone[27] attest.

Partly, this is so difficult because, as the French psychoanalytic feminists Luce Irigaray and Julia Kristeva show, there is almost no symbolic representation of mothers; that is, of mothers as people who nurture, love, have sex, get angry, fail, create, work and exist on their own terms.[28] In the history of art and literature with few exceptions we have idealized Madonnas and sexualised Whores; we have fallen women and women on pedestals, but little that is nuanced and dimensional. Moreover, there is almost no representation of mother/daughter relationships, with the notable exception of Demeter/Persephone, wherein Persephone is abducted by a marauding and lonely Hades and both mother and daughter morn terribly for each other, their bond ripped apart physically and psychically by the patriarchy.[29] This prevailing narrative doesn't change until women got hold of the pen, the marble, the paint brush, the keyboard, and the couch *en masse* in the late twentieth century. Now mother-daughter stories abound, as do mothers as dimensional, desiring subjects.[30]

[26] Lisa Baraitser, *Maternal Encounters: The Ethics of Interruption* (London: Routledge, 2009).

[27] Alison Stone, "Mother-Daughter Relations and the Maternal in Irigaray and Chodorow," *PhiloSOPHIA: A Journal of Continental Feminism* 1, no. 1 (2011): 45–64; Alison Stone, "Psychoanalysis and Maternal Subjectivity," in *Mothering and Psychoanalysis: Clinical, Sociological and Feminist Perspectives*, ed. Petra Bueskens (Bradford, Ontario: Demeter Press, 2014), 325–341.

[28] Stone, "Mother-Daughter Relations." More recently, in popular culture, we have "career women" and "stay at home mums" (as if these were mutually exclusive categories). Again, these stereotypes are unidimensional and unnuanced, and fail to grasp that women encompass and transcend these dualistic categories.

[29] More recently, in popular culture, we have "career women" and "stay at home mums" (as if these were mutually exclusive categories). Again, these stereotypes are unidimensional and unnuanced, and fail to grasp that women encompass and transcend these dualistic categories.

[30] Rachel Cusk, *A Life's Work: On Becoming a Mother* (New York: Picador, 2001); Daphne de Marneffe, *Maternal Desire: On Children, Love, and the Inner Life* (New York: Little, Brown & Co., 2004); Lisa Baraitser, "Oi Mother, Keep Ye' Hair On! Impossible Transformations of Maternal Subjectivity," *Studies in Gender and Sexuality* 7,

Chodorow's work was part of this move to make the maternal subject visible by describing the desire of the daughter to become a mother; and also, as part of her feminist politics, to ameliorate the oppressive and unshared dimensions of mother-work for women. For Chodorow the answer to the problem of exclusive maternal childcare in industrial-capitalist societies was shared parental care.[31] In this schema, bringing fathers into early care would offset our collective narcissistic expectations of women (also internalised by women) for self-sacrifice; that is, for care of everyone but themselves. It would also offset men's more defensive masculinity—the fear of appearing feminine—in the quest to transcend their deep, embodied affinity with their own mothers and, later, their wives and partners. There was a wish, then, to take the daughter out of her sequence in a long line of "patriarchal mothers" and into a life of her own and, concomitantly, to reconnect adult men to intimacy and care of children and for those children, in turn, to internalize a model of masculine care and feminine autonomy (alongside and together with masculine autonomy and feminine care). This was part of a broader feminist politics to reconstruct extant gender roles and free women from their sequestration to the home and, at a more psychological level, to free women (as mothers) from the primitive projections and defenses of adult children of both sexes—i.e., to free women from the kinds of blame, lack of empathy, cruelty, and violence that define misogyny.[32] For Chodorow, as with those who follow, mothers are thus both containing and creating;[33] they are both objects *and* subjects of desire.

no. 3 (2006): 239–248; Baraitser, *Maternal Encounters*; Stone, "Mother-Daughter Relations"; Bueskens, *Mothering and Psychoanalysis*; Christine Moutsou and Rosalind Mayo, *The Mother in Psychoanalysis and Beyond: Matricide and Maternal Subjectivity* (London: Routledge, 2016); Jaqueline Rose, *Mothers: An Essay on Love and Cruelty* (London: Faber & Faber, 2018); Petra Bueskens, "Maternal Subjectivity: From Containing to Creating," in *Dangerous Ideas About Mothers*, eds. Rachel Robertson and Camilla Nelson (Perth: UWA Publishing, 2018), 197–211.

[31] Chodorow, *Reproduction of Mothering*, 211–219.

[32] See also Dorothy Dinnerstein who developed this argument with much more fervor. Dorothy Dinnerstein, *The Mermaid and the Minotaur: Sexual Arrangement and Human Malaise* (New York: Harper & Row, 1976).

[33] I have written elsewhere about the "containing and creating" elements of maternal subjectivity. See Bueskens, "Maternal Subjectivity," 197–211.

Reproducing the Social: Intersections Between Psyche and Society

Chodorow emphasizes the asymmetrical relational trajectories of boys and girls (women and men) and from this develops her theory of the reproduction of mothering. What interests me after four decades of feminism, of which *The Reproduction of Mothering* has itself been influential, is the recursive relationship between mothers and the social. How are mothers, who have benefited from forty years of feminism,[34] recreating and transforming society? In particular, how are mothers *reproducing the social* in ways that reflect their social, political, and psychic interests? How are mothers with political and psychological agency recreating culture and the symbolic? While these questions are too large to answer in a single article, they are certainly worth posing after half a century of feminism in the public and private spheres.

As I have written elsewhere, while contemporary western society has grudgingly accepted the autonomous female "individual" among its suite of legally and culturally legitimate members, mothers continue to suffer serious structural barriers to inclusion and serious economic and career consequences for undertaking mothering work,[35] broadly inclusive of domestic work, care work, emotion work, "kin keeping"[36] and familial organization.[37] Mothers remain, as a consequence of a disproportionate

[34] This assumption is, of course, problematic. Research shows women's happiness levels have declined over the past 40 years. See, Betsey Stevenson and Justin Wolfers, *The Paradox of Declining Female Happiness* (Institute for the Study of Labor, IZA Discussion Paper No. 4200, 2009); Daniel Freeman and Joshua Freeman, *The Stressed Sex: Uncovering the Truth About Men, Women, and Mental Health* (Oxford, UK: Oxford University Press, 2013). Moreover, stay-at-home mothers report higher happiness levels than full-time working mothers, though they are on a par with part-time working mother. This complicates the straightforward assumption that liberal progress—or feminism—makes women happier. Judith Treas, Tanja van der Lippe, and Tsui-O Tai, "The Happy Homemaker? Married Women's Well-Being in Cross-National Perspective," *Social Forces* 90, no. 1 (2011): 111–132.

[35] Bueskens, *Modern Motherhood*.

[36] Catherine J. Rosenthal, "Kinkeeping in the Familial Division of Labor," *Journal of Marriage and the Family* 47, no. 4 (1985): 965–974.

[37] See, Lyn Craig, *Contemporary Motherhood: The Impact of Children on Adult Time* (Hampshire: Ashgate, 2007); Suzanne M. Bianchi, Liana C. Sayer, Melissa A. Milkie, and John P. Robinson, "Housework: Who Did, Does, or Will Do It and How Much

load of unpaid work, second-class citizens because they can't compete on the same terms or from the same embodied subject position as men. Inequality in the domestic division of labor and childcare cuts across "race" and class categories and reconstitutes women as a sex-class.[38] Despite performing crucially important work for families—and, as a result, for society—women pay an ***individualized penalty*** for this work. In the first phase of feminism—and here I am applying a broad brush that is inclusive of both the first and second-waves—women's inclusion into western polities and societies was premised upon separation from the home.[39] Access to property rights (focused in the first instance on property in the person epitomized in the Married Women's Property Acts), citizenship rights (the suffrage), and paid work (including in the professions) formed a tripartite, albeit historically variegated, feminist agenda across the western world from the early nineteenth through to the late twentieth centuries.[40]

However, given that women were the primary carers in the home, and indeed with industrialisation and modernization, everyone else had *left home*[41]—including husbands and fathers, children, extended kin,

Does It Matter?," *Social Forces* 91, no. 1 (2012): 55–63; Leah Ruppanner, "Sharing of Household Responsibilities," in *Encyclopedia of Quality of Life and Well-Being Research*, ed. A. C. Michalos (Dordrecht: Springer, 2014): 258–311; Kathleen Gerson, "There's No Such Thing as Having It All: Gender, Work, and Care in an Age of Insecurity," in *Gender in the Twenty-First Century: The Stalled Revolution and the Road to Equality*, eds. Shannon N. Davis, Sarah Winslow, and David Maume (Oakland, CA: University of California Press, 2017), 13–27.

[38] Sharon Hays, *The Cultural Contradictions of Motherhood* (New Haven: Yale University Press, 1996); Bianchi et al., "Housework." There are significant class differences between women who are mothers in terms of education, employment and, increasingly who gets and stays married, however mothering work remains women's work across diverse cultural, racial, and class and categories.

[39] Feminists fought first for property rights, then for the vote and then for entry into the public sphere, including through paid work and, for those with education and social capital, for entry into the professions. Since the second wave, feminists have fought for not only legal but also cultural change. Current struggles center on culture change.

[40] See, Karen Offen, *European Feminisms, 1700–1950: A Political History* (Stanford, CA: Stanford University Press, 2000); Karen Hunt, "Women as Citizens: Changing the Polity," in *The Routledge History of Women in Europe Since 1700*, ed. Deborah Simonton (London: Routledge, 2006), 216–258.

[41] I am referring here to the period during the day when productive household and agricultural labor took place in and around the home. The gradual emptying of the home occurred in a variegated way in different cultural contexts. I am describing a broad pattern

servants and most unmarried, childless women—mothers were isolated in the home in an unprecedented way (ironically, this is nowadays referred to as the "traditional family"). This novel family arrangement—what Chodorow aptly identified as normalized father absence[42]—was, in fact, not only father absent but also extended kin absent, older child absent and "community-of-women" absent, producing an untenable isolation for mothers (and a corresponding intensification of mothering work), although there were distinct class and race variations with both working class and colored women maintaining closer and more interdependent intergenerational and cross-generational ties.[43] Middle-class women fought to gain access to civil rights, to the suffrage and to paid, professional work in order to ensure their social (re)integration, the realization of their talents and abilities, and for civil and economic autonomy.

Women fought for access to paid work in particular for the simple reason that economic dependence, as was the case for most women—and certainly those in Chodorow's lens—foreclosed autonomy. Working-class women did not alter this pattern of dependence on marriage because they did not earn sufficient wages to head a household.[44] In the U.S. the same was true for African-American women's wages too.[45] The family wage paid to breadwinner husbands was enshrined in law across the western

that followed industrialisation and the movement of production away from the home and into the factory. I elaborate on this point in Bueskens, *Modern Motherhood*.

[42] Chodorow, *Reproduction of Mothering*, 175.

[43] Michael Young and Peter Willmott, *Family and Kinship in East London* (London: Free Press, 2013); C. B. Stack and L. Burton, "Kinscripts: Reflections on Family, Generation, and Culture," in *Mothering: Ideology, Experience, and Agency*, eds. Evelyn Nakano Glenn, Grace Chang, and Linda Reney Forcey (New York: Routledge, 1994), 33–44; Patricia Hill Collins, "Shifting the Center: Race, Class, and Feminist Theorizing About Motherhood," in *Mothering: Ideology, Experience, and Agency*, eds. Evelyn Nakano Glenn, Grace Chang, and Linda Reney Forcey (New York: Routledge, 1994), 45–66; Kathryn Edin and Maria Kefalas, *Promises I Can Keep: Why Poor Women Put Motherhood Before Marriage* (Berkeley: University of California Press, 2005).

[44] Alice Kessler-Harris, *Out to Work: A History of Wage-Earning Women in the United States* (Oxford: Oxford University Press, 2003); H. Berenson, "The 'Family Wage' and Working Women's Consciousness in Britain," *Politics and Society* 19, no. 1 (1991): 71–108.

[45] Elen Mutari, Marilyn Power and Deborah M. Figart, "Neither Mothers nor Breadwinners: African-American Women's Exclusion From US minimum Wage Policies, 1912–1938," *Feminist Economics* 8, no. 2 (2002): 37–61.

world and ensured that men earned wages sufficient to head a family and women did not.[46] Women did not achieve parity—that is equal pay for equal work (in principle)—until the 1970s and, even then, in many countries the work women routinely performed—teaching, nursing, clerical, care and service work—did not earn *a living wage*, producing its own "pink collar ghetto."[47] Access to the "centres of power," in this case defined as access to the labor market, was a central second-wave feminist platform. Arguably, as Chodorow has written elsewhere, this was the period in which "the daughter" rose to prominence—i.e., the young, unmarried, childless, adult woman—differentiating herself, sometimes angrily, from her mother whom she saw as subjected within the institution of (patriarchal) marriage, and therefore also in economic, social, and political life.[48] The angry second-wave feminist daughters rejected mothers and mothering in a quest, Julie Stephens observes, to "give birth to themselves."[49]

This period of psychological and indeed historical "differentiation" released women into a public sphere built by and for men as citizens, subjects, and workers. In particular, the model of paid work was that of a breadwinner with a wife at home. Mothers' inclusion meant the use of institutionalized childcare—or, for the wealthy, nannies—and participation in paid work as disembodied workers ostensibly free of domestic and childcare responsibilities. Several decades of feminism showed us that this produced the double shift (Hochschild 1989), even if more recent work shows this is not a literal double shift[50]—one at work, and then

[46] Nancy Fraser, "After the Family Wage: A Postindustrial Thought Experiment," in *Gender and Citizenship in Transition*, ed. Barbara Hobson (New York: Routledge, 2000), 1–32.

[47] Belinda Probert and B. Wilson (eds.), *Pink Collar Blues: Work, Gender and Technology* (2nd ed.) (Melbourne: Melbourne University Press, 2008).

[48] Nancy Chodorow and Susan Contratto, "The Fantasy of the Perfect Mother," in *Feminism and Psychoanalytic Theory*, ed. Nancy Chodorow (New Haven and London, Yale University Press, 1989 [1980]), 79–96.

[49] Julie Stephens, *Confronting Postmaternal Thinking: Feminism, Memory, and Care* (New York: Columbia University Press, 2011), 44.

[50] Arlie Hochschild, *The Second Shift: Working Parents and the Revolution at Home* (New York: Viking, 2012).

another at home—but is more likely to manifest as multitasking throughout the day.[51] Moreover, women with dependent children typically cut back on work hours, such that men and women's average total paid and unpaid work time is roughly equal, with women performing more unpaid work and men more paid work.[52] This has led some researchers to conclude that we have gained a new, albeit different, equality. What is missing in this picture of seeming "equality" however are the *consequences* of women's unpaid work. There is a heavy and (as yet) societally unacknowledged price paid by women for unpaid care and domestic work; or, in other words, there is a price for the "reproduction of mothering."

Whereas a liberal feminist discourse, evidenced in the second-wave and ongoing, tends to stress women's inclusion in social, political, and economic systems on the same or similar terms as men,[53] newer forms of "maternal feminism"[54] argue for a recognition of women's preferences to care for their children and for social policies that support and reflect these preferences.[55] Conversely, a "matricentric feminism" argues for the

[51] Liana C. Sayer, Paula England, Michael Bittman, and Suzanne. M. Bianchi, "How Long Is the Second (Plus First) Shift? Gender Differences in Paid, Unpaid and Total Work Time in Australia and the United States," *Journal of Comparative Family Studies* 40, no. 4 (2009): 523–545; Bianchi et al., "Housework."

[52] Suzanne M. Bianchi, John P. Robinson, Melissa A. Milkie, *Changing Rhythms of American Family Life* (New York, NY: Russell Sage Foundation, 2006).

[53] Betty Friedan, *The Feminine Mystique* (New York: Penguin, 1963).

[54] Maternal feminism was prominent at the turn of the twentieth century influencing the establishment of the welfare state across the western world and, specifically, provisions for women as "maternal citizens." This feminism was also associated with an essentialist and traditionalist focus centered on women's domestic role; however, the broader vision was: (1) recognition of women's important contributions to citizenship *as mothers*; (2) the economic support of women as mothers alongside and sometimes even outside the institution of marriage, and; (3) the release of women's ethical orientation to care into the world. Contemporary maternal feminism is heir to this earlier incarnation, even as it blends an ethic of equality and cultural liberalism. See Seth Koven and Sonja Michel (eds.), *Mothers of a New World: Maternalist Politics and the Origins of Welfare States* (New York: Routledge, 1993); Marilyn Lake, "'A Revolution in the Family': The Challenge and Contradiction of Maternal Citizenship," in *Mothers of a New World: Maternalist Politics and Welfares States in Comparative Perspective*, eds. Seth Koven and Sonja Michel (New York: Routledge, 1993), 378–395; Marilyn Lake, "State Socialism for Australian Mothers: Andrew Fisher's Radical Maternalism in Its International and Local Contexts," *Labour History: A Journal of Labour and Social History*, no. 102 (2012): 55–70.

[55] Daphne de Marneffe, *Maternal Desire: On Children, Love, and the Inner Life* (New York: Little, Brown & Co., 2004); Anne Manne, *Motherhood: How Should We Care for*

mother as a recognized political subject.[56] A combination of ongoing occupational segregation, inequality in wages and an emergent neoliberal economy meant that, with the exception of an elite professional strata, women did not gain equality through waged work. This has meant that while women are normatively free and equal as "individuals," they are constrained as mothers in the "new social contract." Women can participate, but only on the same terms as men. As we can clearly see, this means that childfree women (broadly speaking, women under age 30)[57] are making great strides in education and paid work, and they have significantly more leisure time than women with dependent children. Highly educated women in well-paid careers tend to delay childbearing (and rearing) into their mid to late thirties, sometimes into their 40s, precisely because of the significant increase in workload and the considerable costs to career, leisure, sleep and well-being.[58]

Conversely, working-class women and those living in poverty, have children much younger and are constrained thereafter to pursue education and employment opportunities unless they have supportive kin, although

Our Children? (Sydney: Allen & Unwin, 2005); Stephens, Confronting *Postmaternal Thinking*; Carla Pascoe Leahy and Petra Bueskens (eds.), *Australian Mothering: Historical and Sociological Perspectives* (London: Palgrave Macmillan, 2019).

[56] Andrea O'Reilly, *Matricentric Feminism* (Bradford, Ontario: Demeter Press, 2016); Bueskens, *Modern Motherhood*.

[57] Working-class and poor women on average have children earlier than middle-class women and those with lower socio-economic status, are more likely to have children early in adult life out of wedlock. Val Gillies, *Marginalised Mothers: Exploring Working Class Experiences of Parenting* (London: Routledge, 2006); Edin and Kafalas, *Promises I Can Keep*; Joan C. Williams, *White Working Class: Overcoming Class Cluelessness in America* (Cambridge, MA: Harvard Business Review Press, 2017).

[58] See Craig, *Contemporary Motherhood*.

The research forms a complex picture here. Parents' happiness declines as does marital happiness, however meaning increases. Infants reduce parents' happiness and marital happiness however, they increase their life meaning and a sense of social connectedness in older age, Martin Seligman, *Authentic Happiness* (New York: Free Press, 2002); Jean M. Twenge, W. Keith Campbell, and Craig A. Foster, "Parenthood and Marital Satisfaction: A Meta-Analytic Review," *Journal of Marriage and the Family* 65, no. 3 (2003): 574–583; S. K. Nelson, K. Kushlev, T. English, E. W. Dunn, and S. Lyubomirsky, "In Defense of Parenthood: Children Are Associated with More Joy Than Misery," *Psychological Science* 24, no. 1 (2013): 3–10; Daniel Gilbert, "Happiness: What Your Mother Didn't Tell You," *World Minds Annual Symposium*, December 13 (2018); C. Becker, I. Kirchmaier, and S. T. Trautmann, "Marriage, Parenthood and Social Network: Subjective Well-Being and Mental Health in Old Age," *PloS One* 14, no. 7 (2019).

they often have a recognized and valued adult status as mothers in their communities.[59] While those in poverty tend to subsist on inadequate welfare provisions and minimal paid work, the working-class often center motherhood but remain compelled to engage in paid work for low wages.[60] Thus, we see the reproduction of the "price of motherhood"[61] remains intact, as does the reproduction of the wage penalty associated with becoming a mother.[62] On the other hand, we see that women are slowly inching toward what I call a "rewriting of the sexual contract,"[63] including their own psychosexual imaginaries insofar as mothers, particularly, but not exclusively, those in the middle-class, now position themselves as partially or wholly autonomous in political, civil, social, economic, familial, interpersonal and psychological terms. Certainly, this is the normative ideal, however unevenly and haphazardly it is being actualised.

Maternal Subjectivity in Late Modernity

Alison Stone contends Chodorow's work is a good foundation for theorizing social change precisely because she defines the social as constitutive of the psychic and therefore influential. In concentrating on the social as much as the psyche, Chodorow foregrounds their reciprocal influence. Stone's own reformulation provides a sophisticated re-reading of Chodorow focused on differentiating maternal from female subjectivity. For Stone,

> Maternal subjectivity is (I take it) a variation on female subjectivity, but it is important to treat the two as distinct, otherwise we lose sight of what is

[59] Edin and Kefalas, *Promises I Can Keep*.

[60] Williams, *White Working Class*.

[61] Anne Crittendon, *The Price of Motherhood: Why the Most Important Job Is Still the Least Valued* (New York: Henry Holt, 2002).

[62] Michelle Budig and Paula England, "The Wage Penalty for Motherhood," *American Sociological Review* 66, no. 2 (2001): 204–225; Michelle Budig and Paula England, "The Motherhood Penalty in Cross-National Perspective: The Importance of Work–Family Policies and Cultural Attitudes," *Social Politics* 19, no. 2 (2012): 163–193.

[63] Bueskens, *Modern Motherhood*.

> peculiar to maternity…for this to be possible the mother must be able to assume a subject position distinct from the daughter.[64]

Stone situates maternal subjectivity in both psychic and social context, building a temporally layered and dynamic account.[65] She marries the two seemingly incommensurate positions in her emphasis on subjectivity as a product of social structure, culture, biology and internal unconscious fantasy. For Stone, our psyches are not straightforwardly malleable (as in Chodorow's contention that shared parenting would de-gender our psyches) rather, as a consequence of our embodied early attachments to our mothers, male and female psyches are ***disposed in particular directions*** (separation/autonomy for the male and identification/attachment for the female).[66] This is determined by unconscious process and given shape in culture. In this formulation, the psyche is not reducible to the social however the cultural realm—what Stone calls, following Irigaray, "the symbolic"—is open to change and therefore so are our psyches. She writes,

> Surely, though, shared parenting would not suffice to undo existing gendered personality structures. Given the patriarchal symbolic, shared parenting would disrupt but not undo the dominant equations man-subject, woman-body. Symbolic change, to challenge and rework dominant representations, is also necessary. Yet on its own, symbolic change would not suffice to undo patriarchy either; without a diversification in family practices (or rather, without political and ideological support for their already occurring diversification), our gender divided family lives will reinforce and reinstall dominant symbolic codes. [Thus] *[t]he projects of symbolic change and social change intersect*).[67]

For Stone, both sides of the social/symbolic equation require change: specifically, changes in parenting practices to generate shared parenting and symbolic change in how mothers (and fathers) are routinely defined. For the latter, she contends, we need to envision mothers as subjects

[64] Stone, "Mother-Daughter Relations." Reproduced here in Chapter 12.

[65] Ibid., 46–47.

[66] Alison Stone, *Feminism, Psychoanalysis and Maternal Subjectivity* (London: Routledge, 2012), 29.

[67] Stone, "Mother-Daughter Relations," 57 (emphasis own).

and, more specifically, as subjects who *differ* from their own mothers. In Stone's terms, "… if the maternal figure were re-imagined as a figure of difference and differentiation rather than fusion, then women could activate and enjoy their identification with their mothers without this necessarily inclining them to become their children's sole or main caregivers."[68] In other words, women would not be condemned to repeat infinitum the cycle outlined so clearly by Chodorow of primary caregiving at the expense of autonomy. This would make space for *mothers as subjects* and, concomitantly, for fathers as caregivers.

Stone suggests that such change is always pushing against the conservative current of our psyches.[69] For example, when reflecting on whether the paternal "no" function elaborated by Lacan (as that which breaks up the mother-infant dyad), and the maternal "yes" function of embodied connection, are necessarily linked to actual mothers and fathers, Stone charts a midway between essentialism and deconstruction.[70] She contends that our historical legacy makes it difficult to break these associations, and indeed that our psyches are disposed against our egalitarian visions in their very formation.[71] However, "it is also possible that we could change the internal significance of these [maternal and paternal] functions, by retaining the idea of two distinct sexuate and parental figures while ceasing to place them in polar opposition to one another."[72] For Stone, it is not actual or symbolic sexual dimorphism that constitutes the problem rather it is the prevailing alignment of mother with "the bodily realm prior to the acquisition of meaning"[73] and, the extent to which this reflects the male psychic trajectory—specifically, the need to separate

[68] Stone, *Feminism, Psychoanalysis and Maternal Subjectivity*, 30.

[69] Stone writes, "… our psychical formation apparently disposes us *against* the sorts of social change that would promote gender justice." Ibid. Here she aligns with Juliet Mitchell's more recent position in which she identifies conservative tendencies in both psychoanalysis and feminism suggesting these reflect an unconscious pull toward stasis or reproduction of the *status quo*. Indeed, for Mitchell, sexual difference is defined by an "underwater tow that makes progress regress on matters of 'gender' equity." Juliet Mitchell, "Introduction, 1999," in *Psychoanalysis and Feminism: A Radical Reassessment of Freudian Psychoanalysis* (London: Penguin, 2000), xviii. See also, Juliet Mitchell, "Reply to Lynne Segal's Commentary," *Studies in Gender and Sexuality* 3, no. 2 (2002), 218.

[70] Stone, *Feminism, Psychoanalysis and Maternal Subjectivity*, 26.

[71] Ibid., 30.

[72] Ibid., 26.

[73] Ibid., 25.

from the mother in the acquisition of a masculine gender identity—that has been imposed on women and girls. For Stone, the imposition of what we might call the masculine "separation paradigm" as the basis—and to date, the only basis—of subjectivity places daughters (as actual and potential mothers) in a conundrum: they are unable to identify with their fathers fully if they want (consciously or unconsciously) to be women, and yet the father represents the only subject position of difference from the mother and thus "girls *qua* female-identified are left unable to differentiate themselves ....".[74]

Against this Freudian-Lacanian paradigm, Stone proffers an alternate vision of subjectivity. She takes on board the feminist and postmodern critique of subjectivity, but rather than jettison "the subject" for its purported rationalist, masculinist, Eurocentric pretensions, Stone's vision is to breathe new life into the subject, specifically in the form of reconnecting subjectivity to maternity and thus to the pre-verbal bodily intimacy of early life.[75] To this end, she offers a clarification of what maternal subjectivity is. This, at its most basic, is a subjectivity that takes root *within* mother-infant relations of bodily and psychic intimacy; it includes the archaic "energies, affects, and repertoires of habit and gesture ... [that] become patterned in significant ways ... prior to and as a precondition of our generating meaning from these body relations."[76] In this sense, she envisages a distinct form of subjectivity; one that arises out of the daughter's early relations with her own mother. These are re-animated when the adult daughter becomes a mother herself, and they are re-worked in her psyche as she assumes care for her own child and simultaneously activates and re-writes her maternal script.

In contradistinction to the standard western paradigm of individuation emerging from a break with the maternal body, then, Stone elaborates on a form of subjectivity that is contiguous and resonant with the maternal, "If mothers are subjects they can only be subjects of a new kind, who generate meanings, and acquire agency *from* their place in maternal body relations."[77] Maternal subjectivity is, then, "a specific form of subjectivity

[74] Ibid., 26.

[75] Ibid., 4.

[76] Ibid., 5.

[77] Ibid., 3.

that is continuous with the maternal body."[78] However, it is a reconceived maternal that is defined by difference,[79] or, as she puts it, "mothers repeat with a difference their past histories with their own mothers."[80] This difference makes it possible to both identify with *and* separate from the mother. It is precisely in the *re*-play that maternal difference lies—motherhood is a second coming, a second significant—yet different—way of being a daughter and, in turn, a subject (and here we see the legacy of Chodorow).

Stone uses the central concept of transference to read the maternal subject as a subject of difference. Here she doesn't use mothering to animate therapy practice, as has so frequently been the case with object relations theory; rather, she uses the psychoanalytic concept of transference to understand *what mothers are doing* when they return—in fantasy and unconscious body memory—to their own infancy in the process of becoming mothers and nurturing their infants.[81] As she says, "[i]nsofar as patient-analyst and mother-child relations are comparable, then, the mother stands to her child as the patient does to the analyst (*not*, as analytic theorists typically have it, the other way round, with the mother as the child's first nurturing therapist)."[82] It is the child, then, who facilitates the emergence of a new self in the mother.[83] For Stone "maternal time" is always a revisiting of the mother's own infancy and sense of being cared for—"a cycling back through the past once more"[84] and, in turn, a reconstruction of the past through the experience of novelty embodied in her own baby and in her care practices. This creates the dynamic quality of both therapy and mothering insofar as both involve a reworking of the past at the level of bodily affect and unconscious process. Stone uses the psychoanalytic concept of transference to highlight the temporal layering

[78] Ibid.; Alison Stone, "Psychoanalysis and Maternal Subjectivity," *Mothering and Psychoanalysis: Clinical, Sociological and Feminist Perspectives*, ed. Petra Bueskens (Bradford, Ontario: Demeter Press, 2014), 325–341.

[79] Stone, *Feminism, Psychoanalysis and Maternal Subjectivity*, 5.

[80] Ibid., 88.

[81] Ibid., 142–147.

[82] Ibid., 145.

[83] I named my first child—a daughter—"Mia Renee." Only later did I realize this literally meant, "my own rebirth," which of course, she was.

[84] Stone, *Feminism, Psychoanalysis and Maternal Subjectivity*, 141.

that animates present experience with the past and, through the unfolding of the child, to an unknown yet imagined future.

In this conception the archaic past of the mother is brought to bear on her relation to her child however, the infant and young child's *difference* reinscribes and thus alters that past, and the affective repertoire that becomes possible thereafter. This gives present interactions their dynamic quality and helps to explain how becoming a mother both reactivates and transforms the past and, together with it, the present; it is a reworking *in vivo* of the mother's relation to her own mother (in and through her relations with her child), in turn producing intra-psychic and social changes in the mother. In this relational dynamic, everyday "lived time" brings together past, present and future to form an "organic unity."[85] For Stone, "the past can be reproduced [in the present] only in being transformed."[86] It is this transformation that anchors the difference of maternal subjectivity—the mother is both continuous with, yet different from, her own mother.

Autonomous Mothers Reproducing the Social

While Stone provides a conceptual framework for intergenerational psychic change, and therefore for the identification of a distinct maternal subjectivity, she does not elaborate on how mothers are reproducing the social (or symbolic) in their own image.

How, then, can we see this change in practice? How is "the social" or "the symbolic" reproducing in terms that reflect maternal subjectivity and interests? The mother, who possesses legal equality, economic autonomy, and personal liberty remains exceedingly rare for all the aforementioned reasons regarding unpaid work in the domestic sphere, the gender pay gap, workplace discrimination and the fact that many women choose to work less once they become mothers (and where that choice is not available, often express it as a preference).[87] Nonetheless autonomous mothers

[85] Talero in Stone, *Feminism, Psychoanalysis and Maternal Subjectivity*, 136.

[86] Stone, *Feminism, Psychoanalysis and Maternal Subjectivity*, 145.

[87] Catherine Hakim, *Work-Lifestyle Choices in the 21st Century: Preference Theory* (Oxford: Oxford University Press, 2000); Lydia Saad, "Children a Key Factor in Women's Desire to Work Outside the Home," Gallup Poll, October 2015; Williams, *White Working Class*.

do exist in the contemporary West, and the ideal of liberty and equality remains hegemonic, and so the great majority of mothers *aspire* to this ideal even if they are unable to realize it. This is borne out in studies on women's preferences, which show most young women prior to having children want marriage, motherhood, *and* a career,[88] and most mothers aim to combine mothering with paid work.[89] Most women, in other words, aspire to "have it all," even as they are routinely told this is not possible.[90]

My contention is that the autonomous mother is an historical birth of deep political import and social consequence. This mother is *reproducing the social*, qua making history, in novel and compelling ways. As autonomous mothers, women are not only reproducing babies—and the maternal, intra-psychic imaginary—they are also *reproducing the social* through embracing, transforming and resisting mainstream culture, including especially the mainstream culture of paid work. The push/pull of these differing strategies reflects the disparate positions women have to market work and family work, and the structural as well as symbolic contradictions between these two spheres. It is beyond the scope of this article to elaborate on these strategies in more than cursory depth. Instead I shall identify these historical developments more broadly with a view to linking their emergence with *autonomous mothers* and identifying the recursive relationship between psyche and society adumbrated by Chodorow, Stone, and others. Mothers, I contend, are subjects of history with the capacity to shape that history.

It is difficult for us to attribute historical agency to women or to feminism. Juliet Mitchell makes the point in a wonderfully illustrative vignette,

[88] Michele Hoffnung, "Wanting It All: Career, Marriage, and Motherhood During College-Educated Women's 20s," *Sex Roles*, 50, no. 9–10 (2004): 711–723; Nicole Arthur, and Christine Lee, "Young Australian Women's Aspirations for Work, Marriage and Family: 'I Guess I am Just Another Person Who Wants It All,'" *Journal of Health Psychology* 13, no. 5 (2008): 589–596.

[89] Hakim, *Work-Lifestyle Choices*; Catherine Hakim, "Women's Lifestyle Preferences in the 21st Century," in *The Future of Motherhood in Europe*, eds. Gijs Beets, Joop Schippers, and Egbert te Velde (Dordrecht: Springer, 2009), 177–195.

[90] See Virginia Haussegger, *Wonder Woman: The Myth of Having It All* (Crows Nest: Allen & Unwin, 2005); Anne Marie Slaughter, "Why Women Still Can't Have It All," *The Atlantic*, July/August, 2012; Kathleen Gerson, "There's No Such Thing as Having it All," 13–27.

I had submitted a university exam question asking how feminism had contributed to post-modernism. The question was returned to me as an error – I should have asked how post-modernism contributed to feminism. Something similar happened on the occasion of celebrating 1968 in 2008 – what, it was asked, had 1968 contributed to feminism? Feminists were major contributors to'68. So perhaps one aspect of the post-political movement undertow is reading second wave feminism, any feminism, as passive. Feminism takes up an object position accepting that it has been influenced by this or that, not that it has done the influencing; it is rarely seen as being in the subject position, of doing something to something else; it is always that something is done to us.[91]

The Transformation of Work Culture

Most mothers in contemporary western societies are in the work force, although the hours and conditions vary between nations with their differing policy frameworks.[92] In the US most mothers work full-time, although, when these figures are disaggregated by class, it turns out that among married mothers, the working class and middle class are much more likely to work full-time, while the upper classes (those with college degrees in the highest 20 percent income bracket) and the poor are more likely to be "stay-at-home" mothers, albeit for different reasons.[93] In the former case, this is about privilege and choice (though it is likely also about supporting a husband's high earning career); in the latter case, low wages and the cost of childcare combine to undermine the value of paid work.[94] We see that when mothers have the capacity to choose their allocation of paid work, part-time work is the majority preference.[95] A recent

[91] Wendy Hollway, Juliet Mitchell, and Julie Walsh, "Interview with Juliet Mitchell *Psychoanalysis and Feminism*: Then and Now," *Psychoanalysis, Culture & Society* no. 20 (2015): 112–130, https://doi.org/10.1057/pcs.2015.3.

[92] Sayer et al., "How Long Is the Second"; Lyn Craig, Killian Mullan, and Megan Blaxland, "Parenthood, Policy and Work-Family Time in Australia 1992–2006," *Work Employment Society* 24, no. 1 (2010): 27–45; Michelle Budig, Joya Misra, and Irene Boeckmann, "The Motherhood Penalty in Cross-National Perspective: The Importance of Work–Family Policies and Cultural Attitudes," *Social Politics* 19, no. 2 (2012): 163–193.

[93] Robert VerBruggen and Wendy Wendy Wang, "The Real Housewives of America: Dad's Income and Mom's Work," Institute for Family Studies, 2019, https://ifstudies.org/ifs-admin/resources/newfinalifsresearchbrief-verbruggenwang-realhousewives.pdf.

[94] Williams, *White Working Class*.

[95] Hakim, *Work-Lifestyle Choices*; Hakim, "Women's Lifestyle Preferences."

Gallup poll, for example, found that close to 60 percent of US mothers with a child under 18 said they would prefer to be at home caring for their family.[96]

In Australia (where the author is based), 66 percent of mothers in couple families and 60 percent of single mothers are in the workforce.[97] However, most of these mothers work part-time, sometimes with only minimal hours. For example, in 2017–2018, 44 percent of employed women worked part-time compared with only 16 percent of men (and most of these men are very young, indeed only in their high school or college years). The gender differences in part-time work increase when children are young. For example, three in five employed mothers (61 percent) with a child under six were working part-time compared to less than one in ten employed fathers (7.9 percent).[98] We see, moreover, that the percentage of mothers in the workforce increases with the age of the youngest child. The movement of mothers into the workforce has therefore been characterized by part-time work (or the preference for it) and also by the rise of flexible work, including working from home and flexible working schedules.

This shift is part of a *reinvention of work culture*, which is especially evident for millennials who also express a majority preference for flexible hours and working from home.[99] Flexible work practices, including working from home, reduced work hours and flexible work hours, are often introduced by and for mothers, but they have the effect of changing workplace cultures more generally. While part-time, flexible and casual employment have historically marginalized women from leadership positions, and are central in the reduction of women's income, assets, and

[96] Saad, "Children a Key Factor."

[97] Australian Bureau of Statistics, *Family Characteristics and Transitions, Australia, 2012–13*, Catalogue 4442.0, 2015, https://www.abs.gov.au/AUSSTATS/abs@.nsf/allprimarymainfeatures/E6A9286119FA0A85CA25699000255C89?opendocument.

[98] Australian Bureau of Statistics, *Gender Indicators, Australia*. Catalogue 4125.0, 2018, https://www.abs.gov.au/ausstats/abs@.nsf/Lookup/by%20Subject/4125.0~Sep%202018~Main%20Features~Economic%20Security~4.

[99] Dennis Finn and Anne Donovan, *PwC's NextGen: A Global Generational Study*, Price Waterhouse Coopers, 17 February (2013), 1–16, https://www.pwc.com/gx/en/hr-management-services/pdf/pwc-nextgen-study-2013.pdf; Deloitte, *Deloitte Millennial Survey*, October 24 (2018), https://www2.deloitte.com/global/en/pages/about-deloitte/articles/millennialsurvey.html.

superannuation, the answer to this problem, as I have argued elsewhere, is not paid work on a male breadwinner model *or* mothers' withdrawal from the labor market; it is, rather, the reinvention of work culture to accommodate care and, additionally, the compensation to women for unpaid work through policies of economic redistribution such as a negative income tax or basic income.[100] Mothers are "rewriting the social" therefore by centring the importance of care and restructuring work practices to reflect this priority. This marks a key reversal in the normative hierarchy of values, which places paid work above unpaid domestic work and mothering. It also indicates key shifts in the lifestyle practices of women over the past half century: on the one hand, mothers are engaging in paid work in ever higher numbers; on the other hand, they are doing that work differently (to men) insofar as they are reducing their hours and re-organizing where, when and how they work. Thus, one significant shift is mothers working; the other, is mothers redefining and re-organizing work in order to prioritize mothering. This project is uneven and ongoing given that paid work has historically been organized on the model of the breadwinner with a wife at home. What I am suggesting here is that mothers are redefining the institution of paid work through the broader inculcation of their values into society. In this, and other ways, mothers are *reproducing the social* to reflect their own interests.

While the move to part-time and flexible work is in part a product of neo liberal economies and the casualisation of labor, for women this also reflects their preference to prioritize mothering and to restructure paid work around this priority. Feminists have also lobbied governments for more "family friendly" policies including breastfeeding breaks and spaces, maternity and paternity leave, carer's leave and unpaid leave, allowing women to prioritize mothering while remaining in the labour market, including in demanding careers. Australia has had a federal government funded maternity leave system since 2011, as do most western nations with the notable exception of the U.S. These policy initiatives have been developed by "femocrats" or feminist bureaucrats working for change inside governments with their roots and support in the feminist movement.

[100] Petra Bueskens, "Poverty-Traps and Pay-Gaps: Why (Single) Mothers Need Basic Income," in *Views of a Universal Basic Income: Perspectives from across Australia*, ed. Tim Hollo (Melbourne: The Green Institute, 2017), 42–51.

While the prioritization of care and the centring of children has the effect of compromising women's economic autonomy (an ongoing major concern for feminists), this also places pressure on governments and policy makers to *take care seriously*—and, as part of this, to take women's preferences seriously. For many women the expectation that they would move from being dependent wives to full-time workers (on the model of a breadwinner with a wife) is unrealistic and has instead produced double shifts, most especially for the working and lower middle-class who often look wistfully to their parents' and grandparents' generations when mothers could stay at home.[101] Under these conditions, the prioritization of care creates a social "problem." While this problem is returned to women and defined as one of poor "time management" or trying (greedily we must assume) to "have it all",[102] or, alternatively, as "opting out"[103] and somehow failing, in fact mothers' duality is a major shift in modern culture that requires innovation and transformation of the social structure. Indeed, in significant ways, women's entry into the workforce *en masse* over the last 40 years *is already* reshaping work culture, reconnecting the formerly differentiated spheres of work and home, separated as a result of the industrial revolution, and re-integrating them around a worker mother/mother worker who is simultaneously and transformatively both roles, functions, identities, and social practices *at once*. This move toward integration of "life/work" roles has been observed by numerous empirical sociologies of motherhood.[104] As Giddens writes

[101] Williams, *White Working Class*.

[102] Slaughter, "Why Women Still Can't Have It All."

[103] Lisa Belkin, "The Opt-Out Revolution," *The New York Times Magazine*, October 26, 2003, https://www.nytimes.com/2003/10/26/magazine/the-opt-out-revolution.html; Pamela Stone and Ackerly Hernandez, L. "The All-or-Nothing Workplace: Flexibility Stigma and "Opting Out" Among Professional-Managerial Women," *Journal of Social Issues* 69, no. 2 (2013): 235–256, https://doi.org/10.1111/josi.12013.

[104] Anne Hattery, *Women, Work and Family: Balancing and Weaving* (Thousand Oaks: Sage, 2001); Alison Morehead, "Synchronizing Time for Work and Family: Preliminary Insights from Qualitative Research with Mothers," *Journal of Sociology* 37, no. 4 (2001): 355–371; Jane Maree Maher, "Accumulating Care: Mothers Beyond the Conflicting Temporalities of Caring and Work," *Time & Society* 18, no. 2–3 (2009): 236–243; Bueskens, *Modern Motherhood*. Integration has also been identified as the "intensification" of women's (mothers') time through "multitasking." See Rachel Connelly and Jean Kimmell, *The Time Use of Mothers in the United States at the Beginning of the 21st Century* (Michigan: W.E. Upjohn Institute for Employment Research, 2010); Liana Sayer, "More Work for Mothers? Trends and Gender Differences in Multitasking," in *Time Competition:*

in his analysis of modern love, the "transformation of intimacy" associated with women's increasing equality, "might be a subversive influence on modern institutions as a whole. For a social world in which emotional fulfillment [and care] replaced the maximizing of economic growth would be very different from that which we know at present.[105] Giddens notes that women have sought, as part of their emancipation, "to constitute love as a medium of communication and self-development – in relation to children as well as to men."[106]

Reproducing Mothers Reproducing the Social

Returning Chodorow to her earlier more sociological concerns, I suggest that autonomous mothers are psychically and socially different kinds of mothers than those who came before. They are qualitatively different from the dependent mothers Chodorow was analyzing and suggest a model of dimensional womanhood that includes access to the symbolic, to means of self-expression and world making (underscored by partial or full economic autonomy) and therefore to the co-creation of the social and political order *in women's—and more specifically, in mothers'—image and interests*. In turn, autonomous mothers offer their daughters a meaningful path to differentiation within the nexus of affinity and connection, while offering society the prospect of "world making women" releasing maternal subjectivity, vision and politics into the world. World making has always been the job of men in public office and, more broadly, in public life. Since the second-wave of feminism, it has also been the job of women, albeit as "individuals" or, in psychoanalytic parlance, as daughters. What we stand on the historical precipice of, is the prospect of *world making mothers*. One key indicator of this is the making and unmaking

Disturbed Balances and New Options in Work and Care, eds. Tanje van der Lippe and Pascale Peters (New York: Edward Elgar, 2006), 41–56; Lyn Craig and Judith Brown, "The Multitasking Parent: Time Penalties, Dimensions, and Gender Differences," in *The Economics of Multitasking*, eds. Charlene M. Kalenkoski and Gigi Foster (New York: Palgrave Macmillan, 2016), 33–59.

[105] Anthony Giddens, *The Transformation of Intimacy: Sexuality, Love and Eroticism in Modern Societies* (Cambridge: Polity Press, 1992), 3.

[106] Ibid., 178.

of paid and unpaid work toward a model where mothers can participate without crippling double shifts, contradictions and career de-railing (and not just an elite strata of mothers). Notwithstanding the "flexibility stigma"[107] and the ongoing economic and status costs associated with part-time work, it is clear that mothers are shaping a new workplace culture and set of policy priorities that centre family life and caregiving. Mothers are engaged in a psychosocial and socio-political re-integration of "work" and "life" to use the currant but flawed parlance. It is precisely the industrial-capitalist separation of "work" and "life" that is being digitally and socially sutured back together, albeit on the basis of their prior differentiation and specialization. In other words, women haven't just joined the workforce on the same model as men but have begun to interrogate, transform, and reshape the institution of paid work to more fully reflect the priorities of caregiving and, in a related sense, work that is meaningful.

Women have led the movement for "postwork" futures and envisaging the separation of wages from work with a view to revaluing not only unpaid work but also creative work, passion projects, idleness, reflection, (re)localisation and embeddedness in family, community and place.[108] Whereas the second-wave of feminism concentrated (I think quite rightly) on opening doors for women to enter the world of paid work as the equals of men (the liberal feminist agenda); in this phase of feminism—what Catherine Hakim calls the "new scenario"[109] and I call the "new sexual contract"[110]—where women have achieved formal legal equality (not to be confused with equality of outcomes or equal respect and recognition), *some women* are rewriting the script. What this looks like in practice is more flexible work, including working from home, the uptake of maternity leave as well as unpaid carers' leave, work integrating with life (with the digitisation of everyday life including in paid work, private leisure and

[107] Joan C. Williams, Mary Blair-Loy, and Jennifer L. Berdahl, "Cultural Schemas, Social Class, and the Flexibility Stigma," *Journal of Social Issues* 69, no. 2 (2013): 209–234.

[108] Kathi Weeks, *The Problem with Work: Feminism, Marxism, Antiwork Politics, and Postwork Imaginaries* (Durham: Duke University Press, 2011); David Graeber, *Bullshit Jobs: A Theory* (London: Penguin, 2019), 274–280.

[109] Hakim, "Work-Lifestyle Choices"; Hakim, *Women's Lifestyle Preferences*.

[110] Bueskens, *Modern Motherhood*.

socialising),[111] as well as the encouragement and/or demand for fathers to be more actively involved in childcare. Increasingly, work and life are merging—and while there are problematic dimensions to this including the intensification of time and pressures to multitask—for many women this opens up possibilities for both *reproducing mothering* (families and children) and *reproducing the social* (institutions and culture) that would be otherwise foreclosed or limited given their more primary roles in the home.

The next task then—if I may be so teleological—is for mothers to not just enter civil society on the terms created by and for men, or even by individualized, childfree women, but *as mothers* (or, in Chodorow's more precise terms, as "daughter-mothers"), with contiguous intergenerational attachments and therefore a fundamental biopsychosocial investment in the past and the future. The mother is the tensile thread between generations. When mothers reproduce the social, they bring new ontologies, new social and political agendas, new psychosocial priorities. Arguably, care of human beings is central to what mothers bring to the socio-symbolic realm as both a necessity and priority in turn calling forth new social, cultural, political and policy responses. What happens when the formal abstract category of the "individual" is (re)connected with his or her generational ties, when she is also seen as a mother with visceral attachments to her suckling infant, her toddler, young child, adult son or daughter, grandchild, great grandchild? This is the work of reintegration after the necessary differentiation and specialization of society that made individualization possible. Mothers call forth the reintegration of care into society (and in particular, into economic production) from its early modern sequestration to the private-domestic sphere. In this way, mothers are reproducing a social re-connected to the value of care and contextual forms of knowing and exchange.

If, as Stone contends, Chodorow's version of the reproduction of mothering requires some disruption of the cycle to permit of a more differentiated and autonomous mother, then here we see the beginnings of practices that are engendering this shift. Just such a mother has been born, I contend, from the first and second-wave feminist "daughters"

[111] Privacy is under assault with digitisation however this is beyond the scope of the article. See Shoshanna Zuboff, *The Age of Surveillance Capitalism: The Fight for a Human Future at the Frontier of Power* (New York: Public Affairs, 2019).

who differentiated themselves, arguably defensively and with ongoing ambivalence,[112] from mothers, mothering and motherhood, and thereby released themselves from the bonds of womanhood in male dominant families and male dominant society. The individuation of women, both politically and psychologically, has arguably been the individuation of (adult) daughters liberated from the shackles of patriarchal families. More recently, however, we have seen the emergence of "autonomous mothers"—a woman who has an education, employment, partial or total economic autonomy and control of her sexuality and fertility. This is a woman who *chooses* when she will become a mother, typically has only one or two children (often in her 30s) and continues in paid work while expecting her (usually male) partner to share childcare and domestic labor. Although she may be a staple in the media, and seemingly "normal," this is a very different kind of mother than all who have come before.

Chodorow in part helped to achieve this through her promulgation of more gender-equal families and a greater involvement for fathers in primary care. Hers was a blueprint for action to release mothers from structural constraints and a gendered family so specialized and intensive it produced defensively sexist men and women without clear ego boundaries, who struggled to differentiate from their own mothers and from the myriad unpaid, unshared and unrewarded demands placed upon them. Now through four decades of the women's movement—and reflecting on forty years since *The Reproduction of Mothering* was published—we see mothers "reproducing the social" through their active participation in social, economic, political, and cultural life. Such mothers have become agents of their own lives and, in turn, agents of history. This produces reciprocal changes in maternal subjectivity allowing for greater flexibility and differentiation. To return to Stone, we see mothers enacting recursive change in both society and the psyche. We are our mother's daughters (reproducing mothering), and the mothers of history (reproducing the social). This is what our feminist foremothers, including Chodorow, fought for.

[112] Chodorow and Contratto, "The Fantasy of the Perfect Mother."

Bibliography

Abrams, L., "At Home in the Family: Women and Familial Relationships." In *The Routledge History of Women in Europe Since 1700*, ed. D Simonton. London: Routledge, 2006, 14–53.

———, *The Making of Modern Woman: Europe 1789–1918*. London: Longman/Pearson, 2002.

Arthur, N., and C. Lee, "Young Australian Women's Aspirations for Work, Marriage and Family: 'I Guess I am Just Another Person Who Wants It All.'" *Journal of Health Psychology* 13, no. 5 (2008): 589–596.

Australian Bureau of Statistics, *Family Characteristics and Transitions, Australia, 2012–13*. Catalogue 4442.0, 2015. https://www.abs.gov.au/AUSSTATS/abs@.nsf/allprimarymainfeatures/E6A928611 9FA0A85CA25699000255C89?opendocument.

———, *Gender Indicators, Australia*. Catalogue 4125.0, 2018. https://www.abs.gov.au/ausstats/abs@.nsf/Lookup/by%20Subject/4125.0~Sep%202018~Main%20Features~Economic%20Security~4.

Baraitser, Lisa, *Maternal Encounters: The Ethics of Interruption*. London: Routledge, 2009.

Becker, C., I. Kirchmaier, and S. T. Trautmann, "Marriage, Parenthood and Social Network: Subjective Well-Being and Mental Health in Old Age." *PloS One* 14, no. 7 (2019). https://doi.org/10.1371/journal.pone.0218704.

Belkin, L., "The Opt-Out Revolution." *The New York Times Magazine*, October 26, 2003. https://www.nytimes.com/2003/10/26/magazine/the-opt-out-revolution.html.

Berenson, H., "The 'Family Wage' and Working Women's Consciousness in Britain." *Politics and Society* 19, no. 1 (1991): 71–108.

Bianchi, S., L. Sayer, M. Milkie, and J. Robinson, "Housework: Who Did, Does, or Will Do It and How Much Does It Matter?" *Social Forces* 91, no. 1 (2012): 55–63.

Bianchi S. M,, Robinson J. P., & Milkie M. A. *Changing Rhythms of American Family Life*. New York, NY: Russell Sage Foundation, 2006.

Budig, M., and P. England, "The Wage Penalty for Motherhood." *American Sociological Review* 66, no. 2 (2001): 204–225.

Budig, M., J. Misra, and I. Boeckmann, "The Motherhood Penalty in Cross-National Perspective: The Importance of Work–Family Policies and Cultural Attitudes." *Social Politics* 19, no. 2 (2012): 163–193.

———, "Work-Family Policy Tradeoffs for Mothers? Unpacking the Cross-National Variation in the Motherhood Earnings Penalties." *Work and Occupations* 43, no. 2 (2016): 119–77.

Bueskens, Petra, *Mothering and Psychoanalysis: Clinical, Sociological and Feminist Perspectives*. Bradford, Ontario: Demeter Press, 2014.

———, *Modern Motherhood and Women's Dual Identities: Rewriting the Sexual Contract*. London: Routledge, 2018a.
———, "Maternal Subjectivity: From Containing to Creating." In *Dangerous Ideas About Mothers*, eds. R. Robertson and C. Nelson. Perth: UWA Publishing, 2018b, 197–211.
———, "Gillard's Dilemma, the Sexual Contract and Maternal Citizenship." In *Australian Mothering: Historical and Sociological Perspectives*, eds. C. Pascoe Leahy and Petra Bueskens. London: Palgrave, 2019, 421–435.
Chodorow, Nancy, *The Reproduction of Mothering: Psychoanalysis and the Sociology of Gender*. Berkeley: University of California Press, 1999 [1978].
Chodorow, Nancy, and S. Contratto, "The Fantasy of the Perfect Mother." In *Feminism and Psychoanalytic Theory*, ed. Nancy Chodorow. Cambridge, UK: Polity, 1989, 79–96.
Collins, H., "Shifting the Center: Race, Class, and Feminist Theorizing About Motherhood." In *Mothering: Ideology, Experience, and Agency*, eds. E. Nakano Glenn, G. Chang, and L. R. Forcey. New York: Routledge, 1994, 45–66.
Connelly, R., and J. Kimmell, *The Time Use of Mothers in the United States at the Beginning of the 21st Century*. Michigan: W.E. Upjohn Institute for Employment Research, 2010.
Craig, L., *Contemporary Motherhood: The Impact of Children on Adult Time*. Hampshire: Ashgate, 2007.
Craig L., and J. Brown, "The Multitasking Parent: Time Penalties, Dimensions, and Gender Differences." In *The Economics of Multitasking*, eds. C. M. Kalenkoski and G. Foster. New York: Palgrave Macmillan, 2016, 33–59.
Craig, L., K. Mullan, and M. Blaxland, "Parenthood, Policy and Work-Family Time in Australia 1992–2006." *Work Employment Society* 24, no. 1 (2010): 27–45.
Crittendon, A., *The Price of Motherhood: Why the Most Important Job Is Still the Least Valued*. Henry Holt: New York, 2002.
Cusk, R., *A Life's Work: On Becoming a Mother*. New York: Picador, 2001.
Deloitte, *Deloitte millennial survey*. October 24, 2018. https://www2.deloitte.com/global/en/pages/about-deloitte/articles/millennialsurvey.html.
de Marneffe, D., *Maternal Desire: On Children, Love, and the Inner Life*. New York: Little, Brown & Co., 2004.
———, "The (M)other We Fall in Love With Wants to Be There." Reply to Commentaries. *Studies in Gender and Sexuality* 10, no. 1 (2009): 27–32.
Edin, K., and M. Kefalas, *Promises I Can Keep: Why Poor Women Put Motherhood Before Marriage*. Berkeley: University of California Press, 2005.
Finn, D., and Donovan, A. *PwC's NextGen: A Global Generational Study,* Price Waterhouse Coopers, 17 February (2013), 1–16. https://www.pwc.com/gx/en/hr-management-services/pdf/pwc-nextgen-study-2013.pdf.

Fraser, N., "After the Family Wage: A Postindustrial Thought Experiment." In *Gender and Citizenship in Transition*, ed. B. Hobson. New York: Routledge, 2000, 1–32.

Freeman, D., and J. Freeman, *The Stressed Sex: Uncovering the Truth About Men, Women, and Mental Health*. Oxford, UK: Oxford University Press, 2013.

Freud, Sigmund, "Femininity." *New Introductory Lectures on Psychoanalysis*, Standard Edition, Vol. 22. London: Hogarth Press, 1964 [1933], 112–135.

Friedan, B., *The Feminine Mystique*. New York: Penguin, 1963.

Gerson, K., "There's No Such Thing as Having It All: Gender, Work, and Care in an Age of Insecurity." In *Gender in the Twenty-First Century: The Stalled Revolution and the Road to Equality*, eds. S. N. Davis, S. Winslow, and D. Maume. Oakland, CA: University of California Press, 2017, 13–27.

Giddens, Anthony, *The Transformation of Intimacy: Sexuality, Love and Eroticism in Modern Societies*. Cambridge: Polity Press, 1992.

Gilbert, D., "Happiness: What Your Mother Didn't Tell You." *World Minds Annual Symposium*, December 13, 2018. https://www.youtube.com/watch?v=b1Y2Z1BGwno.

Gillies, V., *Marginalised Mothers: Exploring Working Class Experiences of Parenting*. London: Routledge, 2007.

Gilligan, C., *In a Different Voice: Psychological Theory and Women's Development*. Cambridge, MA: Harvard University Press, 1982.

Graeber, D., *Bullshit Jobs: A Theory*. London: Penguin, 2019.

Hakim, Catherine, *Work-Lifestyle Choices in the 21st Century: Preference Theory*. Oxford: Oxford University Press, 2000.

———, "Women's Lifestyle Preferences in the 21st Century." In *The Future of Motherhood in Europe*, eds. J. Schippers, G. Beets, and E. te Velde. Dordrecht: Springer, 2009, 177–195.

Hanson, T., "Parenthood and Happiness: A Review of Folk Theories Versus Empirical Evidence." *Social Indicators Research* 109, no. 1 (2012): 29–64.

Hattery, A. *Women, Work and Family: Balancing and Weaving*. Thousand Oaks: Sage, 2001.

Hays, S., *The Cultural Contradictions of Motherhood*. New Haven: Yale University Press, 1996.

Hochschild, A., *The Second Shift: Working Parents and the Revolution at Home*. New York: Viking, 2012 [1989].

Hoffnung, M., "Wanting It All: Career, Marriage, and Motherhood During College-Educated Women's 20s." *Sex Roles*, 50, no. 9–10 (2004): 711–723.

Hollway, W., Mitchell J., and Walsh, J., "Interview with Juliet Mitchell—*Psychoanalysis and Feminism*: Then and Now." *Psychoanalysis, Culture & Society* (2015) 20, 112–130. https://doi.org/10.1057/pcs.2015.3.

Hollway, W., Mitchell, J., & Walsh, J. "Interview with Juliet Mitchell Psychoanalysis and Feminism: Then and Now," Psychoanalysis, Culture & Society (2015) 20, 112130. https://doi.org/10.1057/pcs.2015.3.

Hunt, K., "Women as Citizens: Changing the Polity." In *The Routledge History of Women in Europe Since 1700*, ed. D. Simonton. London: Routledge, 2006, 216–258.

Irigaray, L., "The Bodily Encounter with the Mother," In *The Irigaray Reader Reader*, ed. M. Whitford. Cambridge, MA: Basil Blackwell, 1991, 34–46.

Kessler-Harris, A., *Out to Work: A History of Wage-Earning Women in the United States*. Oxford: Oxford University Press, 2003 [1982].

Koven, S., and S. Michel, eds., *Mothers of a New World: Maternalist Politics and the Origins of Welfare States*. New York: Routledge, 1993.

Kristeva, Julia, and A. Goldhammer, "Stabat Mater." *Poetics Today* 6, no. 1/2 (1985): 133–152.

Lake, M., "'A Revolution in the Family': The Challenge and Contradiction of Maternal Citizenship." In *Mothers of a New World: Maternalist Politics and Welfares States in Comparative Perspective*, eds. S. Koven and S. Michel. New York: Routledge, 1993, 378–395.

———. "State Socialism for Australian Mothers: Andrew Fisher's Radical Maternalism in Its International and Local Contexts." *Labour History: A Journal of Labour and Social History*, no. 102 (2012): 55–70.

Manne, A., *Motherhood: How Should We Care for Our Children?* Crows Nest, Sydney: Allen & Unwin, 2005.

Maher, J., "Accumulating Care: Mothers Beyond the Conflicting Temporalities of Caring and Work." *Time & Society* 18, nos. 2–3 (2009): 236–243.

Mitchell, J., "Introduction, 1999." *Psychoanalysis and Feminism: A Radical Reassessment of Freudian Psychoanalysis*. London: Penguin, 2000, xv–xxxviii.

———, "Reply to Lynne Segal's Commentary." *Studies in Gender and Sexuality* 3, no. 2 (2002): 217–228.

Mitchell, S. A., and M. J. Black, *Freud and Beyond: A History of Modern Psychoanalytic Thought*. USA: Basic Books, 1995.

Morehead, A., "Synchronizing Time for Work and Family: Preliminary Insights from Qualitative Research with Mothers." *Journal of Sociology* 37, no. 4 (2001): 355–371.

Moutsou, C., and R. Mayo, *The Mother in Psychoanalysis and Beyond: Matricide and Maternal Subjectivity*. London: Routledge, 2016.

Mutari, E., M. Power, and D. M. Figart, "Neither Mothers Nor Breadwinners: African-American Women's Exclusion From US Minimum Wage Policies, 1912–1938." *Feminist Economics* 8, no. 2 (2002): 37–61.

Nelson, S. K., K. Kushlev, T. English, E. W. Dunn, and S. Lyubomirsky, "In Defense of Parenthood: Children Are Associated with More Joy Than Misery." *Psychological Science* 24, no. 1 (2013): 3–10.

Offen, K. *European Feminisms, 1700–1950: A Political History*. Stanford, CA: Stanford University Press, 2000.
O'Reilly, A. *Matricentric Feminism*. Toronto: Demeter Press, 2016.
Pascoe Leahy, C., and P. Bueskens, eds., *Australian Mothering: Historical and Sociological Perspectives*. London: Palgrave Macmillan, 2019.
Probert, B., and B. Wilson, eds., *Pink Collar Blues: Work, Gender and Technology*, 2nd Edition. Melbourne: Melbourne University Press, 2008 [1993].
Rose, J., *Mothers: An Essay on Love and Cruelty*. London: Faber & Faber, 2018.
Rosenthal, C. J., "Kinkeeping in the Familial Division of Labor." *Journal of Marriage and the Family* 47, no. 4 (1995): 965–974.
Ruppanner, L., "Sharing of Household Responsibilities." In *Encyclopedia of Quality of Life and Well-Being Research*, eds. A. C. Michalos, 258–311. Dordrecht: Springer, 2014.
Saad, L., "Children a Key Factor in Women's Desire to Work Outside the Home." Gallup Poll, October 2015. https://news.gallucom/poll/186050/children-key-factor-women-desire-work-outside-home.aspx.
Sayer, L. C., P. England, M. Bittman, and S. M. Bianchi, "How Long Is the Second (Plus First) Shift? Gender Differences in Paid, Unpaid and Total Work Time in Australia and the United States." *Journal of Comparative Family Studies* 40, no. 4 (2009): 523–545.
Sayer, L., "More Work for Mothers? Trends and Gender Differences in Multi-tasking." In *Time Competition: Disturbed Balances and New Options in Work and Care*, eds. T. van der Lippe and P. Peters, 41–56. New York: Edward Elgar, 2006.
Seligman, M., *Authentic Happiness*. New York: Free Press, 2002.
Slaughter, A. M., "Why Women Still Can't Have It All." *The Atlantic*, July/August, 2012. https://www.theatlantic.com/magazine/archive/2012/07/why-women-still-cant-have-it-all/309020/.
Stack, C. B., and L. Burton, "Kinscripts: Reflections on Family, Generation, and Culture." In *Mothering: Ideology, Experience, and Agency*, eds. E. Nakano Glenn, G. Chang, and L. R. Forcey, 33–44. New York: Routledge, 1994.
Stevenson, B., and J. Wolfers, *The Paradox of Declining Female Happiness* (Forschungsinstitut zur Zukunft der Arbeit, Institute for the Study of Labor, IZA Discussion Paper No. 4200, 2009). http://ftp.iza.org/dp4200.pdf.
Stone, Alison, *Feminism, Psychoanalysis and Maternal Subjectivity*. London: Routledge, 2012.
———, "Mother-Daughter Relations and the Maternal in Irigaray and Chodorow." *PhiloSOPHIA: A Journal of Continental Feminism* 1, no. 1 (2011): 45–64.
———, "Psychoanalysis and Maternal Subjectivity." In *Mothering and Psychoanalysis: Clinical, Sociological and Feminist Perspectives*, ed. P. Bueskens. Bradford, Ontario: Demeter Press, 2014, 325–341.

Treas, J., van der Lippe, T., and Tai, T. C., "The Happy Homemaker? Married Women's Well-Being in Cross-National Perspective." *Social Forces* 90, no. 1 (2011): 111–132.

Twenge, J. M., W. K. Campbell, and C. Foster, "Parenthood and Marital Satisfaction: A Meta-Analytic Review." *Journal of Marriage and the Family* 65, no. 3 (2003): 574–583.

VerBruggen, R., and W. Wendy Wang, "The Real Housewives of America: Dad's Income and Mom's Work." *Institute for Family Studies*, 2019. https://ifstudies.org/ifs-admin/resources/newfinalifsresearchbrief-verbruggenwang-realhousewives.pdf.

Weeks, K., *The Problem with Work: Feminism, Marxism, Antiwork Politics, and Postwork Imaginaries*. Durham: Duke University Press, 2011.

Williams, J. C., *White Working Class: Overcoming Class Cluelessness in America*. Cambridge, MA: Harvard Business Review Press, 2017.

Williams, J., M. Blair-Loy, and J. L. Berdahl, "Cultural Schemas, Social Class, and the Flexibility Stigma." *Journal of Social Issues 69*, no. 2 (2013): 209–234.

Young, M., and P. Willmott, *Family and Kinship in East London*. London: Free Press, 1957.

CHAPTER 14

Mirroring a Mother's Love: A Chodorowian Analysis of the Complicated Relationship Between Mothers and Nannies

Katie B. Garner

The figure of the nanny is a bewitching one in our collective western imagination, sometimes quite literally, as with Mary Poppins and Nanny McPhee, who appear in eponymous British novels. In these stories, and others, a nanny appears from an unknown place and is depicted as saving the family. Yet, scratch the surface and a potential malevolence lurks. Stepmothers are ubiquitously cast as villains who want their charges harmed so they will be more powerful or so they can eliminate competition for the attention male protagonists, typically the children's fathers. In *The Reproduction of Mothering*, feminist psychoanalyst Nancy Chodorow asserts that this punishing view of stepmothers originates from our own ambivalence about our mothers, whom we love but also hate, because

K. B. Garner (✉)
International Association of Maternal Action and Scholarship (IAMAS), Chicago, Illinois, USA
e-mail: kbgarner@iamas.com

P. Bueskens (ed.), *Nancy Chodorow and* The Reproduction of Mothering,
https://doi.org/10.1007/978-3-030-55590-0_14

of their seeming omnipotence and our uncomfortable sense of dependence.[1] "Children of both sexes," she argues, "will maintain a fearsome unconscious maternal image as a result of projecting upon the hostility derived from their own feelings of impotence."[2] This ambivalence tends to lead to guilt and shame, so to protect one's sense of goodness as well as prevent us from hating our mothers for our own feelings of vulnerability, the "evil" qualities are transferred to a stepmother. This permits the (nearly always biological) mother, to remain pure, good, loving, and kind.[3] Unlike stepmothers, nannies tend to be depicted as benign, but also multi-faceted, and there is good reason for this. In literature, the mother is often still present when the nanny enters, and given that it is in fact her story, she, as the mother, often frames the conflict, whether it regards her ambivalence about motherhood, her wish to continue working despite cultural pressure to stay home, and/or her experience in a unsatisfactory marriage. An increasing number of novels share narrative space with the nanny, but few center exclusively on the nanny. (Fewer yet depict the nanny as being a mother herself.) Socially constructed power differentials favoring the mother also make this relationship problematic.

Extending this analysis, and drawing on the insights of Chodorow, this essay focuses on the ways in which a heterosexually partnered mother's relationship with the nanny she hires includes several traditionally unrecognized benefits, including: (1) permitting an opportunity to recreate the triangulated relationship the mother-employer experienced as a girl with both her mother and her father; (2) fostering an ability to vicariously adhere to tenets of intensive mothering while still maintaining a career; (3) allowing (re-)engagement in a socially sanctioned female-female relationship and; (4) offering a means of being cared for without undermining one's status as an independent adult in ways continued dependence on one's mother would not. In short, as an employer, a woman can reap the benefits of emotionally bonding with a woman whose role is designed to support her temporally, physically and emotionally (as a mother would for a child), even as she maintains control via the class-

[1] Nancy J. Chodorow, *The Reproduction of Mothering: Psychoanalysis and the Sociology of Gender* (Berkeley, CA: University of California Press, 1978), 51.

[2] Chodorow, *The Reproduction of Mothering*, 122.

[3] Fairy tales notoriously feature mothers who have died before the story begins or during the set-up of the story.

and race-based power she holds, thus providing immense psychological benefits that tend to be unremunerated.

One memoir and two novels will be used to elucidate these ideas: *Women's Work: A Reckoning with Work and Home* by Megan K. Stack,[4] *My Hollywood* by Mona Simpson,[5] and *The Perfect Nanny* by Leila Slimani.[6] Within Stack's, Simpson's, and Slimani's texts, readers encounter modern mothers who hire women to help them with childcare. In all three texts, the race of the nanny is different than the race of the mother-employer, with Stack and Claire identifying as white women who hire a woman of color and Myriam being a woman of color who hires a nanny who is white. All the mother-employers are more comfortable financially than the women they hire, as one would expect, but these mother-employers are not rich. All three are in heterosexual marriages that most would describe as fair to good, at least initially, and none of the men attempt to have an affair with the nannies in their employ, despite this being a common trope in many "nanny novels." All the women express insecurity, ambivalence, and intense love regarding their roles as mothers and their feelings for their children. For all these women, work is a place to reassert a former (and valued) identity, claim social privilege, escape the monotony of carework, and generally feel fulfilled as individuals. All three women form deep and complicated relationships with the nannies they hire. None of the women had nannies as children, but their mothers form part of the relational web of the mother protagonists. These relationships differ in the strength and quality. Myriam's mother is entirely absent from the novel, although she has a tense relationship with her mother-in-law. Stack has a good relationship with her mother who lives far away, and Claire feels her mother was deficient due to her mental illness. In other words, despite a few notable differences, these women are peers by virtue of their class, level of education, marital status, identity as mothers (and ambivalence about motherhood), as well as their interest in waged work. This corpus will be analyzed both individually and collectively, drawing on Chodorow's theories in

[4] Megan K. Stack, *Women's Work: A Reckoning with Work and Home* (New York: Doubleday, 2019).

[5] Mona Simpson, *My Hollywood* (New York: Knopf, 2010).

[6] Leila Slimani, *The Perfect Nanny* (New York: Penguin, 2016).

The Reproduction of Mothering regarding enmeshment, triangulation in a heterosexual mother's relationships, and ambivalence.

Chodorow does not address mother/nanny relationships in her canonical text, *The Reproduction of Mothering*, but she does provide a cohesive feminist analysis of why women have been primary caregivers to children and why many mothers value the role despite some second-wave feminists, including Betty Friedan,[7] Dorothy Dinnerstein,[8] and Shulamith Firestone,[9] dismissing motherhood as oppressive.[10] While Chodorow is often criticized for being an essentialist, a close reading of her work demonstrates otherwise. Her argument is that women are not *innately* better mothers or *biologically* predestined to do motherwork, but are *primed* to do so via their psychosexual relationship with their own mothers. Outsourcing childcare is hardly a new phenomenon, but it is different today. Sociologist Cameron MacDonald posits in *Shadow Mothers: Nannies, Au Pairs, and the Micropolitics of Mothering*: "Never before have the daily lives of so many American mothers been so at odds with prevailing beliefs about children's needs."[11] Indeed, female employers have arguably never eschewed class- and race-based differences so markedly, or at least outwardly. This places both mother-employers and nannies in new terrain.

Part of understanding the mother/nanny dynamic requires understanding the mother/daughter relationship and the emotional landscape of mothering. While the sex of an individual does not solely determine one's destiny (contra Freud), it does shape one's life experience. Chodorow specifically refutes Freud's assertion that women are psychologically marred once they realize they do not possess a penis and later desire a baby as a replacement. For Chodorow, penis envy still exists, but it is not the penis girls covet, rather the more abstract *phallus*, which

[7] Betty Friedan, *The Feminine Mystique* (New York: W. W. Norton, 1963).

[8] Dorothy Dinnerstein, *The Mermaid and the Minotaur* (New York: Harper & Row, 1976).

[9] Shulamith Firestone, *The Dialectic of Sex: The Case for Feminist Revolution* (New York: Morrow, 1970).

[10] Like Rich, Chodorow is a firm critic of the institution of motherhood, but not the actual work of mothering.

[11] Cameron MacDonald, *Shadow Mothers: Nannies, Au Pairs, and the Micropolitics of Mothering* (Berkeley: California University Press, 2010), 3.

endows social privilege, freedom, independence, and cultural power.[12] A girl engages with her father *to gain* vicarious *access* to phallic power, which also permits her to vie for her mother's affection—affection she recognizes is shared with her father. Lucy Holmes, an object-relations psychoanalyst, claims a girl only later identifies with her father because he is a "symbol of freedom from the dependence on the merging with the pre-Oedipal mother."[13] This relationship remains secondary for girls, who typically maintain an intense love for their mothers. Girls and women tend to become erotically heterosexual but, Chodorow argues, often retain a profound emotional connection with women (based on the primordial connection with their own mothers).[14] Heterosexual relationships do not fully permit a woman to work out childhood issues, nor do they feel as comfortable or satisfying as a triangular relationship.

Both Chodorow and Holmes assert that the movement from matri-sexuality to heterosexuality is often incomplete, with Holmes stating that girls "remain in a bisexual triangle throughout childhood and into puberty – and though they usually make a sexual resolution in favor of men, they retain an internal emotional triangle throughout life."[15] The transfer of affection from one's mother is more demanding for girls than boys because a girl child must abandon her mother with whom she deeply identifies, convert her primary love for a woman to a man, and, finally, shift from a triangulated to a dyadic relationship. Holmes further claims a woman's "rejection of her mother is a defense against primary identification, hence her own internal affair as much as a relational affair in the world."[16] It is a triangulated relationship that tends to be recreated later via marriage and reproduction. A woman desires a baby because having

[12] Holmes takes a different tact when she argues that the first "phallus" a child envies is the breast, which is taken orally, releases sustenance, can be withheld, and is a physical representation of a mother's potent power. From her perspective, women desire a baby not to replace the penis, but to claim her own ownership of the first powerful phallic object: the breast.

[13] Lucy Holmes, *The Internal Triangle* (Lanham, MD: Rowman & Littlefield, 2008), 17.

[14] Chodorow, *The Reproduction of Mothering*, 200.

[15] Ibid., 18.

[16] Holmes, *The Internal Triangle*, 17.

one permits her to recreate the triangular relationship dynamic she experienced in girlhood.[17] Boys, both Chodorow and Holmes claim, experience a more complete split from identification with their mother, moving at an early age to an identification with their father and the social power his masculinity conveys upon him. Mothers, for both boys and girls, are literal and figurative emblems of their dependence, helplessness, and enmeshed selves.

When a woman becomes a mother, Chodorow posits that she regresses and becomes enmeshed with her baby, which fulfills her previous experience of enmeshment with her mother.[18] Chodorow cites Christine Olden's work, when she explains that, in the infant's early weeks, a mother "gives herself up and becomes one with him" thus permitting "a new kind of love for the child who is at once her own self and yet separate and outside, [and] concentrates entirely on the infant."[19] According to Chodorow, this regression "activates these early constituted internal object-relationships, defenses, and conflicts."[20] This process can be quite fraught, but, it is this process that Chodorow credits for what many consider a woman's "innate" ability to mother. Biology is not the determining factor; object relationships are, according to Chodorow. "A mother identifies with her own mother (or with the mother she wishes she had)," and thereby "tries to provide nurturant care for the child."[21] During this time, a new mother "reexperiences herself as a cared-for child, thus sharing with her child the possession of a good mother."[22]

It is this point that is particularly relevant to this work, because while the woman is in this state of enmeshed regression she is not only empathically reliving the sense of dependence intrinsic to infancy, but is experiencing ambivalence and dependence as a mother. Nannies enter a mother's home believing their role is to care for a child, but the mother's enmeshment with her child as well as her own insecurity regarding motherhood means, regardless of the nanny's age, mother-employers tend to look to the nannies they hire as pseudo-mothers who can alleviate their

[17] Chodorow, *The Reproduction of Mothering*, 201–203.

[18] Ibid., 164.

[19] Ibid., 86.

[20] Ibid., 89.

[21] Ibid., 90.

[22] Ibid.

discomfort, ambivalence, and perceived ineptness regarding mothering. Interestingly, as Chodorow points out, girls commonly separate their familial world with the extrafamilial one, and, simultaneously become "very critical of [...] her mother, and may idealize the mother or the family of a friend." [23] Nannies can be simultaneously a mother ***and*** an external figure free to be admired. With a nanny's entrance, mother-employers also experience several triangulated relationships. The most pertinent is among a mother-employer, her baby, and the nanny because it permits a mother to re-enact early relationships, but, importantly, with the caveats that she is now older and likely individuated,[24] secondly, that she possesses access to a phallus (both a literal penis and the cultural power it bestows) via her heterosexual relationship as well as her baby, which demonstrates a woman's in situ privilege confirming (correctly or not) her heterosexuality, and thirdly, she holds a less dependent role in the relationship due to her cultural, financial, and often race-based power over the nanny.[25]

Women's Work: A Reckoning with Work and Home—Megan K. Stack

In 2019, Megan K. Stack, a former war correspondent, published a memoir of her early years of motherhood titled *Women's Work: A Reckoning of Work and Home*.[26] Married to another war correspondent, Stack had her first baby in Beijing, China and her second in India—two countries in which domestic service is widely available, inexpensive, and socially acceptable. Initially, Stack resists hiring a nanny for the typical reasons Americans do: pressure to adhere to norms of intensive mothering, reluctance to exert class privilege in a domestic setting, and a desire to prove she can do it all herself. Stack's husband, Tom, quickly resumes his work after their son Max is born and is often away from home. After

[23] Ibid., 137.

[24] Ibid.

[25] One could argue that three other relationships exist, including: (1) mother/nanny/husband; (2) mother-employer/baby/her own mother and; (3) mother-employer/her mother/nanny.

[26] Stack, *Women's Work*.

coming home from the hospital, Stack, who one presumes is hardly weak-kneed, given her profession, is overwhelmed emotionally (she is tested for postpartum depression), physically (Max does not sleep well), and temporally (she intends to write a book during her reprieves from hands-on mothering). Chapter two closes with her naked plea: "Help!"[27]

The couple hires Xiao Li, a young mother from a rural village, who leaves her daughter with grandparents. She and Xiao Li quickly work in tandem to ensure Max is cared for, the apartment is clean, and meals are cooked. When Xiao Li is called back to her child, who has health issues, Stack wants to be understanding, but without Xiao Li, she must assume all the work they have shared while forestalling her writing. Tom suggests they replace Xiao Li with a woman with fewer personal demands, but Stack protests vehemently. "Plainly put," she writes, "I loved her."[28] She continues:

> My emotions toward Xiao Li were not sexual or romantic; neither platonic nor familial. But love it was, all the same. It was a love of gratitude and recognition and dependence; a love that tempered the madness and desperation of my love for Max into a survivable emotion. [...] In those fragile, wild months after Max was born, I'd lived in a dreamscape of darkened rooms and feedings, and most of all, terror. And just as surely as Tom could not understand this existence no matter how hard I tried to find the language to evoke it, Xiao Li intuited my state without a single word. I never had to explain to Xiao Li. She knew, the knowledge was in her face and hands, tactful and gentle, and I loved her. [...] I didn't even know her full name, and I don't think she knew mine, [... but] I associated Xiao Li with sanity and health, with my escape from sleeplessness and depression.[29]

Stack then turns to consider her husband, with whom she has good relationship, and writes:

> Tom's intuition was correct. My attachment to Xiao Li had turned into an irrational dependence. And he didn't even know the extent of my treachery. In those days I sometimes imagined Xiao Li, Tom, Max and

[27] Ibid., 38.

[28] Ibid., 102.

[29] Ibid., 102–103.

> me adrift in an overcrowded lifeboat. Somebody had to be thrown overboard. I knew Tom would have to go; I would pitch my one true love into the waves. That is how deeply I had come to depend on Xiao Li.[30]

This stark ranking of nanny above husband seems dramatic, but makes sense with the assistance of Chodorow's analysis.

According to Chodorow, women are primed not only to hold multiple love interests, but more specifically to love both a man and a woman simultaneously, with the latter relationship offering more emotional sustenance. Chodorow argues that women tend to view men as "*erotic* objects," but because "fathers are comparatively unavailable physically and emotionally [...] and because of the intensity of the mother-daughter relationship in which she participates, girls tend not to make a total transfer of affection to their fathers but [...] oscillate emotionally between mother and father."[31] Moreover, because fathers "are not present as much and are not primary caretakers" with "their own training for masculinity" leading them to "deny emotionally," men "tend to remain *emotionally* secondary, or at most emotionally equal" for women[32] She further posits that this "internal situation continues into adulthood and affects adult women's participation in relationships."[33]

When one lays this analysis over Stack's disclosure, it is easy to see how Stack looks for a maternal and female figure with whom she can bond, particularly when, according to Chodorow, she has regressed to a psychological state that mirrors her infant son's. Tom, like all the husbands in the corpus herein, is gone more than not. Stack shared his vagabond spirit, but after their baby's birth, only Tom works outside the home. Stack confesses to jealousy but admits that her desire to stay home had changed her. Whereas Tom "had slipped easily back into his old life," she writes, "I had been bombed back to some prehistoric version of myself."[34] As if summoning Chodorow, Stack writes: "His [the baby's]emotions, my emotions, our symbiotic state" were inconceivable before she held him.[35]

[30] Stack, *Women's Work*, 103.

[31] Chodorow, *The Reproduction of Mothering*, 193.

[32] Ibid.

[33] Ibid.

[34] Stack, *Women's Work*, 52.

[35] Ibid., 36.

She cannot comprehend how Tom moves effortlessly into parenthood, so unchanged. Stack had nurtured a different fantasy of their life as parents in which Tom "was there, too, at every critical moment."[36] She assumed the "disruption" of a new baby "would be evenly shared," and highlights this was "the expectation of my generation."[37] Tom, as well as the husbands in the two forthcoming novels are hardly villains, but each woman wants her husband to be more involved in childcare, the daily events of the home, and their lives as mothers. Chodorow suggests this is unlikely if the traditional gendered division of labor persists.

Practically speaking, mothers thus experience a mundane but grinding need for the physical and emotional work nannies provide. They not only need help with childcare; they desire proxy mothers to guide them. Xiao Li is younger than Stack, but still an adult mother. Xiao Li's age prevents her from being Stack's biological mother, of course, but her experience allows her to still fill the role. She can soothe Stack's fears, show her how to mother her own child, and importantly, tend to Stack herself, a job requirement seldom listed in job advertisements for nannies, but is labor often wrapped up into the daily work, particularly for new mothers. Moreover, while Xiao Li is Stack's ticket to freedom, or at least permits her to continue her work as a writer, it is implied that were she to not be there, Stack would be responsible for the work. Tom does not see much difference in who does the work—as long as he's not the one doing it. Tom and Stack argue about this frequently, with her explaining: "Xiao Li had given me crucial scraps of time and valuable hope for my career, but [...] I saw that, if I pressed Tom to do more housework, he would call for Xiao Li to be fired."[38] Tom is not nearly as close to Xiao Li as Stack, so firing her has little impact on him, which provides him the upper hand in arguments. With Stack's mother half a world away and Tom's scant assistance, Xiao Li is the one who remains by her side (importantly, because she is being paid). Had Stack's mother stayed, it is likely she and Stack would experience conflicts regarding childcare. Chodorow does not address this specifically, but it seems likely that unresolved issues of dependence and enmeshment are stoked as women navigate being both a

[36] Ibid.

[37] Ibid.

[38] Ibid., 56.

mother and daughter. Nannies are not subject to this, despite being proxy mothers.

Stack experiences a desperate sense of need, but she also feels guilty. She is not an infant unable to conceptualize a caregiver as a separate object. As she delves into Xiao Li's life, Stack treads carefully, not out of fear Xiao Li will feel she is prying, but because learning too much, particularly if too "grim" would be "dangerous."[39] "I might conclude that my domestic arrangement was fundamentally unfair," Stack writes, "I could either drown or I could wear Xiao Li as a life vest. There was no third choice."[40] Stack is uncomfortable with the power dynamics intrinsic to being Xiao Li's employer and is vexed when Tom calls her their maid not only because Stack feels it betrays her emotional connection, but the term casts Stack as "an exploiter feeding on the flesh of people."[41] Stack recognizes Xiao Li is not her mother, yet her emotional attachment, desperate need for her help, and her dependence counter the guilt. When Xiao Li becomes pregnant again, she resigns from her post. Stack tries filling the post, hiring a "parade of *ayis* who didn't last."[42] This, too, is a repetition throughout the following novels. In time, the family moves to India. Life moves forward for both women, who are reunited when Stack returns to interview Xiao Li. This reunion is more important to Stack than Xiao Li, who, while cast as a mother to Stack, never adopted the role herself.

My Hollywood—Mona Simpson

Mona Simpson's *My Hollywood* is a lightly satiric novel set in contemporary Los Angeles, with all the de facto trappings. The novel unfolds in alternating chapters between two women: Claire, a new mother torn between her love for her infant son and her music, and Lola, a 52-year-old Filipina nanny who follows the path of many newly immigrated women who export cash in lieu of time with their children while navigating a new culture and completing socially undervalued work. The novel opens with Claire recalling her first date with her future husband, Paul, and their discussion of how housework should be divided. Paul asserts, "With a

[39] Ibid., 46.

[40] Ibid.

[41] Ibid., 56.

[42] Ibid., 114.

woman who worked, it'd have to be fifty-fifty."[43] She informs Paul that maintaining a career as a music composer while being a mother is infeasible, but Paul objects. Like Stack in *Women's Work*, Claire describes her fantasy of shared parenting as "[h]e, the putative he, would work a little less and I'd work a little less and the kid would have long hair, paint-spattered overalls, and be, in general, a barrel of monkeys."[44] She knows the reality will be different.

Despite Claire's troubling childhood with a mentally ill mother, she is reluctant to outsource care of their new son, William. According to Chodorow the desire to mother originates in part as a result of the desire to return to the cohesive, secure, symbiotic, and empathic connection between mother and daughter. Individuation occurs before this return can be successful. Chodorow argues: "Motherhood may be a (fantasied) attempt to make reparation to a mother's own mother for the injuries she did."[45] Claire's mother was never a role model she wished to emulate as a result of her mother's mental illness and mediocre abilities to parent her. Claire austerely notes: "She made it to the finish: she kept me till I was seventeen, then sent me out mostly intact, with an instrument to hold."[46] Unlike Chodorow's semi-fused mother/daughter dyads, Claire resisted and continues to resist the sense of enmeshment. Claire understandably fears she will reproduce her mother's flawed mothering and become unmoored herself. Her battle is framed as one of life and death as she recalls the various times psychiatric professionals contacted her: "My life or hers" she would think each time.[47] "I'd chosen mine."[48] Claire unduly carries the blame for this, believing she caused her mother's unmooring. "My existence," Claire explains, "had caused too much pain. Having a child wobbled and undid my mother, forced her through strenuous marathons, at the edge of her capacity."[49]

[43] Simpson, *My Hollywood*.

[44] Ibid., 10.

[45] Chodorow, *The Reproduction of Mothering*, 90.

[46] Ibid., 166.

[47] Simpson, *My Hollywood*, 13.

[48] Ibid.

[49] Ibid., 166.

Claire is rattled by new motherhood. She does not reference mental illness, but there are echoes of her mother's struggles.[50] "Marriage hadn't changed me," Claire explains, "Having a child did. I was a dandelion blown."[51] She adores William, but is befuddled by swaddling, is shaken by his unremitting crying, and can't sleep out of fear he might die. She does not describe the self-gratifying enmeshment Chodorow claims reproduces the pre-Oedipal pleasure of a mother/child bond, perhaps because she never experienced it as an infant, but also because she "feared that [her] invisible soul could harm him."[52] Chodorow claims "good and desirable maternal care" is a byproduct of a "mother's 'empathy' with her infant and her treatment of it as an extension of herself – as someone whose interests she knows through total regressive identification."[53] Claire suggests she is (unwillingly) mirroring her mother's early anxiety as a mother. Claire wants to return to work, which offers relief and a sense of accomplishment, but struggles to find the same solace she once experienced. Music, she explains, "formed something I'd had since I was a girl, a banister I touched to be calm," she explains.[54] Music provided the comfort a mother often does, but the proverbial pram in the hallway prevents her from clearing the mental roadblocks required for the creativity her work demands. While left unsaid, her ability to thrive is at stake.

Paul oversees the process of hiring a nanny, having had been primarily raised by an African American woman from Mississippi. Claire's description of hiring a nanny is one written from the perspective of a stranger in a strange land, with her admitting that, until recently, she believed nannies were "something English, from long ago."[55] The process also reveals that the women coming to be interviewed are not magical, but, according to Claire, "resembl[e] the hags of Grimm more than Juliet's nurse or any

[50] Paul Mandelbaum in his review of *My Hollywood* claims Claire is "racked with bouts of post-partum depression," but I disagree and feel her response is quite identifiable for many women as they acclimate to motherhood for the first time. Mandelbaum, "Whose Hollywood Is It Anyway?" Full citation needed.

[51] Simpson, *My Hollywood*, 24.

[52] Ibid., 12.

[53] Chodorow, *Reproduction of Mothering*, 82.

[54] Simpson, *My Hollywood*, 92.

[55] Ibid., 10.

Disney nanny."[56] These nannies are not benevolent or charitable; instead, they require charity, just as her mother did. After a failed hire, Claire chooses Lola, stating: "I knew my deficiencies and so I selected a supplement. I hired a happy nanny."[57] Claire's relationship with Lola, albeit via a paycheck, affords Claire the opportunity to mirror another woman after her own mother failed to provide a suitable model.

Claire, who often had to mother her own mother, relishes being cared for. In *The Psycho-Analysis of the Nursery*, Alice Balint credits "coldness" and the ensuing "unappeased love" her child experiences as "prevent[ing] the requisite loosening of the bond between them" since the "child will still eternally seek, even when grown up, for a mother-substitute, and bring a childish immature love to the relationship."[58] Her mother's inability to fully support Claire leaves Claire with few qualms about securing Lola's allegiance via material means. Claire does not just seek help with childcare but emotional relief from the "momumental responsibility" of mothering.[59] She explains: "Now I had my baby and I saw. Why women got so little done. How much my own mother had given. Why so many people feel mad at their mothers; because whatever childhood was or wasn't, they're the ones who made it. Fathers loomed above it all, high trees."[60] She desires a proxy mother who can care for her and help her find her footing. Lola does both while also permitting Claire to be "above it all," like the fathers she envies. Claire feels important to Lola, even if that importance is tinged with the instrumentalism of a paycheck, indeed maybe *because* of the paycheck.

While Claire is aware of the financial puppet strings she is pulling, she cares for Lola and values the close relationship between Lola and William, perhaps believing she cannot offer him what Lola does as *his* proxy mother. Lola comes to care deeply for William, who allows her to transfer the love she has for her children in the Philippines. She even turns down a job that would offer more money. But like Xiao Li, Lola is polite and perhaps even likes Claire, but she does not forget the power differences. Lola claims she does tasks for Paul and Claire that she "would do

[56] Ibid., 7.

[57] Ibid., 12.

[58] Alice Balint, *The Psycho-Analysis of the Nursery*, 90.

[59] Simpson, *My Hollywood*, 6.

[60] Ibid., 10.

only for children small small" back home, and yet she relies on them to provide what matters most to her: her children's success.[61] Unlike Claire, Paul believes Lola takes advantage of Claire's love when she acquiesces to Lola's requests for a raise. But there is a method to what he sees as madness. Claire echoes Stack when she admits, only to herself, that "[p]ushing Lola seemed more promising than pushing Paul."[62] Claire's relationship to Paul permits the financial power that allows her to entice Lola to take on more work since she knows Lola is eager to financially maximize her time in the United States. Paul, like Tom, is reluctant take on additional domestic labor or childcare. In this way, a husband provides not only autonomy via a woman's ability to demonstrate that she has converted to heterosexuality, but she, through him, possesses the phallus she rightly recognizes the social power of. This trade-off is deeply felt, as Claire also claims she is "[i]n the custody of Paul."[63]

As Christmas approaches, Claire purchases a pair of diamond earrings for Lola even as Paul points out that Lola would prefer cash she can send home. Although true, Claire ignores this point as she can only narcissistically imagine that Lola wants what she wants. Through Lola, Claire has the opportunity to recreate the dynamics that left her feeling isolated as a child, just as Chodorow suggests when she claims "[m]otherhood may be a (fantasied) attempt to make reparation to a mother's own mother for the injuries she did."[64] In light of this, Claire's burgeoning identification with Lola encourages her to re-enact the helplessness she felt as a child in her relationship with her unstable mother. This helplessness affected her identity development, but by helping Lola she is able to repair the memories of when her mother needed help and she, as a child, was unable to provide it. Claire wants to provide Lola with material items as a means of "saving" her substitute mother, while also giving her what she would want herself.

This gift also reads as a romantic one; a gift often given by a man to his love interest. Interestingly, when Paul gets called into work on Christmas, he tells Claire to call Lola to fill in. Like Tom, Paul views Lola as a placeholder who permits him temporal and emotional freedom, but Claire is

[61] Simpson, *My Hollywood*, 101.

[62] Ibid., 170.

[63] Ibid., 4.

[64] Chodorow, *The Reproduction of Mothering*, 90.

not placated with Lola as a spousal proxy, even if she welcomes Lola as a substitute mother to herself and William. While Lola provides Claire companionship and lessens the physical demands of mothering a small child, this does not alter what Claire expects of Paul as a husband. Claire does not want Lola to *replace* Paul, but her purchase suggests a triangulated relationship in which Lola is not only a shadow mother but a shadow spouse. Indeed, like Stack who compares her love for Xiao Li as superseding her love for her husband, Claire compares her feelings for Lola to a romantic relationship after Claire reluctantly fires her. As she reflects on the termination and her later separation from Paul, Claire states, "[w]hen Lola left, no one had asked anything. The difference had been profound but private, like the end of an affair that turned out to be the love of your life."[65] Claire rues Lola's departure. She misses their comradery, but she also realizes how much Lola did. In a seemingly desperate attempt to rebalance the scales, however, Claire concludes that Lola's success was because "in the evening she had me."[66] The underbelly of this remark shows a vulnerable wish to be appreciated and feel important. She wants Lola to feel that Claire is as important to her as Lola is to Claire.

In the final chapters, after Claire separates from Paul and is successfully raising William alone, she returns to Lola to petition for a relationship based on parity. She offers to share the work fifty-fifty, mirroring her conversation with Paul in the first chapter. The new relationship proposal is not rooted on her earlier sense of need, but from a sense of pragmatism, newly acquired independence, respect, and love—a love rooted in newfound independence. As it turns out, Lola realizes after returning to the Philippines that her husband had fallen in love with another woman and her grown children did not need her the way she hoped. Lola accepts Claire's offer and returns to Los Angeles. The women thus create a queered triangulated relationship in which Claire can disperse the work of parenting, Lola can recreate the enmeshed relationship that offers her so much gratification (as Chodorow posits), and William can thrive with the two women he loves most.

[65] Simpson, *My Hollywood*, 329.

[66] Simpson, *My Hollywood*, 276.

The Perfect Nanny—Leila Slimani

Leila Slimani's taut novel, *The Perfect Nanny*, opens with: "The baby is dead."[67] After setting the morbid scene, Slimani's subsequent chapter offers swift juxtaposition to normalcy: a married couple discussing what qualities they desire in the woman who will care for their children, Mila and Adam. The mother, Myriam (a nod to the Virgin Mary), is a modern "everywoman" of Moroccan decent, who lives in Paris with her husband, Paul. Despite earning a law degree, Myriam is a stay-at-home mother, and like Claire, feels a desire and responsibility to be an exclusive caregiver. She adheres strictly to the tenets of intensive mothering[68] and "absolutely refused to consider using a babysitter" on the basis that "[s]he alone was capable of meeting her daughter's needs."[69] Myriam knows "everything" about her children and "would like to keep that knowledge secret. She knows their tastes, their habits. She can tell immediately if one of them is ill or sad. She has kept them close to her all this time, convinced that no one could protect them as well as she can."[70] Her love for them is sincere, but she chafes at the strictures of motherhood even as she is loath to relinquish her role. Intensive mothering encourages, even demands, that women complete this emotional work, but Chodorow asserts that this sense of empathy, which borders on telepathy, is rooted in the regression and enmeshment women experience with their children as they re-experience their own infancy. Indeed, this skill not only exists but can be gratifying, she argues. Chodorow highlights that a nonbiological mother may experience this intense empathy, and, while it would not necessarily extend to a nanny as outlined, it does not preclude so either.

Shortly after Myriam shares her trepidation about another woman caring for her children, she reveals that since her children were born she has been "scared that they will die."[71] She is confident others think similarly, and that they too "watched their child sleep and wondered how they would feel if that little body were a corpse, if those eyes were closed

[67] Leila, Slimani, *The Perfect Nanny* (New York: Penguin, 2016), 1.

[68] On this point, see MacDonald, *Shadow Mothers*.

[69] Slimani, *The Perfect Nanny*, 7.

[70] Ibid., 14.

[71] Slimani, *The Perfect Nanny*, 14.

forever."[72] Myriam's fantasy is complicated in its seeming wish fulfillment. Chodorow does not shy away from discussing women's ambivalent love toward their mothers, with these feelings stemming from feelings of entrapment, disempowerment, hatred and more. Chodorow spends less time delving into mothers' ambivalence for their children, which may be a symptom of when she wrote or western culture's reluctance to inspect the dark side of motherhood.[73] In *The Monster Within: The Hidden Side of Motherhood* psychoanalyst/object-relation theorist Barbara Almond posits that "aggression" by mothers is "both psychologically inevitable and socially unacceptable to a *very* marked degree."[74] Indeed, what Myriam describes is not a fit of rage at a child who will not be calmed; it is not violent at all. There exists a passivity, a voyeurism even, as she describes the vision of her children's sleep being everlasting.[75] Her confession carries remarkable weight as Slimani already disclosed the children would be killed.

Myriam never wanted to believe "her children could be an impediment to her success, to her freedom."[76] She rues the injustice of it, but with that insight comes an awareness that she "could never live without feeling that she was incomplete, that she was doing things badly, sacrificing one part of her life for another."[77] Although Paul describes Myriam as "blooming" and a "natural mother," Myriam's internal landscape is decaying.[78] Myriam is "gloomy" and she feels the winter days are "endless."[79] She adds: "Mila's tantrums drove her mad, Adam's first burblings left her indifferent. With each passing day, she felt more and

[72] Ibid.

[73] Adrienne Rich's, *Of Woman Born*, published just one year earlier, was groundbreaking in its candor about mother's ambivalence toward motherhood and even their children. Adrienne Rich, *Of Woman Born: Motherhood as Institution and Experience* (New York: W. W. Norton, 1976).

[74] Barbara Almond, *The Monster Within: The Hidden Side of Motherhood* (Berkeley, CA: California University Press, 2010), 11.

[75] Almond argues that the primary reason for maternal ambivalence is the "conflict between the needs of the mother and the needs of the infant." Almond, *The Monster Within*, 229.

[76] Slimani, *The Perfect Nanny*, 37.

[77] Ibid.

[78] Ibid., 7.

[79] Ibid., 8.

more desperate to go out for a walk on her own. She sometimes wanted to scream like a lunatic in the street. They're eating me alive, she would think."[80] In effect, Myriam has to make a choice but feels she had no good option in the choices available to her. It was not her children's survival or her own, but both of their survival enveloped in one. Her survival was tantamount to theirs. She craves the opportunity to return to her position as a lawyer to escape the boredom and to feel successful at something she's passionate about. When she crosses paths with Pascal, a man with whom she had attended law school, who offers her a position, she takes it.

Like Megan and Claire, Myriam and Paul are not terrifically wealthy. Myriam (perhaps overly cynically and self-pityingly) describes their situation as "the worst of all worlds: too rich to receive welfare and too poor to consider the cost of a nanny as anything other than a sacrifice."[81] Like many women whose work is undercompensated, her salary will barely cover childcare. Paul begrudgingly acquiesces. Like the other husbands, Paul presumes his wife will oversee the children's care. Women, after all, are not the only ones attempting to recreate their childhoods, as Chodorow highlights. A boy's dyadic relationship with his mother is replicated with his wife, and he does not wish to recreate a triadic relationship by hiring a nanny as women do, even as he desires the temporal freedom she permits (and thus replicates what his emotionally disengaged father experienced).[82]

When Myriam and Paul interview nannies, they take the advice of friends to make sure the woman they hire is childless or has grown children—showcasing the ways an employee's personal needs are considered onerous to employers and perhaps mirrors the jealousy siblings have for one another as they vie for a parent's affection. Care, they believe, should be unidirectional, as it is with a parent to a child. Like Claire, Myriam is looking for more than just hired help, in fact, she is described as "awaiting this nanny as if she is the Savior."[83] This, too, echoes Stack's lifeboat imagery and Claire's choice to save herself over providing the care her mother requires. These delineations of life and death run through the

[80] Ibid.

[81] Slimani, *The Perfect Nanny*, 13.

[82] Chodorow, *The Reproduction of Mothering*, 201.

[83] Slimani, *The Perfect Nanny*, 14.

works as mothers fight the opposing forces of enmeshment and freedom, with nannies permitting them both.

Louise's early months with the family are smooth. The children appreciate her playfulness while Myriam and Paul find her "indispensable," likening her to Mary Poppins.[84] "*My* nanny is a miracle-worker," Myriam tells others, with the tell-tale possessive pronoun attached, as she describes Louise's "sudden entrance into their lives" and her "*magical* powers to have transformed this stifling, cramped apartment into a calm, light-filled place."[85] Myriam returns from work to find the "children are calm and clean, not a hair out of place," while the narrator explains, "Louise arouses and fulfills the fantasies of an idyllic family life that Myriam guiltily nurses."[86] Clothes are mended and pressed, bedsheets swapped and washed, and after Myriam tells Louise "she doesn't know how to cook anything and doesn't really want to learn," Louise cooks dinners that "Paul goes into raptures about and the children devour."[87] As with the emotional care that nannies offer mothers, these meals fulfill a core physical need, too.

Food, in a literal sense, interweaves throughout *The Perfect Nanny*. The passage above highlights the ways in which Louise feeds Myriam's family in ways Myriam opts to avoid, and Myriam enjoys being fed as much as everyone else, but trouble lurks under the surface. While Louise's effort is appreciated, it quickly becomes evident that Myriam has no choice but to acquiesce to Louise's "help," and even when she tells Louise she should go home, her request is ignored. It is easier for Myriam to cede her space than fight. Her work at the firm is intense and so she "lets herself be mothered."[88] The degree of agency Myriam has here is debatable, but it is clear she relishes time to focus on her career. Despite being the first into the office, she still doesn't want to go home at the end of the day. Like Claire, she chafes at the responsibility and claims she "would like to have no one she has to call, no one waiting up for her."[89] Her desire

[84] Ibid., 26.

[85] Ibid., 25. Emphasis mine.

[86] Ibid., 26.

[87] Ibid., 27.

[88] Ibid., 53.

[89] Ibid., 37.

and (successful) attempt to eschew her responsibilities as a mother do not go unnoticed.

Myriam has a terse relationship with her mother-in-law, Sylvie, who wishes Paul married a more maternal woman. When they spend a long weekend with her, Sylvie attacks Myriam for working, but Myriam passively takes what she wields claiming she "didn't have the strength to defend herself against those accusations, which she knew were partly true but which she considered as her lot and that of many other women."[90] What she craves is "clemency or gentleness," but none is offered, "[n]ot a single piece of advice was offered from mother to mother, from woman to woman."[91] Instead, she turns to Louise, despite the challenges.

Paul has a more simplistic relationship with Louise, as would be expected of a man adhering to Chodorow's theory. He feels freed by having a nanny, as the other men did, and, like the others, neither tries to seduce nor is seduced by her. Instead, Paul is thrilled to reignite the more spontaneous (and dyadic) relationship he once shared with Myriam. According to Chodorow, this is not unusual, and is based on the theory that men, who do not have an "ongoing inner world to fall back on," as women do, view women as being more emotionally important to them than men are to women, who often nourish relationships with other women. Like Paul in *My Hollywood* and Tom in *Women's Work*, Paul recognizes Louise's usefulness, but seems not to see her as a person per se, rather as a figure that eases the turbulent waters of early parenthood. Childcare is women's work that will get done with or without his involvement. His need for a nanny is less; his dependence, too. Chodorow explains this well when she points out that, for men, the separation from their mothers is more concrete and easily transferred to their romantic partners. Triangulated relationships are not as desirable to men and therefore they view nannies who work for their families more as a means to strengthen their relationships with their wives by freeing up her time, in turn, removing the third figure (i.e., the child) from the preferred one-to-one relationship they previously experienced (and may have favored) with their wives.

Not surprisingly, women are more prone to foster triadic relationships, and Myriam's framing to physical affection showcases this as well as her

[90] Ibid., 127.

[91] Ibid.

ambivalence regarding the love she experiences with her children. Case in point: after a particularly busy week Myriam returns to her children like an "impatient as a lover."[92] She plans to slip into the "big bed," likely hers and Paul's, with them which is transgressive for the coital implications. Her plan is to "tickle them and kiss them, [...] squeeze them against her until they were dizzy. Until they struggled".[93] Tension exists between pleasure and pain, between love and hate. Interestingly, Louise also tends to turn "fun" into something more sinister. Her games of hide-and-go-seek leave Mila "scared" because she and Adam "start to believe that Louise has really gone, [...] that they are alone and she will not come back."[94] As they search, Louise is described as watching them hunt for her, a voyeur taking pleasure in their increasing anxiety. "She watches them as if she's studying the death throes of a fish she's just caught, its gills bleeding, its body shaken by spasms."[95] Even when the children are racked with sobs, she still refuses to emerge. This type of care is what Almond calls vampyric mothering, and occurs when a mother, rather than caring empathically on behalf of her child, subsists from the merging that takes place via what she forces into the child.[96] Drawing plentifully from the fictional figure of Count Dracula, Almond explains that our fear is not only of Dracula's excessive orality, but the enmeshment he requires. His power is a false power that is derived from making others feel weak when in fact their life force is what sustains him. So, too, Myriam views Louise as all-powerful, a woman who "is Vishnu, the nurturing divinity, jealous and protective; the she-wolf at whose breast they drink, the infallible source of their family happiness."[97] Louise is said to "contro[l] the transparent wires without which the magic cannot occur."[98] When Louise becomes ill with a common virus, Myriam panics at Louise's absence.[99] She is abashed

[92] Ibid., 51.

[93] Ibid.

[94] Ibid., 44–45.

[95] Ibid., 45.

[96] Almond, *The Monster Within*, 165–184.

[97] Slimani, *The Perfect Nanny*, 53.

[98] Ibid.

[99] It is not unusual for children to fear that their primary caretaker will vanish, but in *Women's Work*, *My Hollywood*, and *The Perfect Nanny*, a similar fear is demonstrated by the mothers in relation to their nannies as well. Stack, *Women's Work*, 49, 103, 110–111.

at her anxiety, feeling "ashamed [… as] if Louise were infallible, her body immune to fatigue and illness."[100] Her childlike fear mirrors the fear her own children experienced during hide-and-go-seek.

While Louise holds significant power, she is also in debt and Paul and Myriam are providing her much-needed wages. When the government contacts the couple to garnish Louise's wages, Myriam sees deeper fault-lines in Louise's projection of strength and competence. As the novel progresses, readers learn just how trapped Louise is—physically, financially, and emotionally. As winter sets in, Louise is often housebound, like Myriam had been. Whereas Myriam describes Louise as opening up the apartment so it is more spacious, Louise feels "[l]ocked up" and "as if she is going mad" from the "immense solitude."[101] Unlike the glitz of producing records like Paul, or defending clients like Myriam, Louise's work is described as lonely and monotonous, as labor that can hardly be considered work. They relish their adult lives even as these lives are built on dependence that they can shake off with a salary.

Like the husbands in the previous texts, it is Paul who suggests they fire Louise. Myriam opposes this, though. Paul is not surprised, because, according to him, Myriam and Louise "are always in league against him, like two bears. When it comes to the children." He ruefully notes, "they sometimes treat him with a haughtiness that makes him bristle. They act like mothers, treat him like a child."[102] For men, who emotionally separate from their mothers earlier and more completely than women, and identify instead with the power and independence their fathers embody, this push to regress to a place of powerlessness chafes. *The Perfect Nanny*, as well as the other texts, highlight, however, the ways in which women can and do shape the psychological construction of the home. MacDonald, too, found a similar dynamic in the homes of the women she interviewed and theorized that "[c]onspiring this way reinforced the bond between nanny and employers and bolstered the women's sense of the value of the role they shared."[103] She adds: "this kind of collusion increased their awareness that they did indeed share a special role, one

[100] Ibid., 153.

[101] Ibid., 107.

[102] Ibid.

[103] Ibid., 39.

from which the father stood apart."[104] It also creates a triadic relationship between two women, which Chodorow suggests is preferred by many women.

What Paul may not realize, though, is that the power struggle is on two fronts, with Myriam engaging in her own battles. She is primed for this bifurcated war, which is most evident when the two women have a stand-off regarding expired food, which Myriam refuses to allow her children to consume and Louise is fanatical about not wasting. Although Myriam initially identifies with Louise's moral high ground, she soon grows indignant. "Let her search through our garbage," Myriam tells Paul, "I don't have to justify myself to her."[105] When Paul tells Myriam she is afraid of being told off by Louise, Myriam does not deny it but does not waiver either. Louise will not be cowed, either, and forces the children to eat the remains of a chicken carcass Myriam had thrown out. Despite being furious, Myriam does not reprimand Louise; however, while she previously described Louise as having "magical powers" and emerging from the ether, she now "wishes she could make her disappear from her life, with no effort, with a snap of her fingers or a blink of the eyes."[106] Louise plies Myriam with kindness, but a kindness that echoes Almond's vampiric mother. Myriam scoffs at the "irony" of her predicament,[107] namely that she, a fearsome and feared attorney, is "terrified" of Louise.[108] She desires to fire Louise, but muses "Louise has the keys to their apartment; she knows everything; she has embedded herself so deeply in their lives that it now seems impossible to remove her."[109] The combination of phallic keys, vulnerability to those that know more, and

[104] MacDonald, *Shadow Mothering*, 39.

[105] Slimani, *The Perfect Nanny*, 160.

[106] Ibid., 171.

[107] As Cameron notes of the professional women with nannies she interviewed, "For at least some part of the day, their children are being raised by someone else, a fact that left most mothers feeling vulnerable. The fear of powerlessness and lack of control in most areas of their lives. Paradoxically, they felt out of control in a very significant area of their lives BECAUSE of the success they had worked so hard to attain. Striving to make certain that the 'someone else' they were dependent on did the best job possible is the closest these working mothers could come to asserting control and assuring themselves that they were meeting their maternal responsibilities." MacDonald, *Shadow Mothering*, 90.

[108] Ibid.

[109] Slimani, *The Perfect Nanny*, 175.

futility of escaping the enmeshment she once fostered is striking. Even if they "drive her away and she'll come back," Myriam reasons, highlighting her unwanted enmeshment and inability to define the relationship in a way that suits her.[110] This lack of control reaches its apex when Louise murders the children. The detective who arrives examines a picture of Louise and believes she "looks like one of those duplicitous mothers in a fairy tale, abandoning her children in the darkness of a forest."[111] Indeed, this novel most blatantly undermines our collective imagery of what a good nanny should do, even as it successfully casts Louise as the one who fulfills Myriam's (partial) desire to be free of her children. Like the stepmothers of fairy tales, Louise is the scapegoat for dark desires.

Conclusion

The epigraph from Nancy Chodorow's *The Reproduction of Mothering* asserts that our earliest relationships have lasting impacts on us and asserts that the ways we engage with the relationships and experience ourselves in them continues to be replicated throughout our lives. The most critical of these, the mother/child relationship, is profound not because of women's biological propensity to motherhood, but because of the drama of women's enmeshment, ambivalence, and desire for replication. Modern mothers still repeat the cycle Chodorow describes, but variations exist in regard to intensive mothering, neoliberalism, and a cloaking of the power dynamics between employer and employee when care is outsourced. These power differences certainly prevent parity, as Megan Stack highlights when she writes: "But you can't snap at employees the way you might snap at a family member. They are vulnerable to your whims. And, unlike a family, they don't love you. Why should they?"[112] Indeed, while research shows that nannies often grow to love the children for whom they care, that love does not extend to the mothers who employ them.[113] That doesn't prevent these same mother-employers from loving the nannies they hire. In "How Serfdom Saved the Women's Movement," Caitlin Flanagan posits that the mother/nanny "relationship

[110] Ibid., 183.

[111] Ibid., 225.

[112] Stack, *Women's Work*, 214.

[113] Reference.

is in many ways more intense – more vexing, more rewarding, more vital, more fraught – than a marriage."[114] As stated earlier, this is *not* to argue that power dynamics are upended; rather, the dependence and affection mother-employers experience *may* be a place of possibility, a tension that could de-center some of the established arguments regarding how power is allocated and used.

Much of the affection and dependence a mother-employer experiences in her relationship with the nanny she hires results from early relationships with her mother, the dynamics of which are outlined so deftly by Chodorow. As women navigate their relationships with their mothers, feelings of love, hate, anger, enmeshment, dependence, ambivalence, and more are all experienced. Some of these feelings are mitigated as a girl turns her affection to her father, but as Chodorow points out, this does not change a woman's fundamental love for her mother. She continues to crave the triadic relationship of her youth, and Chodorow claims this is one reason women choose to have children. This work herein does not dispute that, but explores another option, namely that women who outsource carework may use the women hired as proxy mothers. In other words, they navigate the relationship as one through which they can relive earlier tensions with their mothers in addition to expecting this woman to do the work of caring for her child (ren).

What stands out in all three of the texts explicated herein is that, while none of the mothers truly regret motherhood, they do begrudge the work, time, and demands of their children—at least at times. It seems worth considering how this ambivalence toward the labor of mothering mirrors our ambivalence of being cared for and being dependent. In other words, we do not want to be dependent or depended upon as mothers. Nannies provide a solution, in limited ways, to the latter, while intensifying feelings of the former. Empowerment is a term often bandied about in relation to mothers and motherhood, but mothers hold deep ambivalence about what that means for themselves and their relationships, particularly with their children. When a woman hires a nanny, she mitigates some of the ambivalence by lessening the onerous work of mothering while still maintaining a close bond as well as adhering, at least by proxy, to the tenets of intensive mothering.

[114] Caitlin Flanagan, "How Serfdom Saved the Women's Movement," *The Atlantic*, March, 2004, https://www.theatlantic.com/magazine/archive/2004/03/how-serfdom-saved-the-women-s-movement/302892/.

Moreover, nannies tend to be welcomed by husbands as well, even though their relationship takes a different shape than the one a mother-employer experiences. Nannies are a means of avoiding the work of childcare[115] and sometimes even the expectations of emotional investment they feel in their marriages. Carework is most certainly not useless, and Chodorow attempts to pushback on some of the feminist critiques that categorize the work as oppressive and find a place of possibility in it. Feminist sociologist Joan Tronto accurately posits that the "use of nannies allows upper-middle-class women and men to benefit from feminist changes without having to surrender the privilege of the traditional patriarchal family."[116] Chodorow argues that because men separate more completely and more thoroughly from their mothers, the gratifying sense of enmeshment that women experience and continue to crave is not present. What these books show, and every nanny novel with which I am familiar, is that Chodorow's claim that, "[w]hen biological mothers do not parent, other women, rather than men, virtually always take their place," remains true.[117] As with Chodrow's insightful and still impactful theory, recognizing the ways in which a nanny shifts family dynamics and permits a transference of men's obligations to home and kin, is important. Fairy tales often end with the sentence: "And they lived happily ever after." This is not the case the books discussed herein. The nanny doesn't just vanish with the family "fixed" forever after. Families are left tattered, re-formed, or destroyed and nannies both help bolster and help obliterate. The gamut is broad, as it is for mothers, who bring their pasts into their present and often beyond.

[115] As Carol Stack observes, "Our private problems are no doubt duplicated in households all over our planet. And yet housework is seldom considered as a serious subject for study, or even discussion. This is an injustice on a grand scale, for housework is everything. It's a ubiquitous physical demand that has hamstrung and silenced women for most of human history. I'd love to believe the struggle for women's equality is concentrated in offices and manufacturing plants, but I've become convinced that this battle takes place, first and foremost, crushingly, at home." Full reference (ix–x).

[116] Joan Tronto, "The Nanny Question in Feminism."

[117] Chodorow, *The Reproduction of Mothering*, 3.

Bibliography

Almond, Barbara, *The Monster Within: The Hidden Side of Motherhood*. Berkley, CA: University of California Press, 2010.

Balint, Alice, *The Psycho-Analysis of the Nursery*. England: Routledge & Kegan Paul, 1953. https://books.google.com/books?id=J6bhCgAAQBAJ&printsec=frontcover&source=gbs_ge_summary_r&cad=0#v=onepage&q&f=false.

Chodorow, Nancy, *The Reproduction of Mothering: Psychoanalysis and Sociology of Gender*. Berkeley: University of California Press, 1978.

Dinnerstein, Dorothy, *The Mermaid and the Minotaur*. New York: Harper & Row, 1976.

Firestone, Shulamith, *The Dialectic of Sex: The Case for Feminist Revolution*. New York: Morrow, 1970.

Flanagan, Caitlin, "How Serfdom Saved the Women's Movement: Dispatches from the Nanny Wars." *The Atlantic*, March 2004.

Friedan, Betty, *The Feminine Mystique*. New York: W. W. Norton, 1963.

Hirsch, Marianne, *The Mother/Daughter Plot: Narrative, Psychoanalysis, Feminism*. Bloomington, IN: Indiana University Press, 1989.

Holmes, Lucy, *The Internal Triangle*. Lanham, MD: Rowman & Littlefield, 2008.

MacDonald, Cameron Lynne, *Shadow Mothers: Nannies, Au Pairs, and the Micropolitics of Mothering*. Berkeley: California University Press, 2010.

Mandelbaum, Paul, "Whose Hollywood Is It Anyway?" *Los Angeles Review of Books*, June, 15, 2011. http://lareviewofbooks.org/essay/whose-hollywood-is-it-anyway/.

Rich, Adrienne, *Of Woman Born: Motherhood as Experience and Institution*. Norton: New York, 1976.

Simpson, Mona, *My Hollywood*. New York: Knopf, 2010.

Slimani, Leila, *The Perfect Nanny*. New York: Penguin, 2016.

Stack, Megan K., *Women's Work: A Reckoning with Work and Home*. New York: Doubleday, 2019.

Tronto, Joan, "The 'Nanny' Question in Feminism." *Hypatia* 17, no. 2 (2002): 34–51.

CHAPTER 15

The Reproduction of Mothering: Unlocking Italian Women's Fiction from the *Fin-de-siècle* Onwards

Ursula Fanning

Nancy Chodorow's *Reproduction of Mothering* was a text that helped me (and several other critics working in Italian Studies, particularly those engaged in feminist criticism) to understand some of the striking recurrent structures and patterns in Italian women's fiction at the turn of the nineteenth and twentieth centuries, and to explain the absolute centrality of the mother-daughter bond in these fictions across the two centuries. I had begun work on a Ph.D. thesis in Italian Studies in the mid-1980s; specifically, I was interested at that point in the output of Matilde Serao, a Neapolitan writer (1856–1927) who had been well-known in her own lifetime, and had attracted a good deal of favorable (as well as some unfavorable, and often blinkered) critical comment in the course of her writing life. Her work was both popular and critically esteemed in France, in

U. Fanning (✉)
University College Dublin, Dublin, Ireland
e-mail: ursula.fanning@ucd.ie

P. Bueskens (ed.), *Nancy Chodorow and* The Reproduction of Mothering,
https://doi.org/10.1007/978-3-030-55590-0_15

the Scandinavian countries, and in the United States.[1] Much of Serao's reading public (though by no means all of it) was female and she often specifically, and consciously, addressed a female audience. Throughout the course of her writing, one of the most obviously recurring (though then critically unnoticed) features of Serao's writing was her investigation of the mother-daughter relationship in a range of permutations, from the perspectives of both daughter-characters and, especially interestingly, those of mother-characters.

Working my way through a body of critical reading, particularly in the area of feminist literary theory and criticism, I was struck by the disparity between what I was reading about (and in) women's writing of the period in English-language fiction, and what I was encountering in my reading of Italian women's writing of the period. Both Margaret Homans and Marianne Hirsch famously note that the perspective of the mother is not one with which we frequently meet in women's writing of the nineteenth and twentieth centuries in English-language fiction by women, nor in its French counterpart. Homans focusses particularly on the nineteenth-century context, and notes that in English fiction, any kind of mother-daughter discourse is "lost to most women writers before the twentieth century."[2] Hirsch, meanwhile, finds that, in English-language as well as in French women's writings of the nineteenth and early twentieth centuries, "mothers tend to be absent, silent or devalued."[3] She goes so far as to define the maternal as "unspeakable," not only within women's fiction but also, to a large extent, within feminist criticism, finding that "feminist writing and scholarship, continuing in large part to adopt daughterly perspectives, ... [keep] mothering outside of representation and maternal discourse a theoretical impossibility."[4]

[1] Henry James, in his 1901 article, in *The North American Review* provides one of the best-known English-language responses to Serao's work (she is, in fact, the only woman writer he discusses at length when he reprints the essay in his collection of essays *Notes on Novelists* in 1914). Henry James, "Matilde Serao," *North American Review* (March 1901): 367–380.

[2] Margaret Homans, *Bearing the Word: Language and Female Experience in Nineteenth-Century Women's Writing* (Chicago: University of Chicago Press, 1986), 226.

[3] Marianne Hirsch, *The Mother-Daughter Plot: Narrative, Psychoanalysis, Feminism* (Bloomington and Indianapolis: Indiana University Press, 1989), 14.

[4] Ibid., 163.

Reading through the large body of Serao's work and later, coming to that of her contemporaries, I found, instead, an obsessional anatomization (sometimes literally so) of the mother-daughter relationship and its significance. Finding Nancy Chodorow's *Reproduction of Mothering*,[5] a text which most assuredly does not "[keep] mothering outside of representation" and which contributes to establishing a maternal perspective, allowed me to begin to posit reasons for this focus (though not to begin to explain the cultural difference that manifested itself around the mother-daughter relationship in these different national contexts). It was through Chodorow that I began to understand the ongoing and intergenerational significance of this bond, and the need (for some women writers) to rework and recast it, and to experiment with it in its different guises.

In this chapter, I will begin by looking at some of Matilde Serao's writings and at the significance of the mother-daughter bond in these nineteenth-century narratives through an interpretative key provided by Chodorow. I will then look at this bond in the work of Sibilla Aleramo at the turn of the century, continuing to draw on Chodorow's insights, and finally I posit the continuation of this bond in Italian women's writings of the later part of the twentieth century, with an eye to developments in theories of the maternal in the works of other critics, including philosophers such as Sara Ruddick whose work inevitably builds on that of Chodorow.

The Mother-Daughter Bond in the Work of Matilde Serao

It is important to give some idea of the discursive context in which Serao and her contemporaries were writing at the turn of the nineteenth century in order to fully grasp the significance and tone of their focus on the maternal and on the mother-daughter bond in particular. In Italy as elsewhere, around the time of the Italian Unification of 1861, motherhood was an important topic, with many prescriptions and proscriptions accreting around it.[6] Women were encouraged to identify themselves not

[5] Nancy Chodorow, *The Reproduction of Mothering: Psychoanalysis and the Sociology of Gender* (Berkeley and Los Angeles: University of California Press, 1978).

[6] Ursula Fanning, "Maternal Prescriptions and Descriptions in Post-Unification Italy," in *Women and Gender in Post-Unification Italy: Between Private and Public Spheres*, eds. Katharine Mitchell and Helena Sanson (Oxford: Peter Lang, 2013), 13–37.

only as literal mothers (and, in that capacity, to raise their children in a proper and "moral" manner[7]), but also to act as mothers of the nascent nation-state. If they were not biological mothers, they were encouraged to look after the children of others, in one of the caring professions. Between 1888 and 1901, indeed, the proportion of women teachers in Italy, for instance, increased from 55 percent of the teaching workforce to 68 percent.[8] Caring for children, in one capacity or another, allowed women to be seen as quasi-respectable members of the workforce if they were in a position where they had to work (as was frequently the case, although official discourses resisted acknowledging this fact for the most part). The discourses around motherhood (both real and symbolic) tended to idealize it, to exalt it above any other role or identity permitted to women. As Fiorenza Taricone notes, the family was regularly figured as a "sanctuary" ["santuario"[9]], the "hearth of the home" ["focolare"] and so on, while women's "mission" was "increasingly to [devote herself] to ... the happiness of man, and the education of her children" ["missione ... anch'essa trasformando e ampliando ... la felicità dell'uomo, l'educazione dei figli"[10]]. Interestingly, Serao (like her female contemporaries) does not reproduce motherhood or the maternal in an unvaryingly hagiographic light. Rather, she is keen to investigate it in all of its permutations and possibilities. She grapples with the topic of maternity, her representation of it, and of the figure of the mother as central to her narrative, from her earliest through to her latest works,[11] and in doing so she anticipates some of the most crucial debates within feminist theory of the late twentieth and twenty-first centuries, both within and beyond the Italian context. Nancy Chodorow's *Reproduction of Mothering* is part of that theoretical debate, and helps us to understood the central negotiations around the maternal ongoing in Italian women's fiction of this period.

[7] Fiorenza Taricone, "I cataloghi femminili dell'ottocento," in *Operaie, borghesi, contadine nel XIX secolo*, eds. Fiorenza Taricone and Beatrice Pisa (Rome: Carucci, 1978), 11–24 (13–14).

[8] Bruna Conti, ed., "Introduzione," in *La donna e il femminismo* (Rome: Edizioni Riuniti, 1978), 7–39.

[9] All translations from Italian are mine, with the exception of the citations from Adriana Cavarero's work.

[10] Taricone, *I cataloghi*, 13.

[11] Serao began writing in the late 1870s and published her last novel in 1926.

One of the most interesting examples of Serao's centralization of the mother-daughter bond in her early work is to be found in the short story "Empty Jackpot" ("Terno secco") of 1889.[12] This jackpot (one of Serao's primary concerns here is the lotto, and its social impact in late nineteenth-century Naples) is "empty" for one of her protagonists because that character has not had the money to play the numbers which she has seen in a dream, and which eventually do come up. Pregnancy and motherhood provide a parallel central focus for the narrative. The pregnancy is that of the servant, Tommasina, who plays the number she has found written on a scrap of paper in the home of her employer and wins. This pregnancy defines Tommasina's character as she frets, in the opening pages of the story, about the deprivation into which her child will be born, and strongly identifies with it: "she shivered, already a mother, already vibrating with love and pity for her creature" ["rabbrividiva, già madre, già fremente di amore e di pietà per la sua creatura"[13]]. This identification with the "creature" in utero embodies, and is explicated by, Chodorow's consideration of the "exclusive symbiotic mother-child relationship."[14] It exemplifies the tendency noted by Chodorow for "a woman to turn her marriage into a family, and to be more involved with ... this child than her husband."[15] Indeed, Tommasina's husband (like many of Serao's father characters) is essentially feckless. He is a failure in what would have been perceived as his primary duty at the time when the story is set, which is to provide for his family and, although he can find money to lend to his friends, Serao tells us that he "allowed his wife to be consumed with fatigue, pregnant, badly dressed, sick" ["lasciava che sua moglie crepasse di fatica, incinta, mal vestita, malaticcia"[16]]. He gives no thought to the child which is due, unlike his wife who is, instead, physically and emotionally consumed by it. When Francesco describes Tommasina in labor, he can only disparage her suffering: "women giving birth always think they're dying – it's to be expected" ["Che volete signori miei, quando la donna

[12] Matilde Serao, "Terno secco," in *All'erta, sentinella!* (Milan: Galli, 1896 [1889]), 123–179.

[13] Ibid., 132.

[14] Chodorow, *The Reproduction of Mothering*, 201.

[15] Ibid., 202.

[16] Serao, "Terno secco," 160.

sta in quello stato, le pare sempre di morire"[17]]. In effect, Serao describes here what Chodorow defines as the "male-dominant but father-absent family where women mother,"[18] that family which, in turn, produces women as mothers, reproducing traditional sex-gender divisions. The other family which is central to this short story is also one in which the father is absent—this time literally so, and with no explanation. The anonymous protagonist (Tommasina's employer) referred to only as "the lady" ["la signora"] or "the mother" ["la madre")] is the mother of an adolescent daughter, Caterina, and there is no mention whatever here of a father/husband/male partner in their family constellation. Moreover, it is precisely on the terrain of the maternal, Serao tells us explicitly, that these women, employer and employee, forge a bond of companionship; Tommasina "looked her employer in the face and the two mothers understood each other, without words, such was the distress of the younger one, and the affectionate compassion of the older" ["Guardò in viso la sua signora e le due madri s'intesero, tacitamente, tanto era il turbamento della giovane, tanto era l'affettuosa compassione della piú vecchia"[19]]. We see here the self-definition of both characters as maternal; the description also functions as an example of what Chodorow would define as a "relational complexity in … self-definition" which she identifies as characteristically female.[20] This crucial notion of relational complexity will find resonance in the Italian context at a much later stage, in the work of Adriana Cavarero who is one of the best-known contemporary Italian feminist philosophers; Cavarero's (now well-known) concept of the relational self is enormously influential in current Italian criticism in both philosophical and feminist critical contexts.[21] The focus of Cavarero is similar, in many respects, to that of Chodorow.

Fascinating in Serao's story, too, is the bond between "the lady" and her daughter which is described as central to both their lives. The mother here is tender and supportive, entirely positive about her maternal role (she is also, and not coincidentally, I think, a teacher). Caterina, the

[17] Ibid., 76.

[18] Chodorow, *The Reproduction of Mothering*, 40.

[19] Serao, "Terno secco," 132.

[20] Chodorow, *The Reproduction of Mothering*, 93.

[21] See, for instance, Adriana Cavarero, *Relating Narratives: Storytelling and Selfhood* (London: Routledge, 2000 [1997]).

daughter, is slow to waken in the mornings and her mother gently prods her: "'Up, little one, up' said the mother, softly, as if she was speaking to a four-year-old child" ["'Su, piccola, su' rispondea la madre, carezzevolmente, come se parlasse con una bimba di quattro anni"[22]]. The two are mutually supporting, in fact, in a fashion reminiscent of that evoked by Chodorow in her description of mother-daughter identification and symbiosis, where the mother experiences "a daughter as an extension or double of a mother herself."[23] We see this as Caterina and her mother leave for work and school respectively: "'Oh, Mama, you're carrying me', she said, as they went down the stairs. 'But you're holding me up, little one' the mother replied" ["'O mamma, tu mi porti' diceva, scendendo le scale. 'Ma tu mi sostieni, piccola'].[24] It is the mother-daughter relationship that closes this narrative, with the revelation of why it is that the mother was unable to bet on the lotto, and hence had an "empty jackpot"—she had given her daughter the last coins she had so that Caterina could buy materials for school. The denouement of the tale is highly dramatic, as the daughter asks the mother why she did not play the lotto, while all around them did:

> "'Did you forget or did you not have the money? Tell me the truth, Mama' ... 'I didn't have the money.' 'How did you not have money? I asked you for money for my drawing-books yesterday and you gave it to me.' The mother said nothing, she didn't utter a word, she didn't move. The daughter fell at her feet like a rag, with her arms open, beating her head off her mother's knees, crying out: 'Forgive me, Mama ...' And the mother replied in a faint voice 'Little one, little one ...' ['Hai dimenticato o non avevi denaro? La verità, mamma' ... 'non avevo denaro.' 'Come non avevi denaro? Non ti ho chiesto una lira per i miei cartoncini di disegno e me l'hai data?' Nulla disse la mamma, non proferì parola, non fece atto. Ma come uno straccio le cadde ai piedi, la figliuola, con le braccia aperte, battendo la testa sulle ginocchia materne, gridando: 'Perdono, mamma ...' E fiocamente la madre diceva: "Piccola, piccola figlia ..."].[25]

[22] Serao, "Terno secco," 130.

[23] Chodorow, *The Reproduction of Mothering*, 109.

[24] Serao, "Terno secco," 133–134.

[25] Ibid., 178–179.

The identification between mother and daughter here could well be seen as excessive; the daughter literally enacts the mother's despair. In one sense, this positive and idealized relationship (based, as is widely acknowledged by critics of Serao's work, on the author's relationship with her own much-loved mother) is characterized by the daughter's overwhelming guilt, coupled with the mother's saintly forgiveness. But it is not so excessive when read in the light of Chodorow's theory, where the daughter is preoccupied with the mother and "experiences a continuation of the two-person relationship of infancy."[26] In fact, Serao presents us, in this story, with that two-person relationship in (appropriately) embryonic form through her depiction of Tommasina and her relationship to the child in utero juxtaposed with the emotionally-absent and disparaging father-figure; it is also writ large in its more developed form through the relationship between the mother and Caterina, where the father does not exist and the exclusive mother-daughter bond meets no obstacle to its symbiotic intensity.

I turn now to Serao's last novel, *Mors tua*, of 1926 where she is a good deal more ambivalent in her representation of the bond between mother and child in general, and mother and daughter in particular.[27] The context of this novel, too, is interesting. It centers on a retrospective presentation of the First World War and reveals Serao's stance as entirely and committedly pacifist.[28] As a result of this pacifism the work was viewed unfavorably by the Fascist regime, and is generally believed to be the reason why Serao did not win the Nobel Prize for literature in 1926 (it went to another Italian woman writer, Grazia Deledda). The novel explores a number of areas: the plight of soldiers at the front, the effect of war and separation on the love relationship, the role of the religious in times of war; but, strikingly, and perhaps unexpectedly for a war novel, its main theme is motherhood, specifically the reactions of mothers to the loss of their children (mothers lose sons and daughters in different ways in this work), and to the dangers with which mothers and children are faced.

[26] Chodorow, *The Reproduction of Mothering*, 96.

[27] Matilde Serao, *Mors tua* (Milan: Treves, 1926).

[28] This marks a departure from some of Serao's earlier work, for example, *Evviva la Guerra!* [*Hurray for War!*] (Milan: Galli, 1896) of 1912 on the Libyan War.

Motherhood frames this text, which opens by depicting a group of mothers and closes (in very negative fashion) by homing in on the pain of one mother in particular. The work is dedicated to the "unknown mother" (as opposed to the more normal remembrance of the "unknown soldier"), and this underlines Serao's focus on the centrality of the maternal. Throughout the novel, Serao filters the narrative through the perspectives of different female characters who watch and analyze other female characters, thus maintaining a sense of female relationality as the text progresses—that ongoing female relationality which is so central to Chodorow's work, especially as it relates to mothers and children.[29] The novel opens with what might seem like an idealization of the mother-child bond once again, as the mothers discuss their fears for their children, and clearly define themselves first and foremost in terms of their maternal identities. The first of the mothers who comes into focus, Marta Ardore, is seen in relation to her sons, Fausto and Giorgio. The elder son is strongly pro-war, and is adamant that he will fight for his country. The younger son is influenced by his elder brother's militarism, and it is he who is eventually killed in battle. What is interesting here is the way in which Marta reacts to this; we learn, through Fausto's words, that she blames him for the loss of Giorgio: "'Mother, as long as I live, wherever I go ... I will hear your accusing cries, I will see the light in your eyes, which aimed to strike me dead" ["'Madre, finché io viva, ovunque io vada ... io udrò il tuo urlo che mi accusava, vedrò il fulgore del tuo sguardo, che mi volea fulminare"].[30] The relationship between the mother and both sons effectively ends with the death of the younger one, since Marta cannot bring herself to forgive Fausto. This is not an idealization of the figure of the mother; she is not all-forgiving; she protects herself as best she can and reneges on her love for her eldest son.

In terms of the mother-daughter relationship, too, Serao is less positive than was the case in the earlier short story (and in much of her earlier work). The crucial mother-daughter relationship in this novel is that between Carolina Leoni and her daughter, Loreta. Here, the mother worries that her daughter will follow her lover to the front (as, indeed, she eventually does). In due course, Carolina learns that Loreta is living with her lover, Carletto. This (shameful, in the mother's eyes, given the

[29] Chodorow, *The Reproduction of Mothering*, 97.

[30] Serao, *Mors tua*, 325.

time and social class represented here) event is what sunders the mother-daughter relationship. Moral and ideological conflicts create an impossible gap between mother and child, and Carolina, fascinatingly, blames herself for loving her child too much. "This," she says, "is the destiny of crazy mothers, like me" ["Questo è il destino delle madri folli, come me'"].[31] The collapsed ego boundaries between mother and daughter depicted by Serao here appear to have induced what she sees as a maternal madness, an over-investment. *Mors tua* turns out to be (one of) Serao's cautionary tales of maternity. Chodorow has noted how mothers, in relation to daughters (like daughters in relation to mothers) experience themselves as "overly attached, unindividuated, and without boundaries."[32] Serao describes this process in considerable detail here, from the perspective of the mother, and considers the toll it takes. Interestingly, too, it is here the heterosexual relationship between Loreta and Carletto which has precipitated the crisis in the mother-daughter relationship. Loreta, in effect, takes refuge (of a sort) in her relationship with Carletto precisely because she feels too close to her mother. Carletto acts (in a functional sense) as a father would for Loreta (and this is another novel, and specifically a family constellation, in which fathers are scarce), according to Chodorow's (and, indeed, Deutsch's) formulation[33]; in her sketching of the father-daughter relationship, Chodorow notes that the "girl's relation to him is emotionally in reaction to ... her relation to her mother."[34] This is certainly how Carletto, too, functions for Loreta—he provides her with a literal escape-route from the claustrophobic bond with the mother.[35]

Over time, then, Serao reconfigures her view of the mother-daughter (and, indeed, the mother-child) relationship. She moves from an idealization of the intense bond to an awareness of the costs associated with

[31] Ibid., 271.

[32] Chodorow, *The Reproduction of Mothering*, 137.

[33] See Helene Deutsch, *The Psychology of Women* (New York: Greene and Stratton, 1944–1945).

[34] Chodorow, *The Reproduction of Mothering*, 192.

[35] In fact, Serao frequently presents the heterosexual relationship as existing in direct competition with the mother-daughter bond. More often than not, in the struggle for emotional primacy, it is the mother-daughter bond that proves stronger than the heterosexual one. See Ursula Fanning, *Gender Meets Genre: Woman as Subject in the Fictional Universe of Matilde Serao* (Dublin and Portland, Oregon: Irish Academic Press, 2002) for more on this, especially 99–102.

that bond (particularly, though, from the perspective of the mother). She finds no way to negate it, or to write it otherwise (it is always intense), but she does represent different kinds of maternal withdrawal in the face of engulfment by the child. It would seem that she hankers after another kind of plot, a different kind of emotional mother-child connection. One could posit that such a connection might be found in a different organization of parenting, of the type envisaged by Chodorow, but unimaginable at the time and in the context in which Serao was writing. The absence of fathers in both emotional and literal senses in her texts is striking, and begs the question of what lies behind that representational absence and what effect it has on Serao's narratives.

In terms of other Italian writers of the late nineteenth-century, and the light which Chodorow can cast on their work too, Katharine Mitchell discusses Chodorow's theories of mother-daughter bonding and how these can be seen to be played out in the works of two other critically-acclaimed women writers of this period, Neera and the Marchesa Colombi, in her volume on gender in fiction and journalism. Mitchell notes that Chodorow's "point about distance between women and men is reinforced from a reading of female friendships in Italian domestic fiction."[36] Her observation underlines the usefulness of Chodorow's work in this context, and highlights some of those recurring features of Italian women's writing of the maternal in the nineteenth century.

Sibilla Aleramo: Reworking the Maternal Story and the Maternal Imaginary

Sibilla Aleramo wrote what is generally considered to be the first feminist novel in Italy but, despite having been translated into English in 1908 and again in 1983, it remains relatively unknown in the English-speaking world.[37] The autobiographical novel tells the story of a woman who leaves her abusive marriage and in so doing, under the legal code of the time, forfeits her rights to her child, a son aged nine at the time of her disappearance. Much of the narrative is taken up with the depiction of

[36] Katharine Mitchell, *Italian Women Writers: Gender and Everyday Life in Fiction and Journalism 1870–1910* (Toronto: University of Toronto Press, 2016), 127.

[37] Sibilla Aleramo, *Una donna* (Milan: Feltrinelli, 1982 [1906]); *A Woman at Bay* (New York: G. P. Putnam's Sons, 1908); *A Woman* (Berkeley and Los Angeles: University of California Press, 1983).

the mother-son relationship, and the consequences of its truncation, but the relationship between the narrator-protagonist and her own mother also proves to be of crucial importance for the novel, and for driving the plot towards its (then very shocking, and still controversial) denouement. To be sure, at the start of the novel and for the first fifty pages or so, the mother-daughter relationship is evoked in predominantly negative terms. The daugher-narrator is keen, above all, to differentiate herself from her mother and to organize her life differently. Tellingly, it is to her father that the anonymous narrator turns for an alternative way of being as she compares her mother to her father and finds her wanting: "I felt her to be … too different in both taste and temperament from my father, and consequently from me" ["La sentivo … troppo diversa di gusti e di temperamento da mio padre, e per conseguenza da me"[38]]. The narrator's father, at least initially, offers her the possibilities of living differently: "my father I adored without limits … He was the shining example for my small self" ["L'amore per mio padre mi dominava unico … Era lui il luminoso esemplare per la mia piccola individualità"[39]]. This daughter models herself physically on her father, chooses to wear androgynous clothes, to cut her hair short because her father suggests she do so, supports him in his choice to move the family away from Milan to the south of Italy (thus severing her mother's connections with friends and family) and goes to work for him. Psychoanalysts explain this kind of identification with the father as, predominantly, an identification with that which he represents. The father is potentially, as Chodorow has it, representative of freedom.[40] Chodorow's following observation encapsulates precisely what is represented at the start of this novel: "A girl is likely to turn to him … as the most available person who can help her to get away from her mother."[41] Other contemporary sociologists also support this view. Martin Richards, for instance, contends that: "From birth, the father will represent separateness and detachment … A father is a representative of the world outside the house, who first brings to the child knowledge about that world. He, and so that world, come to represent

[38] Ibid., 32.

[39] Ibid., 19.

[40] Chodorow, *The Reproduction of Mothering*, 121.

[41] Ibid.

things like independence, activity, and progress."[42] There is evidence in *A Woman* that this is precisely how the father functions. It is he who, initially, directs the protagonist's studies and her reading, and he who encourages her out of the house and into the workforce. As Chodorow puts it: "a daughter looks to her father for a sense of separateness and ... confirmation of her specialness."[43] Aleramo's narrator, indeed, repeatedly tells us that she was her father's favorite child, and the one in whom he confided his hopes and dreams for the future. Chodorow's work helps, thus, to explain the intense father-daughter relationship in this narrative, as well as the complex mother-daughter bond.

The inevitable change of emotional orientation is not long in coming, though, as the daughter moves back to align herself with the mother. Interestingly, it is sexuality (specifically, the heterosexual relationship) which first shakes and then, ultimately, severs the intense bond between father and daughter in this text. The first cracks in the relationship appear when the daughter discovers an unexpected aspect of her father's life—his affair. The affair is a betrayal, for the protagonist, of the mother and of the family. This is the point at which the idol falls: "My father, the glowing example, was suddenly transformed into an object of horror" ["Mio padre, l'esemplare raggiante, si trasformava d'un tratto in un oggetto d'orrore"[44]]. This is also, not coincidentally, the point at which the daughter begins to shift allegiances and to move toward the mother and, by extension, toward the feminine. When she speaks out in public in her mother's defense, her father angrily asserts his authority, announcing his intention to terminate her employment,[45] thus returning her to the "proper," feminine sphere.[46]

The, now shaky, bond is severed altogether with the daughter's own brutal initiation into the sexual domain. Once "possessed" by a man, the narrator can no longer resemble her father. As an object to be taken, "surprised by an unusual, brutal embrace" ["sorpresa da un abbraccio insolito,

[42] Martin Richards, "How Shall We Approach the Study of Fatherhood?" in *The Father Figure*, eds. Lorna McKee and Margaret O Brien (London: Tavistock, 1982), 57–71 (68).

[43] Chodorow, *The Reproduction of Mothering*, 195.

[44] Aleramo, *Una donna*, 44.

[45] Ibid., 46.

[46] See Ursula Fanning, "Sibilla Aleramo's *Una donna*: A Case Study in Women's Autobiographical Fiction," *The Italianist* 19 (1999): 164–177 for more on this.

brutale"[47]], she can no longer be the subject. Chillingly, the narrator sees her harsh sexual initiation (the rape committed by a co-worker) as that which signals her entry into the domain of the feminine and turns back to her mother as model. On discovering the father's affair, the protagonist finds that: "I now felt myself drawn to the unfortunate creature with a full heart" ["Mi sentivo ora attratta verso la sventurata col cuore pieno"[48]]. She begins to form an identification with the mother (or, better, to re-form it, in line with psychoanalytical readings of the pre-Oedipal period when the bond between mother and child is the first, all-consuming passion): "something of her stirred in me, at that time" ["qualcosa di lei palpitava in me, in quell'ora, per la prima volta"[49]], she affirms. This return to the mother can, once again, be read through Chodorow, as an indication of that "relational triangle" in which, for women, the father (and men in general) are emotionally secondary to the mother and women. As Chodorow has it: "a girl never gives up her mother as an internal or external love object."[50] The growing identification between mother and daughter in *A Woman* is not unproblematic in this narrative; in part, it is a response to the narrator's realization that her future simply cannot mirror that of her father (in Italy, at that time). She does not have the resources afforded to him to live a free life. On the contrary, her rape is an inevitable precursor to marriage (a loveless one, like that of her mother, which serves to further underline their commonality). The specter of madness also looms over the daughter, as her mother becomes increasingly unstable and ends up incarcerated in a mental asylum, while the daughter is driven by her own experiences of violence in marriage to attempt suicide. And yet, Aleramo manages to turn this negative link on its head—the fear of madness is sufficiently threatening to push the daughter close to leaving her marriage and, crucially, the final spur to leaving is provided by a letter of her mother's which she discovers, and which seems to speak to her from beyond the grave. In this letter, the mother writes (to her own father) of her desire to leave her marriage and the narrator reflects that, had her mother done this, she might have saved her sanity. The letter from the mother acts as a catalyst for the

[47] Aleramo, *Una donna*, 47.

[48] Ibid., 44.

[49] Ibid., 50.

[50] Chodorow, *The Reproduction of Mothering*, 127.

daughter to save herself, thus the mother-daughter bond, while not always unproblematic nor devoid of ambivalence as represented here, is allowed by the author to function in transformative fashion. The daughter's life is bettered because of what she has learned from her mother. The emotional return to the mother has had a function.

There is another symbiotic relationship explored in this novel, and it is that between mother and son. Aleramo centralizes the physicality of motherhood (both negatively and positively) in her narrative, thus breaking new ground in the context of Italian literature at the turn of the twentieth century and, in doing so, she violates certain taboos around what might be fit subject matter for women writers. On the one hand, childbirth is figured as a sundering of the self: "I had believed I was entering into death at the moment in which my child was entering the world, I cried out in revolt in the name of my torn flesh, my devoured internal organs" ["avevo creduto d'entrare nella morte nel punto in cui mio figlio entrava nel mondo, avevo gettato un urlo di rivolta in nome della mia carne lacerata, delle mie viscere divorate"[51]]; on the other hand, there is a graphic description of the sensual pleasure involved in breast-feeding just a few lines later.[52] This, really, is the libidinal shift identified by Chodorow in the mother-daughter relationship inscribed here,[53] too, in the mother-son relationship. The corporeality of the maternal experience finds its expression for the first time in the Italian context in this novel. The mother-son bond as it is represented here is no less intense than that seen by analysts between mothers and daughters. Indeed, partly because of the violent marriage in which the protagonist finds herself, she engages in an extraordinary fantasy towards the close of the text, breaking yet another taboo in fascinating fashion. The nub of the protagonist's dilemma is that she cannot leave her husband without leaving her beloved son, and so she imagines things otherwise: "*He*, too, my husband might *cease to exist* ... The people who surround us die ... I and my son, alone ... in this immense world, free, free, I and my son ... It was a waking dream" ["Anche *lui*, mio marito, avrebbe potuto *non esistere piú* ... Gli esseri che si agitano intorno a noi muoiono ...] io e mio figlio, soli ...... in questo mondo immenso, liberi, liberi, io e mio figlio ... Era un sogno

[51] Aleramo, *Una donna*, 71.

[52] Ibid., 71.

[53] Chodorow, *The Reproduction of Mothering*, 202.

ad occhi aperti"[54]]. This is a maternally-inspired murder fantasy, with its suggestive ellipses and laden italics. Aleramo wants things differently, and is capable of envisaging a different future for the protagonist and her son, if things were only ordered differently in her world. It is also a symbiotic fantasy, of a return to a state of indifferentiation between self and other, mother and son. The protagonist wants, at the very end, to: "clasp him to me, to enclose him in myself! ... And to disappear myself, so that he can be all *me*!" ["Strapparlo, stringerlo, chiuderlo in me! ... E sparire io, perché fosse tutto *me*!"[55]]. This symbiotic mother-son relationship functions in remarkably similar fashion, in the works of several Italian women writers, to the way in which the symbiotic mother-daughter bond works. It is true that we are not presented with the son's take on this in these writings, and thus the perspective is largely one-sided; hence, any degree of reciprocity cannot be gauged but, for the mother figure, the dynamic seems, essentially, the same.

Late Twentieth-Century Takes on the Maternal

Italian women writers in the second half of the twentieth century (especially post-'68,[56] that year of crucial importance for the women's movement in Italy) politicize and problematize motherhood in various ways, but they rarely ignore it. Through the lens of the maternal, and through exploring maternal voices, they present their readers with a diffuse sense of identity in the personas of their female protagonists. Stefania Lucamante, in her 2008 volume on contemporary Italian women novelists, notes that the mother-daughter relationship "studied in depth by Nancy Chodorow [...] is destined to remain a permanent theme in women's narratives."[57] Likewise, a recent special issue of the journal *Intervalla*, on "Motherhood and Female Identity in Italian Literature and Culture"

[54] Aleramo, *Una donna*, 193.

[55] Ibid., 203.

[56] See Ursula Fanning, "Touching on Taboos: Imagining and Reconceptualizing Motherhood in Some Post-'68 Italian Women's Autobiographical Writings," *La modernità letteraria* 4 (2011): 49–58.

[57] Stefania Lucamante, *A Multitude of Women: The Challenges of the Contemporary Italian Novel* (Toronto: University of Toronto Press, 2008).

focussing on women writers in Italy from the 1970s to the present, foregrounds Chodorow's work in its introduction.[58]

Motherhood is also absolutely central to the formulations of Italian feminist theorists in the late twentieth-century. Most significant, perhaps, in this context is the work of Luisa Muraro.[59] Muraro focusses on the significance of the mother-daughter bond, and uncovers its implications for the transmission of language. She criticizes the cultural repression of the relationship with the literal and symbolic mother. As Graziella Parati and Rebecca West put it in their analysis and collection of theoretical writings from the Italian feminist movement, Muraro holds that "women are privileged by the fact of having been born women and thus having a more immediate connection with the mother through their sex."[60] Parati and West underline the "deeply problematic" nature of this posited bond,[61] but the teasing-out of the mother-daughter relationship is undeniably part of the enterprise of Italian feminism late in the century. Muraro's formulation of the mother-daughter bond is essentialist, rather than rooted in the observation of the formation of the family, and thus differs sharply from Chodorow's position, but the vagaries and apparent ineluctability of the mother-daughter bond are central to the thinking of both critics.

In my view, perhaps the most striking fictional explorations of mother-child bonds in the fictions of this period are to be found in the work of Lidia Ravera, in her 1979 novel *Baby of mine* (*Bambino mio*) and her later *In Which of the Heart's Hiding-Places* (*In quale nascondiglio del cuore*),[62] and here too Chodorow's work proves important in several respects. Ravera, who was actively involved in the Italian feminist movement, was very aware of the denigration of the maternal that was part

[58] Laura Lazzari and Joy Charnely, eds., "To Be or Not to Be a Mother: Choice, Refusal, Reluctance and Conflict. Motherhood and Female Identity in Italian Literature and Culture," *Intervalla* 1 (2016), https://www.fus.edu/intervalla/, 21 February 2018.

[59] Muraro's germinal text, *L'ordine simbolico della madre* (Rome: Editori Riuniti, 1991) was published in English, by SUNY Press, early in 2018. Interestingly, the year in which Muraro's work first appeared is the same year in which Chodorow's *Reproduction* was translated into Italian.

[60] Graziella Parati and Rebecca West, eds., *Italian Feminist theory and Practice: Equality and Sexual Difference* (Madison and Teaneck: Fairleigh Dickinson University Press, 2002), 61.

[61] Ibid., 62.

[62] Lidia Ravera, *Bambino mio* (Milan: Bompiani, 1979) and *In quale nascondiglio del cuore* (Milan: Mondadori, 1993).

and parcel of much of the movement's rhetoric in the 1960s and 70s. As Adalgisa Giorgio has observed: "Feminist analyses of women's cultural and social subordination published in the 1970s put the mother on trial for her complicity with patriarchal norms and for being the agent of their perpetuation, for holding back the daughter's process of individuation, for acting as regulator of her sexuality, and generally for hindering her emancipation and autonomy."[63] Reflections of this "putting on trial" are very much to the fore in Ravera's 1979 work. The protagonist-narrator of this novel refers, early in the narrative, to the very act of thinking about becoming a mother as "the forbidden thought" ["il pensiero proibito"[64]]. The anonymous protagonist also roundly rejects a self-sacrificing kind of mothering: "I deny my mother, I hate sacrifice … I am rootless, free" ["nego mia madre, odio il sacrificio … sono sradicata, libera"[65]]. The narrator firmly turns her back on the traditional institution of the family. In the later novel, too, Ravera's protagonist voices a distrust of conventional family dynamics, and specifically detaches the act of having a child from that of constructing a traditional family, recounting her generation's different attitudes to the process: "we were very happy to have had children, but we didn't tread a traditional path … we were involved in working out an alternative puericulture, with as much vehemence as we rejected a world which hadn't allowed itself to change" ["ci piaceva molto aver fatto dei bambini, ma non marciavamo nella tradizione … ci impegnavamo a elaborare una puericultura alternativa, con impeto pari al rifiuto per un mondo che non si era lasciato cambiare"[66]]. That alternative puericulture implied a greater involvement of fathers, along the lines envisaged by Chodorow in *Reproduction*, where she notes that "the elimination of the present organization of parenting in favour of a system of parenting in which both men and women are responsible would be a tremendous social advance."[67]

However, notwithstanding concerns about traditional mothering, and desires to do things otherwise, Ravera's narrators in both these works

[63] Adalgisa Giorgio, ed., *Writing Mothers and Daughters: Renegotiating the Mother in Western European Narratives by Women* (Oxford: Berghahn, 2002), 5.

[64] Ravera, *Bambino mio*, 10.

[65] Ibid., 11.

[66] Ravera, *In quale nascondiglio*, 10.

[67] Chodorow, *The Reproduction of Mothering*, 219.

indicate a deep, indeed still symbiotic, attachment to their (male) children; the focus here is not on the mother-daughter bond, but rather on the mother and son. In a flashback on the first page of the earlier novel, the narrator notes: "Something, invisible to others, links us" ["Qualcosa ci lega, invisibile agli altri"[68]]. This invisible link is not confined to the early stages of the mother-child relationship, Ravera suggests in the later novel. Here, as the narrator prepares to let go of her adolescent son, she refers to a "patologia dell'eterna gravidanza" ["pathology of eternal pregnancy"[69]]. She explains this as follows: "we never want to give birth to you completely" ["non vogliamo mai partorirvi definitivamente"[70]]. This notion of dualistic identity in motherhood is also to be found in the earlier novel, where the protagonist wonders at her different sense of self once she has given birth: "my I ... ended up goodness knows where. Maybe it stayed in the delivery room" ["il mio io ... è finito chissà dove. Forse è rimasto in sala parto"[71]]. Chodorow suggests that "prolonged symbiosis" is "particularly characteristic of early relationships between mothers and daughters."[72] It is interesting to note that, in Italian women writers' representations of the mother-son relationship, we see this same "prolonged symbiosis," experienced by the mother, if not the child, in these relationships, as well as in representations of the mother-daughter bond.[73] Many of these narratives would suggest that a dual maternal consciousness (along the lines described by Kathryn Rabuzzi)[74] is not confined to the early stages of the mother-daughter relationship, but can also be uncovered in mother-child relationships in general, and at later stages than we might expect. It is especially interesting that Ravera's exploration of this dual consciousness comes as she has her protagonist preparing her

[68] Ravera, *Bambino mio*, 9.

[69] Ravera, *In quale nascondiglio*, 41.

[70] Ibid., 41.

[71] Ravera, *Bambino mio*, 100.

[72] Chodorow, *The Reproduction of Mothering*, 104.

[73] An interesting example of that "prolonged symbiosis" between mother and daughter is also to be found in Gina Lagorio's *A Cyclone Named Titti/Un ciclone chiamato Titti* [1969] (Milan: BUR, 2003). Here the protagonist is emotionally hijacked by thoughts of her teenage daughter, when they are apart from each other and is forced to admit that "I carry [her] still inside me" ["mi porto dentro (Simonetta) anche"], *Un ciclone*, 115).

[74] Kathryn Rabuzzi, *Motherself: A Mythic Analysis of Motherhood* (Bloomington: Indiana University Press, 1988).

son to venture forth into the world, and as she encourages him to look outward, and to look with attention. The protagonist urges her son to: "Travel. Even without going far … what's important is one's baggage: lighten your Self, open your eyes" ["Viaggia. Anche senza andare lontano … l'importante è il bagaglio: alleggerire l'Io, aprire gli occhi"[75]]. This sounds strikingly similar to Sara Ruddick's view of maternal thinking, with the accent on the thinking, as the extending-out of "maternal" attention to the human race as a whole; as such it can be considered both ethical and political. As Ruddick has it, "the identification of the capacity of attention and the virtue of love is at once the foundation and the corrective of maternal thought."[76] Sara Ruddick and Carol Gilligan share with Nancy Chodorow an emphasis on women's relatedness, and all three have been deservedly influential in the Anglo-American feminist theoretical context.[77] Their work also finds echoes in that of Adriana Cavarero, precisely in this common focus on relatedness. Cavarero, like Muraro, reclaims the figure of the mother in her writing, and insists that: "the feminine philosophy of our time … is founded on a maternal figure."[78] Crucial to Cavarero's reclaiming of the mother, and of the birth process, is that focus on relationality; she holds that "in the new philosophical horizon of sexual difference, the basic element of philosophy is a *two*, not a *one*."[79] Cristina Mazzoni has astutely defined Cavarero's position as "the philosophical elaboration of a fluid personal identity and self-understanding based on a dynamic interplay of relations to the other – a feminist metaphysics that, through the ethical bond to the other exemplified by birth, aims to avoid the destructive alternative of either the full subject of metaphysics or the fragmented self of postmodernism."[80]

[75] Ravera, *In quale nascondiglio*, 144.

[76] Sara Ruddick, "Maternal Thinking," in *Mothering: Essays in Feminist Theory*, ed. Joyce Trebilcott (Maryland: Rowman & Littlefield, 1983 [1980]), 213–230.

[77] See Nancy Chodorow, *Feminism and Psychoanalytic Theory* (New Haven and London: Yale University Press, 1989), 263 for a consideration of parallel paths.

[78] Adriana Cavarero, *In Spite of Plato: A Feminist Rewriting of Ancient Philosophy* (London: Routledge, 1995), 5.

[79] Ibid., 6.

[80] Cristina Mazzoni, *Maternal Impressions: Pregnancy and Childbirth in Literature and Theory* (Ithaca and London: Cornell University Press, 2002), 190.

There are remarkable connections here between Italian feminist thought, Italian women's writing and feminist theory in the Anglo-American context, even where their focus differs in terms of gender and of the descriptions of the unfolding of the mother-child relationship, not to mention in their differing views of the desirability/inevitability of the continuation of intense bonds between mother and child/daughter. Read together, these works are mutually provocative and pose questions in relation to each other on which we continue to reflect, and to which there are no easy answers. Their ongoing relevance, and the importance of the dialogue between them, is clear.

Nancy Chodorow, in her early theoretical articulation of the importance of the germinal mother-daughter relationship, has facilitated illuminating insights into Italian women's writings on what, for them, is an ineluctable relational constellation explored from the nineteenth century onwards. Critics in Italian Studies, and the discipline as a whole, have repeatedly benefitted from her thinking and continue to do so.

Works Cited

Aleramo, Sibilla, *Una donna*. Milan: Feltrinelli, 1982 [1906]. Print.

———, *A Woman at Bay*, trans. Maria Hornor Lansdale. G. P. Putnam's Sons: New York, 1908. Print.

———, *A Woman*, trans. Rosalind Delmar. Berkeley and Los Angeles: University of California Press, 1983. Print.

Cavarero, Adriana, *In Spite of Plato: A Feminist Rewriting of Ancient Philosophy*, trans. Serena Anderlini D'Onofrio and Áine O' Healy. London: Routledge, 1995 [1990].

———, *Relating Narratives: Storytelling and Selfhood*, trans. Paul A. Kottman. London: Routledge, 2000 [1997].

Chodorow, Nancy, *Feminism and Psychoanalytic Theory*. New Haven and London: Yale University Press, 1989. Print.

———, *The Reproduction of Mothering: Psychoanalysis and the Sociology of Gender*. Berkeley and Los Angeles: University of California Press, 1978. Print. Translated by Adriana Bottini, *La funzione materna: psicanalisi e sociologia*. Milan: La Tartaruga, 1991. Print.

Conti, Bruna, "Introduzione." In *La donna e il femminismo*, ed. Bruna Conti. Rome: Edizioni Riuniti, 1978, 7–39.

Deutsch, Helene, *The Psychology of Women*, 2 vols. New York: Greene and Stratton, 1944–1945.

Fanning, Ursula, *Gender Meets Genre: Woman as Subject in the Fictional Universe of Matilde Serao*. Dublin and Portland, OR: Irish Academic Press, 2002. Print.

———, "Maternal Prescriptions and Descriptions in Post-Unification Italy." In *Women and Gender in Post-Unification Italy: Between Private and Public Spheres*, eds. Katharine Mitchell and Helena Sanson. Oxford: Peter Lang, 2013, 13–37. Print.

———, "Sibilla Aleramo's *Una donna*: A Case Study in Women's Autobiographical Fiction." *The Italianist* 19 (1999): 164–177. Print.

———, "Touching on Taboos: Imagining and Reconceptualizing Motherhood in Some Post-'68 Italian Women's Autobiographical Writings." *La modernità letteraria* 4 (2011): 49–58. Print.

Gilligan, Carol, *In a Different Voice: Psychological Theory and Women's Development*. Cambridge: Harvard University Press, 1993 [1982]. Print.

Giorgio, Adalgisa, ed., *Writing Mothers and Daughters: Renegotiating the Mother in Western European Narratives by Women*. Oxford: Berghahn, 2002. Print.

Hirsch, Marianne, *The Mother-Daughter Plot: Narrative, Psychoanalysis, Feminism*. Bloomington and Indianapolis: Indiana University Press, 1989. Print.

Homans, Margaret, *Bearing the Word: Language and Female Experience in Nineteenth-Century Women's Writing*. Chicago and London: University of Chicago Press, 1986. Print.

James, Henry, "Matilde Serao." *North American Review* (March 1901): 367–380. http://www.unz.org/Pub/NorthAmericanRev-1901mar-00367, 5 July 2017.

———, *Notes on Novelists*. New York: Scribner, 1914. Print.

Lagorio, Gina, *Un ciclone chiamato Titti*. Milan: BUR, 2003 [1969]. Print.

Lazzari, Laura and Joy Charnely, eds., "To Be or Not to Be a Mother: Choice, Refusal, Reluctance and Conflict. Motherhood and Female Identity in Italian Literature and Culture." *Intervalla* 1 (2016). https://www.fus.edu/intervalla/, 21 February 2018.

Lucamante, Stefania, *A Multitude of Women. The Challenges of the Contemporary Italian Novel*. Toronto: University of Toronto Press, 2008. Print.

Mazzoni, Cristina, *Maternal Impressions: Pregnancy and Childbirth in Literature and Theory*. Ithaca and London: Cornell University Press, 2002. Print.

Mitchell, Katharine, *Italian Women Writers: Gender and Everyday Life in Fiction and Journalism 1870–1910*. Toronto: University of Toronto Press, 2016. Print.

Muraro, Luisa, *L'ordine simbolico della madre*. Rome: Editori Riuniti, 1991. Print.

Parati, Graziella and Rebecca West, eds., *Italian Feminist Theory and Practice: Equality and Sexual Difference*. Madison and Teaneck: Fairleigh Dickinson University Press, 2002.

Rabuzzi, Kathryn, *Motherself: A Mythic Analysis of Motherhood*. Bloomington: Indiana University Press, 1988. Print.
Ravera, Lidia, *Bambino mio*. Milan: Bompiani, 1979. Print.
———, *In quale nascondiglio del cuore: Lettera a un figlio adolescente*. Milan: Mondadori, 1993. Print.
Richards, Martin, "How Shall We Approach the Study of Fatherhood?" In *The Father Figure*, eds. Lorna McKee and Margaret O' Brien. London: Tavistock, 1982, 57–71. Print.
Ruddick, Sara, "Maternal Thinking." In *Mothering: Essays in Feminist Theory*, ed. Joyce Trebilcott. Maryland: Rowman & Littlefield 1983 [1980], 213–230. Print.
Serao, Matilde, *Evviva la guerra!* Naples: Perrella, 1912. Print.
———, *Mors tua*. Milan: Treves, 1926. Print.
———, "Terno secco." In *All'erta, sentinella!* Milan: Galli, 1896 [1889], 123–179. Print.
Taricone, Fiorenza, "I cataloghi femminili dell'ottocento." In *Operaie, borghesi, contadine nel XIX secolo*, eds. Fiorenza Taricone and Beatrice Pisa. Rome: Carucci, 1978, 11–24. Print.

Index

A

Abel, Elizabeth, 27, 35, 37, 38
Adult, 8, 9, 20, 38, 70, 76, 77, 118, 159, 161, 173, 175, 176, 178, 184, 201, 207, 243, 269, 270, 273, 280, 293, 302, 309, 310, 323
Androcentric, 11
Anthropology, 2, 9, 36, 51, 52, 56, 91, 129, 150, 155
Autonomy, 7, 9, 10, 20, 27, 28, 53, 105, 113, 114, 116, 161, 207, 208, 211, 218, 249, 251, 255, 260, 261, 273, 276, 281, 282, 285, 290, 291, 294, 315, 346

B

Balsam, Rosemary, 32, 35, 37, 57, 94, 95, 98, 101, 106, 139
Baraitser, Lisa, 18, 272
Bell, Leslie, 36, 40, 266
Benjamin, Jessica, 1, 11, 21, 40, 84, 114, 139, 196, 207–214, 218, 221, 222, 229
Boy, 5, 59, 68, 100, 131, 141, 152, 196, 210, 243, 268, 319
Breast, 33, 55, 70, 178, 224, 270, 305, 322
  feeding, 254, 256, 258, 289, 343
  milk, 256
Bueskens, Petra, 17, 18, 24, 25, 36, 41, 49
Butler, Judith, 28, 30, 226, 230, 231, 241

C

Care
  deficit, 23
  father, 34
  mother, 21, 22
  parental, 22, 273
Career, 13, 20, 23, 25, 27, 28, 32, 33, 36, 65, 71, 75, 88, 90–92, 104, 113, 117, 137, 138, 154, 163, 182–184, 192, 274, 279, 286, 287, 289, 292, 310, 312, 320

P. Bueskens (ed.), *Nancy Chodorow and* The Reproduction of Mothering, https://doi.org/10.1007/978-3-030-55590-0

Case, 3–5, 38, 59, 95, 103, 106, 129, 131, 135, 142, 161, 176, 177, 276, 277, 284, 322, 327, 332, 337
Child/children, 4, 6, 8–10, 14, 16, 19–25, 27, 33–35, 39, 40, 51, 53, 55, 56, 61, 63–76, 83, 90, 93, 96, 97, 100–102, 104, 106, 107, 113, 118–120, 128, 131, 133–136, 140, 151, 155, 160–162, 164–166, 170–187, 191–201, 208, 211, 220, 225–230, 241–244, 246, 248, 250, 251, 254, 256, 257, 260, 262, 266, 268–273, 275, 276, 278, 279, 282, 284–286, 288, 290, 291, 293, 294, 302, 305, 306, 308, 310, 312–319, 321–326, 333, 335–343, 345–347, 349
  childcare/daycare, 9, 14, 15, 22, 23, 33, 34, 89, 251, 255, 256, 258, 261, 269, 273, 287, 293, 310, 319, 321, 327
Clinical, 2, 30, 36, 37, 39, 53, 56, 57, 63, 65–67, 69, 70, 75, 76, 81, 84, 87, 88, 96–100, 104, 105, 107, 136, 160, 165, 166, 169, 170, 176, 181
  individuality, 31, 32, 65
  practice, 37, 164
Clinician, 37, 39, 63, 91, 100, 139, 163, 170, 187, 223
Commodification, 21
Conscious, 3, 4, 6, 33, 60, 63, 64, 66, 75, 76, 103, 139, 151, 163, 165, 178, 223, 246, 250, 261, 268
Consciousness, 16, 17, 55, 82, 149, 150, 214, 217, 220, 262, 276, 347
  raising, 16, 17, 82, 149, 150, 214, 217, 220
Crittendon, Anne, 25, 280
Culture, 2, 18, 23, 36, 39, 49–54, 58–60, 64, 65, 67, 84, 85, 97, 100, 105, 106, 114, 118, 128, 131, 136, 138–140, 142, 153, 163, 164, 173, 192, 193, 196, 201, 208, 213, 214, 216, 218, 219, 221, 226, 228, 229, 239, 241, 245, 252, 254, 262, 272, 274–276, 281, 286–290, 292, 311, 318

D

Daughter
  becoming a mother, 8, 56, 65–67, 74, 106, 183, 280, 285, 346
  in relation to mother, 61, 326, 338
  sexuality, 14, 294, 341, 346
Defensive, 5, 7, 10, 15, 51, 59, 152, 266, 273, 294
De Marneffe, Daphne, 3, 14, 20, 21, 27, 36, 39, 160–162, 165, 192, 272, 278
Desire, 7–9, 15, 20, 21, 27, 34, 35, 40, 61, 83, 98, 102, 106, 114, 116, 134, 139, 151, 160–162, 164, 182, 192–194, 198, 200, 205–215, 217–223, 225, 229–231, 243, 254, 267–269, 271, 273, 304, 305, 307, 309, 310, 312, 314, 317, 319, 320, 324, 325, 342, 346
Development/developmental, 3–6, 13, 17, 20, 27, 30, 31, 37, 40, 50, 52, 54, 56–58, 60–63, 65–67, 76, 82, 84, 88, 95, 97–102, 105, 113, 125–128, 130–132, 135, 136, 138, 139, 141, 142, 152, 155, 159–163, 165, 166, 177, 196, 199, 201, 205–208, 210–212, 222, 223,

245, 250, 252, 266, 267, 270, 271, 286, 315, 331
Dinnerstein, Dorothy, 10, 14, 21, 22, 81, 114, 160, 273, 304
Dominance, 5, 7, 12, 50–52, 54, 59, 93, 102, 131, 254
  male, 29, 50–52, 54, 59, 93, 102, 114, 131, 257
  maternal, 59
Drive, 53, 55, 65, 83, 106, 150, 154, 156, 184, 185, 201, 223, 224, 227, 265
  theory of, 154, 223, 265
Dyadic, 6–8, 270, 305, 319, 321

E
Economic, 4, 7, 15, 21, 23–25, 27, 28, 32, 35, 41, 50, 53, 150, 192, 193, 201, 216, 274, 276–278, 280, 285, 289–294
  rationalist, 21, 23, 283
Economy, 9, 23, 36, 40, 54, 58, 151, 196, 197
Ego, 5–7, 19, 51, 58, 76, 88, 92, 96, 103, 113, 116, 127, 173, 200, 248, 250, 269, 294, 338
  boundaries, 5, 7, 19, 51, 113, 116, 200, 248, 250, 269, 294, 338
Emotional, 4, 6–12, 19, 23, 27, 32, 39, 41, 50, 53–55, 66, 67, 72, 89, 96, 103, 118, 133, 139, 150, 153, 160, 161, 165, 177, 200, 206, 244, 256, 257, 260, 266, 269–271, 291, 304, 305, 309–311, 314, 315, 317, 320, 327, 338, 339, 341, 343
Empathy, 6, 8, 40, 107, 116, 165, 198, 208, 247, 249, 269, 273, 313, 317
Empirical, 30, 39, 161, 241, 245, 250, 251, 256–258, 290
  research, 39
Empty nest, 27
Ethic of care, 41, 266

F
Fanning, Ursula, 36, 42, 331, 338, 341, 344
Fantasy, 5, 14, 34, 54, 67, 77, 98, 163, 170, 217, 230, 244, 245, 281, 284, 310, 312, 318, 343, 344
Father, 3, 5–7, 11, 12, 23, 28, 35, 40, 41, 59–62, 64–66, 74, 90, 91, 97, 98, 100, 102, 115, 120, 127, 129, 130, 133–135, 140, 155, 172, 175, 178–180, 184, 191, 192, 194, 195, 199–201, 209, 210, 224, 229, 239–245, 250, 251, 255–257, 260, 262, 266, 268–271, 273, 275, 276, 281–283, 288, 293, 294, 301, 302, 305, 306, 309, 314, 319, 323, 324, 326, 333, 334, 336, 338–342, 346
  stay-at-home, 40, 192, 195, 287, 317
Feeling(s), 6, 34, 53–55, 57, 61, 67–69, 71–75, 101, 102, 133, 135, 140, 160–165, 171, 187, 193, 197, 200, 207, 215, 243, 245–249, 259, 268, 302, 303, 315, 316, 318, 323, 324, 326
Femininity, 6, 7, 53, 54, 59, 60, 65, 127, 129, 131, 134, 136, 137, 140, 201, 208, 269
Feminism
  first-wave, 17
  maternal, 20, 278
  second-wave, 11, 15–18, 20, 112, 161, 162, 265, 291, 293, 304
Feminist, 11–17, 20–24, 30, 31, 35–38, 40–42, 50–53, 58, 83–85, 87–89, 91, 98, 99, 101,

103, 105, 106, 108, 111–117, 125–127, 130, 131, 137, 141, 149–151, 155, 156, 161, 162, 196, 201, 208, 210, 213–219, 221, 239–242, 248, 265, 267, 268, 272, 273, 275, 277, 278, 283, 289, 290, 292, 293, 301, 304, 327, 329, 330, 332, 334, 339, 345, 346, 348, 349
foremothers, 13, 15, 21
theory, 30, 216, 345, 348
Fertile/fertility, 3, 11, 33, 70, 73–75, 104, 141, 177, 294
Fiction, 36, 42, 115–117, 322, 329, 330, 332, 339, 341, 345
Italian Women's, 36, 42, 329–332, 344
Firestone, Shulamith, 11–13, 15, 16, 150, 304
Frankfurt School, 21, 36, 51, 52
Fraser, Nancy, 23, 277
Freud, Sigmund, 6, 54, 55, 113, 132, 134, 137, 142, 240, 244, 269
Friday, Nancy, 14
Fromm, Erich, 13, 265, 267

G
Garner, Katie, 22, 36, 41
Gender
female, 10, 41, 50, 51, 90, 97, 215, 262, 281
male, 3, 10, 51, 53, 95, 100, 128, 196, 210, 215, 220, 267, 269, 281
studies, 18, 20, 51, 83, 105, 112, 129, 160, 196, 282
Generation, 3, 4, 13, 14, 20, 21, 25, 27, 35–37, 50, 54, 56, 58, 59, 61, 66, 67, 71, 73–76, 81, 82, 85, 89, 93, 100, 102, 115, 118–120, 137, 153, 162, 177, 180, 206, 208, 225–228, 261, 266, 271, 276, 290, 293, 310, 346
Genital, 57, 137, 141, 142, 160, 207, 214, 244
Gilligan, Carol, 82, 126, 139, 140, 159, 160, 266, 348
Girl, 6, 13, 56, 60–65, 74, 77, 97–99, 101, 103, 139, 141, 165, 172, 175, 196, 208–210, 243, 244, 247, 251, 270, 302, 305, 313, 338, 340, 342
Glass ceiling, 34
Granddaughter, 3, 35, 36, 72
Grandmother/grandmothering, 56, 76, 186
Greer, Germaine, 11, 13, 16, 213, 214

H
Hakim, Catherine, 24–26, 285–287, 292
preference theory, 25, 26, 285
Harris, Adrienne, 3, 35, 37, 63, 84, 99, 139, 220
Heterosexual/heterosexuality
female, 42, 61, 65, 92, 93, 99, 271
genital, 206, 244
male, 195, 207
Hochschild, Arlie, 23, 24, 196, 277
Homophobia, 7, 218, 221
Homosexual/homosexuality, 6, 93, 99, 206
Horney, Karen, 12, 13, 49, 55, 56, 94, 95, 99, 265, 267, 268
Husband, 25, 32, 65, 71, 72, 98, 275, 276, 287, 307–311, 315–317, 319, 323, 327, 333, 334, 343

I
Identification/identificatory, 4–6, 8, 40, 61, 72, 76, 83, 101,

129, 133, 196, 198, 208–210, 222–224, 240, 244, 248–250, 259, 260, 265, 268–270, 281, 282, 285, 305, 306, 313, 315, 333, 335, 336, 340, 342, 348
Identity, 12, 13, 16, 28, 29, 33, 35, 40, 50, 54–56, 60, 63, 66, 67, 95, 97, 100, 101, 105, 114, 120, 129, 139, 140, 152, 153, 160, 161, 194, 197, 199, 201, 214–216, 220, 225, 227, 228, 230, 243, 248, 249, 258, 260, 267–269, 271, 283, 303, 315, 332, 344, 345, 347, 348
Individual/individualist, 15, 18, 21, 24, 32, 34, 36, 39, 53, 54, 63, 65, 67, 76, 94, 102, 105, 107, 112, 113, 121, 128, 129, 131, 132, 136, 138, 161, 163, 164, 166, 174, 177, 206–208, 214, 217, 219, 226, 229, 246, 248–250, 252, 254, 257, 260–262, 274, 279, 291, 293, 303, 304
Infant, 3–6, 8, 9, 21, 26, 40, 55, 60, 70, 93, 95–97, 127, 128, 130, 132–135, 161, 182, 187, 210, 211, 240, 242, 244, 245, 250, 254, 267, 268, 279, 282–285, 293, 306, 309, 311, 313, 318
  infantile sexuality, 5, 121
Inner life, 14, 20, 27, 94, 161, 192, 272, 278
Irigaray, Luce, 40, 41, 130, 240, 242, 244–255, 257–261, 272, 281

J

Jay, Meg, 35, 39

K

Kristeva, Julia, 74, 100, 162, 240, 272

L

Lack, 7, 13, 90, 137, 141, 152, 207, 208, 218, 221, 243, 249, 273, 324, 325
Lazarre, Jane, 14
Lesbian, 30, 126, 137, 192, 206, 215, 219, 221, 270
  families, 216
  love, 206, 214
  sexuality, 212, 218, 219, 221
Libido, 83
Life cycle, 26, 36, 37, 54, 56, 58, 61, 66, 67, 70, 73, 75, 76, 99, 159
Love, 6, 8, 10, 11, 14, 16, 17, 20, 22, 23, 27, 41, 64, 71, 72, 84, 94, 96, 100, 101, 114, 139, 141, 142, 149, 155, 160, 161, 163, 166, 173, 184, 186, 192, 194, 196, 209, 211, 220, 223, 230, 243–245, 247, 250, 252, 254–256, 262, 270, 272, 273, 278, 291, 301, 303, 327
  heterosexual, 194, 244, 270
  lover, 140, 186, 225, 322, 337

M

Manne, Anne, 14, 20–22, 278
Masculinity, 5, 7, 10, 11, 36, 40, 51, 59, 60, 100, 113, 126, 129, 130, 136, 137, 152, 199, 201, 269, 273, 306, 309
Master, 12, 19, 104
  masterful, 19, 37
Maternal, 3, 5, 10, 14, 15, 17–19, 22, 24, 27–29, 33–36, 39–41, 54–57, 59, 60, 62, 63, 65–72, 75–77, 83, 86, 93, 94, 112, 113,

116–120, 128, 160, 161, 222, 240–242, 245–247, 249–251, 253–255, 257–262, 267, 268, 271–273, 278, 280–286, 291, 294, 302, 313, 318, 321, 324, 330–332, 334, 337–339, 343–345, 347, 348
desire, 14, 20, 21, 27, 60, 161, 162, 192, 278
thinking, 348
Maternity, 15, 70, 112, 131, 139, 281, 283, 289, 292, 332, 338
leave, 70, 289, 292
Matrisexual, 242, 244, 250, 268, 270, 305
McGleughlin, Jade, 10, 36, 40, 205, 212, 213, 215, 217, 219, 228–230
Memory, 14–17, 72, 77, 119, 121, 135, 142, 163, 164, 225, 277, 284
collective, 15–17
Millet, Kate, 11, 13, 16, 150
Misogyny/misogynist, 7, 10–12, 22, 51, 53, 273
Mitchell, Juliet, 11, 12, 16, 30, 35, 58, 81, 91, 131, 151–153, 282
Modernity, 8, 18
Mother, 1–8, 12–21, 22, 24, 25, 27, 28, 30–34, 36–42, 50–77, 89, 90, 93, 94, 96–102, 106, 111, 113–115, 118, 119, 121, 127–135, 137, 141, 152, 155, 161, 164, 166, 169, 172, 175, 180–187, 191–195, 197, 200, 205, 208–210, 217, 222–230, 239–262, 265, 267–294, 301–307, 310–327, 330, 332–338, 340–342, 345, 347, 348
Mother-daughter, 4, 6, 19, 32, 34, 36–38, 40–42, 50–54, 56, 59–69, 71, 73–77, 92, 111, 113–115, 117, 120, 205, 206, 239–242, 244–250, 254, 259–261, 266, 267, 270–272, 329–331, 333, 335–341, 343–345, 347, 349
Motherhood, 13–22, 24, 25, 31–35, 42, 49, 55, 57, 65, 68, 73, 75, 77, 81, 103, 104, 106, 139, 162, 225, 228, 254, 262, 276, 278, 280, 284, 286, 290, 294, 302–304, 306, 307, 312, 313, 317, 318, 325, 326, 331–333, 336, 337, 343–345, 347
penalty, 25, 280, 287
Motherhood studies, 49
Mothering, 8–10, 14, 15, 18–21, 23–31, 34, 36–39, 41, 50–52, 54–57, 60, 62, 63, 65–70, 73, 75–77, 85, 90, 92, 95, 97, 103–106, 112, 113, 121, 154, 160–162, 164–166, 170, 175, 183, 185–187, 192, 193, 196–198, 200, 201, 208, 217, 222, 223, 227, 240, 242, 248, 250, 261, 262, 266, 267, 274, 276, 277, 284, 286, 289, 293, 294, 302, 304, 307, 308, 312, 314, 316, 317, 322, 325, 326, 330, 331, 346
male, 27, 40, 191
Mother(s)
good-enough, 39, 51, 173, 185–187, 242
stay-at-home, 192, 195, 274, 287, 317

N

Nanny, 36, 41, 133, 301–304, 306, 307, 309, 311, 313, 314, 317, 319–321, 323, 325–327
Neoliberal/neo-liberalism, 15, 18, 22–24, 28, 289
New York Times, 20, 25, 180, 184

Nordic, 26
 countries, 26
 paradox, 26

O
Oakley, Ann, 16
Object, 3, 6, 8, 19, 34, 37, 38, 55, 62, 96, 105, 111–113, 115, 118–121, 125, 127, 128, 130–132, 154, 155, 165, 209–211, 223, 240–242, 245, 249, 265, 267, 269–271, 284, 305, 306, 311, 341, 342
 relations theory, 3, 38, 112, 113, 125, 127, 128, 130–132, 156, 244, 265, 267, 284
Oedipus, 5–7, 38, 51, 58, 62, 95, 97, 115, 127, 133, 134, 139, 140, 153, 164, 239, 243, 270
 complex, 5–7, 37, 38, 51, 58, 62, 97, 101, 127, 133, 134, 140, 153, 270
Opt-Out Generation, 25
O'Reilly, Andrea, 279
Orloff, Ann, 15, 24

P
Parent, 5, 6, 10, 15, 28, 40, 58, 64, 71, 74, 88, 97, 120, 134–136, 162, 164, 165, 171–173, 177–180, 184, 187, 193, 195–200, 225, 226, 230, 250, 251, 255, 256, 258, 260, 290, 310, 312, 319
Parental, 26, 58, 64, 66, 186, 257, 258, 282
 leave, 26
Patient(s), 32, 56, 62, 64, 65, 73, 87, 92, 106, 107, 116, 139, 163, 165, 171, 230, 284
Patriarchy/patriarchal, 5, 9, 10, 12–14, 18, 41, 63–65, 97, 100, 117, 125, 127–129, 131, 134, 138, 139, 142, 151, 214, 240–242, 246, 247, 249, 252–255, 277, 281, 294, 327, 346
Phallic/phallus, 133, 208, 304, 305, 307, 315, 324
Philipson, Ilene, 3, 35, 38, 39, 154
Postmaternal thinking, 15, 277
Postmodern/postmodernity, 28, 30, 31, 283, 348
Projection, 5, 18, 55, 273, 323
Psychic, 3, 5, 9, 38, 39, 55–57, 66–68, 75, 76, 84, 85, 95, 104, 113, 131, 140, 165, 211, 222, 229, 241, 245, 265, 267, 271, 274, 280–283, 285
 Intra, 4, 267, 268, 285, 286
Psychoanalysis, 1, 2, 4, 11–13, 37, 38, 49–59, 70, 73, 81, 83–85, 87, 89–97, 99–101, 103, 105, 106, 112, 114–118, 125, 127, 130, 131, 135, 138, 139, 141, 151, 154–156, 159, 160, 163–166, 225, 226, 231, 241, 265–267
 drive theory, 13
 relational turn, 155
Psychoanalytic theory, 3, 5, 13, 14, 38, 51, 61, 89, 91, 94–96, 99, 100, 127, 135, 139, 154, 169, 170, 210, 241, 245, 260, 261, 265, 277, 348
Psychology/psychological, 2–4, 10, 12, 13, 20, 30, 32, 34–37, 41, 51, 52, 55, 56, 59, 62–64, 66–69, 76, 82–84, 88–90, 92, 95, 96, 99, 102, 104, 105, 112, 113, 115, 116, 118, 120, 126–129, 131, 132, 139, 141, 142, 150, 153, 156, 159, 160, 163, 165, 169, 170, 173, 175,

176, 181, 193, 197, 198, 201, 205, 206, 218, 223, 229, 230, 269, 273, 274, 277, 280, 294, 303, 304, 309, 318, 323, 338
Psychotherapy, 1, 70

Q
Queer, 136, 205, 206, 210, 219, 220, 222, 223, 225, 228–231, 316

R
Rational/rationality, 18, 151, 211, 247, 266
Rationalist, 21, 283
  economic, 23
Reason, 3, 18, 62, 65, 73, 101, 104, 130, 135, 155, 175, 182, 213, 256, 276, 285, 287, 302, 307, 318, 325, 326, 331, 336
Relational, 6, 8, 9, 40, 50, 51, 53, 56, 62, 67, 68, 83–85, 105, 114, 121, 129, 140, 154, 162, 182, 200, 201, 208, 217, 218, 223, 224, 248–250, 256, 260, 261, 274, 303, 305, 334, 337, 349
Reminiscing, 37
Rich, Adrienne, 14, 19, 112, 113, 304, 318
Rose, Jacqueline, 241, 248, 249
Rossi, Alice, 14
Ruddick, Sara, 29, 331, 348

S
Segal, Lynne, 30, 282
Self/selves, 6–8, 10, 18, 39, 42, 51–54, 56, 59, 62, 63, 65, 69, 71, 76, 116, 119, 121, 153, 161, 162, 199, 200, 207, 210, 211, 223, 226, 227, 230, 231, 240, 241, 243, 250, 261, 262, 269–271, 284, 306, 313, 334, 340, 343, 344, 347, 348
  in relation, 7
Sexuality
  female, 6, 13, 54, 61, 113, 131, 136, 150, 213, 218, 244
  infantile, 121
  latent, 6
  lesbian, 40, 205, 206, 212, 215, 218
  male, 214
Social, 2–5, 7–10, 12, 15, 17, 20, 23–28, 30–32, 34–39, 41, 49, 52, 54, 76, 82, 83, 89, 90, 96, 99, 103, 105–107, 112, 118, 125–131, 136, 138, 140, 142, 150, 152, 156, 159, 161, 162, 164, 171, 193, 199, 201, 206, 212, 214, 217, 218, 220–223, 231, 240–242, 245, 250, 256–259, 262, 265–267, 274–282, 285, 286, 289–291, 293, 294, 303, 305, 306, 315, 333, 338, 346
  structure, 9, 23, 25, 34, 38, 127, 129–131, 136, 161, 162, 281, 290
Sociology/sociological, 2, 13, 36, 37, 51, 52, 54, 56, 76, 83, 87–89, 91, 92, 94, 101, 105, 112, 125, 129, 150, 153–155, 160, 170, 186, 187, 231, 267
Son, 40, 51, 52, 59, 60, 63, 67, 68, 77, 99, 115, 130, 133, 134, 175, 178, 186, 191, 229, 230, 239, 240, 246, 268, 293, 307, 309, 311, 312, 337, 339, 340, 343, 344, 347, 348
  in relation to mother, 51, 59, 60
  sexuality, 76, 99
Splitting, 14, 15, 55, 152, 209, 210, 257

Sprengnether, Madelon, 35, 38, 127, 135, 138, 251
Stephens, Julie, 14, 15, 17, 277, 279
Stone, Alison, 36, 40, 41, 266, 272, 280, 281, 284
Subject/subjectivity
  female/feminine, 11, 13, 18, 19, 40, 41, 118, 240, 257, 266, 280
  individualist, 18
  male/masculine, 247, 257, 258
  maternal, 17–19, 27, 28, 34–36, 39, 41, 55, 57, 160, 161, 246, 250, 251, 254, 255, 257–260, 262, 267, 268, 271–273, 280–285, 291, 294

T
Transference, 52, 64, 65, 178, 284, 327
  countertransference, 65
Triangulate, 6, 8, 41, 270, 271, 302, 305, 307, 316, 321

U
Unconscious, 3–6, 8, 10, 13, 19, 33, 52, 60, 63, 65, 66, 69, 71, 74–76, 82, 83, 89, 98, 100, 102, 106, 107, 134, 135, 139, 151, 153, 156, 163, 165, 170, 205, 206, 211, 217, 223, 224, 227, 230, 243, 245, 246, 253, 268, 281–284, 302
Universal/universalism, 1, 10, 29, 30, 51, 52, 65, 129, 136, 153, 198, 248

W
Wage/wages, 15, 25, 200, 276, 277, 280, 287, 292, 323
  penalty, 25, 280
Warner, Judith, 25
Wife, 8, 16, 24, 98, 171, 172, 182, 192, 269, 277, 289, 290, 319, 333
Winnicott, Donald, 55, 83, 95, 96, 155, 173, 210, 222
Women/women's
  liberation, 9, 37, 82, 206, 212, 213, 215, 217, 220, 221
  movement, 10–13, 15, 40, 81, 82, 103, 206, 212, 213, 215–217, 219, 220, 294, 344
  studies, 126, 129
Woolf, Virginia, 37, 38, 49, 115–117
Work
  domestic, 24, 274, 278, 289
  paid, 9, 15, 18, 20, 23–25, 27, 28, 243, 250, 251, 275–280, 286, 287, 289, 292
  unpaid, 23, 28, 32, 275, 278, 285, 289, 292

The manufacturer's authorised representative in the EU is Springer Nature Customer Service Centre GmbH, Europaplatz 3, 69115 Heidelberg, Germany. If you have any concerns regarding our products, please contact ProductSafety@springernature.com

Printed and bound by CPI Group (UK) Ltd, Croydon, CR0 4YY
30/09/2026
02225451-0018